# PREFACE

Peace is hardly unidimensional. It is a complex set of institutional relationships involving the availability of weapons of violence, the inevitability and continuity of political conflict among human beings, and the maintenance of a system of political order within which most members of a political community can feel collectively and personally secure. In short, peace is nothing less than the problem of creating and operating systems of human self-governance.

For most of us, the parts to this problem and the countless multilateral relationships among these parts are often too much to comprehend all at once. As a result, we adopt partial and limited perspectives from which to tackle the problem, hoping that the whole will be moved if we push against one or more of the manageable parts. This book is an attempt to put some of the larger parts back together for a fresh and comprehensive examination of the problem of safety in this world.

Although Chapter VII of the United Nations Charter places responsibility for international security, peacekeeping, and disarmament under the aegis of the United Nations Security Council, peacekeeping and arms control have become distinct fields of study and policy making over the last three decades. Each field has its own specialists and its own professional literature: each offers its own policies and panaceas. This survey of arms control, peacekeeping, and collective security developments since World War II will endeavor to trace the parallel evolution of events in these two specialized fields and to reestablish the connection between them as integral parts of the larger problem of world security.

In making this survey, I shall be concerned with the subjective and objective aspects of the condition called "security" as well as with the relationship between political distrust and the arms race. This approach will carry us into consideration of the bases of security other than military strength, the question of pricing the cost of "security services," the many sources of internation distrust, the intranation sources of international distrust, and some of the techniques currently used for confidence-building, including third-party involvement in conflict resolution, the development of political institutions, peacekeeping, and the pursuit of arms control and disarmament agreements.

In order to help orient the reader to the sequence of relevant events of recent decades, a Chronology of Significant Security, Arms Control, and Peacekeeping Events is provided at the beginning of this book. If the reader examines this chronology carefully, several trends to be discussed in this study are likely to become self-evident.

This study opens with a concise history of warfare, noting its frequency, its political context, and technological developments. The first chapter of the text concludes with a statement about the dilemmas arising from the relationship between military and other institutions intended to achieve human self-governance. How do military organizations used as instruments of political rivalry become instruments of community order without at the same time eliminating the positive functions of political competition?

Chapter 2 examines the subjective and, presumably, objective criteria for making judgments about the extent of insecurity. The world's military expenditures and resources, the special status of the superpowers, the quantity of nuclear and conventional weaponry extant, and the role of the qualitative aspects of military technology are related to the dynamics of the arms race. Chapter 3 endeavors to make empirically concrete the notion of "trust" as a central element in arms competition and international insecurity. Chapter 4 expands on the many ongoing but often unexamined domestic and internation sources of political distrust. Chapter 5 goes on to describe those political processes that contribute to the promotion of international trust and the creation of conditions for institutionalized trust, the latter a concept of special importance in this survey.

Highlights of the recent history of international peacekeeping are reported and analyzed in Chapter 6. Chapter 7 is devoted to a survey of post-World War II arms control and disarmament negotiations, agreements, and treaties. It reviews the ways they contribute to institutionalized trust and provide a probable avenue to eventual global collective security arrangements similar to the ones achieved within political communities of smaller size than the world.

There are many important technical terms and concepts to which the reader should give particular attention. Many readily available glossaries, dictionaries, and other references provide definitions and discussions of such terms. The full citations for some of these sources may be found in the annotated bibliography at the end of this book. Their authors and titles include: Wolfram F. Hanreider and Larry V. Beal, *Words and Arms: A Dictionary of Security and Defense Terms* (1979); William H. Kincade and Jeffrey D. Porro, eds., *Negotiating Security* (1979); U.S. Arms Control and Disarmament Agency, *SALT Lexicon* (1974); Robert W. Lambert, *Glossary of Arms Control and Disarmament Terms* (1967). A more general source is Jack C. Plano and Roy Olton, *The International Relations Dictionary* (New York: Holt, Rinehart and Winston, latest editon).

As a culminating event of the Disarmament Decade of the 1970s and as an attempt to examine comprehensively the problems of global security and the arms race, the General Assembly of the United Nations conducted a Special Session on Disarmament (SSOD) during May and June of 1978. The *Final Document* adopted by SSOD is a unique and authoritative compendium of the current issues and future agenda regarding global security, arms control, disarmament, and peacekeeping. The *Final Document* is included here as Appendix B. It is significant not only for its substantive content but also for the language its authors employed to achieve consensus among the delegates, and for the issues that did not receive attention.

This book was written to suggest another way of perceiving and coping with mankind's ancient pathology—war. The underlying assumptions of the author are these: Disagreement among human beings is inevitable, and political conflict is perpetual. War and other forms of military violence are primitive, inefficient, and inconclusive techniques of conflict resolution.

# Arms Control and Peacekeeping

# Arms Control and Peacekeeping

## Feeling Safe in this World

**Ralph M. Goldman**
San Francisco State University

**Random House**
New York

First Edition

987654321

Copyright © 1982 by Random House, Inc.

Library of Congress Cataloging in Publication Data

Goldman, Ralph Morris, 1920-
  Arms control and peacekeeping.

  Bibliography: p.
  Includes index.
  1. Arms control.  2.  Security, International.
3.  Peace.  I.  Title.
JX1974.G52       327.1'74       81-13884
ISBN:  0-394-32886-8         AACR2

Manufactured in the United States of America

Weapons and warfare are the symptoms, not the disease. The disease arises from insufficiencies in human relationships, notably distrust, and from inadequacies in the modes of organizing and institutionalizing those relationships for purposes of conflict management and resolution. The pathology of war will respond neither to blame nor to ideology. Its cure requires well confirmed, predictive knowledge; that is, the kind of knowledge about political conflict and its management that solves the dilemmas of feeling safe in this world, which are described in the following pages.

*Ralph M. Goldman*
*San Francisco*

# IN APPRECIATION

Books get written largely because colleagues, friends, and other generous people provide opportunity, resources, deadlines, and good advice. In this instance, help came from several sources. Professor Ellen Dirksen, as chairperson, and her colleagues on the Council on Educational Development, University of California, Los Angeles, provided an opportunity to try out these materials in a course offered at that university during the winter of 1980. Dr. Herbert York, Director, Science, Technology and Public Affairs Program, University of California, San Diego, made funds available for manuscript preparation, under a grant from The Ford Foundation. As Dr. York and a few others will understand, he also indirectly spurred the writing of this manuscript by suddenly becoming head of the American delegation to the Comprehensive Test Ban negotiations. Robert Jervis of the University of California, Los Angeles, Harold Jacobson of the University of Michigan, and Warren Hechrote of the University of California Livermore Laboratory were generous in their comments and chivalrous in saving me from errors of fact and perception, for which I thank them. Mrs. Susan E. Ehlinger of the staff of the Department of Political Science at the University of California, San Diego, performed yeoperson duty on an early draft. Nancy Wilson's Word Processing Center team—Geri Nelligan, Paula Mangini, Kerry Glover, and Wanda Brown—were helpful beyond the call of duty. Feedback from students in my Arms Control and Peacekeeping course has been very helpful to say the least. To each and all, my most sincere gratitude for making the entire enterprise so pleasant.

# A CHRONOLOGY OF SIGNIFICANT SECURITY, ARMS CONTROL, AND PEACEKEEPING EVENTS

**1945**
Germany surrenders to Allies, May 8.
Establishment of United Nations.
Atomic bombs dropped on Hiroshima, August 6, and Nagasaki,
    August 9.
Japan surrenders, September 2.

**1946**
Presence of Soviet Union's troops creates Iranian crisis. United Nations
    pressure leads to Soviet departure from Iran.
Atomic Energy Commission (UNAEC) created by United Nations General
    Assembly. Baruch Plan presented to AEC.
Atomic bomb tested at Bikini by United States.

**1947**
Commission for Conventional Armaments (CCA) created by
    United Nations General Assembly.
Greek civil war leads to establishment of United Nations Special Committee on
    the Balkans (UNSCOB). United States aid to Greece and Turkey announced
    in Truman Doctrine. Marshall Plan for European recovery announced.
Communist Information Bureau (Cominform) created by Soviet Union as
    successor to Communist International. Other transnational political party
    movements—Liberal International, Christian Democratic International,
    Socialist International—being activated.
Cold War begins.
India partitioned into India and Pakistan.

**1948**
Israel declares independence. Arab League commences war with Israel. United
    Nations Truce Supervision Organization in Palestine (UNTSO) established.
Kashmir crisis leads to United Nations Commission for India and Pakistan.
    (UNCIP) and United Nations Military Observer Group in India and
    Pakistan (UNMOGIP).
Malaya civil strife leads to United Nations Commission for Indonesia (UNCI).
Organization of American States (OAS) established as collective security
    system.

**1949**
North Atlantic Treaty Organization (NATO) established.
Soviet Union detonates atomic bomb.
Communist Chinese gain full control of Mainland and occupy
    Tibet.
Council of Europe created.

## 1950

North Korea invades South Korea. Korean War. United Nations General Assembly adopts Uniting for Peace Resolution.

## 1951

Australia, New Zealand, and United States sign ANZUS Treaty.

## 1952

United Nations Disarmament Commission replaces Atomic Energy Commission and Commission for Conventional Armaments.
United Kingdom detonates atomic bomb.
United States detonates first hydrogen bomb.
Civil war commences in Cyprus.

## 1953

Soviet Union reports possession of hydrogen bomb.
Eisenhower presents Atoms-for-Peace proposal at United Nations.

## 1954

Southeast Asia Treaty Organization (SEATO) established.
United States-Japanese mutual defense treaty signed.
Mutual defense treaty between Nationalist China (Taiwan) and United States.
Partition of Vietnam by Geneva Conference.
West Germany invited to join NATO.

## 1955

Baghdad Pact (Iraq, Turkey, United Kingdom, Pakistan, and Iran) formed, later (1959) to become Central Treaty Organization (CENTO).
Soviet Union and its satellites create Warsaw Treaty Organization (WTO).
Diem replaces Emperor Bao Dai and declares Republic of Vietnam.
Guerrilla warfare between North Vietnam and South Vietnam begins.

## 1956

Hungarian Revolution suppressed by Soviet Union.
Suez crisis. Nasser takes over Suez Canal. Britain and France occupy Suez, with collusion of Israel. United Nations Emergency Force (UNEF-1) created for Middle East.

## 1957

United Kingdom detonates hydrogen bomb.
Soviet Union launches first earth satellites, Sputniks I and II.
European Community created by Rome Treaty.
International Atomic Energy Agency (IAEA) established as suggested in Atoms-for-Peace proposal.

## 1958

Conference of Experts to Study the Possibility of Detecting Violations of Possible Agreements on a Suspension of Nuclear Tests (with representatives from the United States, the United Kingdom, France, Canada, the Soviet Union, Poland, Czechoslovakia, and Romania).

Comprehensive test ban talks (CTBT) begun by the United
   States, the Soviet Union, and the United Kingdom.
Lebanese crisis leads to creation of United Nations Observation
   Group in Lebanon (UNOGIL).
Quemoy-Matsu crisis between United States and Communist China.

**1959**

Ten-Nation Disarmament Committee (TNDC) created. In 1961 TNDC
   succeeded by Eighteen-Nation Disarmament Committee (ENDC). In
   1969 ENDC becomes Conference on the Committee on Disarmament
   (CCD) with 26, later 31, members.
Khrushchev proposes complete world disarmament at United Nations.
Antarctic Arms Control Treaty signed.

**1960**

Congo crisis. United Nations Operation in the Congo (UNOC) begun.
France joins "nuclear club."
Sino-Soviet border clashes occur.

**1961**

Kennedy Administration sends military advisers to Vietnam.

**1962**

First meeting of Eighteen-Nation Disarmament Committe (ENDC).
Cuban missile crisis. United States "quarantines" Cuba.
United States and Soviet Union present General and Complete
   Disarmament (GCD) proposals to ENDC.

**1963**

Limited Test Ban Treaty signed ending nuclear tests in atmosphere, in
   outer space, and underwater.
"Hot Line" Agreement signed.
Diem assassinated. Kennedy assassinated.

**1964**

Communist China detonates atomic bomb.
United Nations Force in Cyprus (UNFICYP) established.

**1965**

Last meeting of United Nations D armament Commission.
Special Committee on Peacekeeping Operations (Committee of
   33) set up by United Nations General Assembly.
United Nations India-Pakistan Observation Mission (UNIPOM);
   new Kashmir crisis.
Organization of American States (OAS) sends regional peacekeeping
   mission to Dominican Republic.
United States begins bombing of North Vietnam.

**1966**

France withdraws from NATO military forces.

**1967**
Arab-Israeli Six-Day War.
Outer Space Treaty signed.
Latin American Nuclear-Free Zone established by Treaty of
   Tlatelolco.

**1968**
Non-Proliferation Treaty (NPT) signed.
Rebellion in Czechoslovakia put down by Soviet Union.
U.S. Surveyor 7 lands on moon.
Martin Luther King and Robert Kennedy assassinated.

**1969**
Eighteen-Nation Disarmament Committe membership expanded to
   twenty-six and renamed Conference of the Committee on Disarmament
   (CCD).
SALT I talks begin.
Manned Apollo 11 lands first man on moon.
United Nations General Assembly declares Disarmament Decade.
Nixon begins U.S. troop withdrawal from Vietnam.

**1970**
Soviet and West Germany sign friendship treaty.

**1971**
Seabed Arms Control Treaty is signed.
"Hot Line" Modernization Treaty is signed.
Soviet-American Agreement on Prevention of Accidental Nuclear War is
   signed.
Communist China hosts United States table tennis team.
Communist China replaces Nationalist China at United Nations.

**1972**
United States and Soviet Union sign Biological Weapons
   Convention.
Salt I Interim Agreement and Anti-Ballistic Missile (ABM)
   Treaty signed.
Conference on Security and Cooperation in Europe (CSCE)
   begins in Helsinki.

**1973**
Conference on Mutual and Balanced Force Reductions in Europe
   (MBFR) begins.
Yom Kippur War in Middle East. United Nations Emergency
   Force (UNEF II) reestablished.
Congress passes War Powers Act.
Soviet-American Agreement on Prevention of Nuclear War.
United Nations Law of the Sea Conference begins.

**1974**
India detonates a nuclear device.
Soviet-American ABM Protocol signed.

Threshold Test Ban Treaty (TTBT) signed.
President Nixon resigns.
Vladivostok Agreement between Ford and Brezhnev.

**1975**
Saigon falls to North Vietnamese.
Non-Proliferation Treaty (NPT) Review Conference held.
Helsinki Summit Accords produced by CSCE.

**1976**
Peaceful Nuclear Explosions (PNE) Treaty signed.

**1977**
Environmental Modification Ban signed.
Formal trilateral negotiations begin on comprehensive nuclear test ban.
Sadat visits Jerusalem.

**1978**
United Nations Interim Force in Lebanon (UNIFIL) established.
Camp David Summit Agreement between Israel and Egypt.

**1979**
SALT II signed.
U.S. and U.S.S.R. jointly submit a draft Radiological Weapons
    Treaty to Committee on Disarmament in Geneva.
Radical students hold American embassy staff hostage in Tehran.

**1980**
Soviet Union invades Afghanistan. United Nations General Assembly
    condemns, 104-18, Soviet intervention.
Second Review Conference on Nuclear Non-Proliferation Treaty attended
    by 75 of treaty's 114 signatories.
War between Iraq and Iran. Iran releases American hostages.
Ratification of SALT II Treaty stalled in United States Senate.

# CONTENTS

# CHAPTER 1

# Warfare: A Permanent Human Institution?

To understand the problems of war and safety, we need first to examine the principal human institution for war making; that is, the military organizations that have evolved within human communities and the weapons technologies that have so profoundly influenced the development of military organization and the conduct of warfare. Although the case will not be made here, it may well be that the technology of violence has promoted in human beings their unique opportunities and willingness to kill members of their own species. This chapter has a simpler purpose, namely, to describe some of the major developments in the history of military organization, weapons technology, and warfare, to identify some of the relationships among these three factors, and to appreciate the scope of the challenge that this evolution of military institutions and warfare now presents to the human talent for creating systems of self-governance and nonviolent conflict. This brief institutional history in effect will state the problems: How to hasten the obsolescence of warfare as a technique of human conflict? How to make military organizations agents of political order and justice rather than agents of war?

Warfare has been so much a part of the human condition that the term "inevitable," as in "war is inevitable," seems to be its principal attribute. There are those who accept this inevitability. Consequently, they pursue policies that enlarge their military institutions and that ensnare them in costly and risky arms races. At another extreme, there are those who reject this inevitability, damn their military protectors, and, for their part, become ensnared in a foolish and unsafe theology of community. The middle path among the dilemmas of these opposing policy postures has yet to be found. The working solutions that assuredly would provide physical safety, nonviolent conflict, and ordered self-governance have yet to be invented or clearly recognized—if they already exist. The purpose of this book is to survey and analyze the problem, not to pronounce panaceas. It may also provide background against which we may better understand why it is difficult to feel safe in the world as it is today.

## Primitive and Classical Warfare

"Peoples in primitive societies throughout the world lived more or less in a state of perpetual warfare."[1] As a consequence, warfare became a major function in each culture from the outset of human communal organization, with consequences for many aspects of social and individual behavior. Warfare was the primitive norm rather than a state of disequilibrium as it is considered in modern societies. On the average, primitive warfare accounted for about 30 percent of the deaths in the adult male population of those early societies. Such a dominant social function soon led to specialization in skills and social roles as well as to various forms of primitive military organization. Military institutions, therefore, are among the oldest developed by human society.

The societies that engaged in primitive warfare were small, territorially ill defined, and highly mobile, if not nomadic. Blood revenge rather than territorial or economic motives prevailed as the reasons for fighting. Wife stealing, adultery, and divorce were the most common causes of killing and wars of revenge. Other motives included religious duty, individual prestige, sport, and, later, capture of the positions of chief or other high office in the more organized societies.

The warrior role fell to all men of the tribe who were generally trained from youth in war rituals and skills. Armed conflict became increasingly organized as technical skills—hurling spears, shooting arrows, duels with knives and swords, and so forth—became more demanding. The size of warrior bands grew. The conflicts themselves were, as classified by scholars, of several types: feuding (organized violence between bands within a village or tribal group, akin to civil war); raiding (usually by small bands of 10 to 100 men for some limited objective, such as revenge for adultery); and open pitched battles (involving from 200 to 2,000 warriors meeting in some prescribed area, with each side usually drawing men from allied villages or tribes).

Raids and pitched battles required a limited amount of leadership and organization, even though most of the fighting took place on a man-to-man basis. Elaborate formalities often initiated and ended battles. Warriors had to be notified, convened, and moved to the place of battle in unison. Although the principal objective was revenge, captured food and women also had to be systematically shared or carried off. Treachery (attacks on guest villagers) and alliancing required coordination and leadership, which in turn rapidly led to the emergence of a military elite.[2]

As primitive peoples settled in fixed territories to engage in agriculture and herding, societies began to acquire stability and hierarchical structure under the leadership of a tribal chief or a monarch. Agriculture, herding, and commerce were carried on in defined territories with boundaries. Warriors became more specialized in function and training, weapons and tactics became more complex and efficient, economic and political motives gained in importance, and battle casualties increased in magnitude. Territorial boundaries were patrolled and cities were fortified. Wars were conducted for territorial acquisition, plunder, promotion of trade, or the advancement of a religion or an ideology. Military equipment such as siege engines, heavy archery, and chariots became intricate, engineered, and manufactured—the beginning of the arms industry. Horses, camels, chariots, and ships moved armies from place to place. Soldiers had to be trained in their specialized military skills. Supplies and logistics—whether from a home base or from a conquered population—became vital considerations in military strategy.

Armies came to consist of specialized, trained, disciplined, and organized groups of men whose occasional warfare activities were carried on even as the rest of the society performed its routine affairs. Military leaders were usually chieftains, kings, or other senior nobility or public officers. Armies began to assume great size as early as 3,000–2,000 B.C., when battles between Egyptians and Syrians brought out contingents of 10,000–15,000 men on each side. By the eighth century B.C., the Sargon Dynasty of Assyria maintained a regular army of from 50,000 to 100,000 fighting men, with another 50,000 in auxiliary contingents.[3]

Large-scale conquest, the political consolidation of great empires, and the expansion of militant religions dominated the development of military institutions from the fourth century B.C. through the fifteenth century A.D. In the fourth century B.C., Alexander the Great led a force that usually consisted of 30,000–40,000 infantry and 5,000–7,000 cavalry to gather, through conquest, an empire that stretched from Egypt to India. His "secret weapons" were two innovations: the Macedonian phalanx infantry formation and the siege engine.

In Rome, from about the third century B.C. to the regime of Julius Caesar in the first century B.C., the development of military organization, tactics, and military administration reached new levels of sophistication and professionalism. From the outset, each Roman tribe or clan furnished units with a certain number of horsemen (traditionally 10 of the richest men) and footmen (legend sets their number at about 100 sentries); 30 of these units of horsemen and footmen comprised a legion. The king or general who led the legion rode at the head of the cavalry. The infantry—less wealthy and less skilled than the cavalry—was divided according to age into advanced troops and reserves, and according to weapon skills into swordsmen, javelin throwers, engineers, and even musicians. By 216 B.C., when Hannibal engaged Varra at Cannae, a Roman legion consisted of 5,000 infantrymen. There were 16 Roman and allied legions (80,000 men) plus 6,000 cavalry deployed against Hannibal's 40,000 infantrymen and 10,000 cavalry; Hannibal won. In 48 B.C., Caesar's 22,000-man army defeated Pompey's force of between 36,000 and 45,000, indicating the approximate size of military units of that day. As the jurisdiction of the Roman Empire spread around the Mediterranean basin from Spain to the Middle East and from Carthage to Gaul, encompassing some 150 million people, the Empire never had less than 300,000 men under arms and must have required some type of central staff to manage this vast military enterprise.[4]

Other famous large-scale military operations included: Attila, whose army of about 200,000 Huns and Germans was defeated in A.D. 451; Muhammad and his successors, whose horsemen extended Islam across North Africa and Southern Europe during the years 622#732; Charlemagne, whose army of feudal knights brought together an eighth-century empire encompassing France, Germany, and Italy; the Viking Norsemen of the ninth to eleventh centuries who left permanent political establishments in Normandy, England, and Iceland; the Christian Crusades against Islam in the eleventh to thirteenth centuries; Genghis Khan's invasion of Iran and Russia in the thirteenth century; and the English attempt to conquer France in the Hundred Years' War from 1337 to 1453.

## Medieval Transformations

The economic structure of feudal Europe from the eighth to the thirteenth centuries altered the nature of military organization and leadership in significant ways. The essential economic relationship of feudalism was the cultivation of land by a tenant farmer who paid fixed dues, rents, or taxes to a local lord who held title to the lands of all his tenants. Over the centuries, a hierarchy of tenancy developed, with local and regional lords holding land titles or being tenants themselves under grants from or contracts with higher nobles, kings, or the Church.

Associated with this system of landholding and agriculture was a tradition of military service, or vassalage. Each local lord owed military service to a more senior noble or king. At the same time, each lord, noble, and king maintained a band of armed retainers attached to his household who protected his landholdings, maintained local order, and, with him, rendered military service when called upon by the superior noble. The number, equipment, skills, and leadership of each band of armed retainers varied widely, in part dependent upon the lord's income from rents, his personal martial interests and skills, and his alliances with other nobles. In short, military officership or leadership was contingent upon noble and landholding status. While the nobility spent much of its time in individual military exercises as a source of sport and self-glorification, there was little occasion or opportunity for training large contingents of infantrymen or cavalry except in actual battle.

The practice of hiring soldiers of fortune or mercenaries developed in response to the lord's occasional need for skilled soldiers on short notice. The high cost of mercenaries' salaries and maintenance in an era of primitive tax arrangements limited the growth of this practice for some time. Several of the major medieval military campaigns, on the other hand, were carried out by volunteer armies recruited under special circumstances. The army of 50,000 men that followed William the Conqueror to England in 1066 were motivated in large part by promises of land in that country if conquered. Religious reasons and tales of the exotic East drew volunteers for the Crusades.

By the end of the twelfth century, however, Philip II of France and Henry II of England, spurred by advancing and more costly military technology and manpower specialization, had managed to organize tax structures that enabled them to hire large numbers of mercenaries on a permanent basis, thus freeing them substantially from dependency upon the military resources of the nobility. By 1202, Philip's professional army was estimated to consist of about 2,800 men, some 2,000 of them infantry and 800 with other skills. The force included knights, mounted sergeants, mounted crossbowmen, foot sergeants (ordinary spearmen), foot crossbowmen, and sappers.[5]

The thirteenth and fourteenth centuries saw a decline in the use of cavalry tactics. Both rider and horse had become too heavily armored for maneuverability or staying power—together their iron could weigh as much as 100–140 pounds. At the same time, the invention of the longbow, with accuracy at 250–300 yards, returned the infantry archer to a major role on the battlefield. The longbow, along with new forms of infantry recruitment, came into prominence during England's Hundred Years' War against France. In 1346, Edward III not only hired mercenaries but also initiated an indenture system of recruiting. Under this system, the king contracted with a number of his subjects to raise troops for him. The contractor would command the troops he raised, keep them in the field for a fixed time, and receive a stipulated sum from the royal treasury. This system enabled Edward to gather about 7,000 men-at-arms, the squires and other attendants of the men-at-arms, 10,000 archers, 4,000 infantry, smiths, artificers, and other specialists, for a total of 35,000. This was the force he used for his first raid on France, hardly a large-scale beginning to a long-term war.[6] But such were the dimensions of military operations of that day. Edward's successes rested upon the longbow as a weapon and his return to organized and disciplined infantry. Edward's other winning weapon was the cannon.

Gunpowder had been known for centuries and used primarily for setting fire to ships and other targets. The first time gunpowder was used to fire a projectile was during the reign of Alfonso the Wise, King of Castile (1221Z–1284). Edward III, at the battle of Crécy in 1346, was the first to use a cannon. His five cannon ended an age of castle fortification and introduced an age of artillery and firearms.[7]

## Renaissance Military Technology

The fifteenth and sixteenth centuries were a period of prolonged transition from medieval to modern military technology and organization. Cannons were refined, standardized, put on wheels, and drawn by horses; artillery units grew in number. Stronger fortifications were built for defense against siege and cannon. Turkish influences were manifest in the development of light horse cavalry, that is, lightly armed, highly mobile, and open in formation.

This variety of technology was compelling changes in the organization of battlefield units, the coordination of command, and the maintenance of supply lines. France continued to rely upon heavy cavalry formations and the mounted charge. The Swiss and Germans developed the infantry phalanx and file formations, requiring substantial discipline. French and Italian foot soldiers were usually archers, crossbowmen, swordsmen, and javelin throwers involved in less coordinated actions. Hand-firearms were available by 1500 but not widely used.

Armies tended to range in size from 10,000 to 20,000 men, and much of the fighting of the sixteenth century was between France and Spain over control of the rich Italian states. Systems of officership—not yet a profession—began to emerge: captains led companies; groups of companies were led by colonels; the king led the army. There were branches and each had a chief: supply marshal, scoutmaster general for intelligence, camp marshal, and so on. Mercenaries were the principal recruits, but their recruitment was still the privilege and responsibility of nobles. Armies were raised for specific campaigns rather than for permanent service. Attempts were made early in the seventeenth century, without success, to create officer training schools.

Great strides in military organization were made under Maurice of Nassau (The Netherlands), King Gustavus Adolphus of Sweden, Cardinal Richelieu of France, and the Spanish army during the seventeenth century. Similar reforms, under different conditions, were initiated by Cromwell in England. Much of this change reflected the arrival of the musket as a hand weapon using prepared cartridges and the development of the infantry as a highly disciplined and mobile body. Navies were also growing in importance, not only for troop transport and supply, but also as fighting units in their own right.[8]

In the eighteenth century the most significant changes in armament were the substitution of the flintlock for the matchlock musket and the introduction of the bayonet in place of the pike. These further underscored the major role of the infantryman and motivated greater attention to his training and deployment. Larger armies went hand in hand with the political integration of several nation-states in Europe. Military organization became more hierarchical and complicated, and military leadership began to acquire a professional *esprit*.

## America's Revolutionary Revolution

Perhaps the most unsettling development for European military leaders was the American War of Independence. Here was a war in which a government, fearful of a permanent army, refused to recruit a small but well-trained and well-supplied army as General Washington requested. Instead, the Continental Congress preferred to let recruitment go on haphazardly and for short terms of services; some 400,000 men in a population of about 3,000,000 passed through army service for short and long periods from the beginning to the end of the war. American officers were chiefly the wealthy and the politicians rather than nobles or mercenary soldiers. Infantrymen were reluctant, short-term volunteers who brought their own weapon, the musket. Battle formations were loose and in the twentieth century would be considered guerrilla warfare. For European armies of the eighteenth and nineteenth centuries, the American example assigned new importance to tactical light troops, that is, local partisan irregulars who attached themselves to the regular army for brief local actions. Above all, the War of Independence ended with a clear constitutional definition of civilian supremacy over the military and a representative democracy whose very existence was a threat to Europe's monarchies.[9] However, it must be remembered that France, Spain, and the Netherlands were at war with Britain at the same time as the Americans and thereby contributed substantially to the latter's success.

The nineteenth century was the beginning of very large-scale wars in which great armies moved in and out of areas densely populated by civilians. Civilian casualties often exceeded the military. Light and heavy weaponry began to be mass-produced, and arms industries flourished. Political ideology became a major justification for declarations of war. Once started, wars tended to draw in large numbers of countries to maintain or restructure balances of power. The French Revolution and the Napoleonic Wars spread the ideas of liberty, equality, and fraternity among the autocracies of Europe. The Crimean War halted Russian intervention southward. Nationalism was the ideological motivation for the Italian and German wars of unification. Slavery and a conflict of cultures were in part responsible for the American Civil War, one of the bloodiest of that time. This was exceeded, however, by the Taiping Rebellion in China (1850–1864) which was responsible for 20 million deaths. In Paraguay, most of that country's population died in the Lopez War (1865–1870). The century also saw the Russo-Turkish War in 1878 and the Spanish-American War of 1898.

Another striking development in the evolution of military institutions during the nineteenth century was the emergence of military officership as a profession. "Prior to 1800 there was no such thing as a professional officer corps. In 1900 such bodies existed in virtually all major countries."[10] No longer was officership achieved on the basis of aristocratic status, wealth, purchase, mercenary skills, or political connections. In Prussia in 1808, a system of open recruitment, education, and examination was initiated to assure a highly competent officer corps for that country. The concept spread slowly. France and Great Britain eventually established their own military academies in the last quarter of the century. Meanwhile, the Prussians formulated a professional ethic and produced a professional literature that includes classics in military theory and philosophy.

## War in the Twentieth Century

The twentieth century has been a continuation of the warring nineteenth century, but on a more massive scale. World War I cost nine million military and thirty million civilian lives. World War II cost seventeen million military and thirty-four million civilian lives. The airplane added a third dimension to military operations that had hitherto been confined to land and sea. Advanced military technology, radio, and mass production industries brought entire populations into the orbit of military operations and management. Vast military bureaucracies were required to conduct wars and to maintain states of preparedness and military leaders became increasingly pervasive influences in the political, economic, and even cultural lives of major nations.

Since the end of World War II, nuclear fission, the atom bomb, jet airplanes, intercontinental ballistic missiles, space satellites, television, and laser technology have made it militarily possible to destroy most of human civilization in a matter of hours or days. This fearsome possibility has not, as we shall see, slowed the competition in military technological development or the escalation of commerce in armaments. Nor has this possibility discouraged limited wars such as those in Korea, Vietnam, and the Middle East, or the countless military confrontations that have increasingly engaged United Nations peacekeeping efforts. In so hostile and warlike a world, with few global military institutions for collective security and peacekeeping, each of the more than 160 nations, large and small, has been forced to look to its own defense. The motivation for strengthening national military organizations and institutions, at whatever cost, appears to be compelling and overriding.[11] The record of human warfare, as of 1960, was equally compelling: 14,531 wars in 5,560 years of recorded human history; only ten years of complete peace in the 185 generations covered by this period.[12]

The technological search for security has, ironically, become one of the principal propellants of the qualitative arms race. The meaning of "qualitative" is perhaps best suggested by comparing the bow-and-arrow to the atom bomb. The arrow is lethal to one person at a time; the atom bomb may destroy a city full of people at one time. Both weapons are human artifacts produced at different stages of mankind's technological advancement. The potential lethality of military weapons is the principal motive for developing them, and students of this morbid subject have developed a "lethality index" with which to evaluate different weapons.

A United States Army colonel, P. N. Dupuy, created such a lethality index in the early 1960s. The lethality score took into account six attributes: (1) a weapon's effective sustained rate of fire, that is, the number of arrows, bullets, and so forth it could shoot in one hour, (2) the number of potential human targets it could hit per strike, (3) the relative effect—death, incapacitation, or other result—of each strike, (4) the effective range of the weapon (in thousands of yards), (5) its accuracy, (6) its reliability expressed as a probability that the weapon would not misfire. In Table 1 we can see examples of Dupuy's lethality index applied to selected known weapons as of 1964. Some sixteen years later, Julian Perry Robinson of Sussex University applied the same lethality scoring procedure to weapons developed since Dupuy's evaluation. Robinson's results are included in Table 1. The progression in the lethality of weapons is the essence of the qualitative arms race.

# Military Institutions: A Dilemma of Self-Governance

Our brief survey of the military side of human evolution reminds us that the motivations for organized social and political violence have for millenia been stirred by the fear and anger arising from actions ranging from wife stealing to attempted world domination. Whatever the motivation, people need not look far for a reason to fight. Such reasons are the inevitable consequence of different

**Table 1.   The Lethality Index***

| Dupuy's List: 1964 | | Robinson's List: 1978 | |
|---|---|---|---|
| Broadsword | 20 | Assault rifle | 4,200 |
| Longbow | 34 | Medium howitzer, nerve gas shell | 1,400,000 |
| Flintlock, 18th century | 47 | Fighter bomber with napalm firebombs | 1,900,000 |
| Breechloading rifle | 230 | Main battle tank | 3,200,000 |
| Machine gun, World War I | 13,000 | Multiple missile launcher | 12,000,000 |
| Tank, World War I | 68,000 | Fighter bomber, nerve gas bombs | 28,000,000 |
| Field gun, World War I | 470,000 | Tactical guided missile, nerve gas warhead | 91,000,000 |
| Howitzer 155m, World War II | 660,000 | Heavy bomber with cluster bombs | 150,000,000 |
| Ballistic missile, high explosive warhead | 860,000 | Heavy bomber, high explosive load | 210,000,000 |
| Fighter bomber, World War II | 3,000,000 | Tactical guided missile, 20 kiloton warhead | 830,000,000 |
| Fission explosive 1-megaton airburst | 666,000,000 | Strategic guided missile, 1-megaton warhead | 18,000,000,000 |

*Index values calculated on basis of known or estimated performance of six factors: effective sustained rate of fire (how many arrows, bullets, etc. can be shot in one hour); number of potential targets per strike (target referring to one person standing unprotected in mass formation each occupying four square feet of ground); relative effect of strike (the possibility of the victim being incapacitated, with a 50 per cent probability of death); effective range (using a formula based on thousands of yards); accuracy (probability of the strike hitting its target); reliability (probability that the weapon would not misfire).

SOURCE: *San Francisco Examiner* (July 4, 1978) based on Julian Perry Robinson report in *Bulletin of Atomic Scientists* (March 1978), pp. 42–45.

perceptions of reality, different value priorities, distrust of the intentions of others, and fear for one's own safety and survival.

Given that many stimuli escalation of human conflicts tends to be limited only by an adversary's capacity to overcome the opposition. The major elements of this capacity have been (a) weapons technology, (b) military organization, and (c) willingness to assume the risks and costs of violence, that is, warfare. Our survey points up the breathtaking quality of the human genius for developing weapons technology from spears to multi-megaton nuclear missiles, from weapons capable of killing only a single person at a strike to those able to kill several millions. Military organization, too, has grown from tiny raiding parties to massively mobilized armies, navies, and air forces. Military organization, we have seen, has responded in large measure to the changing requirements in the supply and handling of increasingly lethal weaponry. In turn, modern economies have been largely organized in response to the production and other requirements of military organizations and their weaponry.

What seems to remain unchanged but profoundly in dispute today is the willingness to assume the risks and costs of warfare. There are those who consider wars of any type to be inhumane and obsolete. Others believe that there are some values worth fighting for: the liberty-or-death type of choice. But it is clear that nuclear war could readily end life—and liberty—on this planet. It is increasingly evident that limited wars, such as Vietnam and Afghanistan, are not only difficult to limit but also less and less predictable in their political outcomes. Are there, therefore, risks and costs of warfare that political communities should be willing to assume? Or are there alternative human institutions for conducting serious conflicts without endeavoring to destroy the adversary?

Warfare is a form of conflict interaction between human beings. Weaponry and military organizations are instruments for, rather than causes of this form of, conflict interaction. The conflict is between people, not weapons. Arrangements for arms control and disarmament tend to focus on matters pertaining to weaponry and military organization whereas arrangements for peacekeeping tend to be concerned with the management of conflict between people. One of the most fundamental dilemmas of human self-governance arises out of the manner in which political communities employ their weaponry and military institutions. Do the military serve as instruments of safety, security, and order, protecting the community's system for carrying on its inevitable disagreements and conflicts nonviolently? Or, are the military tools of oppression and aggression in the hands of self-aggrandizing, lawless, foolish, or primitive leaders? These questions have absorbed political philosophers and political leaders since ancient times.

The military organizes and controls the community's resources for physical coercion. This fact raises two issues: (1) Who controls the military? (2) Against whom do the military exercise physical coercion? With respect to the first issue, as we have seen in our brief history of warfare, in most political communities, at least historically, the principal political leaders have also been the principal leaders of the military, for example, kings and nobles, totalitarian dictators, and the like. However, in communities that are constitutional democracies, the principle of civilian ascendancy over the military has been the key to establishing and preserving the lawful and constrained exercise of physical coercion for purposes about which there is community consensus. That consensus is usually manifest in the popular, competitive, and constitutional election of the chief executives of the community, its legislative process, its system of justice, and, most importantly, its use of political party institutions as the vehicle for carrying on its more serious conflicts. "Ballots instead of bullets" are the preferred instruments of coercion in constitutional democracies, at least in their internal conflicts. What makes the emergence of "military-industrial complexes" (MIC) so worrisome for some contemporary constitutional democracies is the tendency of MICs to weaken the institutions—political parties and legislatures—of civilian control of the military. In dictatorships, however, the military managers of the means of physical coercion are usually one and the same as the political leaders, and they are unconcerned about community consensus. The relationship is one of military ascendancy over the civilians, and the consequence is almost invariably political oppression, that is, a police state. There are also those political halfway houses, such as the Soviet Union and the People's Republic of China, where authoritarian regimes maintain substantial but hardly complete civilian control over the military. The political meaning of the civilian-military, oppression-order mix in these regimes will undoubtedly remain unclear for some time to come.

All political communities, regardless of whether constitutional or totalitarian, require resources of physical coercion, that is, a military institution, to provide protection from external enemies and attackers. Here, too, it is inevitable that political communities such as nations will have conflicting interests from time to time. But how inevitable is the exercise of military power in the conduct of these intercommunity conflicts? The world has yet to clarify its definition of the differences between "aggression" and "defense," although, as we shall see in a later chapter, the General Assembly of the United Nations, after twenty years of discussion, adopted in

1974 a definition of "aggression" as part of a code of international law. The world has yet to construct a constitutional system of self-governance wherein there would be (a) civilian ascendancy over the military, (b) community consensus in the selection of and policy making by civilian leaders, and (c) the employment of the military as instruments for the protection of systems of orderly and nonviolent disagreement. Instead, the world continues to engage in warfare, seeks to prevent or ameliorate war through arms control agreements, and attempts to create institutions for peacekeeping and conflict management. Even a world without war will surely have military institutions. The uncommonly difficult question is how to convert the world's many military institutions from instruments of international warfare into constitutionally controlled police services for the maintenance of world collective security. It is to the latter question that we now turn.

# References

1. William Tulio Divale, *Warfare in Primitive Societies: A Bibliography* (Santa Barbara, CA: ABC-Clio, 1973), p. xvii.
2. *Ibid.;* Quincy Wright, *A Study of War* (Chicago: University of Chicago Press, 1942); also, same author, "The Study of War," *International Encyclopedia of the Social Sciences* (New York: Macmillan, 1968), Vol. 16.
3. Oliver L. Spaulding, Jr., H. Nickerson, and J. W. Wright, *Warfare* (New York: Harcourt, Brace, 1925), pp. 10, 25.
4. *Ibid.,* p. 215 and *passim.*
5. John Beeler, *Warfare in Feudal Europe, 730–1200* (Ithaca: Cornell University Press, 1971), pp. 40–43. Also, Spaulding *et al., op. cit.,* Chap. V.
6. *Ibid.,* pp. 374 ff.
7. Ludwig Renn, *Warfare* (Freeport, N.Y.: Books for Libraries Press, reprinted 1971), p. 122; Spaulding *et al., op. cit.,* pp. 375 ff.
8. This survey of the development of military technology and institutions emphasizes the organization of armies for the conduct of land warfare. From time to time in history, however, control of the seas has been the dominant organizing influence in the growth of specific military institutions. Not until the height of the Roman Empire was a naval fleet clearly distinguishable from the mercantile. At that time, navies fought each other in phalanx and other formations imitative of those used in land warfare. The Norsemen, who invented the longboat as a new type of warship, gave a new importance to piracy and land raids launched from the sea; there was little distinction between sailor and soldier in these operations. To promote and protect their sea-borne commerce, the Hanseatic League of north

European towns developed large sailing vessels to serve both mercantile and naval purposes. During the sixteenth century, Italians,
Spaniards, Turks, and English began to give serious attention to
matters of sea exploration, colonial trade, piracy, and naval warfare; vessels were armed with cannon, heavily armored for defense,
and designed for maneuverability. The English defeat of the
awesome Spanish Armada in 1588 was a turning point in that it
confirmed the importance of naval warfare and inaugurated a new
era of British naval power. England's first military academy, in fact,
was created to train naval rather than army officers. From the
seventeenth century on, naval organizations were an integral part of
the military institutions of most major powers. Renn, *op. cit.*, pp.
212–234.

9. Alfred Vagts, *A History of Militarism* (New York: Meridian Books,
1959), Chap. 3.

10. Samuel P. Huntington, *The Soldier and the State* (New York: Vin-
tage Books, 1964), p. 19.

11. The trend has stimulated the study of military institutions in several
of the social sciences. For a review of the growing literature, Kurt
Lang, *Military Institutions and the Sociology of War* (Beverly Hills:
Sage Publications, 1972).

12. A report on "war as a permanent condition," *Time* (September 24,
1965), pp. 30–31. No survey of warfare can fail to refer to Quincy
Wright's monumental *A Study of War* (2 vols., Chicago: University
of Chicago Press, 1942) which, for the first time, provided a thorough
history of war and an interdisciplinary analysis of war's characteristics. J. David Singer's Correlates of War Project at the University
of Michigan has drawn together substantial quantitative data about
attributes of wars: participants, length, destructiveness, etc. See J.
David Singer, "The 'Correlates of War' Project," *World Politics,*
Vol. 24 (January 1972), No. 2, pp. 243–70. Also, J. David Singer
and Melvin Small, *The Wages of War 1815–1965* (New York: John
Wiley, 1972), which is a handbook of the data collected. David W.
Zeigler, *War, Peace, and International Politics* (Boston: Little,
Brown, 1977) provides a comprehensive introductory survey of the
role of war and various approaches to peace as these relate to the
conduct of international politics. On the "inevitability" of war and
the views of various philosophies on the subject of war, Donald A.
Wells, *The War Myth* (New York: Pegasus, 1967).

# CHAPTER 2

# The Condition of Insecurity

Our Nation's safety continues to depend upon a strong, modern military defense, capable of meeting the full spectrum of our military needs. We have had that strength in the past. We have it now. And we will maintain it. Yet we cannot assure our security by military strength alone. New weapons systems acquired by one side stimulate the other side to develop more sophisticated countermeasures. The net effect is the expansion of weapons systems on both sides without a real increase in the security of either.[1]

The contemporary pursuit of national and global security is generally perceived as a "hardware" problem, that is, a matter of possessing sufficient weaponry and the military organization to use that weaponry. This chapter examines the assumption that military resources are the best objective measure of security and introduces the subjective aspects of "sense of security." This subjectively manifests itself in "hawkish" and "dovish" estimates regarding the amount of military strength needed to be secure. Out of the debate between Hawks and Doves comes the public budget for "security services," that is, for police and the military. The international competition for security is the propellant of the arms race, actually two races, both stated in terms of hardware: the nuclear race and the conventional arms race. As a consequence, two superpower coalitions—the North Atlantic Treaty Organization and the Warsaw Treaty Organization—hold sway over the world, responsible for two thirds of the world's military expenditures. Other nations, particularly in the Middle East, are racing along behind. The other propellant of the arms race, in addition to the search for security, is technological, commonly referred to as the qualitative arms race. Huge research budgets and unbounded human ingenuity pour forth new weapons technologies and each new weapons system upsets some nation's sense of security. Turning off human ingenuity is about as difficult as turning up a political community's sense of security. Such are the circumstances of insecurity in the world today.

## Security as Subjective Judgment

Does a gun in the home add to the safety of its occupants? Put this question to any group and it will provoke a heated debate within seconds. Perhaps not surprisingly, the sides will divide up *not* between those who own a gun on the one hand and those who do not on the other, but rather between those who *feel* that a gun will add to their security and those who *feel* that the gun will increase their insecurity. In short, the issue reveals itself not as a matter of weapon possession but rather as one pertaining to a "sense of security."

What is most striking about such a debate is the highly and necessarily subjective character of the views held about the sense of security. It matters not whether the individual or family actually possesses a weapon. The argument of one side will be that the weapon will serve as a deterrent to violence or illegal entry into the home. The other side will argue that the presence of a weapon is likely to be unknown to an intruder and an incitement to instant escalation as soon as the intruder discovers this. One side will argue that the weapon is necessary for retaliation and revenge. The other side will decry these actions as meaningless once an exchange of gunfire begins. One side will feel better about having the "protection" of a weapon; the other side will prefer to live with the "risks" of being weaponless. Finally, the proponent of arming is likely to take some pride in the technology and skills associated with weapons possession while the disarmer will cite the countless accidents and intrafamily deaths—in the United States someone is killed by a handgun every 50 minutes—resulting from the availability and/or mishandling of guns.

What is the basis for feeling more safe or less safe, with or without weapons? Obviously the conclusion about one's safety is arrived at on the basis of subjective beliefs and feelings stimulated by *ostensibly* relevant objective conditions or events. The leaders of the two nuclear superpowers, for example, feel relatively secure from nuclear attack because of the relative size of their stockpiles of nuclear warheads: 11,000 possessed by the United States and 5,000–6,000 by the Soviet Union. Smaller nations, as neighbors, will watch closely and suspiciously the build-up of nearby armed forces, assuming that one's own strength and security necessarily declines as the neighbor's military power increases. In short, the active search for a sense of security can, under such conditions, be the principal cause of the insecurity of others. Out of this relatively simple dynamic have come history's recurrent arms races.

So significant a subjective judgment as arming or not arming oneself deserves closer examination. What is the judgmental or psychological process involved in such a choice? Behavioral scientists refer to this process as "subjective probability." In their daily lives, people must constantly estimate the probability of events. How do these private assessments conform to the laws of probability, that is, mathematical or objective probability? Often not very well.

One reason is that we often confuse the intensity of our wishes or hopes with the probability that some desired event will take place, a confusion that may frequently be observed in children around Christmas Eve or political candidates trying to keep up the morale of their campaign workers. We also make subjective probability estimates on the basis of personal experience or skills in statistical reasoning, as described below.[2]

The judgmental consequences of personal experience were revealed in an experiment in comparing risk taking of a group of beginners just starting training as bus drivers with that of trained drivers and of an experienced instructor. The test task was to drive a bus between two posts. The posts were set at various distances, ranging from gaps that the bus could clear very easily to openings narrower than the bus. The experienced drivers not only performed more successfully than the inexperienced but also took less risk. The beginners sometimes tried to drive the bus through an impossibly narrow gap; the trained drivers seldom did; the instructor never did. Such "experience" undoubtedly involves a subconscious measuring and counting process that improves one's judgmental accuracy as the number of assessment experiences increases. In this experiment, for example, the more experienced the driver, the less risky (inaccurate) his subjective probability estimate regarding the narrowest gap through which he could safely drive.

Improvement in subjective probability assessment resulting from cumulative experience illustrates, too, one of the rules of mathematical probability, namely, the additive theorem. This theorem states that small, independent probabilities of an event add up to a larger probability. For example, assume that you are drawing for a winning ticket in a pool. Your chances of success will increase in proportion to the number of tickets you purchase. Two tickets will double your chances, three tickets will triple them, and so forth. However, ask your friends if they would prefer to draw 1 ticket from a box of 10 or 10 tickets from a box of 100, in the latter case putting back the ticket drawn before making the next draw. Most will prefer to make the single draw from the box of 10, even though the chances of drawing the winning ticket is exactly the same in both cases. They prefer a single large probability (1 in 10) to what they perceive as a set of smaller probabilities (10 in 100). Their subjective probability assessment does not match the mathematical probability. Juries and politicians are constantly having to weigh one large item of evidence (and the probabilities associated with it) against the sum of several small items (and the probabilities associated with that sum). For example, should one friendly summit meeting between superpower leaders be the basis for important detente policies, particularly since it is impossible to have such meetings frequently? Or should detente policies be premised upon the success or failure of many more meetings by lesser officials?

There is another kind of situation in which chances are multiplicative rather than additive. For example, a general may have to decide whether to stake success on a single big battle or a succession of smaller ones. Assume that he must win *each* of the smaller battles in order to undertake the next in the series. His chances of success are multiplicative, not additive. Assume that the chance of success in each battle is 50–50, that is, ½. The overall chance for a series is ½ x ½ x ½ . . . . On this basis, the more battles he has to win, the smaller is his chance of final success. People very often choose the series with multiple chances rather than the single chance, even though mathematically the series' chance is smaller.

These examples are offered simply to illustrate that there may be—and often is—a significant difference between mathematical or objective probability and a person's subjective probability estimate about the prospect of an event occurring. In internation relations, such estimates are made regarding the extent of a nation's security, with a number of psychological factors that tend to promote arms races. Some of these factors consist of "evidence" that is presumed to be objective. One factor is the degree of hostility of one nation toward another. A second is the degree of trust or distrust between the two nations. The third factor, thought to be the most objective, is the quantity and quality of the other's weaponry.

The perception that another nation seeks to inflict destruction upon or deny resources to one's own nation may readily be based upon the behavior of posturing leaders, threats and name-calling, ideological enmity, military maneuvers, and even normal competition. When leaders of the Soviet Union speak of "capitalist encirclement," "capitalist ruling circles," and "imperialist aggression" in comments about the United States, Americans are hardly about to interpret such talk as anything but hostile. Conversely, when American leaders embark upon Communist witch hunts, warn against "the Red menace," and threaten "massive nuclear retaliation" against any Soviet aggressions, the Russians have no difficulty identifying their principal enemy. However, Anwar Sadat's famous trip to Jerusalem from Cairo and the ensuing peace process between Egypt and Israel suggest that internation hostilities can be reversed.

Distrust is a distinct attitude of one party toward another, as we shall see later in greater detail. Distrust consists of two major elements: a prediction regarding the future conduct of the other party, and a judgment that the expected conduct will have negative consequences for oneself. Senate discussions regarding SALT II, for example, include many predictions that the Soviet Union is likely to try to cheat and the judgment that such cheating can have profound negative consequences for the survival of the United

States. In short, many senators distrust the Soviet Union's leaders. As the next chapter will explain, political distrust is a major generator of the arms race and a principal analytical theme of this book.

Some will argue that it is difficult to measure with precision such factors as hostility and distrust, but there can be no mistake about the quantity and quality of an adversary's weaponry. Hence, the other's weapons stockpile is usually considered the most "objective" measure of that party's intentions and of the degree of one's own security. Weaponry can be seen, counted, and evaluated for quality. *Prima facie*, the greater the quantity and quality of the other's weapons, the more serious is the threat to one's safety. But how much is "more?" Unfortunately, the answer almost invariably involves a great amount of subjective probability assessment. As a consequence, the search for a "military balance" becomes a comparison of apples and oranges (tanks versus neutron bombs, for example) and soon flounders on the unmeasurable. Arms races thus become inexorable.

## The Search for Objective Sources of Security

Possibly the most costly of human endeavors is the search for objective bases for feeling physically safe. Powerful and famous persons surround themselves with bodyguards, usually at great private or public expense. Corporations and other propertied organizations expend large sums for plant and other security systems. Communities pay taxes for expensive police forces. Nations carry the weighty burden of military budgets and expensive weapons systems. One of the most widely held of human propositions is that might makes right. A corollary proposition is that military power assures security. The side with the most guns is presumably the safest. Because military strength lends itself readily to quantification, the tendency is to correlate physical safety with size of military forces. The assumption is that degree of military strength is the most objective and reliable measure of physical security.

However, there are those who will vigorously argue, on both empirical and logical grounds, that such an assumption is not only in error but also dangerous. This point of view usually starts from the assertion that an escalating arms race decreases rather than increases security. The further contention is that there are many sources—objectively observable and measurable—of physical security other than or in addition to the military. These other foundations of security include a nation's economic resources, technological and educational capacities, cultural and social values and practices, and adaptive political institutions. These sources of strength are, it is argued, along with the military, highly significant for security.

It is hardly a novel proposition that a prosperous and equitable economy is a source of strength and security. But throughout history, hasn't the possession of natural resources and national wealth invited attack from the predatory and the greedy? In other words, is not a prosperous economy a source of insecurity? The answer depends upon a number of factors. The citizens of a society in which wealth is widely distributed are more likely to pay the taxes and man the defenses that will assure the safety of that community. However, concentrated wealth is likely to be less secure among an envious or angry citizenry unwilling to protect that wealth from greedy outsiders, or even insiders. Another factor is the extent to which the citizenry is the principal source as well as beneficiary of the community's resources. What sense does it make to try to capture a nation of highly productive farmers if these farmers go on strike or slow down production when they fall under the military rule of some hated foreigner? To offer a more specific illustration, would the United States remain the "breadbasket of the world" if its farmlands and farmers were captives of some odious military conqueror? Whatever one's answer to these questions, the point remains that economic strength is perceived by many as a principal source of national security even in the absence of great military strength. Witness the contemporary success of Germany and Japan in the world's economy. Witness the dramatic rise in influence of the Arab oil-producing states.

Witness also the difficulties of the economy of the Soviet Union and their relationship to military spending. During the 1950s the Gross National Product of the Soviet Union was growing by about 5.8 percent annually compared to a United States rate of 3.2 percent annually. Khrushchev boasted that the Soviet economy would soon surpass the American and that the Communists would "bury" the capitalists. But at about that time U.S. growth moved up to about 4 percent and by early 1970s the Soviets were down to 3.7 percent GNP growth annually. Soviet economists placed the blame on the leveling off of Soviet capital growth (no new technologies, no new industries, too little equipment replacement in old industries), the stabilization of the labor force (very little occupational mobility, low birthrate, much manpower tied up in armed forces), rigid bureaucracy (discouraging individual enterprise), and accelerating military expenditures—growing at 4.5 percent annually. Both Soviet and American economists agree that an arms race could compel even a totalitarian economy to spend itself into a self-destroying depression. "Reducing military expenditures, however, would weaken the Soviet Union's principal claim to world power . . . . This appears to be quite incompatible with the conservative leanings of the Soviet gerontocracy.''[3] The current interest of Soviet leaders in detente and arms control may reflect their concern for limiting, if not reducing, military costs and forestalling domestic economic crises.

Another frequently cited foundation of national security is the technological and educational achievements of a society. Life in a modern industrialized and civilized community requires a literate and well-educated populace. One need only look at the tribulations of the many nations in which only 1 to 5 percent of the people are literate or educated to conclude that ignorance is a major source of instability and insecurity for these communities. In contrast, the United States is clearly the technological and educational envy of the world, the nation with the greatest number of colleges and universities, the most varied educational enterprise, the greatest investment in research and human inventiveness, the producer of computers, moon landings, lasers, and other grand achievements of high technology by an educated, free, and inventive people in what is becoming an Information Society. We may argue over the quality or quantity of these claims but, overall, the objective evidence and the world's envy tend to confirm the validity of the claims. However, technology and education are hardly an American monopoly. Witness the surprise and shock experienced in the United States when, in 1957, the Soviet Union sent aloft its Sputnik. It immediately became a matter of American pride that the United States catch up; politicians and taxpayers were never more willing to pay out the funds necessary for education and research. Ironically, a highly educated and inventive populace is essential not only to produce high technology but also to carry forward what is commonly referred to as ''the qualitative arms race,'' that is, the contest for superiority in new and ingenious military technologies. We shall return to the qualitative arms race later.

One troublesome aspect of American technological superiority is the question of with whom it should be shared. Our less-educated and less-skilled allies—for example, the late Shah of Iran—do not have sufficiently trained people to handle, let alone develop, advanced equipment. Our industrialized allies—for example, Japan and France—starting without technology, often outinvent us. Most difficult, however, is the issue of transferring United States technology and knowhow to our adversaries, particularly the Soviet Union. For example, during summer 1979, Dresser Industries of Dallas began to design and equip a $144 million plant near the Volga River to produce oil drill bits for the Soviet oil industry. The same facility may be quickly converted to the manufacture of projectiles capable of penetrating the latest United States tanks. This transfer of American technology will help increase Soviet oil production and make available a potential military projectile plant. Is this good or bad for United States security? Can we trust the Russians? Of the $1 billion in manufactured goods sold to Communist governments in 1978, about one-third was considered high technology. Although the Export Administration Act prohibits technology sales to Communist governments if such transfers make a "significant contribution" to their military potential, according to one senior Pentagon official it has become increasingly difficult to tell "whether an item is a sword or a plowshare."[4]

A further source of security, many will argue, are the cultural and social values and practices of a society. Without freedom and respect for the individual, few societies have succeeded in becoming affluent, creative, or cultured. Invention and the arts flourish in those communities where basic social attitudes promote tolerance, respect for others, optimism, and freedom of association and discussion. It is the basic position of Andrei Sakharov, the developer of the Soviet H-bomb, that the lack of freedom in the Soviet Union is detrimental to the achievements and the very safety of that nation. Knowledge cannot grow well or spread freely in a closed and isolated society; science is an open process that malfunctions under conditions of secrecy. Not many cultures value freedom and creativity, nor do some national elites care to risk the revolutionary consequences of educating their people. Such societies are also among the least stable or secure in the world.

Many of the above arguments, we are told, make it easier to comprehend in what ways a society's political institutions may be an additional objective source of security. The political community that is willing to distribute its shares of power widely among its citizenry, that has a capacity for expressing and resolving profound disagreements, and that produces leaders skilled in the discovery and pursuit of widely held political goals is also likely to have strong and highly adaptive institutional arrangements to accomplish all this. For Americans, many of the relevant institutions are specific and well known: a free press and academy; a competitive political party system that succeeds in harnessing dissent, insurgency, and innovation; an open bureaucracy that is fair game for the dissatisfactions of legislators and taxpayers; a judicial system and legal profession accustomed to victories, defeats, and compromises; and the most varied and numerous array of organized interest groups in the world. As a consequence, the United States has perhaps the noisiest, most visible, and, according to some, the most revolutionary political system in the world. What may seem to be sound, fury, and confusion to some is more likely the inevitable friction of a complex society adapting to new conditions and goals. At least such were the institutions that Woodrow Wilson had in mind when he called upon his fellow-citizens to fight to keep the world safe for democracy. He was not alone in assuming that democratic political institutions are a source of society's strength and security. It is also the goal of these institutions to make violence obsolete as a technique for resolving human conflict and change.

These are merely brief summaries of the assumptions and contentions of those who argue that safety and security in this world is derived from objective sources other than military strength. Each of these other resources is objective to the extent that it may be observed and quantified: the economy in dollars and standards of living; education in terms of numbers of literate citizens and years of formal education; culture in terms of degrees of consensus about particular attitudes and practices; and politics by participation, votes, and capacity for conflict resolution. Some may doubt the validity and reliability of some of these quantifications, but the argument is that these sources are measurable, hence objective.

The more psychologically sensitive among us will, however, continue to wonder how much of the derived sense of security comes from objective measures and how much from highly subjective probability estimates. The world is full of irrational, trigger-happy, and dangerous persons, groups, and regimes that are gratified by destroying wealth, burning books and other repositories of knowledge, inflicting primitive and totalitarian values upon others, and closing down venerable political institutions. In such a world and against such forces, only clearly overwhelming military might seems to provide the best protection and the most clearly measurable sense of security. Hence, bigger armies, air forces, and navies, better weapons, and more powerful military alliance systems become the order of the day. From this point of view, Switzerland is presumably safe only because every one of its citizens is a soldier. Germany and Japan, although disarmed, are presumably safe only because they are protected by the American defense umbrella.

Such are the arguments back and forth regarding the nature of security and the objective and subjective foundations upon which our sense of security is premised. "Hawks" tend to perceive the world as risky, specific adversaries as evil and dangerous, and the objective military sources of security as the most important. "Doves," on the other hand, seem more willing to live with a higher degree of risk, see potential adversaries as misguided but educable, and count most sources of security, particulary the military, as only temporary assurances in what is essentially, in their view, a subjective judgment.

With such divergent points of departure, each side arrives at quite different policy conclusions regarding such practical issues as weapons development, military strategy, defense budgets, foreign policy, and, most generally, the investment of all kinds of community resources for the support of "security services." The fact that the world as a whole currently spends over $480 billion a year for military purposes and that the arms race is one of the most serious preoccupations of mankind today clearly suggests that the predominant perceptions and policies are hawkish.

## The World's Military Outlays

World military expenditures are thoroughly and authoritatively reported eleswhere in great detail and on an annual basis.[5] The purpose of citing some of the specific data about world military expenditures is to provide a general and relatively concrete impression of the size, content, and scope of the financial outlays that the world seems willing to expend for its security services. There are, of course, other costs of a nonfiscal kind: social and psychological consequences, such as collective fear or collective sense of insecurity; possible alternative uses of funds; and the crisis climate generated by a world of garrison states.

In 1978, 145 of the 160 nations of the world were spending about $480 billion annually (current dollars) for the support of military forces and the purchase of weapons and military equipment. This contrasts with the 1967 world military expenditure of $201 billion, that is, 7.1 percent of the gross world product. The 1978 military expenditure amounted to 5.4 percent of the world's gross product, that is, the gross dollar value of all the goods and services produced by the normal productive activity of the world. Only the world's expenditure for education, 5.3 per cent of the world gross product, matched the military. Other special expenditures trailed; for example, only 3.0 percent for health services. It is expected that world military expenditures during the 1980s will exceed $600 billion a year.

Who were the Big Spenders? The North Atlantic Treaty Organization (NATO) was, collectively, responsible for 38 percent of the $480 billion total. The Warsaw Treaty Organization (WTO or Warsaw Pact) was its equal at 37 percent. Other spenders, grouped by region, followed far behind: East Asia at 12 percent; the Near East at 7 percent; South Asia at 2 percent; Latin America and Africa at over 1 percent each. Of course, embedded in the NATO and Warsaw Pact alliances are the two truly Big Spenders: the United States and the Soviet Union. We shall return to a comparison between these two shortly.

On what is the $480 billion spent? There are wages to be paid to the 27 million persons who make up all the world's regular military forces, the 10 million others who comprise paramilitary forces, the 30 million employed in civilian support work for the military, and the 24 million in the ready reserves. Another $25 billion is spent annually for research and development, that is, to support human inventiveness and adaptiveness, a remarkable spur to the qualitative arms race. Yet another $80 billion constitutes the annual procurement expenditure for weapons and military equipment. As a consequence of these procurement programs, the world had, in 1976, spread among its nations 124,000 tanks, 12,400 combat ships, 35,000 combat aircraft, and nuclear weapons the equivalent of more than 50 billion tons of TNT. By way of contrast, annual expenditures for United Nations peacekeeping in recent years has been approximately $150–200 million (repeat: million, not billion).

There are other comparisons that can be made. About one dollar in every six for public expenditures throughout the world goes for military aspects of security, or what is familiarly referred to as the arms race. In two days the world spends on arms the equivalent of a year's budget for the United Nations and its specialized agencies. The world's military budget of $480 billion equals the annual income of 1.8 billion people in the thirty-six poorest nations in the world.

Is there a more appropriate scale for measuring the cost of world security services and equipment? For example, how much do American cities spend on the security services provided by police departments? How does this compare to the global expenditure? Table 2 offers some recent data and comparisons.

From the table, it is evident that cities allocate for police protection some 19 percent of their total budgets. The 1977 per capita expenditures reveal where cities put their priorities: $57 per person for education, $47 for police protection, $43 for sanitation, $34 for

**Table 2.    The Cost of Security Services, 1977–1978**

| Community (number of dollars) | Police/Military Expenditures Current (M) | Total Budget Governmental Expenditures (B) | Percent for Security Services (M/B) |
|---|---|---|---|
| San Francisco police—1978 (millions) | 185 | 974 | 19.0 |
| All U. S. cities police—1977 (millions) | 454 | 2,386 | 19.0 |
| World military–1977 (billions) | 434 | 1,640 | 26.4 |
| U.S. military—1977 (billions) | 101 | 381 | 26.5 |
| U.S.S.R. military—1977 (billions) | 140 | 252 | 56.0 |

SOURCES: U.S. Arms Control and Disarmament Agency, *World Military Expenditures, 1968-1977*; U.S. Bureau of the Census, *City Expenditures of 1977*; San Francisco City Budget, 1978-79.

welfare, $31 for highways, $26 for fire protection, and so forth. If we consider military expenditures as a security service cost comparable to police and fire protection, we find, perhaps surprisingly, that the world expenditure of $434 billion—the 1977 figure—represents a similar proportion of the governmental budgets of all nations in the world taken together, specifically 26.4 percent. The United States military budget as a portion of the total national budget also falls within this range: 26.5 percent. By contrast, in 1977 the Soviet Union put more than half of its national government budget—56.0 percent—into security services.[6] Thus, it would seem that most political communities in the world, whether local, national, or international, tend to view from 19 to 26 percent of their government budgets as an appropriate level of expenditure for police and military security services. If sense of security could be objectified as a simple budgetary issue, such questions as "How much is enough for security services?" could be more easily debated as a public issue. Of course, this is not likely, given the highly subjective aspects of sense of security, not to mention the difficulty in comparing such significant national budgets as those of the United States and the Soviet Union.

However, debate does occur at the local community level and usually reveals the difficulty of either validly connecting cause and effect or reaching objective public policy conclusions. San Diego, California, was the scene of just such a debate recently. Between 1970 and 1977, serious crime in San Diego rose by nearly 182 percent. Over this same period, the city's police force also rose from about 850 officers in 1970 to some 1,250 authorized in 1978. The occasion of the recent debate was the City Council's vote to add another 100 officers to the force. Even the sponsors of the increase were reluctant to correlate crime rate with size of police force. "There's nothing that says the crime rate will go down if you add more cops," said one. "How do you measure crime that doesn't take place?" complained another. On the other side of the debate, a sociologist offered data that showed *arrests* for serious crimes in San Diego rose only 18 percent, from 4,053 to 4,789, during the 1970–1977 period while the number of serious crimes *reported* jumped 150 percent, from 14,131 to 35,248. The sociologist: concluded "People derive a certain sense of security from police but it's a false security."[7] Even more tantalizing is the relationship of weapons to the sense of security of police officers themselves. Only 430 of London's 21,500 officers are authorized to use firearms; most carry wooden truncheons. Yet, during the four years from 1974 to 1978 not one London police officer was killed in line of duty. Do people also derive a false sense of security from the possession of weapons?

Another way of evaluating the cost of security is to compare police and military expenditures to gross world or gross national product. This is a debatable comparison on at least two grounds. First, the dollar value placed on the same goods or services may vary from country to country. Second, many of the more primitively produced goods and services in the developing nations of the world are omitted from censuses of economic activity in those places. Nonetheless, the available statistics are interesting and do give a more concrete impression of the dimensions of the military costs borne by the productive societies of the world. We have already noted that the $480 billion total world military expenditure represents about 5.4 percent of the gross world product. The 1978 military expenditure of the United States represents 5.1

percent of the American gross national product. The comparable figure for the Soviet Union is 12.2 percent. Stated in terms of per capita military expenditures, these percentages represent 1978 military outlays of about $103 per capita worldwide, more than $460 for each U.S. citizen, and close to $550 per Soviet citizen. By comparison, Japan's per capita military expenditure is only $57, one of the lowest in the world. Saudi Arabia's per capita expenditure is $1,088, and Israel's is $984, the world's two highest.

The Soviet percentage has been at about the same level for more than a dozen years and is, of course, a matter of great attention and debate among American security policymakers. Some dismiss the high Soviet outlays as a short-term effort to reach parity with the Americans (presumably with the unstated acquiescence of American policymakers). Others view the rate of Soviet expenditure as evidence of a Soviet drive for military superiority. The Soviet leaders keep reminding everyone that they have to worry about China and Europe as well as the United States. These kinds of data lead to extensive, heated, and often arcane discussions about the *relative* military strengths of the United States and the Union of Soviet Socialist Republics. Such fiscal and hardware comparisons inevitably fuel the arms race since these are the dimensions that best lend themselves to the postures of "worst-case" analysts and Hawks.

## Comparing the Superpowers

The simplest, albeit probably the least valid, yardstick for comparing American and Soviet military strength is the fiscal one. In 1978, according to the U.S. ACDA report cited earlier, the American military budget stood at $101 billion in constant 1977 dollars. The Soviet military budget was $143 billion, also in constant dollars. These 1978 figures were merely a passing phase in escalating outlays on both sides. Thus, President Carter requested $126 billion for the defense budget for 1980; the Soviet Union, $164 billion.

A sharper picture comes into focus when we examine military expenditures for the period from 1960 to 1975. Over these fifteen years, the United States spent more that $1 *trillion* on its military budgets while the Soviet Union spent about $860 billion. Together, these two giants spent about two-thirds of all the military outlays worldwide for this period. These vast sums exclude costs for both domestic civilian expenditures and domestic security forces.

Over the same 1960–1975 period, the United States exported $41 billion worth of arms to other countries. By 1978 the United

States was supplying some 32 per cent of all of the arms transferred from one country to another throughout the world. The Soviet Union was a close second, exporting $27 billion worth of arms to other countries during the 1960–1975 period and supplying 34 per cent of the arms transfers of 1978. During the fifteen years covered, other suppliers were significant, but to a far lesser degree: France exporting $3.8 billion; followed by China, West Germany, Czechoslovakia, Poland, Canada, and others in decreasing amounts. By 1978 France was supplying 7 percent of the world total in arms transfers and the United Kingdom and West Germany 5 percent each. Who imports these arms? Currently, the developing countries of the world—despite their great need to improve the education, health, and prosperity of their people—import arms at the rate of $17 billion a year. The economic and political motivations for such arms supplying and buying are obviously substantial and will be discussed below.

Returning to the comparison of American and Soviet military strength, another traditional yardstick is military hardware. A few of the major manpower and weapons statistics are summarized in Table 3. Since China is a large concern for the Soviet Union, recent data for it are also presented.

Even a cursory interpretation of these figures will reveal how difficult it is to determine the "military balance" between the superpowers. The Soviet Union has a far greater number of troops in its military services. It is also a landlocked country with borders many thousands of miles longer than those of the United States, with presumably hostile neighbors at its eastern border (the People's Republic of China with some 4 million troops) and, just beyond its Warsaw Pact allies, western border (NATO). Although this is rarely mentioned, the Soviet Union also has some internal policing problems not experienced by the United States, namely, several hostile nationality groups among its Soviet republics and a few satellites in Eastern Europe whose reliability as allies is likely to diminish rapidly under wartime conditions.

A similar difficulty of comparison applies in connection with tanks. Again, the Soviet Union is a landlocked country, largely dependent upon land mobility for its troops. However, an American analyst could easily wonder about the need for such an overwhelming superiority in tanks. Tanks are usually considered attack weapons; there must be other factors involved in this imbalance. Adding data about the balance of tanks between NATO and the Warsaw Pact leads to an even less encouraging interpretation. The Warsaw Pact has 20,500 tanks to NATO's 7,000. Why so many Pact tanks if their intentions are defensive rather than offensive?

**Table 3.   Comparison of Superpower and Chinese Military Forces; Selected Components, 1978-1979**

| General Purpose Forces | U.S. | U.S.S.R. | P.R.C. |
|---|---|---|---|
| Troops (in millions) | 2.1* | 4.7 | 4.3 |
| Tanks | 12,675 | 45,000 | 10,000 |
| Warplanes | 4,900 | 8,500 | 5,100 |
| Surface Combat Ships | 172 | 243 | 23 |
| Submarines (Nuclear and | 70N | 85N | 1N |
| Diesel) | 5D | 158D | 74D |
| **Strategic Nuclear Forces** | | | |
| Strategic Vehicles: | | | |
| ICBM | 1,054 | 1,477 | 70 |
| SLBM | 656 | 1,015 | 0 |
| Bombers | 417 | 135 | 80 |
| Total vehicles | 2,127 | 2,627 | 150 |
| Deliverable warheads** | 9,200 | 5,000 | 500 |

*The United States troop level reached 3.1 million during the Vietnam War. In terms of combat-ready troops, as of 1979, the United States was estimated to have a force of 220,000 and the Soviet Union 1,560,000.

**As of 1980, the United States had about 11,000 warheads and the Soviet Union 6,000.

SOURCES: U.S. Department of Defense, Congressional Budget Office, and Institute for Strategic Studies, as reported in *U.S. News and World Report* (October 30, 1978); *Newsweek* (February 5 and June 25, 1979); also, U.S. Department of Defense *Annual Report, Fiscal Year 1980.*

The American-Soviet balance in tactical aircraft seems close enough, but Soviet superiority in surface combat ships and submarines must surely reflect a desire to compensate for being landlocked. It is a classic issue in Russian military affairs for that nation to seek warm water ports and sea outlets to the rest of the world. It may also be true that the Soviet Union builds a substantial naval force—243 combat ships and 243 submarines—in order to extend its political and diplomatic influence into regions and nations far beyond its immediate borders. At least, such is the American Hawk view of Soviet naval forces, particularly when one takes into account the 1,015 Soviet SLBM missiles reported lower down in the table.

The balance in superpower strategic nuclear forces is an entirely separate ball game and the principal concern of SALT II negotiators. Here the United States, creator of the nuclear bomb, is clearly the dominant force in number of deliverable nuclear warheads: 9,200 to the Soviet's 5,000, as of 1979. While the warheads have different explosive power, or megatonnage, the United States is still out in front. However, it must be noted that the Soviet Union tends to prefer a bigger megatonnage bang for its nuclear warhead buck.

It is with respect to strategic delivery vehicles that SALT negotiations and verification techniques become pertinent. While it is extremely difficult to measure from a distance the size and explosive power of a nuclear warhead, it is quite possible to verify the number and placement of delivery vehicles, and the latter have been the principal subjects of SALT negotiations. As part of their drive to overtake the American nuclear force over the past decade, the Soviet Union has actually passed the Americans in numbers of intercontinental ballistic missiles (ICBMs) and submarine-launched ballistic missiles (SLBMs). On the other hand, the United States continues to be ahead in number of bombers, accuracy in reaching targets, and, as indicated above, number of warheads. These three components of the strategic nuclear force—ICBMs, SLBMs, and bombers—are usually referred to as the three-legged Triad. The achievement of a rough balance in American and Soviet strategic nuclear forces is the purpose of the policy of "essential equivalency," that is, a rough but sufficient balance in the size of the forces such that neither side may expect or claim an overriding superiority.

Military strategists consider the comparisons in Table 3 relatively meaningless unless one also takes into account such factors as long-term trends in force size, changes in hardware technology and effectiveness, and a comparison between alliance systems—NATO versus Warsaw Pact—rather than the two superpowers alone. Perhaps the most visible and awesome trend to follow is the race in strategic weaponry described in Table 4. Soviet "catch up" is vividly presented by these figures.

The most striking comparison in Table 4 is the long-run stability in the number of American strategic nuclear delivery vehicles in contrast to the manifold increase in numbers of Soviet vehicles from 550 to 2,523. The United States policymakers obviously made a determination in the mid-1960s that about 2,200 delivery vehicles would be more than enough to deter a Soviet attack or devastate most Soviet cities, industrial centers, and population in a counterattack. In fact, such a number of delivery vehicles is considered from five to ten times as many as needed, that is, sufficient to provide substantial overkill. The Soviet Union, on the other hand, has been determined to demonstrate that it is equal to

**Table 4.   The Strategic Weapons Race, 1965-1982 Without Salt II**

| | 1965 | | 1972 (SALT I) | | 1975 | | 1982 est. (SALT II) | |
|---|---|---|---|---|---|---|---|---|
| | US | USSR | US | USSR | US | USSR | US | USSR |
| Number of weapons | | | | | | | | |
| ICBM | 854 | 270 | 1054 | 1618 | 1054 | 1599 | 1054 | 1350 |
| SLBM | 496 | 120 | 656 | 740 | 656 | 784 | 800 | 950 |
| Bombers | 936 | 160 | 457 | 140 | 465 | 140 | 546 | 100 |
| Total strategic nuclear vehicles | 2285 | 550 | 2167 | 2498 | 2175 | 2523 | 2400 | 2400 |
| | | | | | | | (Vladivostok) | |
| | | | | | | | 2250 | 2250 |
| | | | | | | | (Proposed SALT II) | |
| Total deliverable warheads | 4480 | 870 | 5880 | 2220 | 10312 | 3083 | 17478 | 9330 |
| Total megatonnage | 4547 | 2700 | | | 3415 | 9385 | 6480 | 5925 |

SOURCES: John Barton and L. Weiler, *International Arms Control* (1976), p. 57, for 1972; J. I. Coffey, *Arms Control and European Security* (London, 1977), assuming continuation of U.S. programs for B-1, TRIDENT, etc., and Soviet programs for SS-17 as of 1976. As of 1978, USSR had about 200 MIRV-type vehicles, U.S. about 1,000 MIRVs. US wanted to limit MIRVs to about 1,200 each side. As of 1980, the United States had about 11,000 deliverable warheads and the Soviet Union 6,000.

the United States as a nuclear superpower on the one hand and capable of carrying on a two-front nuclear war on the other hand. A fundamental and perhaps compelling Soviet argument at SALT talks is that they need more strategic weapons than the United States because they have more potential enemies than does the United States.

The other terrifying factors in Table 4 are the number of deliverable warheads and their respective total megatonnages. A single megaton is the equivalent of one million tons of TNT in explosive power. As of 1975, the Soviets had 3,083 warheads with a total megatonnage of 9,385 whereas the United States, with as many of 10,312 warheads, had a lower total megatonnage of 3,415. The greater Soviet megatonnage, in fact, subsequently became a source of American dissatisfaction in the course of the SALT II negotiations. The Table 4 projections for 1982 show the two superpowers with a joint stockpile of 26,808 warheads and a total explosive capacity of 12,405 megatons (or 12,405 millions of tons of TNT). The atomic bombs that destroyed Hiroshima and

Nagasaki had explosive yields equivalent to 14,000 and 20,000 tons of TNT, respectively. Little wonder that all who understand the implications of the current stockpiles are so certain that any super-power nuclear exchange would end life and civilization on earth as we know it.

In addition to the trends in escalating nuclear stockpiles, there are technological features that make it extremely difficult to measure the "equivalency" of American and Soviet forces. The United States has always been more advanced with respect to the accuracy with which its nuclear vehicles reach their designated targets, but there is substantial evidence that the Soviet Union is catching up in this technology, too. Because an ICBM force is literally fixed in concrete, it is the most vulnerable component of the Triad. Hence, both sides plan to introduce mobile missile systems, known in the United States as the MX missile. The MX plan is to build trenches or underground tunnels about thirteen miles in length; the missile silos are to be kept moving around among the tunnels so that the enemy has greater difficulty making a direct hit, unless, of course, new devices are invented for detecting and locking onto the moving missile targets. At the present time, submarines are the leg of the Triad most difficult to detect, but both sides are working determinedly to improve submarine detection and antisubmarine weapons systems. One vigorously espoused and presumably cheaper alternative to the land-based shuttle concept of MX call for substantially augmenting the submarine leg of the Triad. This alternative would increase the number of submarine-launched ballistic missiles (SLBMs) and would have nuclear-armed submarines on constant patrol.

The bomber leg of the Triad is also undergoing rapid technological change. The Soviet Backfire bomber is capable of completing a one-way flight from the Soviet Union to Cuba, raising questions about its exclusion from classification as a strategic bomber (which are considered capable of completing an attack and returning to home base). On the American side, the F-111 fighter-bombers stationed in Western Europe are able to complete round trips to the Soviet Union and raise similar questions regarding their strategic classification. Further, the development of cruise missiles with a capacity for delivering nuclear bombs has also raised issues of classification. A cruise missile is an unmanned, self-propelled, guided missile that is small enough to be launched from aircraft, submarines, or ground platforms. Present cruise missiles are few in number and have a range of only several hundred miles, but the technology is available to lengthen delivery distance to several thousand miles. Because of their small size and ease of conceal-ment, verification of numbers of cruise missiles and their capacities is at present almost impossible. How shall limits be placed upon numbers and capacities of cruise missiles in an arms control agreement? Such are some of the more obvious difficulties spurred by technological developments.

There is further complexity in issues associated with such new devices as the neutron bomb, a small nuclear warhead that can fit into existing NATO artillery. This is a weapon that explodes overhead, emitting a burst of neutrons that penetrate armor and buildings sufficiently to kill or disable their crews or occupants by enhanced radiation. Is the neutron bomb a strategic or a tactical weapon? Should it be dealt with in SALT talks or in the negotiations for a mutual and balanced force reduction in Europe (MBFR)?

One feature of the military balance that may be easily overlooked by the inexperienced observer is civil defense. Measures for protecting potential population and economic targets without employing weapons systems are the concern of civil defense. Such efforts are intended to improve the survivability of the war-making capacity of the attacked nation. Survivability assures that the attacker will experience whatever terror the victim may be able to launch in a counterattack. Some typical civil defense measures include evacuation arrangements, fallout shelters, dispersal or redundancy of production facilities, concealment of manufacture and storage facilities in hardened underground locations, and similar efforts. The Soviet Union's defense system is reputedly elaborate and places highest priority on the survival of the political and technical elite. However, despite allegations of large Soviet civil defense planning efforts and expenditures, there have been no large-scale Soviet drills that would give observable evidence of this preparation. In the United States, too, civil defense has been a relatively neglected aspect of military preparation. The underlying assumption seems to be that shelters and other measures capable of withstanding the blast and fallout effects of a nuclear exchange are technically and economically not feasible. These assumptions and difficulties notwithstanding, it remains true that any serious effort to build up civil defense could have a significant influence upon the military balance.

The more one gets into the subject of military hardware and comparisons of military forces, the more one realizes the impossibility of achieving precisely measurable balance or an objective military measure of sense of security. In other words, if arms control negotiators pay attention only to the military hardware and military forces in the problem, it is a certainty that they can *never* arrive at a quantitatively and psychologically satisfying security arrangement. The ingredients for imbalance and destabilization are *permanently* built into so limited a definition of the security problem.

But the problem gets magnified as we move on to a third aspect of comparison, namely, alliance systems. Alliancing is an ancient and standard approach to augmenting one's military capacity as a counter-force or deterrent to a potential enemy. During World War I, the Allies (Russia, France, England, Italy, the United States, and others) were aligned against the Central Powers (Germany, Austria-Hungary, Turkey, and Bulgaria). In World War II, it was the Allies (the United States, England, most of Western Europe, Russia, and others) against the Axis (Germany, Italy, and Japan). Even the United Nations, when created at the end of World War II, was generally conceived as a collective security alliance system of the former Allies intent upon preventing further aggressions by the defeated Axis powers. The two Germanys, Italy, and Japan were disarmed and for a long time excluded from the United Nations. The U.N. collective security arrangement, particularly as implemented in the Security Council, lost its effectiveness as soon as the former allies became adversaries during the Cold War era.

For its part, following World War II the United States pursued a policy of *collective defense* arrangements and alliances that reached into every corner of the world. The Rio Treaty of 1947 was a multilateral extension of the Monroe Doctrine wherein the United States and the twenty-one nations of Latin America agreed that an armed attack against any American state "shall be considered as an attack against all the American states and . . . each one . . . undertakes to assist in meeting the attack . . . " In 1949 the United States and fourteen other nations established the North Atlantic Treaty Organization (NATO) with the understanding that "an armed attack against one or more of them in Europe or North America shall be considered an attack against them all." The ANZUS Treaty among Australia, New Zealand, and the United States in 1951 and the bilateral Philippine Treaty of the same year concluded similar mutual defense arrangements. A more complicated alliance was the Southeast Asia Treaty Organization (SEATO) among seven nations: United States, United Kingdom, France, New Zealand, Australia, Philippines, and Thailand. The war in Vietnam and the changing structure of power in Southeast Asia led to the disbandment of SEATO in 1977. Two other important bilateral alliances for the United States were its treaties with the Republic of China on Taiwan (1954) and Japan (1960). Although the United States was the militarily most powerful member of each of these defense alliances, American *national* security was also well served in each case, providing the United States with strategic outposts and military friends in many corners of the world. These alliance obligations explain why slightly over 500,000 U.S. troops were based in overseas locations at the end of 1980.

The Soviet Union has not been dormant in its own search for allies. The eight-nation Warsaw Treaty Organization, created in 1955 as a counter to NATO, is the most substantial of the Soviet alliances, although here, too, the superpower is clearly the dominant member.

Just how to weigh the contribution of an alliance system to one's national security again reduces itself to criteria that turn out to be highly subjective. What does seem objectively indisputable is that in the contemporary world the two most powerful alliance systems are NATO and the Warsaw Pact. Atop each of these is of course one of the two superpowers. As though the rest of the world hardly exists, most military analysts leap to make a hardware comparison between the two alliance systems, as in Table 5. These comparisons for 1978–1979 and others for subsequent years tend to be of contested accuracy and offer incomplete statements of the military realities. For example, as of 1978, Warsaw Pact tanks, some of them quite old, were said to number 16,000 compared to NATO's 7,000. These figures, however, do not recognize that NATO possesses nearly 200,000 highly accurate antitank missiles. Other comparisons are similarly misleading. Yet the numbers of weapons and military forces are a basis—inescapably—for estimating one's security against a potent adversary.

**Table 5.  Comparison of NATO and Warsaw Pact Military Forces, Selected Items, 1978–1979**

|  | NATO | Warsaw Pact |
|---|---|---|
| Combat troops | 790,000 | 960,000 |
| Tanks | 7,000 | 16,000 |
| Tactical aircraft | 1,000 | 2,800 |
| Tactical nuclear missiles | 7,000 | 3,500 |
| Artillery pieces | 2,700 | 10,000 |

SOURCES: *Newsweek* (April 17, 1978); According to U.S. Arms Control and Disarmament Agency, *Annual Report 1979.*

After centuries of warfare in the "cockpit of Europe," NATO and the Warsaw Pact exist on the assumption that yet another war may take place on the continent. The victim of several invasions from Western Europe, the Russians leave no doubt that they now wish to protect their European borders and those of their satellite states with a preponderance of military manpower and hardware. However, NATO insists upon parity and seeks to balance the Pact's 16,000 tanks by maintaining a preponderance of tactical nuclear missiles: 7,000. The newly developed neutron bomb, designed primarily to serve as an antitank weapon, will eventually have to be added to NATO's total. This is a very expensive military standoff and led to initiation in 1972 of East-West talks through MBFR. Although both sides seemed eager to achieve a lower and less costly balance of military forces, the negotiation quickly became one of comparing apples and oranges as each side indicated their requirements for having a sufficient sense of security. The negotiations have continued to this day under the assumption that one of the alliance systems may possibly attack the other, but a conception and institution of collective security that could leave both sides feeling thoroughly safe is missing.

## Conventional Weaponry and Its Sale

We have already observed that the Soviet Union is the world's largest supplier (34 per cent) of arms to other countries and the United States (32 per cent) a close second. Other major suppliers include France, West Germany, the United Kingdom, and, in more recent years, smaller developed nations such as Israel. "Conventional weapons" are everything other than nuclear bombs and their long-range delivery systems. The most costly part of the world's arms race is in the transfer, that is, export and import, of nonnuclear weapons systems. Table 6 provides an overview of the arms trade, particularly between developed and developing nations.

Thus, in a world population of over 4 billion, over 26 million persons are in the armed forces, more than half (15,884,000) in the service of the developing nations that can least afford it. On the other hand, the Big Spenders for military purposes are among the 28 developed nations—to the tune of $324 per capita compared to the $31 per capita spent by the 117 developing nations.

Perhaps the most striking data in the table are the figures for arms exports and imports, which show clearly that the suppliers are developed nations and the purchasers the developing nations. According to the U.S. Department of State, during the 1950–1976 period the United States alone transferred abroad over $110 billion in arms and related military services. During 1978 United States sales totaled over $6.7 billion to 68 countries. Most of this weaponry went to countries in the Middle East, specifically Israel, Iran, and Saudi Arabia, while about one-third went to NATO,

**Table 6.   World Arms Transfers, 1978 (Current dollars)**

|  | World | 28 Developed Nations | 117 Developing Nations |
|---|---|---|---|
| Population (in millions) | 4,315 | 1,063 | 3,252 |
| Armed Forces (in thousands) | 26,639 | 10,755 | 15,884 |
| GNP, per capita (1977 dollars) | 1,934 | $ 4,752 | $ 571 |
| Military Expenditures, per capita (1977 dollars) | $ 103 | $ 324 | $ 31 |
| Arms Exports (in billions) | $ 20.6 | $ 19.7 | $ 0.9 |
| Arms Imports (in billions) | $ 20.6 | $ 3.9 | $ 16.7 |

SOURCE: U.S. Arms Control and Disarmament Agency, *World Military Expenditures and Arms Transfers, 1969-1978* (December 1980), pp. 75, 113.

South Korea, and Japan. However, only about 3 percent of United States arms sales were made to countries in Latin America. Shipments to particular countries can reach astronomical figures. For example, between 1968 and 1977, the United States shipped to Israel a total of at least $4.2 billion worth of arms. This particular flow of arms was at a low figure of $28.6 million in 1968, reached $303.2 million in 1971, shot up to $977.9 million in 1974 immediately after the 1973 Arab-Israeli war, and dropped to $875.3 million through 1977. Between 1950 and 1975, American military sales to Iran totaled $9.5 billion and to Saudi Arabia $2.4 billion.[8]

What motivates such a costly arms trade? Despite their tremendous need for economic and social development resources, the developing countries that are big arms purchasers have relatively clear motivations, namely, defense against external attack, maintenance of internal order, and increased diplomatic prestige. Nothing stimulates arms purchases as quickly as the acquisition of weapons by one's neighbors, particularly if such neighbors have been enemies in the recent past. If India arms, Pakistan is driven to do so as well; if Israel arms, Egypt feels compelled to follow a similar course. A nation's substantial military strength presumably deters its more trigger-happy neighbors.

A less visible motivation is internal security. American

weapons sent to Nicaragua, for example, may have had more to do with maintaining the incumbent regime there than with the defense of that country against predatory neighbors. The presence of Soviet troops in or near East European satellite countries or in Afghanistan may serve more to deter internal disorder than external attack. The international arms trade may have more to do with the discouragement of domestic revolutions and civil wars than with the maintenance of peace in the international arena. However, excessively sophisticated weapons may prove to be utterly useless for maintaining internal order—witness the recent revolution against the Shah in Iran.

A third motivation that spurs the purchaser of arms is international prestige. Only nuclear Big Shots (pun intended) are admitted to the Nuclear Club, and this is a major consideration in the pressure for nuclear proliferation. Atom bombs are a great equalizer in the power politics of the world. To a lesser degree this also motivates the purchase of sophisticated conventional weaponry.

From the point of view of suppliers, the motivations to sell are equally compelling. For example, in the United States labor force of some 80 million, more than 700,000 jobs are defense-related; jobs and profits are major inducements for arms production and sales. Supplier nations are also interested in improving their balance of payments, for example, exchanging high technology weapons for oil. Further, selling weapons abroad reduces the per-unit production cost of military equipment, a savings in the price of purchases for the supplier's own armed services. Another motivation for the supplier is to gain friends and prestige among the nations of the world. A fifth motivation relates to the management of relations among one's allies. For example, if a supplier wishes to constrain military conflict between two allies, as the United States has in the case of Greece and Turkey over Cyprus, it becomes possible to do so by cutting off the supply of equipment and spare replacement parts to one or both allies.

In general, however, there is growing evidence that conventional arms transfers encourage local arms races, aggravate regional tensions, and lead to the misallocation of scarce resources within developing countries. In 1977, President Carter initiated a policy that would consider arms transfers as "exceptional" foreign policy actions, placing the burden of persuasion upon those who favor a particular export sale. Such conventional arms transfers were no longer to be considered "useful" foreign policy instruments. This first small step toward reducing the role of the United States as the major conventional arms supplier in the world is, however, likely to have little impact until such time as *all* major suppliers adopt collective criteria for determining when such transfers should or should not be made.

## Technological Advances and the Qualitative Race

In the field of weapons development, the world, as noted earlier, spends $25 billion or more annually for research and development. This is a tremendous investment in human ingenuity and inventiveness and, as has been amply demonstrated, produces some remarkable results. The investment is aimed at producing and improving military hardware. However, it may be a kind of global derangement to have so much ingenuity and inventiveness motivated by fear for national security. Hardly any of these resources are directed toward figuring out how the world can be made much safer at much reduced cost, probably through new institutional arrangements.

In its broadest sense, the qualitative arms race extends to every facet of military equipment development. This may range from improved vehicles for delivering nuclear bombs to improved surgical instruments intended to repair wounded bodies. So comprehensive are the concerns of military research and development that it becomes well-nigh impossible to distinguish the military from the civilian uses of much of the improved technology and discoveries. In fact, among the positive arguments often used in support of large budgets for military research and development (R&D) are the peacetime civilian payoffs of such research. In the ordinary course of civilian research, according to the military R&D people, such technological advances would be far less likely than under the pressures of military need. Furthermore, it is argued, Congress is far less likely to appropriate funds for civilian research as readily as for military purposes.

From another point of view, the question arises whether and how to halt the qualitative arms race. It may have taken a few million years to "advance" from throwing rocks to throwing nuclear bombs at each other, but, if nothing else, Table 1 indicates that the pace of "improvement" is quickening and even more devastating. Even if military research and development received not another penny, would such a policy also require a halt to human inquiry, discovery, invention, creativity, and competitiveness? Perhaps the question about halting the technological race is the wrong question; human discovery and technological progress are clearly here to stay. Perhaps the more appropriate question is "How do we make it unnecessary and undesirable for human beings to throw *anything* at all at each other?"

Controlling the relationship between advancing technology and global security is becoming increasingly complex and difficult, even for those with the most peaceful of intentions. The line between military and peaceful uses of technology seems to be disappearing. Efforts to control the growth and dissemination of currently available weaponry are undermined by wholly new technologies that make the existing weapons systems obsolete. Two examples may be drawn from developments in laser and satellite technology.

*Particle-beam weaponry* (PBW) is one of the current technologies experiencing rapid development. PBW is based on lasers (*light amplification through stimulated emission of radiation*). Lasers are directed beams of electrons, protons, or neutrons that have been concentrated together to produce high levels of energy emission. In recent years laser technology has demonstrated its usefulness in fields as wide-ranging as metallurgy and surgery. It is also well known that the United States, the Soviet Union, and other nations are engaged in a race to develop military applications, that is, PBW. Theoretically, PBW would be capable of instantaneous transfer of energy to a target at essentially 100 percent efficiency. The ability to hit and destroy any and all targets is, of course, every military strategist's dream.

What are some of the military uses of PBW? PBW could hit incoming missiles almost without fail, attack enemy satellites, serve as a ship-borne anti-cruise-missile weapon, carry out successful air-to-air attacks, and, ultimately, in strategic missions, destroy an enemy entirely. Although difficult to imagine, PBW could make nuclear weapons—today's "ultimate" weapon—obsolete. Conceivably, the laborious efforts to achieve SALT arms control agreements may simply turn out to be a discussion of an "outmoded" weapons system. The first feasibility demonstrations of PBW are expected to take place in the early 1980s.

Among the great achievements of modern science and technology are the satellites that carried the first men to the moon and back safely, scan every inch of the earth's surface and near-surface for the discovery of new natural resources and for meterological purposes, and unilaterally verify arms control agreements. The peaceful uses of satellite technology, including instantaneous communication to all parts of the world, have only begun to be discovered and applied. The same is true, unfortunately, of their military uses. In order to keep dangerous nuclear and other weaponry out of the skies, the superpowers agreed in 1967 to a Treaty on the Peaceful Uses of Outer Space and Celestial Bodies. The object was to keep the moon's surface and outer space free of weapons of mass destruction and other objects that could be orbited and possibly drop unexpectedly out of the sky. One nuclear-powered Soviet Cosmos satellite, for example, fell out of the sky in northern Canada in January 1978. Cosmos 954 was a reconnaissance satellite, not a weapon. Its nuclear reactor was used to power an ocean-scanning radar. The United States SkyLab fell out of the sky on July 11, 1979.

The Soviet Union has also tested "hunter-killer" satellites designed to destroy orbiting reconnaissance, communications, and navigational satellites at any time. This is one of the more striking examples of the qualitative arms race. The Soviet Union began testing its current generation of hunter-killers in 1976. Two days before he left office, President Ford approved an American program to develop and deploy a similar weapon. President Carter rescinded the deployment order but allowed the Pentagon to continue development of several antisatellite systems. Proponents of the American program have argued convincingly that American forces are "critically reliant on space for surveillance, reconnaissance, early warning, navigation, meteorology, mapping, communications, and command and control."[9] There are also ongoing efforts to develop, on both the American and Soviet sides, hunter-killers armed with lasers capable of shooting down nuclear missiles and enemy satellites at scores or hundreds of miles' distance. Given such imaginative and technologically feasible developments in the field of lasers and satellite weaponry, it is difficult to see how this aspect of the qualitative arms race can be successfully brought under control by the slow-moving antisatellite negotiations that were recently initiated between the United States and the Soviet Union.

Finally, yet another example of the profound difficulty of disentangling peaceful from military uses of advancing technology is the problem of using nuclear fuel to produce energy without also producing the plutonium byproduct that is necessary for building nuclear weapons. Both nuclear fuel and atom bombs are made from uranium that comes out of the ground There are two types of atoms in natural uranium, U-238 and U-235. Only U-235 splits naturally, resulting in energy that may be converted into electric power or used as an explosive. Less than 1 percent of the atoms of natural uranium are U-235. Through an expensive diffusion process, the United States government is able to "enrich" the natural uranium by separating and discarding some of the U-238 so that the remaining uranium has a greater or more enriched percentage of U-235. If natural uranium is enriched beyond a certain degree—20 per cent— the uranium can be used to make bombs. Current commercial nuclear reactors, called *l*ight *w*ater *r*eactors (LWR), require uranium fuel that is enriched only to 3 percent of

U-235 and therefore cannot be used for bombs. This low level of enrichment requires 1200 stages and a very great amount of electrical power. Thus, it is possible to sell nuclear reactors and uranium fuel without danger of their being *easily or quickly* diverted to the manufacture of nuclear bombs. But a determined purchaser could, with difficulty (4000 stages and enormous amounts of electricity) and time, indeed make bombs.

Bombs can be manufactured from highly enriched uranium and also from plutonium, a manmade element that does not exist in nature. Plutonium is created in a nuclear reactor when some of the "useless" U-238 captures neutrons set free in the fission process, an event that transforms U-238 into plutonium-239. Once plutonium is separated from the spent fuel that is discharged from a reactor, the plutonium can readily be shaped into an explosive. A dozen pounds or so of plutonium can make a bomb of the 20-kiloton capacity of the one dropped on Nagasaki. The separation of plutonium from the spent nuclear fuel is called reprocessing.

Plutonium can also be used as a fuel for reactors. Separated plutonium can be recycled back into light water reactors. It can also fuel another type of reactor called a breeder reactor. A breeder reactor, by transforming U-238 into plutonium, can create more fuel than it uses and thereby increase the energy output from uranium fiftyfold. The commercial success of breeder reactors, because of their projected high capital costs, is still undemonstrated. Many nations with little fossil fuel or uranium resources are, of course, eager to achieve energy independence through the development of breeder reactors, and this raises all the hazards of making available a plutonium stockpile for weapons purposes.

Military and peaceful motivations for acquiring nuclear fuel and facilities are likely to be overwhelming in the absence of some system of stringent international controls. Plutonium in the hands of terrorists or an unstable national leadership could become a potent instrument of international blackmail. The excessive stockpiling of plutonium can be dangerous to the community around it. The availability of plutonium could facilitate the proliferation of nuclear weapons. Some steps have been taken to hold back the nuclear floodgates. The International Atomic Energy Agency (IAEA) has developed and been given responsibility for a safeguard system under which countries must file regular reports about their civilian nuclear activities and allow international inspectors—now numbering between 200 and 300—to visit their nuclear facilities to verify the reports and ensure that there has been no diversion of materials from civilian to military purposes. In 1977 the Carter administration proposed an International

Nuclear Fuel Cycle Evaluation (INCFE) to study ways of improving the design and management of nuclear materials for peaceful purposes in ways that would prevent nuclear weapons proliferation. By 1980 some sixty-six nations and five international organizations were involved in the study.

INCFE set up eight Working Groups to investigate such issues as (1) fuel and heavy water availability, (2) enrichment availability, (3) assurances of long-term supply of technology, fuel, and heavy water, (4) reprocessing, plutonium handling, and recycling, (5) fast breeders, (6) spent fuel management, (7) waste management and disposal, and (8) advanced fuel cycle and reactor concepts. In preparing their reports, the Working Groups achieved substantial consensus on many issues: that the international trade in plutonium and highly enriched uranium poses a significant threat of nuclear-weapons proliferation; that stronger IAEA safeguards are needed; that breeder reactors may be appropriate only in the most highly developed nations; and that there is an immediate need to assure nuclear fuel resources to many nations over the long term.

Meanwhile, President Carter initiated a "plutonium pause," that is, a policy of limiting the number of newly licensed commercial facilities capable of producing plutonium or enriched uranium. Specifically, that administration announced that it would "defer indefinitely the commercial reprocessing and recycling of plutonium being produced in U.S. nuclear power programs . . . and will restructure our own U.S. breeder program to give greater priority to alternative designs of the breeder other than plutonium."[10]

In sum, rapidly advancing technologies in such fields as lasers, satellites, and nuclear fuel, to mention only the better known examples, are introducing security risks and problems of which it is increasingly difficult for policymakers, military strategists, and arms controllers to keep abreast. Theoretical definitions that try to distinguish between offensive and defensive weaponry, strategic and tactical forces, and civilian and military uses are falling by the wayside as a consequence of accelerating technological change.

The consequences for the security problem are also profound. What constitutes a "balance" of military forces sufficient to assure security? There is simply no way to answer this question quantitatively or technologically. How much should a nation or the world spend for security services? Much depends on whether the security expenditure is a collective one in which all share equitably or a competitive one that assumes a direct connection between size of military forces and sense of security. A third dilemma arises from the propensity to make hypothetical worst-case analyses of security situations. The principle here is to assume the worst that a potential enemy can do to you and then prepare thoroughly to overcome such an eventuality. Worst-case analysis often leads to demands for zero-risk preparation; it is also contingent upon the human imagination's boundless capacity to hypothesize worst-case scenarios.

Perhaps the arms race is *not* a race at all but rather a process that has become institutionalized by a political inability to comprehend and redefine the essential elements of the problem of security and safety in this world. As we shall see in the next chapter, the security problem may have less to do with technology, weapons, balance of military forces, and all of the hardware issues that are now the central focus of attention and more to do with social and psychological relationships, attitudes, and institutions that influence the subjective as well as the objective aspects of people's sense of security.

# References

1. Secretary of State Cyrus Vance before the American Society of Newspaper Editors, April 10, 1978.
2. Analysis and examples are based on John Cohen, "Subjective Probability." *Scientific American* 197, no.5 (November 1957), pp. 128ff. Also, the same author's *Chance, Skills, and Luck; The Psychology of Guessing and Gambling* (Baltimore: Penguin, 1960).
3. An analysis by Arrige Levi, former editor of *La Stampa* of Turin, in *Atlas World Press Review* (February 1979), pp. 35–36.
4. Report by H. Josef Hebert, *Los Angeles Times,* July 2, 1979, Sec. 3, p. 14.
5. The most authoritative sources include: United Nations; Stockholm International Peace Research Institute; United States Arms Control and Disarmament Agency; International Institute for Strategic Studies in London; North Atlantic Treaty Organization; United States Central Intelligence Agency; and the United States Agency for International Development. Two particularly relevant and available sources are: Ruth Leger Sivard, *World Military and Social Expenditures* (Washington, D.C. 20036: Arms Control Association, published annually); U.S. Arms Control and Disarmament Agency, *World Military Expenditures and Arms Transfers, 1969–1978* (Washington, D.C. 20451: December 1980).
6. Obviously, the question arises as to which expenditures each of the superpowers classifies as military and which as nonmilitary governmental expenditures. In 1976, for example, the nonmilitary central

government expenditures of the United States were $258 billion whereas the comparable Soviet nonmilitary outlays came to $101 billion. There is litttle doubt that a great deal of American "nonmilitary" spending is actually in support of the defense program while, in the Soviet Union, much that is "military" also serves civilian purposes. The complexity and significance of evaluating Soviet military expenditures is carefully analyzed in Milton Leitenberg, *USSR Military Expenditure and Defense Industry Conversion* (Political Issues Series, Vol. 6, No. 4, Center for the Study of Armament and Disarmament, California State University Los Angeles, Los Angeles, CA 90032). Leitenberg notes that the USSR has reported its military budget at between 17.2 and 17.9 billion rubles since 1969, a fixed figure that flies in the face of the Soviet Union's manifest escalation of its military forces. Western sources estimate an expenditure rise from 35 billion rubles in 1967 to 58 billion rubles in 1979. Converting rubles into dollar figures is, of course, another difficulty since the inflation rate in the Soviet Union is practically zero when compared to the frequent double-digit rates occurring in the United States.

7. *Los Angeles Times* (February 11, 1979), Sec. 2, pp. 1ff.
8. U.S. Department of Defense figures for Israel reported in *Newsweek* (March 20, 1978); p. 28.
9. Statement by Robert Kirk, President of Vought Corporation, reported in *Newsweek* (February 13, 1978), p. 53.
10. S. Jacob Scherr and James M. Cubie, "President Carter's 'Plutonium Pause'," *Arms Control Today* 8, No. 3 (March 1978); pp. 1–3.

# CHAPTER 3

# Political Distrust as Generator
# of the Arms Race

Both Hawks and Doves have much to say about political distrust. Hawks will identify an "enemy," call attention to that enemy's "misconduct and treachery," and conclude that greater military strength is necessary because that enemy cannot be trusted. Hawks will tend to interpret the designated enemy's behavior as "proof" of untrustworthiness. Doves, on the other hand, will tend to emphasize good faith and trust, argue that the circle of fear must be broken by a reduction in military forces, even unilaterally, and conclude that trust must be "given," even at some risk, in order to assure and calm the anxious enemy.

The phenomena of trust and distrust are among the most frequently mentioned and least dealt with elements in the problem of security and arms control. Distrust clearly leads to worst-case analysis, military buildups, and acceleration of the arms race; we have a great deal of evidence of how this process works. We have much less evidence to support a prediction that international political trust would produce arms control, security, and peace. This chapter will describe some of the components of trust and distrust that are identified in behavioral theory. The decision-making predicament of the policymaker responsible for security will be analyzed and illustrated by the case of the Prisoners' Dilemma. Some examples of security policies that generate distrust and others that promote trust and cooperation will be given. The chapter will conclude with an argument favoring greater attention to the trust-distrust aspect of the arms race.

## Prisoners' and Security Dilemmas

The Prisoner's Dilemma, which is a special case of the theory of games of strategy, affords an excellent model for better understanding some of the difficulties associated with the question of security and safety in this world. In the usual formulation of the Prisoners' Dilemma, two prisoners have been caught and charged with some crime such as armed robbery. Lacking evidence, the district attorney realizes that he has a weak case against the two, whereupon he has the prisoners placed in separate cells and held incommunicado. He then offers each prisoner the following deal. "The evidence against you is not complete, so each of you has a choice of confessing or not confessing to the crime. If you both confess, your sentences will be five years each. If neither of you confesses, your sentences will be one year each. If one of you confesses, the one who confesses will get a light sentence of only half a year for helping us clear up this case, but the other will dealt with harshly and receive a sentence of ten years." Because the prisoners are kept separated, each must make his own decision about confessing without information about what the other prisoner has decided.

**Figure 1.    Prisoners' Dilemma Payoff Matrix**

|              |             | Prisoner II | |
|--------------|-------------|-------------|-------------|
|              |             | *Confess*   | *Not Confess* |
| **Prisoner I** | *Confess*   | 5, 5        | ½, 10       |
|              | *Not Confess* | 10, ½     | 1, 1        |

The first number in each cell represents the possible sentence for Prisoner I and the second the possible sentence for Prisoner II. Obviously each prisoner's greatest preference is likely to be the half-year sentence, followed by the one-year sentence, and the five-year sentence next. The least desirable outcome for each prisoner would be a ten-year sentence. "Rational" behavior, by definition, requires that a person strive exclusively for his first preference on a scale of preferences. In this case, a "rational" prisoner must strive exclusively for the payoff that maximizes his own self-interest without regard for the other party, that is, the half-year sentence. However, neither prisoner can escape the hard fact that the outcome for himself is also contingent upon what his partner in crime decides. In other words, the dilemma each has is how to reconcile the two self-interested "rationalities."

Ordinarily, individuals in such a situation proceed to communicate with each other in order to arrive at some *collective* action. Such is the central role that communication plays in the achievement of cooperation in human affairs. In our hypothetical Prisoners' Dilemma, however, communication is not possible, and each must consider other factors in arriving at his own decision to confess or not confess.

Each prisoner must consider two antecedent questions. First, what will be the other prisoner's *probable behavior*? Second, will that probable behavior have *positive or negative consequences* for oneself? These two questions are, in fact, the principal elements of *trust*. "Trust" has been defined as consisting of at least two elements: (a) predictability of another's behavior and (b) the positive or negative consequences of that behavior for the trusting individual.[1]

To predict another's probable behavior requires observation of the past behavior of that individual. This is an *empirical* process. One must also make a judgment as to whether or not the predicted behavior will have positive consequences for oneself. This is a *normative* judgment. Taken together, the empirical and the normative conclusions will generate an attitude of trust or distrust toward the other person. Obviously the possibility of error in predicting how another will behave depends a great deal on how well one knows the other, and such empirical knowledge is rarely perfect or without risk. Further, the extent to which one wishes to risk trusting another may depend a great deal upon the weightiness of the positive or negative consequences for oneself that may ensue from such a trusting attitude.

Thus, in the case of the two prisoners, much will depend on how long they have been partners in crime, how well they have "stuck together" under trying circumstances in the past, the extent to which they share common goals, and the degree to which they like each other. If they trust each other not to confess, each would give up his "rational" first preference for the half-year sentence in favor of a second best, but collective, preference: the one-year sentence. However, if they distrust each other, each is likely to try to "get the jump" on the other by confessing, and both are likely thereby to get their third preference, the five year sentence. If one is trusting of the other while the other is distrusting of him, the trusting (not confessing) prisoner will be "exploited" in that he will receive a ten-year sentence while his partner gets off with only a half year.

Distrust continues to be a major hurdle to cooperation most familiarly in international affairs. In fact, distrust is the central feature of the arms race. Consider the following observations by former U.S. Secretary of Defense Harold Brown in his annual report to the Congress:

> There remains the question of how large the collective deterrent should be. The answer to that question depends, in turn, on how we interpret the policies and assess the capabilities of the Soviet Union . . . . We face great uncertainty as to the intentions of [the Soviet] leadership . . . . [After reviewing the growth in Soviet military forces since 1964] the Soviets may be less well-intentioned than we would wish them to be. Our planning must take that possibility into account . . . . Exactly what the Soviets are trying to accomplish with their large and growing capabilities is uncertain.[2]

The secretary of defense has said that the Soviet Union is not to be trusted. Its future behavior cannot be reliably predicted on the basis of its past behavior, particularly in the light of its rapidly growing military forces. The consequences of Soviet behavior for the United States are likely to be negative, that is, reduced American security as well as reduced American influence in world politics. Of course, Soviet leaders express a similar analysis, with certain variations, arguing that they are surrounded by past and present enemies, namely, Germany and NATO on the west and China on the east—not to mention the other superpower in North America.

Thus, the parties to an arms race are in a predicament similar to that described in the Prisoners' Dilemma. Thinking strictly on a unilateral, self-interested, "rational" basis, the leader of a nation might say: "We have two choices: to arm or to disarm. If the other nation disarms, we are better off by remaining armed. If the other nation arms, we are even more obviously better off remaining armed." Hence, in an environment of international distrust, the outcome is an arms race, even though both parties may prefer to use their respective resources for other than military purposes. Robert Jervis has formulated this security dilemma as described in Figure 2.[3]

**Figure 2.    Payoff Matrix In The Security Dilemma**

|  |  | Nation B | | | |
|---|---|---|---|---|---|
|  |  | Cooperate | | Defect | |
|  |  |  | 2 |  | 1 |
|  | Cooperate | CC | | CD | |
| **Nation A** |  |  |  |  |  |
|  |  | 2 | | 4 | |
|  |  |  | 4 | | 3 |
|  | Defect | DC | | DD | |
|  |  | 1 | | 3 | |

In Jervis' formulation, the numbers represent the ranked order of preferences of Nations A and B. Thinking strictly in terms of its own maximum self-interest, each nation most prefers—as represented by the numeral 1—to defect and thereby exploit the cooperative inclination of the other nation. At the other extreme, however, each nation would least like—numeral 4—to be exploited for being cooperative while the other nation defects. Each nation's second preference would be to cooperate *if and only if* the other nation can be *trusted* to cooperate as well. However, under conditions of distrust, each nation is likely to defect and go its own way, resulting in the third preference in the defect-defect cell, that is, engage in a competitive arms race.

Jervis' excellent analysis of the security dilemma makes it clear that the essential task of Nations A and B is to do all that is necessary and possible to increase their opponent's incentive to cooperate. In recent years, the popular term for this type of effort has been "confidence building." Nations A and B also need to increase the costs that each nation risks by exploiting the other nation.

What happens to nations that allow themselves to be exploited, as indicated in the DC and CD cells in Figure 2? The most obvious results are loss of territory or loss of sovereignty. A more subtle consequence is the loss of international prestige and influence that, in the volatile and fickle world of international politics, may also have serious consequences for the security and prosperity of the victim. It is the profound fear of such exploitation that drives nations to arm, join alliance systems, or seek protection from superpowers.

However, nations that cooperate successfully may be able to achieve safety and security at reduced cost, allocate resources to desirable nonmilitary purposes, and achieve all the benefits of nonviolent human community. Territory is thus more likely to be shared by the cooperating nations in a more civilized manner for the economic and cultural good of all. In a universally cooperative world community, the preservation of national sovereignty may become a less treasured stake because it would no longer be equated with national survival. Finally, the contest for prestige and political influence can, among cooperating nations, proceed in arenas other than the battlefield.

## Policies for Promoting Cooperation

What are some of the factors and policies that are likely to encourage nations to cooperate successfully, that is, pursue the payoffs of the CC matrix? One consideration relates to the central problem of the security dilemma identified by Jervis. The security dilemma arises because an increase in one nation's ostensive security decreases the security of others. That is to say, every time a nation adds to its military or other security-relevant capacity, joins an alliance, or aspires to territory that may improve its safety, such actions automatically decrease the security of others. Since every nation must do its utmost to maintain and improve its security, the dilemma is how to avoid an apparently inevitable arms race and prevent inadvertent war.

To encourage the cooperation needed to prevent such disasters, one recommended policy is for a nation to give up some of its ability to inflict damage on the other. In some respects this is what the United States did when it leveled off its rate of military spending relative to its gross national product following the end of the Vietnam War. A similar policy was the American freeze on the number of its strategic delivery systems following SALT I, thereby allowing the Soviet Union to catch up and, according to the Hawks, possibly surpass the American arsenal.

A second policy designed to encourage nations to cooperate is to understate the gains one's own side could achieve from ever exploiting the other. In other words, the leaders of powerful nations ought not to go around, as Khrushchev did, bragging that "we will bury you," referring to the day when, in his opinion, the Soviet Union would "win" its contest with the United States.

A third policy promotive of cooperation is also an argument for an open society. The general availability of information about a nation's military and other resources, that is, the elimination of secrecy about security resources, can be a major contributor to the reduction of national anxiety about the capacity and intentions of another nation. In many areas of human behavior, information tends to reduce anxiety. A similar tendency applies in the security field. If information is not openly available, nations expend great sums, as we shall see below, on verification systems, KGBs, and CIAs in order to obtain the required information.

A fourth cooperation-producing policy would be to break up large issues and big transactions into smaller ones, thereby reducing the scale of possible losses for each party if exploited by the other. This is a familiar principle in the theory and practice of negotiation. The principle assumes that there is small likelihood that suspicious and hostile adversaries can ever reach Grand Settlements of *all* their outstanding controversies *at one time*. The greater probability is that small issues, if successfully resolved, will tend to build attitudes of trust that encourage the resolution of larger issues at a later time. Often the larger issues lose much of their saliency and significance as the momentum of smaller resolutions goes forward. Such is the argument for the Camp David agreements that led to the treaty between Egypt and Israel, leaving such "large" issues as the disposition of the Palestinians and of Jerusalem for later negotiation. Such also is the argument for the SALT I and SALT II agreements. Opponents of these agreements insist that all outstanding issues with the Soviet Union need to be linked one with the other in order to get the Russians to concede on any of them. Proponents of the SALT agreements consider such linkage to be insurmountable obstacles to making any progress toward halting the arms competition with the Soviets. The nonlinkage posture is presumably the one that is more likely to advance the cooperative relationships of the CC cell in the Figure 2 payoff matrix.

A fifth policy recommendation offered by Jervis is that each nation's leaders study and comprehend the nature of the security dilemma itself. An understanding of the security dilemma is likely to lead to humility and caution about this extremely complex and dangerous problem. In a world that resounds with bravado propaganda and strutting statesmen, such humility and caution could be great contributions to the sense of world security in general.

## Policies to Discourage Exploitation

In an imperfect world in which human judgment is fallible, it is necessary to make *explicit and relatively certain* that exploitation of one nation by another, as in the DC and CD situations, will incur grave costs for the exploiter. What policies are likely to accomplish this? The issue is essentially one of reward-and-punishment conditioning. Just as the several policies suggested above would reward nations for cooperating with each other, the policies that follow below are intended to deter or punish exploitation of one nation by another.

"Drawing-the-line" is one of several familiar policies for making clear to a potential attacker or predator the risks of exploitation This is one of the principal functions of geography and territorial boundaries. The military force that crosses a boundary is *prima facie* an aggressor. An unfriendly boundary crossing legitimizes such countermoves as "hot pursuit" or a general invasion of the attacker's territory. Thus, when Idi Amin's troops crossed over from Uganda into Tanzanian territory, this act legitimized the Tanzanian counterinvasion that ultimately unseated Amin and gave the Ugandans a new regime. Similarly, the principle of hot pursuit in international law permits the victim to not only resist the attack but also to pursue the invader into the latter's own territory without necessarily embarking upon a general counterinvasion.

Drawing-the-line is one of the functions of demilitarized zones. These zones are usually a result of military engagements at the end of which the parties separate in such a way as to minimize the recurrence of further military incidents. Presumably, entering or tampering with the demilitarized zone by either side signals a warning to the potential victim and is likely to provoke countermeasures. Border incidents and breaches of demilitarized zones are familiar techniques by which potential exploiters test the resolve and military capacity of a prospective victim. Buffer states, buffer zones, and boundaries made up of mountains, rivers, and oceans are geographical conditions that make such tests difficult for potential aggressors to carry off. These conditions also give the prospective victim an opportunity to mobilize his defense.

"Trip-wire" arrangements are another type of punitive warning system. This usually involves a relationship between a powerful and a weak ally. The powerful ally will agree to defend the weaker ally by placing a small contingent of troops or a few military installations at exposed and vulnerable places within the territory of the weaker nation. The presence of American troops and military installations in Europe and South Korea, although large enough to have a substantial fighting capability, serve as trip-wires for NATO and South Korea, respectively. As a consequence, any attack on NATO or South Korea automatically includes an attack on the forces of the United States as well and serves as grounds for immediate American military action against the attacker.

A third type of potential punishment is preemption, that is, the offense that presumably makes the best defense. When one nation observes a neighbor going through all the motions of military preparation for an attack, the best defense may be attacking first. Such was the basis for Israel's preemptive attack against Egypt in the Seven Day War of 1967. With the help of Soviet military equipment, Egypt had reoccupied Sharm-el-Sheikh, closed the Gulf of Aqaba to Israeli shipping, requested the withdrawal of the United Nations Emergency Force that had been patrolling the Israeli-Egyptian border, declared a state of national emergency at home, and agreed to carry on common military operations with Jordan, Syria, and Iraq. As a consequence of these threats to its security, Israel launched a preemptive attack. Israeli forces captured the Sinai, the West Bank, and the Golan Heights, destroyed the Egyptian air force, and captured or destroyed most of the Soviet-supplied military equipment. Preemption is, of course, a high-risk policy. It requires starting a war on the basis of inferences and guesses about the probable military behavior of a potential attacker. In the case of the Seven Day War, were all the Egyptian maneuvers merely for the purpose of threat and pressure, or were they actual preparations for a military attack? Rather than wait and consequently have to fight a war on its own tiny territory, Israel decided that an attack was imminent, struck first, and carried the war into the enemies' territories. The cost to the Egyptians and their allies was devastating.

A fourth type of punitive action is publicity. In this approach, a potential or actual attacker is exposed as such to the entire world. The assumption is that exposure will trigger negative world opinion and thereby embarrass or otherwise hurt the aggressor. In such instances, the "smoking gun" scenario is the most damaging. The aggressor is either caught red-handed in the midst of an act of aggression or, after the deed, found with a "smoking gun" in his hand, that is, with overwhelming circumstantial evidence that he committed the evil deed. The latter was the approach the United States was able to use during the Cuban missile crisis. The Soviet ambassador to the United Nations categorically denied American charges that the Soviets were building intercontinental ballistic missile sites in Cuba. For a few days it was the word of the United States against that of the Soviet Union. Then Ambassador Adlai Stevenson dramatically presented U-2 reconnaissance photographs revealing the Soviet missile launcher emplacements. The exposure did much to undermine Soviet credibility and eventually led to their agreement to withdraw the missiles.

Yet another approach intended to warn or deter a potential aggressor is explicitly and publicly to express concern over the other's behavior. If we glance back at the definition of distrust, such expressions amount to stating the belief that the other's behavior is predictable and likely to have negative consequences for the party expressing concerns. In the Soviet Union, these statements of concern usually take the form of speeches before the Supreme Soviet or propaganda pieces in official publications such as *Pravda*. In the United States, the usual occasions for such statements are senate debates over presidential appointments to agencies such as the Arms Control and Disarmament Agency or the approval of arms control treaties such as SALT II. Anticipating statements of senatorial concern about Soviet behavior, principal arguments in support of the SALT II treaty were that (a) it did not assume that the Soviet Union could be trusted and (b) American intelligence could amply verify all aspects of the treaty. Significantly, on the eve of the senate debate, Soviet leaders made several moves obviously intended to demonstrate their trustworthiness, including the release of a number of Soviet dissidents and the first voluntary announcement of the precise type and size of their nuclear arsenal (which previously was known only from United States intelligence reports).

A final, and in some ways ultimate, warning to potential aggressors takes the form of the arms race itself. A nation's willingness to expend its precious and limited resources in order to invent and stockpile vast quantities of weapons is presumably the most fundamental kind of demonstration of national resolve and capacity to defend itself under any and all circumstances. In traditional arms races, this has meant maintaining clearly visible and measurable military equality with one or *any combination of* potential attackers. The escalatory trap of this approach is that a nation's leaders may hypothesize any one of a number of potential combinations of enemies. This worst-case analysis spurs the drive not only to match the principal adversary but also to surpass the adversary in order to match the combined strength of the hypothesized hostile coalition. It is a favorite theme of Soviet arms control negotiators, for example, that Russia has more enemies—the United States, Western Europe, China, and others—than the United States, and hence Russia must arm itself sufficiently to be able to repel an attack from all of them at once.

In such situations, the security dilemma prevails, that is, any increase in one state's security (through the invention and stockpiling of arms, for example) decreases the security of others. In response to such situations, the other state or states respond with their own arms buildup. The traditional assumption in making such a response is that overt preparation for a strong defense will make clear to potential aggressors the high price they would pay if they were to launch an attack.

However, as Jervis points out, in an age of nuclear weapons and deterrence theories, the distinctions between offense and defense and between offensive and defensive weaponry have become entirely obsolete. In any nuclear exchange, no side can adequately defend itself. This is the strategic conclusion that emerged from the 1960s debate over antiballistic missile systems that led to the SALT I agreements. Under such circumstances of defenselessness, the number of missiles and warheads that a nation has can only serve as an index of its military capacity and political resolve.

So much for models of the security dilemma and policies for dealing with it. What emerges from this analysis is the central importance of trust and the extreme difficulty in designing political conditions that promote trust, deter physical attack, and improve the security of all.

## The Behavioral Study of Trust and Distrust

The terms "trust" and "distrust" are frequently part of discussions and analyses of security and arms control. Consider the following quotations in which the term "trust" is the central, yet most ambiguous, element.

*Item:* In an address at Princeton University on March 22, 1979, Undersecretary of State for Political Affairs David D. Newsom spoke on the problems of dealing with political change throughout the world. He commented on the widespread distrust of the United States.

> If one sees political change in geopolitical terms, it is natural to expect a response in the same terms. Is an abrupt change in a country the result of

internal circumstances or is it a calculated extension of the power of an adversary? Will a display of American power assist our friends in maintaining control? Will it inhibit the subversion of those opposed to us? Or will it awaken fears of intervention in an internal matter?

Two facts are important in assessing our use of power—whether by the movement of military forces or the imposition of sanctions on aid or food or exports.

In many of the countries of the world we face an endemic problem of suspicion of our motives. We may feel that our motives are clear and justified. We may assert that the day of manipulating other regimes has long passed. Sufficient suspicion exists in countries where those who would embarrass us have the seeds to do so. Our power moves can be easily exploited against the backdrop of history of actions and propaganda which maintain deep doubts in turbulent nations about our own objectives.

*Item:* On September 7, 1979, Lane Kirkland, representing the AFL-CIO, offered testimony to the Senate Foreign Relations Committee on SALT II. Here are some excerpts of his exchange with Senators Charles Percy and Jacob Javits.

*Kirkland:* . . . Defense goals must, of course, be gauged and judged as relative to the threat that one perceives. We perceive that the threat presented by the rate of expansion and improvement of strategic nuclear arms is real and is growing.

*Percy:* . . . Do you believe that presence of Soviet combat troops in Cuba should be linked in any way with the SALT debate?

*Kirkland:* . . . (Soviet troops in Cuba) calls into question two elements that are very important considerations of arms control negotiations with the Soviets: the question of intentions and the question of our prudence in relying on their (the Soviet's) observance of any agreements that we make. . . . I suspect that the existence of those questions has far more to do with what misgivings there may be in the public mind about arms control negotiations than anything else—any appraisal of the particular balance of forces in the treaty, the general suspicion and lack of confidence in the Soviet Union as a negotiating partner. . . .

*Javits:* . . . What is the attitude of the American people toward the risk taking which is implied in your statement? . . . The way the Kremlin works, as we see from Cuba in this highly surreptitious way, you don't know what they are liable to spring. And you are always confronted with the worst-case hypothesis . . .

*Item:* At the conclusion of the joint meeting of NATO foreign and defense ministers in Brussels on December 12, 1979, at which it was decided to deploy 108 Pershing II ballistic missiles and 464 ground-launched cruise missiles in Europe, Secretary of State Cyrus Vance commented: "The two years of intensive consultations which led up to these decisions give evidence of the mutual trust that prevails in the alliance." Here is a case in which trust is correctly identified as a major element in a complex system of cooperation.

*Item:* In his syndicated column of August 28, 1979, Jack Anderson cites a top-secret document on "Understanding Soviet Strategic Policy," prepared by Central Intelligence Agency analyst Fritz Ermath, in which three distinct perspectives are found in the American intelligence community. One contends that the Soviet leaders seek clear superiority over the United States within as short a span as a decade. A second believes the Soviet leaders expect no superiority but are determined to resist being placed in an inferior position. A third part of the intelligence community thinks the Soviets wish to hedge against uncertainty and maintain overall parity with the United States. Ermath observes:

> The subject of Soviet strategic policy and objectives is very elusive. Pertinent evidence is voluminous, but it almost never speaks for itself. Interpretation of the evidence always involves our preconceptions about the Soviet Union as a nation, international politics, the meaning of military power, and the condition of our own country.

*Item:* Testifying before the Senate Foreign Relations Committee on July 9, 1979, regarding the proposed SALT II Treaty, Secretary of Defense Harold Brown commented, "I would not recommend this treaty if it required us to trust the Soviets. Too much is at stake for us to have to rely on their good will or scruples. The SALT II treaty is designed to assure that we do not need to rely on trust. It is verifiable. . . . "

The prevailing military assumption in international relations is that *no nation* can be fully trusted; hence, nations insist upon procedures for verification of compliance with arms control agreements, inspection of military facilities, and creation of international police forces or collective security systems designed to constrain or punish "lawbreaking" nations. In an evaluation of the provisions of the proposed SALT II Treaty, Thomas W. Milburn and Kenneth H. Watman stated the issue succinctly: "The first and most self-evident principle for verification is that we do not trust the Soviets. Indeed, it is precisely because we do not trust them that verification, a substitute for trust, is incorporated in the agreement."

However, verification and inspection, when successfully implemented, may provide the basis for promoting trust. Examples of such results are the activities of the Agency for the Control of Armaments (ACA), a council operating under the Western European Union. WEU—consisting of Belgium, France, Luxembourg, the Netherlands, and the United Kingdom—was established as a defense alliance in 1948. In separate agreements signed in 1954, the Federal Republic of Germany undertook not to manufacture in its territory nuclear, chemical, biological, or certain other classes of weapons. ACA was created as an agency of WEU in order to monitor these arms control agreements. The verification system has worked so well that both NATO and Warsaw Pact have been increasingly trusting of West Germany's military policies and operations. Given Germany's militaristic past over the last century, ACA's success may be considered a major achievement in world security affairs.[4]

Despite the obvious and profound significance of political trust in these situations, there has been very little systematic study of the behavioral attributes and dimensions of political trust.[5] Given its relevance to the problem of arms control and collective security, we return to the matter of defining and estimating the influence of trust and distrust in political and security relationships.

Earlier, we defined "trust" as consisting of at least two elements: (1) predictability of another's behavior and (2) the positive or negative consequences of that other's behavior for oneself. We also noted that prediction of another's behavior is essentially an empirical process whereas the determination of what is positive or negative—good or bad—for oneself is essentially a normative judgment. In other words, trust is attitudinal in nature. It is an expectation about the future consequences for oneself of another's probable behavior.[6] While the two attributes of trust — predictability of another's behavior and the judgment about the consequences of that behavior for oneself—can be made explicit and intersubjectively observable, each of the attributes has ambiguities that deserve further examination.

Will the other behave as predicted? If we carefully observe the past behavior of the other party, we often can, within a specifiable range of probability, predict how that individual or nation may behave under similar circumstances in the future. Predictions of this kind are the aspiration if not yet the full-blown achievement of the behavioral sciences. For example, to answer the question whether the Soviet Union will adhere to its treaty obligations, one must examine the past behavior of Soviet leaders with respect to treaty compliance. Such an examination of past behavior is likely to reveal that the Soviet Union tends to adhere to most of its treaty obligations, although it may very deliberately test or stretch some treaty provisions in order to determine what the other party's level of tolerance will be. If the Soviet Union is seriously displeased with a treaty, it is more likely to abrogate the treaty than breach it. If these generalizations are valid (and there is yet no research that tests them), then we may expect that the odds are favorable that the Soviet Union will adhere to any present or future treaties that it signs. Element One of trust—predictability of the other's behavior—is present.

Now, for the sake of illustration, let us assume that a fictitious investigation of Soviet treaty compliance over the last thirty years reveals that the Soviets have adhered to their obligations 85 percent of the time. Since the score does not achieve the 100 percent mark, chances are 15 in 100 that the Soviets may breach present and future treaties. What does a policymaker do with this estimate?

A dovish policymaker will consider the odds favorable and future Soviet performance fairly predictable; he or she will be inclined to accept the 15-in-100 risk and trust both the prediction and the Soviet Union. A hawkish policymaker, on the other hand, will be inclined to demand perfect Soviet performance and magnify the significance of the 15-in-100 risk in the light of the importance of the stakes, namely, the national security and survival of the United States. This policymaker will continue to distrust the Soviet Union and refuse to assume the margin of risk predicted. Notice that even in circumstances where data is as quantified as in this illustration, the interpretation and application of the findings are nonetheless highly subjective, as in the case of judgments about sense of security discussed earlier.

The second ambiguity relates to Element Two: the normative aspect of trust. Will the consequences of the expected behavior of the other be positive or negative for oneself? What is good for oneself turns out to be the ultimate subjectivity. Each of us makes our own individual judgment about what is "good" or "bad" for us according to our own particular and private yardstick.

As evident in every debate about the ratification of an arms control agreement between the Soviet Union and the United States, Hawks and Doves have very different understandings about what is good or bad for America in these treaty agreements. In a less public way the same kind of debate unquestionably goes on between Hawks and Doves in the Soviet Union where fear of encirclement still drives the Hawks toward escalation on the one hand, but pressures of the excessive military budget on the Soviet economy reinforces the Dove position on the other.

The hawkish view about the positive or negative consequences of another's expected behavior is invariably premised upon the perceived evilness, treachery, ambition, stupidity, and general untrustworthiness of the other, particularly if the other has already been identified as "The Enemy." According to Hawks, The Enemy's behavior is bound to be aimed at producing negative consequences for oneself. The dovish premise, on the other hand, avoids designating enemies and emphasizes the general riskiness and fearsomeness of the human condition: we are all in this together. In this view, the expected behavior of the other is likely to become positive if given a fair chance but negative only if there are gross errors of human judgment. The Hawk cannot trust The Enemy and usually can point to a history of the other's "misbehaviors"as the basis for his judgment. The Dove *wants to trust* the other but is handicapped by the necessity of explaining this desire as an expectation about the *future*, that is, as a hope or a prediction, neither of which can ever by asserted with the certainty that is the Hawk's as the latter brings forward evidence about The Enemy's past misbehaviors.

A discussion of trust and distrust in human affairs cannot avoid making reference, albeit a disturbing one, to the views of social Darwinists and contemporary sociobiologists, particularly with regard to the issues of trust and deception.[7] In their view, confirmed, they claim, by the entire evolutionary process, deception about reality and exploitation of the trusting have been widely prevalent throughout the animal kindgom and a key factor in the survival of species. In a world rampant with betrayal, exploitation, and violence, the deceiver usually appears to have an impressive advantage and success rate, particularly in the short run. However, does the deceiver have the same advantage over the long run? Are not deception and exploitation the principal stimuli for propelling animals of all kinds into coalitions and cooperations designed for protection and survival? And is not trust an essential component of such cooperative systems, including those we call societies and political communities? If the answers to these questions are affirmative, then beliefs about cooperation and trust, too, may claim to be confirmed by the entire evolutionary process which seems to preserve those species with the greatest skills in developing and maintaining cooperative systems.

One must conclude from this analysis that the Doves clearly have the harder row to hoe. In a world beset by long histories of distrust and enmity among peoples and nations and by the chauvinistic language of nationalism and patriotism, the Hawks can readily make a strong case for their suspicions and their policies. The Doves must face the countless theoretical and practical difficulties of trying to create unprecedented universal conditions that promote political trust among peoples and elites at the same time that they assure everyone's physical safety and security.

In short, it falls to the Doves to produce globally the conditions that have made human order and self-governance possible in communities of smaller size—a large and frustrating undertaking at best.

# References

1. Morton Deutsch, "Trust and Suspicion," *Journal of Conflict Resolution*, 2 (1958), 265-279.
2. Secretary of Defense, *Annual Report to the Congress: Fiscal Year 1979*, pp. 33-34, 62.
3. Robert Jervis, "Cooperation Under the Security Dilemma," *World Politics* (January 1978), pp. 167-214. For a survey and evaluation of the debate about deterrence theory and mutual assured destruction (MAD), Donald M. Snow, "Current Nuclear Deterrence Thinking: An Overview and Review," *International Studies Quarterly*, 23, no. 3 (September 1979), 445-486.
4. Thomas W. Milburn and Kenneth H. Watman, "SALT II: Verification," *Mershon Center Quarterly Report*, 4, no. 4 (Summer 1979), 1. The description of the work of the Agency for the Control of Armaments is from Harold K. Jacobson, *Networks of Interdependence: International Organizations and the Global Political System* (New York: Knopf, 1979), pp. 183-185. The Kirkland testimony is reported in *AFL-CIO Free Trade Union News*, 34, no. 10 (October 1979), 8-9.
5. Scientific research on the attributes and dimensions of individual trust as a human attitude and judgment is modest. Almost nothing seems to be available on the more complex phenomenon of trust and distrust as an aspect of collective behavior. Morton Deutsch's "Trust and Suspicion" (*Journal of Conflict Resolution*, 2 (1958), 265-79,) has been cited above. Deutsch's most fully developed theoretical statement about the psychology of the trusting process may be found in his *The Resolution of Conflict: Constructive and Destructive Processes* (New Haven: Yale University Press, 1973), Chap. 7 on "Trust and Suspicion: Theoretical Notes." This seminal statement is probably the best point of departure for future psychological inquiries. On the matter of trust and distrust in the behavior of collectivities, a substantial theoretical statement is offered by Harold Garfinkel, "A Conception of, and Experiments with, 'Trust' as a Condition of Stable Concerted Actions," in O. J. Harvey, *Motivation and Social Internation* (New York: Ronald Press, 1963), Chap. 7. For a thorough review of the literature pertaining to the concept of "political trust," Thomas O. Jukam,

"The Effects of Vietnam Policy on the Decline of Political Trust in American Political Life" (Ph.D. dissertation, Michigan State University, 1977), Chap. 2. Jukam found trust, regardless of poorly operationalized definitions, central to the theories of students of personality such as Erik H. Erikson, and students of social exchange such as Peter Blau, as well as others focusing on such phenomena as legitimacy, alienation, and dissent. Jukam conceives of political trust as "a sentiment consisting of a set of evaluations about the trustworthiness of governmental incumbents, about their ability to perform and fulfill anticipated obligations in accordance with expected norms of behavior." Jukam includes among these norms such qualities as honesty, credibility, responsibility, competence, and integrity (p. 63).

In the behavioral literature, attitudes of trust are intimately related to matters of perception—what we see—and cognitive structure—what we already know. See Robert Jervis, *Perception and Misperception in International Politics* (Princeton, N.J.: Princeton University Press, 1976) and David Finlay, Ole Holsti, and R. Fagen, eds., *Enemies in Politics* (Chicago: Rand McNally, 1967). The relationships among attitudes of trust, perceptions, and cognitive structure underscore the significant influence of subjectivity, particularly subjective probability, in judgments of trust and distrust.

A body of behavioral theory that is significantly related to the phenomenon of trust is exchange, or transaction, theory. The relevant proposition in this theory is that political trust is a principal attitudinal consequence of a series of successful (read: profitable) transactions of behavioral and political currencies over time. George Homans, *Social Behavior: Its Elementary Forms* (New York: Harcourt, Brace & World, 1961); Peter M. Blau, *The Dynamics of Bureaucracy* (Chicago: University of Chicago Press, 1955) and *Exchange and Power in Social Life* (New York: Wiley, 1964); Ralph M. Goldman, "A Transactional Theory of Political Integration and Arms Control," *American Political Science Review,* 63, no. 3 (September 1969), 719-33, and *Contemporary Perspectives on Politics* (New Brunswick, N.J.: Transaction Books, 1976), Chap. 4.

6. An attitudinal study of political trust could conceivably be quite straightforward, yet make a significant contribution to our understanding of the relationships among such variables as political trust, sense of security, hawkish and dovish predispositions, and specific nations and national leaderships as objects of trust or distrust. The two elements of trust could readily be operationalized by a number of questions of a fairly obvious kind. For example, Element One—predictability of another's behavior—could be documented by such forecast-type questions as: "If there were a treaty banning all nuclear tests, what are the odds that the Soviet

Union would somehow cheat and conduct a secret test explosion?''
Element Two—positive or negative consequences of the other's behavior
for oneself—might be explored by such evaluative questions as: ''Is the
Soviet Union's interest in negotiating arms control agreements good or
bad for American national security?'' The respondent's place on a
hawkishness-dovishness scale could be determined by a cluster of questions on such relevant matters as his or her view of worst-case analyses,
amount of security risk the United States can safely take, and related
topics that distinguish Hawks from Doves. This inquiry could readily
become cross-cultural and might even be attractive to Soviet researchers
if, of course, ''United States'' replaced ''Soviet Union'' in the questions.

7. More precisely, sociobiological theories tend to be significant
   modifications of the Darwinian theory of natural selection.
   Sociobiologists evaluate apparently altruistic self-sacrificial acts by
   individual members of a species as acts intended to protect the survival chances of the species' gene pool. To illustrate, consider what
   is genetically involved in some acts of human altruism. A mother
   has, on the average, half her genes in common with her offspring
   and a quarter with her grandchildren. Siblings share half their
   genes, cousins one-eighth, and so on. An act of sacrifice by an individual member of the family nevertheless increases the survival
   and reproductive prospects of related individuals carrying some of
   the same genes. If the cumulative increase in fitness of the survivors
   exceeds the loss of the altruistic individual organism, the species is
   the beneficiary.

   In the case of unrelated organisms, one organism helps another in
   the expectation of receiving help in return, that is, on an assumption that the beneficiary of the help may be trusted to reciprocate.
   Cheating—defined as a failure to reciprocate—is likely to be selected
   against, that is, trust toward such cheating organisms will be
   diminished in the future. In this way, sociobiological theory seems
   to destroy current notions of altruism and replace them with a con-
   firmation of the central role of trust in the collective survival of
   species, even where cheating and deception are significant aspects of
   cooperation. Richard Dawkins, *The Selfish Gene* (New York: Oxford University Press, 1976), and R. L. Trivers, ''The Evolution of
   Reciprocal Altruism,'' 46, no. 1, *Quarterly Review of Biology*
   (1971), 35-37.

# CHAPTER 4

# Sources of Political Distrust

Built into the politics among nations and within nations are elements that create and perpetuate political distrust. A brief examination of these elements may lead us to a better understanding of some of the causes of the arms race and some of the institutional and behavioral hurdles that must be surmounted if collective security is to be achieved.

## Sources of Distrust among Nations

There are several features of relationships among nations that, sometimes clearly, sometimes imperceptibly, affect the extent of distrust and conflict among them. Some of the factors that are usually presumed to reduce distrust and conflict include common culture, common language, similar racial characteristics, and similar social, political, and economic institutions. Conversely, when these factors are neither common nor similar, the occasions for fear, distrust, and conflict seem to multiply. There are a number of the latter factors that bear upon questions of security and military strength and that appear to induce the kind of political distrust that concerns us here. These include: competition among the political leaderships, or elites, of the world; the concept and practices of national sovereignty; the inexorable march of technological advancement; and the widespread practice of keeping military and political secrets.

### Competing Elites

One of the most common pitfalls in analyzing and trying to resolve the problems of security and arms control is the almost exclusive focus upon their military hardware aspects. A familiar analogy may be drawn from the field of medicine where, very often, for lack of well-confirmed knowledge about the causes of a disease, practitioners spend a great deal of time and effort diagnosing and treating symptoms. In E.B. White's more felicitous language, "I am afraid that blaming armaments for war is like blaming fever for disease."[1]

Symptomatic relief may make the disease more tolerable for the patient but it almost never cures the disease that causes the symptoms. Similarly, to focus on the diagnosis and treatment of the military hardware issues of an arms race may bring "symptomatic relief" through the treatment we call "arms control." However, this approach fails to deal with causes. The cause of the arms race is to be found in the beliefs and behaviors of the human beings who feel their sense of security requires that they mobilize weapons and military forces. More specifically, the particular human beings who pursue this mode of "treatment" of the security problem are the competing elites of the world community.

Who comprise these elites? Are they an identifiable and finite group of persons? The answer to the latter question is "yes." A small expenditure of effort could compile a *Who's Who* of the entire world community. In fact, it is a major duty of the Central Intelligence Agency to make just such a compilation. Our hypothetical *Who's Who* would probably number only several thousand names. It would include: senior governmental officials of the more than 160 nations of the world and its supranational organizations such as the United Nations (a roster is already available in such periodical publications as *Current World Leaders* and the *Political Handbook of the World*); senior officers of several score major multinational corporations; leaders of world churches and other transnational organizations and movements; and famous personages with worldwide reputations (usually entertainers, athletes, and artists).

Not all of these leading persons compete politically or on a worldwide basis, nor are most of them concerned with problems of national or world security. However, close examination of these world leaders would probably reveal that those who are most concerned with security and safety are the very ones who are most competitive with each other with regard to control and management of the world's wealth, policy-making processes, and institutional arrangements. These are familiar functional concerns of politicians and businessmen. These are the types of leaders who would most often be included in any roster of "competing world elites."

These world elites have different conceptions of reality and the human condition which they make known through their respective ideologies. They have different notions about how the economic resources of the world should be developed and distributed, notions that are given such names as "capitalism," "communism," "socialism," and so on. These competing elites have fundamentally different attitudes towards religion, education, and the goals that human society should seek. And, historically, these elites have had some painful experiences dealing with each other, usually as a consequence of wars, religious or racial bigotry, or economic exploitation. As consequence, various elite factions perceive each other as serious adversaries as they carry on their competition and conflicts.

The forms that these conflicts take in actual practice tend to fuel the potitical distrust that already exists among them. For example, Soviet and American political leaders are keenly aware that their respective nuclear stockpiles are excessive, well beyond the overkill range. Further, they are also fully cognizant of the fact that their respective nuclear delivery systems are aimed directly at each other. Mutual deterrence from attack and rough "equivalence" of types and quantities of strategic weaponry have clearly been achieved. The SALT process and treaties are intended to take these clearly discernible conditions into account. Then why do the nuclear superpowers insist upon pursuing the nuclear arms race, even after that race has been slowed to a walk?

If we consider that these are *competing political elites* for whom weaponry is but one of several instruments of power, we may discover that the nuclear arms "walk" (rather than "race") may have much to do with the competitive prestige and influence each superpower wishes to maintain or promote among the less mighty nations, organizations, and movements of the world. SALT and the strategic nuclear balance may simply reflect an implicit agreement between superpower leaders that the time has come to stabilize the nuclear instruments of influence, particularly since other instruments of competition—international trade, regional organizations, transnational political parties, and so forth —are beginning to emerge as alternatives to military modes of superpower ascendancy in world affairs. If the superpowers can halt their nuclear competition, for example, they can better demand that others—China, Brazil, and South Africa, for example—do so as well. In addition, whatever the two superpowers can save in military expenditures can better be used in their worldwide competition with such rapidly growing economic giants as Japan, West Germany, China, Brazil, and others.

At the risk of slight oversimplification, one can argue that the principal sources of distrust, arms races, and war are embedded in the perceptions of and relationships among competing world elites. These perceptions and relationships include their different subjective senses of security, their reliance upon military hardware as an objective measure of safety and power, and their failure or inability to build alternative institutions of conflict and competition, such as world party systems or international marketplaces to serve as arenas other than the battlefield for the conduct of their competitive activities. In short, world security and the arms race can *only* be understood and controlled if we investigate their sources among elite relationships rather than focus upon the symptoms that appear in the form of military hardware.

## National Sovereignty

Historically and literally, the king was "sovereign" in his

realm. By definition, the king—or queen—had the "final say" in matters of public or governmental policy and presumably in the resolution of conflicting interests within their realm. Political philosophers and institution-builders have since expanded and refined in theoretical as well as practical detail many meanings of the concept "sovereignty." In the last analysis, sovereignty refers to prerogative, that is, the capacity to make ultimate, final, decisive political choices to the extent that any human choices can be ultimate, final, and decisive.

In the course of time, monarchs came to delegate or share their sovereign prerogatives with royal ministers, houses of parliament, cabinets, political parties, and popular electorates. As the system of feudal relationships that prevailed for many centuries was transformed into the modern nation-state, the attributes of sovereignty that once adhered to royal persons came to be the principal characteristics of organized nations. As the nation-state system and the ideologies of nationalism began to dominate the structure of world politics over the last two or three centuries, the symbols and practices of *national sovereignty* acquired paramount importance. The essential trait of the nation—as of the person—is assumed to be its capacity and freedom to choose for itself, that is, to be its own ultimate sovereign in matters of conduct, internal organization, self-defense, and relationships with others.

The separation of sovereign national organization from sovereign royal persons proved to be a great convenience for practicing politicians. Modern politicians, particularly in egalitarian and democratic societies, prefer to depersonalize the exercise of power. Rather than claim prerogatives for themselves as persons, they prefer to exercise those prerogatives on behalf of some constituency or organization such as the nation.

The formal relations among sovereign nations are far more ponderous than the informal relations among competing or friendly world leaders. The exercise of private policy or preference, particularly in the facilitation of friendships, proceeds more easily on the informal side of internation affairs. It is when internation leadership relationships are hostile and distrustful that the barrier of national sovereignty is quickly erected. A vivid example of this, drawn from the history of arms control, was the Soviet Union's refusal to agree to inspection of its nuclear and other military facilities as would have been required under the Baruch Plan for turning over the United States nuclear monopoly to an international agency following World War II. The Soviet Union considered such inspections a flagrant breach of its national sovereignty and, in a sense, an invasion of its national right to privacy. What this posture, premised upon national sovereignty, reflected was a profound distrust of Americans, capitalists, and the U.N. majority by the Soviet Communist leaders and their certainty that their own scientists would shortly break the American monopoly by producing a Soviet atom bomb.

Since the end of World War II, the number of sovereign nations has increased from approximately 50 to more than 160. Even as empires built during the eighteenth and nineteenth centuries continued to disintegrate, postwar nationalist movements and leaders decried the evils of imperialism. These local leaders struggled, with greater or less success, to put together the symbols and organizations necessary to advance their new nationalisms, achieve the full status of sovereign nation-states, and join the world community of nations as equals. In that world community, as structured by the United Nations System, these newcomer nations are indeed treated as sovereign equals by the older and much more influential states. The one-nation, one-vote principle prevails in the United Nations General Assembly as well as other United Nations agencies. In these settings, the voice and vote of tiny Burundi is equal to the voice and vote of either mighty superpower.

In less than two generations, the membership of the world community, in the form of nation-states, has trebled. Nationalism and national sovereignty have been fundamental features in their integration as well as in their incorporation into the political affairs of the world. The practical and symbolic requirements for becoming integrated nations prompted their leaders to choose anti-imperialist and antisuperpower postures. Such, for example, has been the motivation for the organization of nonaligned states as a working coalition in world affairs and also for the emergence of a North-South debate over the distribution of the world's economic resources. Here again political distrust continues to be generated by the memory of unhappy past relationships, the pervasiveness of cultural and economic differences, and the need to use national sovereignty as a weight in the balance of international power and influence.

However, even as new nations promote nationalism and older nations stand behind a shield of national sovereignty, the evolution of supranational organizations and worldwide relationships proceeds with each passing day. As soon as nations become members of a supranatural organization, their sovereignty and freedom to behave without constraint are diluted by the obligations and advantages of membership in such organizations. For example, although in the past the Soviet Union has exercised its veto power with great frequency in the Security Council, that defensive practice has declined significantly in recent years: 77 vetoes in the first decade of its U.N. membership; 26 vetoes in the second decade;

only 17 vetoes in the third. Given the increase in the number of its potential U.N. allies and the many alternative methods of asserting its views, the Soviet Union is obviously more relaxed about its U.N. participation. Today, like every other nation in the United Nations, the Soviet Union has become constrained in its exercise of political choice by the events, coalitions, and policies developed in that organization. Contrarily, in more recent years the United States has found itself in an increasingly defensive situation, exercising its veto increasingly as a consequence: from zero in the first two decades to twenty-one vetoes between 1966 and 1977. Americans have become more suspicious and less supportive of the United Nations.

Just as membership in supranational organizations constrains the exercise of national sovereignty, other forms of international collaboration also nibble away at the prerogatives of nation-states. The growth of regional organizations such as NATO and the Warsaw Pact, the European Community, the Organization of American States, the Arab League, and the Organization of African Unity also tends to diminish the freedom of action of member states. Another similar development is the growth in numbers of multilateral treaties, each of which creates a national commitment to a transnational process that, bit by bit, diminishes the sovereign prerogatives of national political leaders.

Yet another sovereignty-diluting development has been the phenomenal proliferation of *multinational corporations* (MNCs). Since the end of World War II, literally thousands of corporate enterprises have come into being to conduct manufacturing and other economic functions in two or more nations. As of 1978 corporations, not countries, comprised nearly 40 percent of the 100 largest organized economic units in the world. Thus, for example, General Motors Corporation, with sales of $63 billion, was the largest corporate economic unit, with only 22 nations larger than it by this standard. General Motors ranked ahead of Yugoslavia, whose gross national product was $56 billion. The ten largest corporations in the roster of 100 included: General Motors, Exxon, Royal Dutch Shell, Ford, Mobil, Texaco, British Petroleum, Standard Oil of California, National Iranian Oil, and International Business Machines. The decisions of these corporate enterprises regarding the extraction of mineral and other natural resources, the location of plants and other labor-intensive units, the setting of prices and wages, the disbursement of dividends on stocks and bonds, and so on, have far-reaching strategic as well as economic consequences. Officers of governments and officers of corporations have only begun to become accustomed to dealing with each other in ways that affect national security and world peace. There are those business enthusiasts who claim that the world will eventually have an end to war and violence largely because these are bad for business.

This trend in the weakening of national sovereignty notwithstanding, the sovereign nation is bound to be with us for generations to come. National sovereignty, its requirements, and its manifestations are likely to continue to generate political distrust in international relations. Nations will continue to insist upon their national privacy by resisting arrangements for international inspection and verification of their military or other resources. Even as the mass media of communications become increasingly capable of reaching into every corner of the world to observe and report events, national leaders, in the name of national sovereignty, will for some time undoubtedly continue to insist that only their own versions of reality be communicated; national censorship will continue to reduce the flow and shape the bias of information going across borders. National sovereignty will also continue to be the basis for claims to equality in forums such as the United Nations, despite the unequal contribution of support and influence that most nations make to such forums. Further, for some time to come, sovereign nation-states, rather than political parties or organized group interests, will comprise international coalitions, alliance systems, and voting blocs. Above all, national sovereignty will continue to stimulate, as it always has in the past, the search for the military resources that national leaders consider so vital for the exercise of their influence in international affairs and for the safety of their regimes and populations against predatory neighbors. In sum, national sovereignty is bound to be a major source of political distrust among nations for a long time.

## Technological Development

Table 1 summarized for us the tremendous "advances" in the lethality of weapons. The entire history of military technology has been the development of new and ingenious ways of throwing rocks at each other in order to destroy or injure persons and property. The more of an adversary's persons and property a military device can destroy or injure, the more "powerful" the rock-thrower presumably is.

The remarkable assumption of many military strategists has been that nuclear bombs are simply bigger and better rocks. As soon as unthinkable nuclear exchanges became theoretically "thinkable," it became feasible for military strategists to plan and produce nuclear weaponry as though these could be used for the most part like any other bomb in traditional wars. Nuclear bombs were, according to this view, simply another phase in the advancing qualitative arms race. Thus, as recently as 1977, one leading but hawkish American strategic analyst could still write a magazine article entitled "Why the Soviet Union Thinks It Could Fight and Win a Nuclear War."[2] Or, consider the United States Joint Chiefs of Staff Emergency War Plan known as "Halfmoon", prepared *in 1948*, which called for "a main offensive effort" by *dropping 50 atomic bombs on targets in 20 Soviet cities*.[3] The "thinkability" of nuclear war came early to military strategists, and they—both Soviet and American—have been frightening the dickens out of each other and the rest of the world ever since.

Since Hiroshima, fear and multibillion dollar *r*esearch and *de*velopment (R&D) budgets—usually 10 percent of major-power military budgets—have spurred the search for military knowledge and the exercise of human inventiveness on behalf of an accelerating qualitative arms race. The $25 billion world R&D current annual expenditure for military research noted earlier reports only the governmental part of expenditures along these lines. The figure represents governmental budget items and does not include the military-related R&D outlays of private corporations or backyard inventors. This is a tremendous investment in human inventiveness for the purpose of coping with only the symptomatic aspects of security and safety. It is the kind of investment that produced the atom bomb and all of its successor technologies and also placed men on the moon. However, for reasons about which we may readily speculate, similar R&D resources are *not* available to those seeking the cause and cure of cancer, the treatment of mental illness, the development of safe sources of energy, or the identification of nonmilitary remedies for the pathology of international insecurity and war. Few things provide as accurate a measure of a community's priorities as its governmental budget. Clearly, we and other budgetmakers around the world fear our well-armed enemies more than we do the loss of life and happiness as a consequence of cancer, mental illness, shortages of energy, or the collective insecurities of *all* peoples and elites.

Given these military security priorities and enormous R&D resources, the pace of military technological development has been swift and dramatic. In turn, advancing military technology has constantly fueled the arms competition, destabilized military balances, unsettled almost everyone's sense of security, and, above all, sustained attitudes of political distrust. With such priorities and budgets, it is almost a certainty that nations will continue to create new weapons. Add to this empirical certainty the equally assured normative judgment that new weapons produced by one nation will be "bad" for others. Such a sequence of developments is bound to lead to aggravated political distrust.

A short inventory of major military technological developments since World War II illustrates the above point. In July 1945, when the United States detonated the first A-bomb experimentally, it became the possessor of a nuclear monopoly that would last only a few short years. A month later it dropped a 14-kiloton (equivalent to 14,000 tons of TNT) A-bomb on Hiroshima causing 135,000 casualties and, shortly thereafter, a 20-kiloton bomb on Nagasaki resulting in 64,000 casualties. These city-destroying bombs were measured in kilotons at that time; they are now measured in megatons (each equivalent to one million tons of TNT). In August 1949, Soviet scientists detonated that nation's first A-bomb. The British followed in November 1952, the French in 1960, China in 1964, and India in 1973. The technological monopoly had become nuclear proliferation, with about thirty other nations presently in the wings on the point of producing their own nuclear weapon capability. Fusion bombs soon succeeded the earlier fission type, and the United States detonated its first hydrogen bomb with a 10 megaton yield in November 1952.[4] The Soviet Union followed suit in 1955, and China did so in 1967.

The same technological contest and escalation has taken place for other weapons systems. It was one thing to create bombs that could destroy entire cities but another to deliver these bombs directly to cities halfway around the earth. In August 1957, the Soviet Union launched a test intercontinental ballistic missile that traveled the length of Siberia. In August 1958, the United States fired a test ICBM, the Atlas, with a range of 6,000 miles. The era of intercontinental ballistic missiles had begun. The R&D engineers of nuclear delivery systems concerned themselves with CEP (Circular Error Probable), that is, the distance from the target within which, on the average, half of the nuclear warheads would most probably fall; at first, CEPs were five miles or less, and now they are as low as 0.15 mile), range, and throw-weight (the megatonnage of nuclear explosive force carried in the warhead).

By 1960, the notion of multiple warheads entered the technology. *m*ultiple *r*eentry *v*ehicles (MRVs) were developed to land in a specific pattern around the same target. The next technological leap was MIRV (*m*ultiple, *i*ndependently-targetable *r*eentry *v*ehicles), which could be aimed at different targets after being fired and conveyed by the same missile "bus." Development of MIRVs has proceeded so rapidly that the SALT II Treaty places a limit of ten to fourteen warheads on any single missile.

The advancing nuclear bomb and delivery system technology is matched by developments in other areas. High-resolution photo reconnaissance systems have been developed that are capable of observing human individuals on the ground from orbiting satellites more than 100 miles up. These flying cameras are essential for military intelligence and verification of arms control agreements. Yet, even as the technological capacity to observe and gather intelligence improves, the technology of concealment advances as well. Cruise missiles with diameters as small as 21 inches are now available for delivering nuclear bombs over a distance of up to 2,000 miles. Cruise missiles are small enough to be hidden underground, in submarines, or in aircraft, and launched from any of these. The MX missile is at hand in various designs intended to move ICBM launchers about underground, in open trenches, or in submarines in secret patterns making them difficult to locate for targeting purposes. Research and development is also producing tactical warheads of the neutron bomb type.

All the advancement is not reserved to the field of nuclear weaponry. We have already noted that the age of lasers is almost upon us as the superpowers race to develop this technology. More broadly, however, the advancing technology in conventional weapons is also awesome. The roster of military marvels is overwhelming: (a) "smart" bombs or *p*recision *g*uided *m*unitions (PGMs) capable of seeking out and striking targets with almost infallible accuracy through the use of television cameras, radar, laser beams, and similar electronic technology; (b) planes (Boeing 707s) carrying *a*irborne *w*arning *a*nd *c*ontrol *s*ystems (AWACS) capable of detecting low-flying planes up to 250 miles away and with sufficient military command and communication equipment to serve as key command headquarters; (c) night vision devices and other equipment that create electronic battlefield sensors capable of detecting day or night the presence and movement of troops or equipment; (d) ships that are able to speed over water at 90 miles per hour on a cushion of air. The list of ingenious devices goes on and so does their lethality. For example, in World War II an estimated 300,000 bullets were required to kill a single infantryman. But in 1967, during the Mideast War, a Russian Styx surface-to-surface "smart" PGM-type missile (cost: $20,000) sank the Israeli destroyer Elath (cost: $150 million). In the 1973 Mideast War similar Soviet-made *s*urface-to-*a*ir *m*issiles (SAMs) brought down 90 Israeli fighters in 2 days, and a 20-pound, infantry-fired, wire-guided Soviet Sagger missile destroyed 130 Israeli tanks in several hours. Technology moves onward toward higher accuracy, miniaturization, improved penetration of targets, and lower cost per weapon unit.[5]

The momentum of the qualitative arms race is difficult to

analyze, negotiate, or halt. In contemporary industrial societies, it is something of a sacrilege to suggest that technological progress of any kind be slowed down or stopped. It would be as though Alexander Graham Bell, Thomas Edison, Henry Ford, and Jonas Salk were being required to put an end to their creativity and inventiveness at the risk of going to jail if they failed to stop. In an open and technologically sophisticated society it is well-nigh impossible to constrain human creativity and inventiveness. Even in closed societies such as the Soviet Union the inevitable pressures of military competition, consumer demand, and imitation of the living styles of other societies conspire to promote technological change. How else can a society cope with the persistent fear that some adversary will create the Ultimate Weapon (as though the nuclear bomb is not), the certainty that technological progress will continue unabated, and the likelihood that adverse developments in the military field may weaken one's own security.

Precisely because it *is* the most creative and technologically advanced society in the world, the United States is unfortunately the principal source of this type of technological destabilization and distrust. Some proud and chauvinistic policymakers have even proposed that the United States concentrate its military chiefly on research and development, creating new hardware wonders at such a pace as to make previous wonders obsolete even before they go into full production. At such a pace, the Soviet Union presumably could never catch up and the United States would be forever secure. This argument is both gratifying and terrifying.

## Military Secrecy

Secrecy and spying are forms of informational warfare. As such, their practitioners assume that a situation of conflict exists, enemies or potential enemies may be specified, and suspicion is the order of the day. As a consequence, vast sums of money and effort are expended throughout the world (a) to keep military technologies and strategies "secure," that is, secret, and (b) to carry on the intelligence operations aimed at ferreting out each other's secrets.[6] This secrecy-intelligence circle is probably the most enduring and pervasive perpetuator of political distrust.

One of the strongest arguments in support of the functions of national intelligence agencies may be found in Simmel's paradox: "The most effective prerequisite for preventing struggle, the exact knowledge of the comparative strength of the two parties, is very often attainable only by the actual fighting out of the conflict."[7] In more contemporary strategic language, the most effective deterrent to war is exact knowledge of the relative military resources of the most likely adversaries.

Historically, there are many tragic examples of misperception of the strength of the other side—either as underestimates or overestimates—that have contributed to gross policy errors. In 1914, the Germans overestimated the size of the French army by 121,000. The French overestimated German strength by 134,000. The actual strength of each side became evident only in the process of military combat. In later years, the world overestimated Hitler's military resources after the German occupation of Czechoslovakia, and then Hilter underestimated the strength and the resolve of England and the Soviet Union. Here again the final measurements came on the battlefield.

In the light of such considerations, the multibillion dollar intelligence activities of the United States Central Intelligence Agency, the Soviet KGB, and the intelligence communities of other nations throughout the world are considered essential for the prevention of errors in strategic judgment by national leaders and the deterrence of international military adventures that employ violence and terror as instruments of influence. However, such intelligence acitivies are conducted in secret and their findings are treated as national secrets. In turn, these secrets aggravate the "distrust dilemma" and escalate the arms race. This is the basic relationship among military secrecy, military and political intelligence, and the arms race.

If we probe more deeply into the management of secrets and spies, other substantial risks are revealed. Secrecy may be and has been a cover for bureaucratic and military misjudgments or breaches of the law of one kind or another. Secrecy can also be a tool of power, a barrier between those who have a "right to know" and those who do not. This barrier may determine who is a member of the more influential political ingroup and who must remain the outgroup. Similarly, as recent investigations of the CIA have revealed, spying may carry substantial risks for civil liberties, too. The McCarthy investigations of the early 1950s and the Watergate scandal indicate how spying on foreigners may easily flow over into spying against one's own citizens. Civil liberties thus endangered may created a climate of suspicion and fear that spreads all too rapidly among the citizenry. Another bureaucratic qualm about spying is that the validity and reliability of the information gathered may be questionable, yet, because of secrecy, remains unchallenged. Worst of all, the function of information gathering by spies may readily slip into forms of political coercion and violence domestically and internationally.

What are some of the principal motivations and justifications for military secrecy? A prime motivation is the maintenance of technological advantage over others. Governments, corporations, and even individual scientists keep secrets for as long as possible in order to deny a competitor some perceived advantage. It took the Soviet Union four years to break the American A-bomb monopoly, but meanwhile, American military and political ascendancy in world affairs could hardly be challenged by the Soviets in any significant way. Corporations spend millions of dollars in the development of new inventions and products, an investment that they try to protect with secrecy until their discoveries can be patented. As for scientists, the glory of being first to discover new knowledge is unquestionably a major motivation for the inquiries they pursue.

Another motivation for secrecy is bluff and surprise. By leaking partial or incorrect information about a secret weapon, one side can keep the other uncertain and anxious about what the latter might be up against in a military confrontation. Such is the central purpose of bluffing. Surprise requires that a secret be well kept so that an adversary is overwhelmed when discovering it during a military confrontation, as exemplified by the devastating and surprising accuracy of Soviet-supplied "smart" antitank missiles described earlier and used by the Arabs against Israeli tanks in the 1973 Yom Kippur war.

Yet another motivation for secrecy is the rarely acknowledged political need for mystery and conspiracy as instruments of national cohesion. Few attitudes unite a nation as quickly as fear of some perceived enemy. The question that often ends any debate between Hawks and Doves is the hawkish "but can you trust the Russians?" This question, together with the recurrent discovery of spying by the other side, paves the way for witch hunts and spy scares. The Palmer raids against suspected Communists after World War I and the McCarthy "Red" hunt following World War II, both stimulated by popular fear and the political ambitions of their namesakes, were prime examples of such use of secrecy, spying, and fear.

In general, then, secrecy and spying reinforce political distrust, accelerate the arms race, encourage public investment in costly intelligence organizations, and, frequently overlooked, obstruct the advancement of knowledge generally, particularly in nonmilitary research. There is also the very risk of nuclear war, as the Cuban missile crisis of 1962 so amply demonstrated. Given the large intelligence budgets for the CIA and the KGB, each of the superpowers is extremely well informed about the disposition of the other's forces. Any major changes in these dispositions are usually signaled by one side publicly and well in advance, as in the case of the CENTO (Central Treaty Organization) treaty permitting the placement of American missiles in Turkey within range of the Soviet Union. One of the most disturbing aspects of the Cuban missile crisis for American leaders was that the Soviet Union was secretly making a major change in the disposition of its strategic weapons. Not only was the placement of Soviet missiles in Cuba a flagrant challenge to the Monroe Doctrine and a real military threat to American security, the move also raised profound questions about the Soviet leadership's effort to accomplish all this in secrecy.

The trends, fortunately, have not all been in favor of secrecy, spying, and suspicion. Much has been accomplished since World War II with respect to unilateral reporting, arrangements for "hot lines," verification techniques (particularly by observational satellites), and on-site inspection. In other words, there are tendencies toward sharing "exact knowledge," as suggested by Simmel, for preventing conflict. A fundamental byproduct of such tendencies will inevitably be the promotion of trust among nations and competing elites.

Unilateral reporting of one's military resources is an inescapable part of politics in open societies where priorities and budgets are debated publicly and where military research, development, and procurement contracts must be made part of the public record. Although bureaucracies in all societies tend to proliferate the secret classification of documents and other information, this tendency is not likely to go unchallenged or persist forever. The press is always eager to disclose and expose. Opposition political parties are curious to learn if secrecy has been a cover for policy blunders on the part of the incumbents. Taxpayers are extremely reluctant to pay for the high cost of document classification programs, miscarriages of civil rights that are often associated with such programs, or intelligence agencies preoccupied with keeping or discovering secrets. Such tendencies in the open society make it easy for intelligence operatives of totalitarian regimes to ascertain types, quantities, and uses of the military hardware of such societies. Communist intelligence operatives need do no more than make a trip to the local library, a request to the Government Printing Office for a copy of the secretary of defense's latest annual report, a subscription to the *New York Times*, an examination of the *Federal Register*, and so on.

However, the Soviet Union has surely been the champion secret-keeper of the world for decades. It has been a remarkable feature of most arms control negotiations between the United States and the Soviet Union that the weapon names and stockpile quantities data used by *both sides* have been those presented by the United States. Soviet negotiating practice has strictly accepted the American names and figures as the basis for negotiations. From the Soviet point of view, this practice has been a cheap way of checking the competency of American intelligence operations while at the same time playing their own military cards close to the chest. From the American point of view, the practice has been multipurpose: a proud demonstration of American intelligence competency; a deterrent to Soviet trickery; but, above all, a policy designed to compile "exact knowledge" and promote trust between the two nuclear giants. The Soviet leadership may well be catching on, for they recently announced a willingness to publish data about their nuclear inventories as part of the Soviet contribution to the continuation of the SALT process. The day may come when all nations, as a procedure for promoting global trust and preventing war, unilaterally and regularly report their weapons inventories to some international agency such as the Military Staff Committee of the United Nations Security Council.

A "hot line" is a direct and constantly open communication system between the leaders of the United States and the Soviet Union for use in emergencies. The original hot-line system consisted of underseas cables, one line following a northern route between Washington and Moscow and a second line on a southern route across North Africa. The first hot-line agreement between the superpowers was signed in 1963. A modernization treaty, aimed at bringing the communication technology up to date, was completed in 1971. At the present time satellites as well as cables serve to keep several channels open between the White House and the Kremlin.

The importance of this ostensibly simple arrangement should not be underestimated. When two powerful parties, ordinarily described as "enemies," make arrangements to communicate with each other instantaneously in emergencies, there must exist a substantial stake and shared interest that surpasses any gain that may be served by their enmity. In this case, any one of a number of simple human or mechanical errors could unleash a nuclear exchange that is unintended and unwanted. Even in less urgent situations, a hot-line system may permit the superpowers to avoid the kind of face-off that occurred in the Cuban missile crisis and, as it actually did, in the 1973 Mideast War, or that could occur in any one of a number of crisis spots in the world. The practice of using the hot line for direct communication between superpower leaders is a profoundly positive measure aimed at sharing "exact knowledge" as well as responsibility for preventing major wars triggered by errors of information or failings of judgment of one of the parties, such as those that led to World War I and World War II.

"Exact knowledge" through verification has been a tale of reconnaissance technology. The Mata Haris have been for the most part replaced by less scintillating "national technical means" of data gathering about weaponry: U-2 planes, orbiting satellites, line-of-sight radar stations, over-the-horizon radar stations, a variety of sensors, high resolution cameras capable of providing a clear photograph of an object one foot across from an altitude of 100 miles, and a cafeteria of computer-generated analytical systems that produce maps, interpret photographs, and analyze many forms of evidence. Rumor and hearsay have been replaced by direct visual or electronic observation. In the words of Congressman Les Aspin:

> In short, the "national technical means" of surveillance available to this country for observing Russian missile tests are multiple, redundant and complementary. They enable the U.S. to detect all long-range missiles fired from the U.S.S.R. They are, in fact, far more reliable than most human intelligence gathering (that is, spying), which may yield second-hand, dated information or even false, slanted information.[8]

The technological revolution in reconnaissance has had a profound impact on the issue of trust. It is now possible for arms control negotiators to claim, with only slight exaggeration, that all agreements may be sufficiently verified by national technical means so that the risk of cheating is reduced almost to zero. In other words, distrust need no longer be an issue in the negotiation of arms control agreements; distrust is simply assumed, and verification is arranged. However, as we have seen, Hawks are not easily satisfied. Theoretically, and even practically, there is always *some* possibility for cheating, and Hawks manifest their profound distrust of an adversary by focusing their arguments on this risk, as illustrated earlier in our discussion of Soviet treaty compliance. For the extreme Hawk, anything less than 100 per cent verifiability is too risky to accept.

Hawkish demands notwithstanding, the trend is in the other direction. The advance of reconnaissance technology has strengthened national technical means for the verification of arms control agreements and facilitated the acquisition of other vital intelligence information. Improved verification capabilities have in turn encouraged arms controllers to broaden the scope of their negotiations and agreements, including the specification of a growing number of ground rules for noninterference with each other's national technical means of verification. As the number, scope, and verifiability of arms control agreements increase, the scope of political trust also expands.

Perhaps the touchiest approach to the reduction and elimination of military secrecy is inspection. Proposals for direct, on-site inspection of national military forces by some international agency elicit all of the negative responses that a family experiences when presented with a warrant to search its home. For the family, searches and inspections are generally perceived as annoying and demeaning invasions of privacy. The same is true for nations, particularly for closed societies that also see an added insult to their national sovereignty.

Inspection usually requires that qualified observers, representing either an international agency or one of the parties to an arms control agreement, be permitted to examine personally and directly the weapons and/or military personnel of the nation being inspected or be allowed on-site during weapons tests and similar exercises. Theoretically, the process of inspection could put an end to all military secrecy. It hardly follows, though, that an end to military secrecy means an end to military strength; the weapons and military forces would continue to be present and capable of destruction. What would decline in importance and cost, however, would be high-risk bluffing and the expensive intelligence operations presently associated with military secrecy.

The notion of inspection had an unpromising beginning with the Soviet rejection of the on-site inspection requirement of the Baruch Plan put forth by the United States in 1946. Under this plan, the United States would have agreed to place all atomic resources under the control of an international agency, the United Nations Atomic Energy Commission. As a condition of this grant of its nuclear monopoly, the United States required that all national territories be open to AEC inspection teams. Preoccupied with its own A-bomb development program and conservative about its national sovereignty, the Soviet Union rejected the proposal. During the course of the discussions, however, the concept of inspection was thoroughly aired and produced a sustantial literature. The 1950s and early 1960s witnessed the advancement of reconnaissance and verification technology, as noted. In some respects, the Cuban missile crisis was a Soviet test of United States capacity for unilateral reconnaissance, and the high-resolution U-2 photographs of the Cuban missile launcher sites were a dramatic demonstration of that capacity.

During the 1960s and 1970s, the acceptability and legitimacy of inspection advanced considerably. The International Atomic Energy Agency (IAEA) has been charged with responsibility for keeping careful account of all fissionable materials transferred from one country to another for nuclear energy purposes. This responsibility includes the inspection of security systems for nuclear power plants, accounting procedures (to detect the diversion of plutonium for explosive uses), and safety provisions for the handling of fissionable materials. The inspection force of the IAEA is already understaffed and overworked.

The Soviet Union's attitude toward inspection has also been changing. In the Peaceful Nuclear Explosions (PNE) Treaty of 1976, wherein a 150 kiloton limit was placed on PNEs for projects such as extraction of underground energy sources, the Soviets agreed for the first time to a provision for on-site inspection. These inspections, by American observers, are to be scheduled whenever a PNE takes place. This treaty also calls for the mandatory exchange of relevant technical data. The PNE Treaty was a companion to the Threshold Test Ban Treaty, signed in 1976, which limited Soviet and American underground nuclear tests to a maximum yield of 150 kilotons.

Verification and inspection are likely to be major technical issues for the negotiators of the Comprehensive Test Ban (CTB) Treaty. These negotiations, currently in progress among the United States, the Soviet Union, and the United Kingdom, would presumably put an end to all nuclear testing for a given period, probably between three and five years. CTB is expected to consist of two separate treaties. A trilateral treaty among the three negotiating powers is likely to be verifiable through present national technical means. Further, these three nations now have large, if not too large, stockpiles of nuclear weapons, reducing their need for further tests. The three powers can afford to postpone or terminate nuclear tests, contingent upon whether or not the two absent nuclear powers, France and China, go along with the ban in fact if not in formality. The second CTB treaty is where difficulties are likely to be greater. This multilateral treaty will invite all nations to cease nuclear tests, which in effect means foregoing the possibility of possessing nuclear weapons, the goal of the Nuclear Non-Proliferation Treaty (NPT) of 1970. With some thirty countries on the threshold of nuclear weapon capability, this is indeed a large demand. The inspection system proposed in the multilateral CTB treaty will consist of a chain of seismic stations throughout the world capable of reporting underground nuclear test explosions. Joint American and Soviet satellite reconnaissance would presumably discover surface or atmospheric nuclear tests.

Overall, therefore, the sources of political distrust among nations—competing elites, national sovereignty, technological developments, and military secrecy—continue to be potent. The odds favor the continuation of international political distrust for decades to come. However, these sources of distrust are being challenged and constrained as the world grows smaller and its capacity for self-destruction grows larger. World elites are beginning to find the military levers of power either awkward or obsolescent, often playing second fiddle to economic considerations or to nonmilitary political coalitions in supranational organizations. National sovereignty, which will hardly ever be *declared* obsolete, continues, like old soldiers, to fade away. Military technology advances almost unabated but increasingly in competition for tax dollars and with consumer needs. Secrecy and spying also continue to have a substantial place in world affairs, but here, too, the principles of disclosure and publicly shared information seem to be gaining ground.

## Sources of Distrust from within Nations

More often than most politicians and statesmen would be willing to acknowledge, foreign policy is made more for the folks back home than for any internation motivation. Patriotism and national chauvinism still describe powerful popular attitudes within nations throughout the world. Furthermore, like all public policy, foreign policy touches and affects different domestic interests in very different ways, benefiting some and disadvantaging others. In the United States there are Democrats and Republicans, factions within each major party, thousands of organized interest groups, a national government of divided powers and separate banches, a federal system with fifty states, and many other sources of political division that in some way relate to the conduct of foreign affairs. In the Soviet Union a similar, albeit less visible, complexity exists: party, bureaucracy, the military, regions, and nationality groups function actively, each with its own interest and perspective, in what otherwise appears to be a political monolith. Two other old adversaries provide another example: Israel and Egypt. The political friction within Israel and its Knesset, particularly with regard to foreign policy, is audible throughout the world. In Egypt, despite the very rare passing press reference to President Sadat's tenuous hold on that country's economy, all political judgments appear to be tightly within his grasp. Yet political parties exist, ministers come and go, popular protests occur, and, like most politicians, Sadat must maintain a successful political coalition in order to govern.

## Hawks versus Doves

Cutting across the domestic political diversity within all nations are Hawks and Doves. Their differences are fundamental and pervasive in the conduct of foreign policy.

As we have already noted, Hawks tend to be nationalistic, deeply committed to national security, and suspicious of all past or potential foreign enemies. Hawks rely heavily on military techniques of international influence and national security. They also tend to be most demanding regarding the terms of treaties and other international agreements.

Doves tend to be internationalists, humanists, more inclined to see parties to a conflict rather than enemies, promotive of non-military techniques of conflict management—for example arbitration, international law—interested in economic and social methods of international influence, inclined to trust their opposite parties in the negotiating process, and often more interested in concluding agreements per se than in the fine details of their specific terms.

Hawks suspect whereas Doves trust, usually on the basis of the same empirical evidence. Doves call Hawks paranoid; Hawks call Doves fools. The simple fact that both perspectives exist in every country and set the tone of every domestic foreign policy debate is itself sufficient to keep alive the problem of political distrust among competing elites.

The research of James N. Rosenau and Ole R. Holsti confirm and elaborate upon these impressionistic distinctions between Hawks and Doves. Using a 111-item questionnaire to inquire into the post-Vietnam foreign policy orientations of 2,282 leaders in all walks of American life, they found three quite distinct foreign policy belief systems: Cold War Internationalists, Post-Cold War Internationalists, and Isolationists. The Cold War Internationalists were akin to Hawks in that they perceived the international system as bipolar, the global issues as primarily East-West in character, the Soviet Union as the main threat to the United States in a zero-sum conflict, and keeping up militarily with the Soviets as a basic premise of United States foreign policy. The dovish Post-Cold War Internationalists added North-South issues to those of East versus West in a multipolar world, poverty and Third World antagonism as the main threats to the United States, a non-zero-sum conflict in which the Soviet Union was militarily powerful but also a developing country, and the promotion of economic and political institutions as the basis of United States foreign policy. Isolationists resembled the Post-Cold War Internationalists in many beliefs but favored keeping foreign involvements to a minimum and focusing on handling problems at home. What keeps

American opinion toward the Soviet Union shifting between hawkish and dovish are changing views about Soviet intentions, according to Rosenau and Holsti.[9]

The postures of Hawks and Doves flow logically from their respective assumptions about an adversary's intentions and their interpretations of self-interest, the very issues that created a dilemma for our hypothetical prisoners. In fact, the two sets of postures may be built in to the professional responsibilities of particular individuals. What president of the United States or the Soviet Union and what citizenry would want a defense minister and a military high command that fails to speculate about worst-case scenarios? It is the professional responsibility of the military to engage in this type of exercise and to provide appropriate advice accordingly. Whether a president or a citizenry accepts the advice is another matter. On the other hand, what president and citizenry would want economic advisers who fail to point out that economic ruin brought on by excessive military spending may be worse than some degree of military insecurity or even some kinds of military defeat? The assumptions, the interpretations, and the debates are illustrated by the following instances.

We referred earlier to the 1948 Emergency War Plan "Halfmoon" prepared by the Joint Chiefs of Staff. It is important to recall the historical setting in which Halfmoon was proposed. At the end of World War II in 1945, the United States, as it had in every previous war, began a rapid demobilization of its armed forces, returning millions of soldiers and sailors home and disposing of weapons and equipment it had sent to all corners of the world. The Soviet Union only partially demobilized despite its cruel losses and damage suffered during the war.

As early as 1946, American military strategists began advising President Truman, as it was their responsibility to do, that the Soviet army was capable of taking Western Europe (except for Great Britain), Turkey, Iran, the Persian Gulf, Manchuria, Korea, and North China in a matter of weeks or months.[10] The United States, they reported, had left itself only enough forces to defend the Western Hemisphere. Recalling some of the wartime difficulties in cooperating with the Communists against the Axis and observing the Soviet postwar threats to occupied Berlin (the Berlin Crisis came in the summer of 1948), Greece, Turkey, Iran, and other countries on its periphery, American military and political leaders became deeply distrustful of the intentions of dictator Stalin and the rest of the Soviet leadership. Soviet unwillingness to negotiate about the Baruch Plan for establishing an international agency to take over the American nuclear monopoly, along with other evidence, convinced United States leaders that the Soviets were striving to develop their own nuclear capability. Lubricated by mutual distrust, Soviet-American competition over the future of Europe and other strategic areas of the world, worst-case military analyses on both sides, and the professional obligation of military planners to take such cases into account, the wheel of the Soviet-American arms competition and the Cold War began rolling faster and faster and, it seemed, irreversibly.

Preparedness to counter Soviet conventional forces became the prime concern of American military planners between 1945 and 1949. Concern for Soviet nuclear capacity came later. The atom bomb was perceived as the sole United States advantage in these early plans. Between 1946 and 1948, it is estimated that only about a dozen A-bombs were available. This fact was not reported to President Truman until April 1947! Truman was shocked to learn how small the stockpile was. Further, only about 27 to 32 B-29 bombers capable of delivering A-bombs were on hand. Many of the A-bombs were unassembled and would require twenty-four, specially trained men about two days to prepare each bomb for action. Under pressure to develop a feasible nuclear attack force, in October 1947, the Joint Chiefs of Staff informed the chairman of the U.S. Atomic Energy Commission that there existed a military requirement for approximately 400 atomic bombs (20 kilotons). Soon after, in May 1948, came the plan for Halfmoon under which 50 atomic bombs (probably the entire stockpile at that time) would be dropped on targets in 20 Soviet cities.

President Truman rejected Halfmoon and requested an alternate plan using conventional forces. By September 1948, however, following the nasty Berlin Crisis and airlift, Truman found that he had to assure his defense officials that he would be willing to use atomic weapons if it became necessary. Henceforth, and anticipating the massive retaliation doctrine of President Eisenhower's secretary of state, John Foster Dulles, United States military strategists, reinforced by new nuclear technologies, became absorbed in discussions about the number of A-bombs needed, the specific Soviet cities to be destroyed, and the procedures for giving the fatal command. Not many Communist spies were needed, if any at all, to communicate all this to the already paranoid Soviet leadership. By the early 1950s, with the United States embroiled in Korea and the Soviet Union vetoing all collective security moves at the United Nations, fear and distrust were rampant.

Leaping ahead to the mid-1970s—thousands of nuclear bombs and megatons later—we find that the American strategic debate had also escalated to keep abreast of the weaponry. The issue had become whether a nuclear war was any longer thinkable, survivable, and winnable. The issue is stated by Professor Richard Pipes of Harvard, who at one time was director of the Russian Research Center at that university.

> The classic dictum of Clausewitz, that war is politics pursued by other means, is widely believed in the United States to have lost its validity after Hiroshima and Nagasaki. Soviet doctrine, by contrast, emphatically asserts that while all-out nuclear war would indeed prove extremely destructive to both parties, its outcome would not be mutual suicide: the country better prepared for it and in possession of a superior strategy could win and emerge a viable society. "There is profound erroneousness and harm in the disorienting claims of bourgeois ideologies that there will be no victor in a thermonuclear world war," thunders an authoritative Soviet publication. The theme is mandatory in the current Soviet military literature. Clausewitz, buried in the United States, seems to be alive and prospering in the Soviet Union.[11]

What should the United States do? "It is high time to start paying heed to Soviet strategic doctrine," advises Professor Pipes. Scientists and accountants have been too influential in the formulation of current United States strategic theory; it is important that the military be given a central role. Pipes then cites analyses of Soviet military literature as evidence that the Soviet ruling elite regards conflict and violence as natural regulators of all human affairs: "war between nations, in its view, represent only a variant of wars between classes. . . ."[12] Because *they* think a nuclear war can be won and may be willing to make a preemptive nuclear strike in order to win it, *we* must "make it impossible for them to succeed."[13]

When we hear from the Doves, we learn that Professor Pipes may have been selective in the evidence he offered regarding Soviet strategic doctrine and intentions. In fact, it may be a matter of American Hawks citing Soviet Hawks, and vice versa. Worst-case analysis feeds on worst-case analysis and gets to be nerve-wracking for the reader of these analyses. Robert L. Arnett, a Soviet specialist at the Library of Congress, responds to Pipes directly and, also looking at the Soviet literature, concludes that Pipes's inferences are incorrect.[14] Arnett then quotes the writings of a Soviet defense minister, a leading Soviet military text writer, and others, in which all agree that the rejection of nuclear war is dictated by the realities of the era. Although it is unpopular and even ideologically incorrect to speak of Communist defeat under *any* circumstances, a number of Soviet strategic thinkers have expressed doubts about Soviet chances for survival and meaningful victory in a nuclear war.

Given that the Soviet Union is still a closed society, it seems more difficult for American Doves to find and cite the thought and writings of their dovish Soviet counterparts. The hawkish evidence for perpetuating fear and distrust seems so much easier to come by and so much easier to believe.

## Domestic Order and Domestic Oppression

A second source of international political distrust originating from within domestic politics is the question of domestic order. One of the principal traits of government is its monopoly of the basic instruments of violence within its community. The government that does not have such a monopoly cannot long maintain domestic order or itself in power. As history amply demonstrates, it is not a very long road from domestic law-and-order to domestic political oppression. Hence the constitutional importance placed upon civilian control over the military, the separation of civilian from military leadership, and the practice of legislating military appropriations for short terms of one or two years.

Whether called police or armies, weapons and militarily trained personnel are indispensable elements in any system of domestic order. Revolution, civil war, terrorism, subversion, riots, and crime are very real and ever-present threats to societies and governments no matter how long established. As a consequence of these possibilities in domestic politics, governments necessarily become the principal producers, purchasers, and users of military equipment. But the more a government may arm itself for domestic purposes, the greater it appears to be a military threat to the security of its neighboring countries or traditional international adversaries: the security dilemma. In this way, the maintenance of domestic order may become a significant stimulator of the arms race.

Examples abound. Mao's "wars of national liberation" were nothing more than civil wars in which one side was supplied by outside Communists. Vietnam was essentially a civil war won by the North Vietnamese as soon as American military support was withdrawn for the South; the Soviet Union made no equivalent withdrawal from support of the North. The Samoza regime in Nicaragua used American-made military gear in its battle with the Sandinista revolutionaries who, in turn, were supplied largely by Cuba.

In these and other examples, the role of arms changes with the occasion and the possessor. A well-armed central government is difficult to overthrow without the aid of outside suppliers to the revolutionaries. Without strong democratic institutions, a well-armed regime is likely to become oppressive to its citizens, thereby giving cause for discontent and revolution. For example, fourteen past and present recipients of United States arms aid are regimes that have acquired their power by military takeover of nationalist or constitutional governments or simply by declaring martial law. These nations and the dates of takeover are: Iran (1953), Argentina (1955), Dominican Republic (1963), Bolivia (1964), Brazil (1964), Indonesia (1966), Nigeria (1966), Greece (1967), Mali (1968), Thailand (1969), Chile (1972), Philippines (1972), South Korea (1972), and Uruguay (1973). However, if it is poorly armed, a regime quickly finds it difficult to maintain order or defend itself in a civil war. The cycle of arming, oppressing, and rebelling becomes circular within the nation. Unfortunate side effects of this process are the undermining of international confidence in the regime and the escalation of the arms race in the neighboring region.

An interesting special case is that of the Shah of Iran. Spurred by the billions of dollars earned by his oil-rich country and ambitious to become the leading military power in the Middle East, the Shah indulged himself in the purchase of highly sophisticated weaponry, mainly from the United States. He was also able to equip a small and loyal royal guard and secret police, both of which enabled him to maintain an oppressive regime for many years. However, when the Muslim ayatollahs led by Khomeini united to challenge the Shah, the latter found to his dismay that the weapons he had purchased were too sophisticated for domestic purposes and his royal guard and secret police too small to deal with the mass demonstrations against his regime. What the Shah lacked was a citizen militia loyal to a central government in which it had a vested interest. This was a case where the resources for a powerful international military organization were available but grossly mismanaged by the purchase of inappropriate weapons and insufficient training of troops for domestic order purposes. The Shah's military buildup, of course, disturbed his neighbors, generated distrust of his intentions and judgment, and generally strained international relations in that region.

## Multiple Functions of Military Establishments

Armies do more than fight wars. There is substantial validity to some of the claims in the military recruitment advertising: learn while you serve; see the world at Uncle Sam's expense; get yourself a patriotic job; reap the benefits of employment in one of the world's largest organizations, and so on. The hard fact is that military institutions throughout the world serve many functions in addition to those of defense, security, and the maintenance of order. If armies were no longer needed for security and order, new institutions would undoubtedly have to be created or old ones adapted and expanded to fulfill some of these other functions.

If we were to examine the military institutions of every nation and society, we might be shocked to realize that the military in most nations are the most organized and stabilizing influence in the community. This has been true historically and continues to be so today. There are, of course, societies in which the church is the principal organization, or a close second to the military. In modern times civil governments have been created to manage and advance the community's common causes. In the last two or three centuries corporate enterprises and political parties have also become significant mobilizers of communities. In the American experience prior to the Civil War, governments and political parties were the predominant organizers. The two became so interwined that the failure of one—the political parties—led to the failure of the other, and to the Civil War. In the latter half of the nineteenth century, American parties were revived, but corporate enterprise came on strong until harnessed to some degree during Wilsonian and New Deal periods. Significant for our understanding of American attitudes toward security and arms control, it was not until World War II and the Cold War that followed it that United States military institutions became a major and regularly present organizing influence in American life. When President Eisenhower warned about the influence of "the military-industrial complex," he was reporting on a new fact of American political life, namely, the emerging coalition between military and corporate organizations. It is the unqualified view of this author that only a revival and strengthening of the political parties will constrain the military-industrial complex and, extended transnationally, provide the world with an alternative to war for conducting and resolving its elite conflicts. However, what is new for Americans has been "old hat" for most other societies, that is, the predominance of military institutions as the major organizing influence in the political community.

Armies, particulary the more successful ones, have traditionally performed important educational functions. One often hears the claim that the U.S. Department of Defense supports probably the largest educational budget in the world. The raw youth recruited for most armies in the world often become literate through military training programs. The requirements of even the simplest military technology lead to training for a large range of occupations. This is more true in the sophisticatedly equipped armies of the developed nations. It costs tens of thousands of dollars to train an airplane pilot, for example, and the acquired skills are worth an annual income of between $30,000 and $50,000 for the pilot who returns to civilian employment. The United States military also provide a variety of scholarships and fellowships through assignments to various military academies and through such programs as ROTC (Reserve Officers Training Corps). For those soldiers and sailors who become veterans, the GI Bill has, in the American case, afforded further civilian education and opportunity for achievement to more than 10 million individuals.

In yet another direction, the military is a principal socializing force in the community. A young person's experience in the military services comes at a highly formative period of his or her life. The socialization that takes place during this period and under these circumstances tends to endure. Habits of personal care and hygiene are acquired as a result of military instruction and pressures. A variety of experiences in group living are acquired under different circumstances of tension, various mixes of races and nationalities, and different degrees of social preparation. Respect for authority on the basis of organizational necessity, individual merit, and other criteria are explicitly communicated. The successful army also knows how to make the ordinary citizen into a proud patriot. Although we may disagree about the merits of the content of the military socialization process, the fact remains that the military does socialize its troops. The individual who goes into the services as a raw recruit comes out a veteran and a different person.

Yet another function of the military is employment. In many societies the financial resources are simply not available for employing full-time employees to perform certain public functions, for example, emergency disaster relief, road building, fire fighting, the distribution of food and medicine, and so on. Yet, the necessary manpower to perform these functions may be readily available and unemployed. Enlistment into the armed forces has been a traditional, cheap, and convenient way of putting together the unemployed manpower to serve the public need.

We have noted elsewhere that some 700,000 jobs in the United States labor force are defense-related. The term "defense contract" is a euphemism for the development, manufacture, and acquisition of military weapons. In awarding defense contracts, the Department of Defense is careful to take into consideration the employment consequences of the contract, and is particularly concerned that the resulting employment is widely distributed around the country, although perhaps a bit more so in the districts of friendly congressmen. Communities that are neglected are quickly heard from. Labor unions whose members' employment depends upon such contracts tend to support military budgets that result in high employment in defense industries.

This relationship between the military and employment often is the basis for a rebuttal to the argument that military spending is noneconomic and a waste of human and natural resources. The rebuttal usually points to all of the economic payoffs that flow from high employment in the defense industries: expendable income in the hands of 700,000 workers and their families; the development of skills and products that may be used for both defense and nonmilitary purposes; the stimulation of employment and production in other parts of the economy as a consequence of spending by defense employees and contractors. Further, the argument goes, the production of military equipment is no more wasteful than the production of cosmetics, smoking and alcoholic products, most patent medicines, and countless other wholly unnecessary and even harmful consumption goods of contemporary life.

We must conclude that the multipurpose military establishment performs a sufficient number of functions for the community to guarantee being kept around for a long time. The acceptance of the military as a "normal" feature of community life and organization also assures that the military will be at hand to make substantial claims upon the public budget. Their presence, their claims, the public support given, and the political and economic influence that results all combine to make the military a highly significant element in the domestic politics of most nations. However, the acceptance and success of military institutions at home may well generate distrust and insecurity abroad.

## The Destabilizing Behavior of Public Bureaucracies

Another source of political distrust originating from the dynamics within nations is the role and behavior of national governmental bureaucracies. Competition for resources and competing career ambitions occur within these bureaucracies and tend to have consequences that inflate military budgets. In addition, bureaucrats in different agencies come to the problems of security and arms control from different perspectives with different perceptions and modes of analysis and diverse procedures for arriving at public policy. Whether Soviet or American, a domestic "arms race" within these bureaucracies is often as vigorous as the arms competition between nations.

The sheer number of agencies centrally concerned with the making of foreign policy in any sizable nation is often breathtaking. Under the Constitution of the United States the president is responsible for the conduct of foreign affairs, but the Congress appropriates the funds for these matters in addition to holding the prerogative of declaring war. Within Congress the two houses and a number of their respective powerful committees, not to mention factions within the major political parties, play a vital role in shaping foreign policy. Lobbies and other special interests have particular access to members of Congress, although they also reach into the federal bureaucracy as well. The Department of State is a major instrument of foreign policy, but this status hardly diminishes the influence of the Department of Defense (with its allies in the military-industrial complex, as President Eisenhower called it), the three services—Army, Navy, and Air Force—within Defense, the Central Intelligence Agency, the Arms Control and Disarmament Agency, and, increasingly, such departments as Commerce and Treasury. Outside the government, but very influential in their policy-making impact, are such consulting organizations ("think tanks") as the RAND Corporation, the Institute of Defense Analysis, and the Hudson Institute. There are also the experts at universities. Last in this listing, but often first in influence, is the press, where the manner in which events are reported may predetermine the course of foreign policy. Needless to say, the array of foreign policy agencies within the Soviet Union, the People's Republic of China, the United Kingdom, France, and nearly every other nation compound the problem of bureaucratic competition.

Like any other group in society, agencies within a bureaucracy compete for limited resources. One approach to claiming and obtaining additional resources is to acquire or create additional functions. One of the chief types of controversy in the Defense Department, for example, revolves around issues of function. To cite an instance, should the Air Force Tactical Air Command (TAC) be allowed to develop an overseas theater-based nuclear delivery capability such as the Strategic Air Command's (SAC)? To cite another, in the Navy, who shall deliver nuclear missiles against the Soviet Union: carrier-based fliers or submarine launchers? Questions of function and mission involve not only the esprit de corps of the competing agencies but also the funds, personnel, and technology necessary to implement the functions. The stakes, from a bureaucratic point of view, are usually substantial.

Financial resources in the form of congressional appropriations are another bone of contention among agencies. The defense budget, now $125 billion large, is presented to Congress after passing through an elaborate Defense Department system for program and budget development—PPBS (Planning, Programming, and Budgeting System)—which presumably strengthens civilian control over the services and moderates the intensity of interservice bargaining. Over 50 days of hearings are conducted by House and

Senate Armed Service Committees and Appropriations Committees, listening to 200-400 witnesses—mainly from the Pentagon. Approximately 10,000 pages of testimony are printed as a result, not including the reports of the committees themselves. Reports and commentary are received from the recently established Congressional Budget Office (CBO) and the General Accounting Office (GAO).

While each of the services within the Department of Defense and each of the agencies within the services has presumably had a full opportunity to present and defend its budget requests via the Pentagon's PPBS system before the defense budget goes to Congress, it has frequently happened that a bureaucratic faction within the Defense Department, in collusion with friendly congressmen on the respective legislative committees, has objected during hearings to the amount of money requested by the secretary of defense for its agency. The protest is usually made in terms of some strategic doctrine or some technological considerations, but the bottom line is the question of more or less resources for the particular agency and the congressional district that may be the greatest beneficiary of contracts, installations, and other military expenditures.

Similar struggles over agency resources arise in connection with issues of personnel. For example, should two or more agencies be consolidated and staffing for each reduced, or should the staffs remain separated despite duplication of duties by some? How many troops should different branches of the Army, Air Force, or Navy be allocated? The impulse of every bureaucratic agency is, of course, to retain staff and add more.

Even in the negotiation of arms control agreements, competing agency interests must be represented. It is not unusual for an arms control negotiating delegation to include officials from the National Security Council, the Department of Defense, the Department of State, the Arms Control and Disarmament Agency, NASA, and possibly a personal representative of the president. Each agency has a point of view to present, a function to perform, possibly some responsibility for the implementation of treaty provisions, and a budget to request after the arms control agreement is signed. In addition, there is the usual bureaucratic concern for recognition and influence, that is, for being present "where the action is" and "having a say" about the action taken.[15]

Even when they are not struggling for resources, bureaucratic agencies, as others groups in society, approach problems and decisions with biases in perception and modes of analysis. Bureaucrats are popularly assumed to be informed, objective, rational, and neutral; hence, most working bureaucrats would probably be reluctant to acknowledge their lack of information, the presence of bias, the subjectivity of their judgments, and the network of political friendships that characterize their actual working conditions. Or, if they do acknowledge these less-than-perfect characteristics, they might be inclined to argue that most of the shortcomings are dealt with in the cauldron of bureaucratic consultation and decision-making procedure.

Differences in the training of bureaucrats in various agencies may have important consequences for their approaches to data gathering, analysis, and interpretation of findings. Military, strategic, and technological functions and programs are particularly subject to such differences in professional skills. Natural scientists, mathematicians, engineers, and professionals trained in related disciplines are among the principal makers of defense, security, and arms control policy. They are trained in logical and linear thinking. As a consequence, much security and military doctrine is based upon systems analysis, game theory, and similar rigorous but often inappropriate modes of thought. Among these bureaucrats there is little place for the less tidy intellectual approaches of historians, psychologists, political scientists, anthropologists, and the like. The differences in the consequent policies may be profound, as different as *increasing* weapons based on conclusions drawn from one kind of thinking or *reducing* them on the basis of conclusions derived from an entirely different intellectual perspective. These differences pertain to differences in intellectual training, not differences of ideology and perception as we find between Hawks and Doves.

The importance of theories and analytical viewpoint for how a bureaucratic analyst arrives at his explanations, predictions, and public policy decisions has been demonstrated by Graham Allison.[16] Allison identified three conceptual models which, when applied to the analysis of policy decisions taken during the Cuban missile crisis, would have led not only to different perceptions of events but could have led to several different policy decisions.

Allison's first model of decision making assumes that national policy is made by a single actor through a rational thought process. Applied to the Cuban missile crisis, this simply identifies the primary American objective (removing the missiles), considers the alternatives available (do nothing, employ diplomacy, invade, blockade), and concludes that the final choice (blockade, or "quarantine," as it was called) was the only rational choice for the United States. The conclusion was presumably that of a single national actor.

Allison's second model focuses on organizational process. It views policy decisions as the outputs of large organizations rather than as rational choices of single actors. Thus, different bureaucratic organizations initially structure the "situation of choice" by raising the problem and gathering the information upon which action is to be taken. From this perspective, the decision in the Cuban missile crisis would call for an understanding of the CIA-Air Force disagreement about obtaining intelligence data (a disagreement that established the day of the missile discovery), the options of various organizations, and their organizational implementation (in this case, the Navy's desire for autonomy, an agency interest that altered the plan for the blockade). This model sees the policy decisions as the outputs of a mosaic of organizations.

The third model sees policy as the consequence of bureaucratic politics, that is, a series of bargaining negotiations. Policy decisions are the result of a bargaining process in which all aspects of information, analysis, and choice are subject to the skills and influence of the negotiators, or players. Thus, the choices made in the Cuban missile crisis were the bargains concluded by the president and representatives of the State Department, the CIA, the Defense Department, the Navy, and others.

Irving Janis describes yet another way of arriving at policy decisions.[17] Bureaucrats and political leaders, he notes, are reluctant to be wrong, different, or the object of peer disapproval. Thus, when a group or committee of them considers a policy decision, the small-group dynamics operate in such a way as to produce concurrence as a defense of self-esteem and as a demonstration of humanitarian impulses. This usually occurs at the expense of critical thinking and leads to decisions at the lowest common denominator, that is, the choice of that option which is least resisted by most of the members of the decision-making group and is the most conservative of the policies available. Insight, innovation, and risk taking are *not* the forte of bureaucratic committees.

Thus far we have seen how the struggle for agency resources and the differences of perception and analysis within different parts of a bureaucracy tend to lead to "safe" security decisions. Usually a "safe" choice leads to expansion of military functions, increase in military budgets, acquisition of new technologies, and emphasis upon primarily military objectives, namely, defeating an enemy. As these behaviors are conducted within the bureaucracies and within the nation, the consequence for relations among nations is escalatory. Further examination of the destabilizing bureaucratic processes leads us into the realm of bureaucratic procedure, the pursuit of bureaucratic careers, and the political ambitions of some bureaucrats.

Briefly, bureaucratic procedures usually involve the collection of information, the analysis of evidence, the identification of policy options, and the search for a consensus regarding an option to be chosen. Bureaucratic procedures may also serve as a method for concealing bias and subjectivity as well as for sheltering bureaucrats from personal responsibility for their choices. It is one thing when a decision is the deed of a person, quite another when it is the "output" of a blameless procedure.

Then there are the usual career concerns of employees in large organizations. In this respect, a public bureaucrat is no different from any other employee interested in pleasing his boss, holding onto a job, and possibly earning a promotion from time to time. The hierarchical character of bureaucratic organizations discourages independence and innovation, which in turn promotes the "safe" and escalatory choices noted above. Bureaucrats who have political ambitions, enjoy dealing with the presidential and congressional politicians, or grab personal publicity whenever the opportunity presents itself often take controversial, hence newsworthy, postures and are inclined to prefer hawkish policies. Principled controversy and patriotism are, after all, positive grist for the publicity mill. For such individuals, the availability of an "Enemy" represents another opportunity for controversiality and patriotic posturing. The internation consequence is, of course, distrust and escalation.

Thus, certain familiar patterns of interaction between nations and within nations contribute to the environment of distrust, fear, and growing stockpiles of weaponry throughout the world. Usually the factors surveyed here are considered remote from and irrelevant to the problem of security and arms control. Once we recognize that these are indeed influential factors, it may become more feasible to constrain and guide them.

# References

1. *Essays of E.B. White* (New York: Harper & Row, 1977), p. 102.
2. Richard Pipes, in *Commentary* (July 1977), pp. 21-34.
3. David Alan Rosenberg, "American Atomic Strategy and the Hydrogen Bomb Decision," *Journal of American History*, 66 (1979), 68.
4. For the story of the American decision to go ahead with the super-bomb program, see Herbert F. York, *The Advisors: Oppenheimer, Teller and The Superbomb* (San Francisco: W.H. Freeman, 1976).
5. Paul F. Walker, "New Weapons and the Changing Nature of War-fare," *Arms Control Today*, 9, no. 4 (April 1979), 1, 5-6; Richard Burt, "Nuclear Proliferation and the Spread of New Conventional

Weapons Technology," *International Security* (Winter 1977), pp. 119-39.

6. The literature on espionage, the Central Intelligence Agency, and military and political intelligence generally is vast. A useful bibliography is Ronald M. Devore, *Spies and All That . . . ; Intelligence Agencies and Operations*, Political Issues Series, vol. 4, no. 3, Center for the Study of Armament and Disarmament, California State University Los Angeles, Los Angeles CA. 90032, 1977. An authoritative history and organizational analysis is Tyrus G. Fain, ed., *The Intelligence Community: History, Organization, and Issues* (New York: R. R. Bowker, 1977). For a more popular overview of the issues, Tom Braden, "What's Wrong with the CIA?", *Saturday Review* (April 5, 1975), pp. 14-18, and the special issue of *Society* (March/April 1975) on "Espionage/USA."

7. Georg Simmel, "The Sociology of Conflict," *American Journal of Sociology*, 9 (January 1904), 501, quoted and discussed by Lewis A. Coser, *Continuities in the Study of Social Conflict* (New York: Free Press, 1967), Chap. 12 on the dysfunctions of military secrecy. Stanton K. Tefft, ed., *Secrecy; A Cross-Cultural Perspective* (New York: Human Sciences Press, 1980), offers a broad-ranging examination of secrecy as a feature of social and political interaction from the perspectives of anthropology, political science, and sociology. Using the Prisoners' Dilemma as an analytical model of the arms race, Brams and colleagues endeavor to demonstrate the wisdom, under certain circumstances, of the superpowers sharing intelligence data in order to achieve conditional cooperation. Steven J. Brams, Morton D. Davis, and Philip D. Straffin, Jr., "The Geometry of the Arms Race," *International Studies Quarterly*, 23 (December 1979), 567-600.

8. Les Aspin, "The Verification of the SALT II Agreement," *Scientific American*, February 1979, no. 2, p. 38.

9. James N. Rosenau and Ole R. Holsti, "Public Opinion and Foreign Policy: The Presumption of Constancy Versus the Acceptance of Change" (Paper presented at Annual Meeting of International Studies Association, March 23, 1979). Also, Ole R. Holsti, "The Three-Headed Eagle; The United States and System Change," *International Studies Quarterly*, 23, no. 3 (September 1979), 339-359.

10. The following account is based on Rosenberg, *op. cit.*

11. Pipes, *op. cit.*, p. 21.

12. *Ibid.*, p. 26

13. *Ibid.*, p. 34. Pipes' analysis is a model of the Hawk position and logic.

14. "Soviet Views on Nuclear War," in William H. Kincade and Jeffrey D. Porro, *Negotiating Security* (Washington, D.C.: Carnegie Endowment for International Peace, 1979), pp. 115-120.

15. For a succinct description of the handling of the defense budget by Congress, Nancy J. Bearg and Edwin A. Deagle, Jr., "Congress and the Defense Budget," in John E. Endicott and Roy W. Stafford, Jr., eds., *American Defense Policy*, 4th ed. (Baltimore: Johns

Hopkins University Press, 1977), pp. 335-354. For another view and criticism of the same process, Congressman Les Aspin, "The Defense Budget and Foreign Policy: The Role of Congress," *ibid.*, pp. 321-334. Aspin expresses his disenchantment with the Armed Services Committees and the Defense Appropriations Subcommittees "as molders and disposers of the defense budget." ·

16. Graham T. Allison, *Essence of Decision* (Boston: Little, Brown, 1971).

17. Irving L. Janis, *Victims of Groupthink: a Psychological Study of Foreign-Policy Decisions and Fiascoes* (Boston: Houghton Mifflin, 1972).

# CHAPTER 5

# Confidence-Building: The Promotion of Political Trust

If a major cause of the pathology of insecurity and arms races lies in the distrust among the world's competing elites, then therapeutic steps must include creating the conditions of political trust in a realistic and lasting way. "Confidence-building" is the popular rubric for such policies and action. Perhaps the most difficult and elusive confidence-building measure at this time in human history is the development of systems of institutionalized trust, as illustrated in our reference to the granting of mortgage loans by banks. Peacekeeping, as presently practiced by the United Nations, is another incipient but increasingly significant approach to confidence building, having thus far saved untold millions of dollars and countless lives. Finally, as we shall see, the arms control process itself has confidence-building consequences that transcend matching weapons systems, maintaining verification programs, or developing credible nuclear strategies. As we survey these confidence-building policies and actions, we may well conclude that the "secret cure" for insecurity, arms races, and wars may be nothing more or less than reducing and eliminating political distrust among the world's leaders.

What architectural principles can we learn for building institutions of political trust from the experience of banks that provide mortgages and car loans? What kinds of governmental systems have succeeded in replacing internal civil wars with trust-promoting systems of political representation and partisan contest? The institutionalized trust represented by bank loans stimulates the community's economy and increases the happiness—to the extent that homes and automobiles are an index of happiness—of its citizens. The trust found in well-integrated political systems reflects institutional arrangements that permit serious elite conflict, without need for violence, on the one hand, and the vigorous pursuit of justice and freedom on the other. Are such institutional developments pertinent and possible on a world scale?

Political institutions rarely, if ever, come into being, full grown, around a conference table. Rather, they evolve because they are functional. Even the classic cases of the Federal Convention that wrote the Constitution of the United States and the San Francisco Conference that produced the Charter of the United Nations for the most part recorded in contractual form many of the political institutional developments that had already evolved up to that point in time. Today we continue to have a number of evolving world institutions that are likely to be promotive of international political trust, as we shall see. At this time, however, international confidence building consists of many not-yet-fully-institutionalized policies, programs, practices, and political transactions.

Our concern for the evolution of political institutions warrants a brief definition of "institution." Karl W. Deutsch offers such a definition. "An *institution* is an orderly and more or less formal collection of human habits and *roles*—that is, of interlocking expectations of behavior—that results in a stable organization or practice whose performance can be predicted with some reliability." Examples of such organizations are governments, corporations, legislatures, courts, and the family. Buying in marketplaces, voting in elections, getting married, and holding property are types of institutional practices. "To *institutionalize* a practice, process, or service is to transform it from a poorly organized and informal activity into a highly organized and formal one."[1]

David B. Truman characterizes an institution as a human group whose patterns of membership and interaction have become formal, uniform, stable, and general.[2] *Formality* refers to the relatively highly organized character of most institutions. Positions are designated and persons are chosen to fill the roles called for by these positions. Rules are written to help clarify behavioral expectations and to reveal those who depart from these expectations. *Uniformity* refers to the similarity of behavioral patterns within particular types of institutions, for example, the nurturant behavior of parents in the family or the bargaining behavior of transactors in the marketplace. *Stability* alludes to the tendency for members and behaviors to revert to a prior pattern or equilibrium following a disturbance. Stability also refers to the durability of institutional behavior patterns, for example, voting for a representative in Congress in 1980 is not much different from voting in 1880. Finally, *generality* is that quality of similarity that certain institutions have regardless of the society or place in which they may be found, for example, a family is recognizable as such in every society, a legislature is a legislature wherever one is found, and so forth.

Once the attributes of institutions are specified, it is simple to recognize how they contribute to the development of trust. The qualities of uniformity, formality, and stability contribute to the predictability of most patterns of behavior within an institutional framework. Predictable behavior is one of the elements in an attitude of trust. Another element is the judgment that the behavior will have positive or negative consequences for oneself. Any institutionalized group is, by definition, a cooperative system in which shared goals are pursued by common effort. Thus, any appropriate behavior within the institution is highly likely to be aimed at achieving the shared goal, that is, to have positive consequences for all members. "Institutionalized trust," therefore, is nothing more than the attitude of trust that is a consequence of and reinforced by the predictable behaviors making up the activity of the members of the institution.

## Negotiating Profitable Transactions

One of the important lessons of behavioral theory and research is that successful communication, negotiation, and transaction between parties, whether adversary or competitive, tend to reduce the conflict aspects of their relationship and eventually lead to attitudes of trust and inclinations to cooperate.[3] According to these theories, successful communication leads the parties to shared meanings regarding language and symbols, to common perceptions of reality as described in the content of the communication, to better understanding of each other's value preferences, to mutually profitable transactions between them, and, in time, to more trusting predispositions toward each other. Even though the communication process may start out negatively, and even angrily, the interactions slowly, and often imperceptibly, tend to co-orient the parties to similar realities and values.

Such, of course, is one of the fundamental merits of the United Nations as a world communication center. An analysis of the content of Soviet Union statements in that forum over the past thirty years would probably reveal a decrease in the amount of Soviet invective directed at the United States. This decrease reflects not only a growth in Soviet strength and self-confidence since the days when strong language was their leaders' principal counter to the American nuclear giant, but also the success of Soviet-American transactions in many areas that have lead the parties out of the Cold War into an era of detente. The growth in communicative activity between the superpowers and among all the nations of the world is, therefore, gratifying.

Advancing technology promotes this. Television and radio sets may be found in the remotest corners of the world and in the most totalitarian of societies. Satellites bring into the home pictures of events in every part of the globe. The world press and news-reporting services are numerous and competitive. Local events may acquire worldwide significance in a matter of hours or days. To protect and facilitate the coverage of news, international rules of reporting are currently being developed under the auspices of UNESCO. Before long, this trend is likely to make disclosure and worldwide publicity the significant political weaponry they are in open societies where Watergates are discovered and briberies exposed. Such world communication developments may eventually lay secrecy, military or any other, to rest forever and provide the world with one of the traditionally most effective instruments for promoting political trust, namely, a free press.

Internation communication is also advancing along other fronts: social, cultural, economic, political, and even military. Consider, for example, the highly personal social interactions associated with international travel. In recent decades, tourism and travel in other forms have become major industries throughout the world. Whether high school or college students hitchhiking from country to country or retirees on group tours arranged by travel agents, the number of individuals visiting and sightseeing places distant from their homes has multiplied dramatically in recent years. For some communities and countries, tourism has become a major source of income. Peoples and cultures previously fearsome to each other have begun to become familiar and unthreatening. A residual network of friendships around the world often follows each individual's trip abroad. In fact, some tourists can hardly wait until a peace treaty has been signed between former enemy states in order to be able to travel to the other's land: witness the backlog of tourist reservations for travel between Israel and Egypt following their treaty signing.

Cultural exchanges are a well-established means of reaching out and communicating. Such exchanges are often a first step in the improvement of relations between two hostile powers. Ballet companies and symphony orchestras are permitted to perform and tour in the "enemy" country, much to the delight of appreciative elite audiences. Artists and art collections are sent on loan and leave the impression that "any culture that produces such beautiful art can't be all that bad." Athletic events are arranged, suggesting that there may be more civilized forms of competition than warfare, for example, the Olympics and the memorable Ping Pong matches that led to the opening between mainland China and the United States. Scientists, physicians, and academic specialists are permitted to visit, heightening the common ground from which the search for knowledge and the good life may be pursued together. As familiarity with other cultures spreads, trust and the sense of human brotherhood may be expected to deepen.

Readers of "the bottom line" tend to believe that *real* payoffs are those of an economic and material character. What brings in the bucks is what counts. For promoting the growth of international political trust, few processes pave the way as smoothly as international commercial transactions and trade generally. In the eighteenth and nineteenth centuries, this was a fundamental precept of free trade doctrine, namely, that trade, even though competitive, leads to friendships and prevents war. Although sometimes considered occasions of tension, trade between the superpowers, the

Third World's demands for a "new international economic order," the consultations among the OPEC nations regarding world oil prices, and the North-South dialogue regarding the more equitable distribution of the world's resources are, in the final analysis, communicative activities among nations aimed at defining and coping with unprecedented international trade problems. The resulting negotiations and transactions among nations are likely to be profitable for all concerned and, hence, help build the environment of trust. From this perspective, it is a positive condition when nations around the world owe, the United States as they now do, $45.7 billion in war debts, reconstruction loans, development loans, and the like. This includes $1.1 billion owed by the Soviet Union. Most of these were constructive loans in the first place and any future negotiations about them are likely to be associated with improved trade relations between the debtor and the United States.

Multinational corporations have grown in number—to thousands at this time—and in share of international trade activity in recent decades. It is the contention of liberal freetraders that as the proportion of multinational corporations producing and distributing nonmilitary goods increase, those corporations involved in military production will presumably become a diminishing minority within the framework of international trade. Under such circumstances war would be bad for business. What is bad for business is likely to be vigorously discouraged by business and the governments they influence. Selling Coca Cola rather than tanks to China may have more than symbolic significance for the promotion of international political trust.

Political modes of communication and transaction promotive of trust are exemplified by the following trends: the growing frequency of summit conferences among world leaders; the widening scope of bilateral, multilateral, and universal negotiations dealing with political, economic, and military issues; and the intensifying participation of nations in supranational organizations, including the United Nations system and regional organizations such as the European Community, the Organization of American States, the Organization of African Unity, and the Arab League. The frequency and significance of these communicative interactions have increased from year to year and have received growing attention from the world press. Rather than brandish weapons and diatribe at each other, international politicians are more and more turning to the United Nations and to regional organizations to make their case and solicit allies and support. Although battlefields continue to be very much in the foreground, these institutional forums have already become the principal platforms for appeals to world opinion and for the conduct of international argument. In similar fashion, during centuries past the English nobility moved their disagreements from the battlefield to Parliament. In Western Europe the same process evolves today as old national enemies become accustomed to conducting their disagreements within the European Council, the European Commission, and the European Parliament.

As for communication and transactions about military matters, this is what military alliance systems, peacekeeping operations, and arms control negotiations are all about. Because these are so central in contemporary security issues and so important for feeling safe in this world, we shall give these topics closer examination at a later time.

In retrospect, then, it appears that the volume, pace, and significance of international communication, negotiation, and related transactions are increasing rapidly and, in many respects, becoming institutionalized. Tourism, cultural exchange, international trade, and treaties among nations are likely to be difficult to turn off or discard as the years pass. The trend is positive: toward intensification and institutionalization.

## Raising the Cost of Betrayal

From our description of the Prisoners' Dilemma we learned that the most self-interested behavior of a nation is to exploit rather than cooperate with another nation, particularly if the other nation is acting cooperatively. Such exploitation may be interpreted as stark betrayal of trust. But this would be true only if the two parties had an established agreement to cooperate and enough experience with each other to expect such cooperation. The Prisoners' Dilemma model makes no such assumption. On the contrary, the model creates a paradox that tests whether trust or distrust exists in the mind of one or both parties. In the real world of international politics, such gross betrayals of trust are rare simply because the working assumption of most national leaders is that their adversaries, and often their friends, *cannot* be trusted. Distrust is the working hypothesis.

However, there does exist a substantial body of international "law" that brings some order and ordered expectations to international relations. This is not a legislated body of law, nor does the world have a judicial system for testing laws or enforcing them. International law consists of traditional practices in the conduct of affairs among nations but, more precisely and explicitly, it is made up of a large body of contractual agreements for the most part enforceable only by an aggrieved party to the contract itself. In this respect, technically, the Charter of the United Nations is a multilateral treaty among sovereign nations; it is not a constitution for an integrated system of government.

Each of the traditional practices and all of the provisions of treaties and similar formal agreements, like any contract between two or more parties, are designed to specify with some clarity the conduct that the parties may expect of each other (the empirical aspect of trust) and prescribe only such conduct that in given situations would bring positive advantage to the parties (the normative aspect of trust). Clearly understood traditional practices and well written treaties thereby serve as a form of institutionalized trust which, bit by bit, may promote enduring political trust among participating nations. However, traditional practices may be misunderstood or rejected, treaties and agreements may be ambiguous and broken, and nations may respond to the impulse or the opportunity to exploit each other. If such internation exploitation is to be discouraged and the environment of international trust improved, it becomes necessary to devise ways of raising the cost of betrayal.

Several such means are employed from time to time with varying degrees of effectiveness. Publicity, as we have seen, is one punitive tactic that is frequently used. One nation describes the breach of trust incurred by another and points the finger of guilt. The accused nation replies with denials, a different version of events, and reciprocates the charges against the accusing nation. These exchanges get nowhere until such time as the intelligence agencies of neutral countries, the press, or some supranational organization independently investigates what happened and makes a public report of its findings. As we shall see in our discussion of United Nations peacekeeping, publicity may be extremely influential in identifying the offending parties, bringing pressure for better conduct, and perhaps leading to a nonviolent and equitable resolution of the conflict between the parties. In the absence of publicity, world leaders and world opinion flounder in misinformation and doubt about the circumstances of a conflict and the account of it that should be believed. With neutral and authoritative publicity of the facts of the case, implications can be understood, sides can be taken, and pressures brought to bear.

It is not often that nations censure one of their number, but when they do, the censure resolution either may or may not function as a weighty fact of international politics. When the League of Nations condemned the Japanese for invading Manchuria in 1931 and Italy for attacking Ethiopa in 1936, the censures were ignored. Instead, the incapacity of the League of Nations to prevent aggression and, later, World War II, became evident. Yet the United Nations censure of South Africa for its apartheid policies has admittedly been a source of discomfiture for that nation. The purpose of a censure resolution may be more symbolic than practical, as in the case of the Arab-sponsored United Nations resolution condemning Zionism as a form of racism.

A boycott is a punitive technique that has frequently increased the cost of exploitative behavior. The boycott may be economic, that is, refusal to trade with generally or to sell or buy specific products of the boycotted nation. A military boycott is a refusal to sell weapons to the exploiter. A boycott is rarely 100 percent effective. Some countries, for example, will side with the boycotted nation and serve as its supplier or as a channel through which supplies from elsewhere may flow. These difficulties notwithstanding, boycotts do serve as a means for raising the price of betrayal.

A more serious action against nations that embark upon major breaches of political trust is military. When the North Koreans attacked the South Koreans, the United Nations, under the requirements of Chapter VII of its Charter, declared the former an "aggressor" and responded militarily with what President Truman called "a police action." In the Cuban missile crisis, President Kennedy ordered a naval quarantine, a military action that fortunately fell short of war when the Soviet Union backed off. President Johnson's escalation of American involvement in the Vietnam War was, in his words, intended to discourage further North Vietnamese incursions upon the South and to demonstrate to the North Vietnamese that it would be cheaper for all concerned if they came to the negotiating table. The recurrent Arab-Israeli wars in the Middle East have in part been tests of American resolve in supporting the existence of Israel as a sovereign nation, a test that Egyptian President Sadat eventually considered dispensable. In each of these cases, the usual military objective of total victory over an enemy has given way to the diplomatic objective of raising the cost of breaches of international trust to a level that discourages or punishes the exploiter.

## Systematizing Conflict Resolution

Conflict is an inevitable part of human social life. Conflict arises out of scarcity of resources, different perceptions of reality, and different value priorities. If constrained adequately, social and political conflict may actually advance human progress or satisfaction, as in the case of competition in economic marketplaces, contests in sports arenas, conflicts in courts, and debates over the validity of an empirical theory or the merits of different values.

Serious conflicts are those in which the parties consider the stakes high or are determined to eliminate each other entirely. The conflicts that occur among leaders in world affairs usually involve high stakes and often a desire to eliminate the adversary. The perceived seriousness of internation conflicts is precisely the motivation for arming. Weapons provide a way of influencing the distribution of high stakes, eliminating an adversary, or preventing an adversary from eliminating oneself. An international program for confidence building usually seeks to reduce the perceived value of the stakes, end the capacity of any one nation to destroy another, and develop techniques of conflict resolution that help the parties in a serious conflict find their way to a transaction that can prove profitable to both.

Conflict management is a rapidly growing field of study and practice.[4] Henry Kissinger's role in bringing a cease-fire to the 1973 Yom Kippur War and President Carter's Camp David summit negotiations leading to the Egyptian-Israeli peace treaty are recent dramatic examples of international conflict management at its best. However, countless less dramatic international conflicts are mediated by similar third-party interventions. The busiest of these mediators are the officers, particularly the secretary-general, of the United Nations and several regional organizations. Friendly, interested, or neutral superpowers may perform a similar function, as did the United States in the Middle East and the Soviet Union in the Indian-Pakistan dispute over Kashmir. Although parties to a conflict rarely choose to do so, they may, if they wish, turn to the International Court of Justice in search of a more or less binding settlement of their dispute. In such instances, ICJ acts as an authoritative interpreter of existing international law if applicable to the case. Unlike judicial systems within nations, ICJ has no enforceable statutory law to interpret.

In a comprehensive survey of internation conflicts during the period 1945 to 1974, Robert L. Butterworth analyzed 310 conflict cases. He found third-party conflict management interventions numbering as follows: 122 by the United Nations; 26 by the Organization of American States; 16 by the Arab League; 13 by the Organization of African Unity; 7 by the Council of Europe; 10 by the United States; 2 by the Soviet Union; 4 by the United Kingdom; 5 by NATO; 2 by the Warsaw Pact; and 12 by the International Court of Justice. Miscellaneous third parties intervened in many of the remaining cases, but as many as 55 conflicts had no third-party involvement whatsoever.[5]

Within the short span of three decades, then, the world experienced more than 400 internation conflicts of sufficient seriousness to engage or nearly engage military forces. Given such a high frequency of conflict, it is indeed impressive that a catastrophic world war has been avoided. The batting average of the conflict-managing parties, particularly the United Nations, has been better than usually recognized. Several of the major internation conflicts involving U.N. peacekeeping interventions will be described in detail in the next chapter. As internation conflict resolution continues successfully, as third-party conflict managers sharpen their skills and as institutions of conflict resolution become more systematic and stable, we can look forward to a significant advancement of international political trust. The weight of the stakes will be reduced because the very survival of parties will no longer be at issue. The need for military solutions will appear too costly and even unnecessary. On the latter point, might not Japan and Germany have been as prosperous as they now are without having gone to war?

## Developing Systems of Institutionalized Trust

Political distrust, as we have argued, is the principal generator of the arms race and a major obstacle to the resolution of serious conflicts among the world's political elites. If this argument is valid, then political trust must take the place of distrust before the present arms competition can be replaced by an integrated and constitutional system of global security services and before elite conflicts can be resolved by regular rather than crisis procedures. However, trust is not a gift that can be given nor is it a condition that can be willed. Trust is an attitude that, as behavioral scientists explain, is an outcome of successive mutually profitable transactions between human beings. Trust develops with certain types of experience. We tend to trust those persons with whom we have had satisfying (profitable) exchanges. In the typical commercial transaction, Person A pays money for a product being sold by Person B. If the product satisfies A's needs and if the money is sufficient to give B a profit from which he derives his livelihood, then both transactors will be happy with the exchange, consider the deal "profitable" according to their respective criteria, and be sufficiently trusting of each other to be predisposed to future favorable transactions between themselves.

Social and political transactions differ somewhat from economic ones in that the things (currencies) exchanged are less explicit, less specific, and usually less quantifiable. For example, in a social exchange, Person A may give advice to Person B in exchange for the latter's deference. This is a real social transaction but one that is difficult to describe in precise units (how much advice is worth how much deference?). A familiar political example is legislative "logrolling" wherein Legislator A gives his vote to Legislator B's bill in exchange for B's vote favoring one of A's projects. In international transactions, treaties are little more than written contracts recording political currencies that have been exchanged between participating nations.

The simplest transactions are those in which two parties simultaneously transfer currencies between themselves, for example, money to a cashier in exchange for a bag of groceries. However, when the transfers take place at different times, anticipation and trust become significant attitudes in the situation. If your grocer knows and trusts you on the basis of good longstanding customer relations, he will be inclined to extend you credit, that is, trust you to pay later for goods that you purchase now. You have the convenience of paying your food bill in a single monthly lump sum; he has the profit that comes with selling you food. If this trust arrangement works to your mutual satisfaction over time, he may even trust you enough to provide you with check-cashing and similar services. The attitudes of mutual trust are reinforced with each fulfilled obligation: he, in giving you groceries now for payment later; you, in paying the monthly bill regularly and on time. A political analogy to this transaction may be found in any international treaty that sets down present expectations about future national conduct, for example, the limitation or reduction of weapons systems, observance of specified border delineations, compliance with prearranged procedures, and so on.

As we noted in the earlier discussion of the Prisoners' Dilemma, trust is an attitude toward another person that is premised upon two evaluations: (1) an empirical evaluation based upon the predictability of the other's behavior and (2) a normative evaluation regarding the positive or negative consequences of that behavior for oneself. We tend to trust persons whose behavior is reliably predictable and whose good behavior is likely to produce outcomes that we consider "good" for ourselves. The more predictable the other's behavior and the more positive the consequences seem, the stronger is our attitude of trust toward that other person. Transactions are occasions for such twofold evaluations, and each mutually satisfying transaction reinforces and strengthens the existing attitudes of trust between the parties. In this way, nations that fulfill treaty obligations to each other over time tend to become staunch allies and enter into cooperative relations with each other in activities beyond those prescribed in treaties.

"Institutionalized trust" is a term that describes those ways of organizing social, economic, and political transactions so as to maximize the predictability of each party's behavior and encourage favorable evaluations of the profitability of the exchange for each of the transacting parties. Predictability of behavior usually requires sound information about the person's previous patterns of conduct in matters relevant to those in the exchange; for example, a record of unblemished bill paying for consumer purchases. Accurate credit records, such as those institutionalized by the recent growth in credit agencies, facilitate the gathering of such data about a person. Evaluations of positive consequences for oneself (profitability) are, of course, private and subjective but can be aided by precise quantitative units for measuring value and by readily available market information. For example, the prices of automobiles are precisely stated in dollar units and the current market values of particular automobiles are widely available; the institutionalization of the automobile business has made all this possible. This makes it quite easy for seller and buyer to judge the "goodness of a deal" that they may be negotiating.

In our daily lives we may observe many forms of institutionalized trust. Banks and credit agencies will trust almost anyone under clearly defined conditions. Mortgages, automobile loans, personal loans, and credit cards—all are based upon the empirical determination of whether or not an individual is a good "credit risk," that is, predictable in loan repayment behavior. The usual procedure is as follows: A person entirely unkown to the officers of a bank applies for a mortgage to buy a house (a positive consequence for the borrower). In order to earn interest on its loans (a positive consequence for the bank), the bank will be happy to make the long-term loan *if* (1) the borrower, upon investigation, is found to be an established member of the community with a relatively stable job, (2) has no record of having defaulted upon other loans or extensions of credit, (3) is willing to sign a loan agreement in which the property purchased, in this case a home, will revert to the ownership of the bank if mortgage payments are defaulted, otherwise known as foreclosure, and (4) the borrower's normal income seems to be sufficient to cover the payments on the mortgage. Notice how each of these requirements helps evaluate or influence the predictability of the borrower's repayment behavior. While the bank is eager to earn interest on the money it lends, it does so at almost no predictable risk precisely because the borrower's past and present behavior show him to be a good "credit risk" who would stand to lose a valuable equity in his home if he were to default on the mortgage payments. The bank extends its trust on the basis of the borrower's empirically observed past behavior: regular employment and income; faithful repayment of other loans or credit; willingness to have home repossessed by the bank if mortgage payments are defaulted.

In the world of commerce, institutionalizing the elements of a trust relationship appears to be simplicity itself. In the example of banks offering mortgage loans on the basis of verifiable empirical and normative information, it is possible to (a) determine what a borrower's future behavior is likely to be on the basis of the record of his past performance (good credit risk) and his willingness to take a substantial penalty (foreclosure on his home) if he betrays the trust (defaults) and (b) arrive at the judgment that the predicted behavior of both borrower and bank after the mortgage loan is made will have positive consequences for both (a home immediately for the borrower and interest earned by the lender). ·

This commercial relationship of trust is so well institutionalized that millions of mortgages are outstanding, millions of homes have been built, and society has prospered as a consequence. Foreclosures are few in relation to the volume. Refinancing is possible for those who are temporarily unable to meet the conditions of the loan. It all seems so reasonable. Yet, the institution of mortgage lending was not created out of whole cloth in a single sitting. Like all systems of institutionalized trust, it evolved slowly. The stakes were money and goods. In the evolution of political institutions of trust, on the other hand, the stakes seem to be much greater: power, the distribution of community resources, human lives, and, lately, civilization itself. This may be why institutionalized trust develops much more slowly and cautiously in the realm of politics.

Politics has its examples of institutionalized trust. When a political party in control of a government willingly gives up public office to a challenging party that has won an election, the expectation, usually based upon observed past behavior, is that the newly incumbent party will do the same if it is defeated in the next election. The normative judgment is also usually made that such peaceful changes of regime are in the best interest of the political community. Similar attitudes of trust may be found in legislative and judicial situations. Again, "logrolling" is the most familiar example, one legislator promising to vote for another's bill in exchange for a subsequent return of the favor. Plea bargaining and other forms of pretrial negotiation have become highly institutionalized transactions calling for trust among the parties to a judicial proceeding.

Which, then, are the political institutions that promote political trust and often serve as nonviolent alternatives to revolution, civil war, or international war as modes of political conflict? The answer is at hand in every textbook about human self-governance: *court systems*, wherein disputes and breaches of civic trust are dealt with in a public fashion according to principles consistent with the mores of the community; *representative assemblies*, to which significant persons, groups, and other constituencies send agents to articulate their interests and achieve public policies that bring the greatest profit to the greatest number; *political party systems*, which serve as the vehicles for mobilizing ballots rather than bullets and through which competing elites may conduct their drive for power. These are the principal political institutions that function as arenas of political conflict. When they are poorly designed or malfunction, the community may become irreparably divided and may even cease to exist. When they are well designed or evolve adaptively, the community flourishes, its competing elites come to trust each other, large stakes are broken up into more manageable smaller ones, and the diverse interests in the community carry on their conflicts with less seriousness (as defined above) and a greater sense of security.

Such political institutions and the institutionalized trust that they promote are present on a worldwide basis today only in the most primitive form. The outline of a world court system is perceptible in the existence of an International Court of Justice and a difficult-to-enforce body of international law and practice. The Security Council and the General Assembly of the United Nations are representative bodies although, of course, representative of nations rather than electoral constituencies. In dimmer outline are the elements of a world party system that may follow from the recent growth of transnational political party activities: the Communist, Socialist, Christian Democratic, Liberal, and other internationals. It remains to be seen whether these political institutions develop to a degree that enables them to promote international institutionalized trust. The merits of their contributions along these lines since the end of the World War II continue to be a much debated issue.

Is this then a prescription for world government? Are not these political institutions the hallmark of government? Not quite. The model of the Founding Fathers and the authors of the United Nations Charter notwithstanding, entire governments do not come into being at a single sitting nor do political systems become integrated in a single generation. Political institutions that eventually become part of a governmental system may evolve at an uneven pace. One institution or a combination of two or more may emerge prior to becoming the core of a viable government. For example, in England the political system's core has been the representative assembly, that is, Parliament. In the United States, however, governmental stability was achieved only after Congress and the political parties began to operate in tandem more effectively. Hence, the issue is not one of putting together a world government, a prospect that is undoubtedly generations away, but rather of adopting policies that encourage the development of one or more of the trust-promoting political institutions on a worldwide basis. *The more immediate goal is not world government but rather trusting elites, effective conflict management, an end to the arms race, and a universal sense of security.*

To better understand how certain political institutions promote trust and security, we need to separate out the development of these institutions from the establishment of governments. We also need to look at historical cases in which the long process of institutional development has successfully resulted in trusting elites, enduring governments, integrated political communities, arms control, and an end to warfare. Examples are not hard to come by. We need only review the strife-torn histories of some of the world's older national communities to discover the nature of the process.[6]

Before doing so, we need to add one other institution to our observations, namely, the military. Military institutions are *not* an arena *within* which conflicts are resolved. Rather, military organizations and their armaments are *instrumental* in the conduct of conflicts and the protection of institutions. On the one hand, the military may serve as instruments of hostile leaderships engaged in serious conflicts. As such, military organizations become a source of fear, distrust, arms races, and war. On the other hand, the more civilized function of military organization is to preserve safety, enforce constitutional and legal decisions, and maintain order so that the conflicts of hostile leaderships may be carried on in less destructive arenas. With this distinction in mind, it becomes a matter of empirical examination to determine how military institutions have historically related to the other institutional arenas of conflict, that is, court systems, representative assemblies, and political party systems.

Let us use the English experience as an example. That community was ostensibly an established nation as early as the sixth century. Yet, for a full millenium, until the Glorious Revolution of 1688-1689, England endured civil war after civil war. Whether over the royal succession or landed property or their personal prerogatives, the English nobility took up arms against each other with deadly regularity. Political insight as well as dramatic artistry led William Shakespeare to immortalize many of these struggles by focusing his audiences' attention upon the relationships among the competing nobles rather than their military hardware or battlefield strategies. When peace did prevail in England, it was usually during the reign of a monarch who understood how to deal with the nation's principal leaders, interests, and representatives as they appeared in Parliament. The king or queen who related well to that representative assembly and managed well the conflicts therein was facilitating the development of a conflict-resolving, trust-promoting political institution.

The nobility were also the military leaders of the land, each with his personal guard or feudal army. The monarch, who came to be perceived as the first among equals, could call up these "private" armies only under carefully specified circumstances, for example, invasion or with the consent of the nobility. Military forces for expeditions to foreign lands were usually made up of volunteers and financed in a variety of ways, only one of which was appropriation by Parliament. The nobility and local sheriffs also performed functions related to maintaining domestic order in their communities. The capacity of a monarch to maintain nation-wide domestic order depended a great deal upon whether or not he was supported by a substantial coalition of nobles. When such coalitions fell apart or were challenged, civil war ensued.

During the seventeenth century, the revival of the principle of the divine right of kings and the low regard in which the Stuarts held Parliament, led to century-long internal war moving back and forth from battlefield to Parliament. The settlement of the Glorious Revolution established a new relationship between the monarchy and the representative assembly, with the latter assuming full control of the nation's military institutions.

Several significant institutional developments converged during this period. There occurred a critical transition from civil war to a stable governmental system and an integrated political community. The numerous armies of the nobility were incorporated into a centralized military organization which, in turn, was placed under civilian control of Parliament. It was declared incompatible for a person to have active military status and parliamentary membership at the same time, thereby legally separating the personnel of the two institutions. Biennial parliamentary appropriations for the military kept the latter on a short leash under a classic form of separation of powers.

More significant than noticed was the emergence of parliamentary political parties during the latter half of the seventeenth century and the beginning of the eighteenth. The parties were initially coalitions of personal factions in Parliament, with military alliances and other resources backing them up. The factional coalitions became fairly stable in composition, that is, political parties. When party leaders became interested in dominating parliamentary votes on public policy, they turned to electing as many of their fellow-partisans to Parliament as possible. This took the parties beyond the halls of Parliament into electoral constituencies. During a period of about half a century, the English party system emerged, stabilized, and became a meaningful and effective vehicle for elite competition; in short, a nonmilitary alternative to civil war. The Glorious Revolution was England's last internal war.

Remarkably, a similar institutional process occurred in a very different political culture—Mexico. There, internal wars, carried on by the semiprivate armies of competing *caudillos*, were common from the time of independence from Spain in 1821 to the selection in 1929 of a successor to President Calles. Mexico's critical transition into governmental stability took place between the Revolution of 1910 and the last attempted civil war in 1929. During these two decades, the difficult task of centralizing the nation's military institutions was carried forward by succeeding Mexican presidents. The national party system that emerged during this transition proved even more representative than the Mexican Congress and became the principal arena of nonviolent political conflict. In England, Parliament had become the conflict-resolving, trust-promoting political instition; in Mexico, the majority party performed this function. In both cases, the broad constitutional outlines of governmental structure existed long before particular political institutions permitted that outlined structure to stabilize and reach maturity.

We see a similar experience in the United States. The Founding Fathers wrote a Constitution, but the political parties and Congress eventually provided the conflict-resolving, trust-promoting functions. When the American party system collapsed in 1860, so did Congress. A brutal Civil War left the country deeply scarred. Stability returned only after the Reconstruction Period was liquidated, and the party system again achieved balance and strength.

As a congenital self-disarmer, the United States failed to develop centralized military institutions until the beginning of the twentieth century. Volunteer armies and state militia reflected the highly decentralized character of the American military system prior to World War I; the Civil War was in fact started as a conflict between Northern and Southern state militias. During and after World War II, the United States experienced the first large-scale centralization of a permanent military institution. *It is likely to become one of the most significant institutional issues in American politics: whether or not the party system and Congress are together capable of maintaining effective civilian ascendancy over a new institution, the military-industrial complex.* However, until now, the nation has undoubtedly had the last of its civil wars and has successfully passed through a critical transition that reestablished Congress and the party system as the central institutions of conflict resolution and promotion of political trust.

What lessons are learned from these thumbnail case histories of institutional development?

**1.** Competing elites require an alternative to the battlefield for the vigorous and serious pursuit of their inevitable disagreements. An effective political party system serves as such an alternative.

**2.** By military victory of one faction over the others or by constitutional agreement among them all, *the community's military institutions may be converted from competing armies into instruments of internal order and safety. This transition requires that the military be centralized under civilian control that is widely shared. Such shared control is perhaps the most comprehensive definition of "arms control."* The sharing is best accomplished through the organization of an efficient representative assembly. "Efficiency" in this situation refers to the adequate representation of all significant political interests in the community.

**3.** Stable government and integrated political communities follow rather than precede the development of mature and effective political parties and representative assemblies. It is in the parties and the assemblies that the most critical arrangements for systematic conflict resolution and institutionalized trust can be made.

How does all this apply to international arms control and global security? The history of the development of these political institutions *within nations* suggests that we examine the status of similar developments at the international level today. Although there may be much debate about the stage, pace, and future integrative consequences of these international institutional developments, they are undeniably in progress.

At the regional level, for example, the European Community, made up of nations that formerly were at war with each other time and again over the centuries, has begun to centralize its military institutions within the North Atlantic Treaty Organization and has debated the merits of a separate European Defense Community. In the multilayer structure of the European Community, the European Parliament has been perhaps the politically weakest component. That Parliament, however, in June 1979 expanded its membership from 190 to 410 representatives from nine nations and conducted the first direct popular election of representatives to that supranational body. Significant within the Parliament, and more so now as they try to mobilize voters throughout the Community, are the transnational parties that have been increasingly active in Europe and the world since World War II: Social Democrats, Christian Democrats, Liberals, Eurocommunists, and others.[7]

Thus, in little over a single generation, Europeans have been centralizing their military institutions, assigning greater responsibilities to their representative assembly, and developing transnational parties as instruments of elite competition. Formerly hostile national leaderships are now trusting collaborators for the advancement of Western Europe's prosperity, the improvement of their collective security, and the maintenance of internal order and peace. The model is bound to catch on in other regional communities.

The broad outlines of similar institutional developments exist, less visibly, in and around the United Nations system. Despite the strong mandate of Chapter VII of the Charter, the collective security system promised is still relatively nonexistent, lost in the shadow of the nuclear superpowers. Yet, the United Nations' military experience with peacekeeping must be counted as a significant, albeit unapplauded, beginning. When the Military Staff Committee of the Security Council is revived some time in the future, we shall have a sign that collective security is again alive at the United Nations. We shall comment further on this later.

As for providing an arena for conflict management and conflict resolution, both the Security Council and the General Assembly, representative assemblies of a special kind, have a respectable record of achievement. Again, it may be generations before the representatives to one or both of these bodies are directly elected by the peoples of the world, but the general structure and the conflict-resolving, trust-promoting functions are already being performed.

What is perhaps most lacking is the presence of effective transnational political parties. But these, too, are at hand. There are approximately 90 Communist parties throughout the world claiming a total membership of 60 million, not including some 40 million supporting voters in capitalist countries. Social Democrats, Socialists, and Laborites report some 57 party affiliates in 50 countries, with a membership of nearly 20 million and some 80 million other voters supporting Socialist tickets in their respective nations. Christian Democrats, with regional organizations in Western Europe, Latin America, and Eastern Europe, have affiliates in about 60 nations. The Liberal International runs a strong third or fourth to the other parties in many nations, with its strongest affiliates in Great Britain, Canada, West Germany, and one or two other countries. American political leaders, unfortunately, have attended to these transnational party developments mainly as an aspect of CIA covert operations.

Thus, even with the prospects for world government far in the future, the most relevant political institutional developments for promoting international political trust, increasing collective security, and moderating the arms race are presently in progress. The ingredients for international institutionalized trust are available. There are tested institutional arenas in which internation and interelite conflicts have been resolved and "deals" transacted. Large, high-stake transactions have been broken up into smaller ones to reduce risks and costs. Expectations about elite behavior are becoming increasingly apparent; dangerous breaches of trust are being discovered in time for deterrents to be applied. All of these institutional developments are beginning to stabilize and make predictable the political behaviors of the world's elites. Further, the growing volume and pace of successful transactions and conflict resolutions are improving the positive consequences of each party's behavior for the others. In sum, the environment of political trust is growing.

## Returning to Collective Security

When the League of Nations and the United Nations were created, the political leaders of the world were in effect acknowledging that unilateral "national security" could no longer provide the full measure of safety that it had in previous times. Weapons had become too destructive, alliance systems too unreliable. "Collective security" became a significant concept following World War I. It was written into the United Nations Charter with a degree of explicitness never before achieved in an international agreement. However, a working system of international collective security has yet to become operative. "Peacekeeping," with its special contemporary meanings, has become a replacement concept describing what the United Nations undertakes in the security field. For the most part, though, unilateral approaches to national security remain as the predominant technique for achieving national safety.

The political leader who speaks of "national security" usually refers to the assumption that his nation has the primary responsibility for its self-defense. Self-defense includes the protection of the nation's territory, citizens, social and political institutions, economic interests, and all else that a predator nation might destroy or take away from it. When a leader refers to national security, he usually implies other conditions and some strong policies. He implies that weapons and military preparedness have the highest national priority because the nation's survival is at stake. Under threatening circumstances, he argues that the emergency powers of the nation's leadership should be expanded as much as necessary, including a suspension, at least temporarily, of individual and group interests, even to the extent of setting aside civil liberties. Although essentially a unilateral responsibility, national security may justify building alliances with others and placing armed forces and installations overseas to ward off or discourage potential aggressors. Self-reliance, however, is the basic posture. The only limit to defense preparations, he would insist, is the perceived strength of the suspected enemy. With such postures and policies, national security rests upon and promotes international political distrust and arms races.

"Collective security," on the other hand, is best described as a mutual insurance contract among states. Under the terms of such a contract, each state agrees to guarantee the safety of all the others in exchange for a similar commitment by the others. Collective security assumes that the maintenance of security and order is a fundamental and legitimate common interest meriting shared responsibilities. It also assumes that an internation conflict may have an "aggressor" on the one hand and a "victim" on the other and that the identity of the aggressor may be determined by a collective judgment. It further assumes that the military forces of the collective security system will be sufficient to enforce the judgment and punish or discourage the aggressor. In addition to this capacity for collective sanctions, the concept of collective security seeks to supplant the balance-of-power as a system for maintaining the peace, but doing so without creating a comprehensive government with a monopoly of the instruments of force. Finally, collective security assumes universality of membership in the system, that is, all members of the community are part of the security contract.[8]

The official collective security system for the world is prescribed in Chapter VII of the Charter of the United Nations, a large part of which is quoted below. The brief comments in brackets are this author's. The title of Chapter VII is "Action with Respect to Threats to the Peace, Breaches of the Peace, and Acts of Aggression."

*Article 39.* The Security Council shall determine the existence of any threat to the peace, breach of the peace, or act of aggression. [The Cold War soon made such determinations almost impossible because of the veto power of the Permanent Members. This development prompted the General Assembly's Uniting for Peace Resolution of 1950.]

*Article 40.* In order to prevent an aggravation of the situation, the Security Council may . . . call upon the parties concerned to comply with such provisional measures as it deems necessary or desirable. [The Security Council was to be the United Nations' principal arena for deterring aggression and resolving conflicts.]

*Article 41.* The Security Council may decide what measures not involving the use of armed forces are to be employed to give effect to its decision. . . . [This is the authorization for boycotts and similar collective pressures.]

*Article 42.* Should the Security Council consider that measures provided for in Article 41 would be inadequate or have proved to be inadequate, it may take such action by air, sea, or land forces as may be necessary to maintain or restore international peace and security. Such action may include demonstrations, blockades, and other operations by air, sea, or land forces of Members of the United Nations. [The ultimate authority for the United Nations "police action" such as described by President Truman with respect to Korea. The capacity for military sanctions is recognized here as an ultimate response to an act of aggression by one of its members.]

*Article 43.* All members of the United Nations . . . undertake to make available to the Security Council, on its call and in accordance with a special agreement or agreements, armed forces . . . necessary for the purpose of maintaining international peace and security. Such agreement or agreements shall govern the numbers and types of forces, their degree of readiness and general locations, and the nature of the facilities and assistance to be provided. [Neither the Security Council nor the General Assembly has yet determined how these special agreements are to be accomplished on a regular basis nor what their provisions about the disposition of forces should be.]

*Article 44.* [Any Member providing peacekeeping forces may participate in Security Council decisions regarding their employment.]

*Article 45.* In order to enable the United Nations to take urgent military measures, Members shall hold immediately available national air-force contingents for combined international enforcement action. [This Article, as does Article 43, raises fundamental issues about the nature of national standby forces.]

*Article 46.* Plans for the application of armed force shall be made by the Security Council with the assistance of the Military Staff Committee.

*Article 47.* There shall be established a Military Staff Committee to advise and assist the Security Council on all questions relating to the Security Council's military requirements for the maintenance of international peace and security, the employment and command of forces placed at its disposal, the regulation of armaments, and possible disarmament. The Military Staff Committee shall consist of the Chiefs of Staff of the Permanent Members of the Security Council or their representatives. . . . The Military Staff Committee . . . may establish regional subcommittees. [The Military Staff Committee was to be the beginning of the world's "Department of Defense," that is, the central military bureaucracy responsible, on the one hand, for peacekeeping planning and operations and, on the other, for arms control. Article 47 fits the historical experience about the necessity for centralizing the military institutions of the community. This Article has yet to be put into effect. The MSC meets fortnightly at the United Nations, often in full military regalia, for about ten minutes, as required by the Security Council's rules. Meanwhile, as we shall see, peacekeeping has become a major concern and activity of the General Assembly and the Secretary-General. As for arms control, this MSC responsibility has been dispersed among numerous other agencies and forums, on the unsound premise that arms control is a problem separable from peacekeeping. The provision for regional subcommittees was particularly prescient, recognizing that most armed conflicts are likely to be relatively local in character and best handled by local "police forces."]

*Articles 48–51.* . . . the members of the United Nations shall join in affording mutual assistance in carrying out the measures decided upon by the Security Council. . . . Nothing in the present Charter shall impair the inherent right of individual or collective self-defense if an armed attack occurs against a Member of the United Nations, until the Security Council has taken measures necessary to maintain international peace and security.

Chapter VII thus establishes a world collective security system that, if implemented, could be a first major step toward the centralization of global military institutions. This process of military centralization, at some time in the distant future, could become part of the kind of critical transition described earlier. At such time, the world's representative assemblies (presumably the General Assembly and the Security Council) and its transnational political party system could converge to share civilian control of the military and turn the world's military institutions to their civilized function as instruments of *internal* order and safety rather than warfare between competing elites.

Unfortunately, the leaderships of the world are not yet prepared to implement the provisions of Chapter VII. The hurdles have been several, and, in many respects, understandable. Each of the hurdles has been further heightened by the pervasiveness of international political distrust. Yet, one by one, the hurdles are apparently being surmounted.

One hurdle has been the problem of universality of membership. How could the safety of *all* be guaranteed by *all* if (a) a Cold War undermines the willingness of principal members to support the guarantee or (b) a country like China, with one-fourth of the world's population, and other significant states are not members of the collective security system? Rousseau's parable of the stag hunt illustrates the problem.

In the parable, all members of a hunt are required to remain at their assigned positions to prevent the stag from escaping and to thereby completely assure that all hunters will share in the delicious venison that is the purpose of the hunt. If *any one* of the hunters is distracted or defects (presumably because he is misinformed, disloyal, or simply chases a more available passing rabbit), the stag will escape and none will enjoy venison. This requirement of universal participation means that any one member of the cooperating group may deny the collective goal (the stag; safety and security in international affairs) to all the members.

Universality and unanimity are heavy burdens for any human system to carry. Recognition of the People's Republic of China rather than the Republic of China on Taiwan as the proper representative of China at the United Nations in 1971 achieved a "great leap forward" for the principle of universality. However, the uncertain political nature of China's participation and the continued exclusion of other significant states still leave the success of the global "stag hunt" in doubt.

The second hurdle relates to the problem of defining aggression and identifying an aggressor. The United Nations' effort to brand North Korea and the People's Republic of China as aggressors in 1950 was the first and last serious attempt to apply this principle of collective security. The Korean War demonstrated that the United Nations did not have adequate criteria for making a judgment about aggression by one sovereign nation against another. While there could be parties to an internation conflict, it was not certain that there need be an aggressor. Further, it became clear that the United Nations did not have the means to enforce collective sanctions against an aggressor, particularly, as in the case of Korea, when only one superpower provided the military forces while the other (in this case the Soviet Union) refrained from direct involvement or actively objected.

The question of defining "aggression" has nonetheless troubled the United Nations, particularly the General Assembly. A definition of "aggression" capable of commanding general acceptance by the international community has been sought without success for more than 150 years. It was attempted at the Congress of Vienna (1815), at the Hague peace conference of 1899, at the Versailles peace conference of 1919, and by the League of Nations. The San Francisco conference of 1945 decided not to try to include a definition in the United Nations Charter, noting that "the progress of modern warfare renders very difficult the definition of all cases." In 1951, the General Assembly referred to its International Law Commission, consisting of twenty-five law experts, the tasks of drafting a Code of Offenses Against the Peace and Security of Mankind as well as the Question of Defining Aggression. In 1954, the General Assembly appointed a special committee of thirty-five members to speed along the process of defining aggression. Not until April 1974, more than twenty years later, did the General Assembly adopt a definition in eight articles. The long process reminds one of the difficulties that physicians have in writing a code of professional ethics which must define "malpractice." The U.N. definition of aggression alluded to many types of acts: invasion, bombardment of territory, blockade of ports, attacks on the armed forces of one state by those of another, and sending terrorists into another state. The definition also acknowledges that its list of acts was not exhaustive, leaving it to the Security Council to expand the list or apply it to specific acts as it saw fit.

Another hurdle is the extreme difficulty, particularly because of the veto, in achieving consensus about a judgment that one or another nation has been an aggressor. The veto power held by the five permanent members has the political and military capacity to challenge and halt any action of the United Nations, even to the point of war. From the outset, the Security Council's efforts to exercise its collective security functions were frustrated frequently by the Soviet Union's use of its veto power. It must be remembered, of course, that in the years immediately following World War II, the United Nations was largely dominated by the United States, with the Communist bloc a distinct minority. While the United States openly supported its friends and allies with military and economic aid as well as favorable votes in the United Nations, the Soviet Union was actively supporting Communist parties and revolutionary guerrillas, aided by the exercise of the veto whenever necessary. The Greek civil war was a case in point.

At the end of the German occupation in 1945, the Royalist party and the king's government-in-exile returned to Greece. They found that Communist-led resistance groups had already established a provisional government of their own. In the civil war that ensued, the left-wing forces received supplies and sanctuary from Yugoslavia, Albania, and Bulgaria, which were in turn receiving arms from the Soviet Union. When the British were no longer able to give the Royalist party sufficient support, the United States enunciated the Truman Doctrine (March 1947) and began sending large-scale aid to Greece and Turkey. In one phase of the conflict, when a Security Council commission investigating border violations recommended that all external assistance to the Greek guerrillas be ended, this recommendation was vetoed by the Soviet Union, accompanied by protests over American aid to Greece and Turkey. Such was the tone, the pattern, and the political dynamics of the Cold War and the Security Council's incapacity to determine, as called for in Article 39, the existence of a threat to the peace, breach of the peace, or act of aggression.

That the Security Council was able to act at all in response to the North Korean attack on South Korea in June 1950 was the result of a fortuitous set of circumstances. Three months earlier, in March, the Soviet Union began a boycott of the Security Council in protest over the Council's unwillingness to seat the representative from Peking in place of the one from Taiwan as the legitimate Chinese delegate. In the absence of the Soviet representative, the Council was able to pass unanimously resolutions calling for a cease-fire, the withdrawal of North Korean forces, and a call to all United Nations members to help the Republic of Korea. The United Nations forces, led by General Douglas MacArthur, not only drove back the North Koreans but seemed on the verge of conquering them when the People's Republic of China, in October 1950, sent massive waves of troops against the United Nations forces for a successful counterattack. By January 1951, the Communists had recrossed the 38th parallel and captured Seoul, the South Korean capital. Meanwhile, the Soviet delegate had returned to the Security Council, and the Soviet veto once again effectively paralyzed that body.

It was under these circumstances that the General Assembly, on November 3, 1950, adopted the Uniting for Peace Resolution which provided, among other things, that if the Security Council, because of the lack of unanimity of its Permanent Members, fails to exercise its responsibility in the maintenance of peace, the General Assembly shall consider the matter immediately in emergency session for the purpose of recommending to members collective measures to be taken, including the use of armed forces. This was a radical assumption of the Security Council's peacekeeping function by the General Assembly and marked, as we shall see, the beginning of a new era and new conceptions of the peacekeeping and collective security responsibilities of the United Nations. In effect, collective security, as conceived in Chapter VII, was laid to rest, with hope for a reincarnation some day. An alternate concept of peacekeeping came into being at this time.

Finally, perhaps the most serious hurdle on the road to a feasible world collective security system are the requirements for large collective military forces sufficient to deal with military conflicts of all sizes and types. Two or three hypothetical scenarios will suggest how difficult it is to conceive of a practical system.

The most elementary scenario puts the nuclear superpowers in an all-out nuclear exchange. Since such a catastrophic exchange could take place within a matter of an hour or two at the most, it is difficult to conceive of a military role for the United Nations at all. Even with its own stockpile of nuclear weapons, a highly unlikely prospect, the United Nations could hardly step in to threaten or punish an "aggressor" or both parties. Nor is the day close when all nuclear powers would be willing to turn over their entire nuclear arsenals to the United Nations, giving that body a monopoly of the world's most powerful instruments of violence. Such a gift and such a monopoly would, of course, be the hallmark of a functioning and viable world government. While history and logic suggest that such an arrangement is the only solution for the world's collective security dilemma, most of us can readily agree that lessons of history and logic are not likely to be acted upon for many generations. Meanwhile, collective security arrangements at the nuclear level will have to rely on SALT treaties, comprehensive test bans, nuclear nonproliferation treaties, and reconnaissance systems capable of verifying all of these. With extraordinary luck, humanity may survive those many generations before all national nuclear weapons are turned over to a world collective security agency.

A second scenario that demonstrates the difficulties of putting together sufficient military forces to implement a collective security system relates to possible conflicts between middle-sized nonnuclear powers. The Middle East wars have been examples of this type of conflict. North Korea, Vietnam, and South Africa, while still nonnuclear states, possess some of the largest armies in the world. The military force that a United Nations collective security system would require to break up a fight between powers of this size would have to be substantial indeed: several hundred thousand if not millions of troops, substantial air force contingents, and so forth.[9] The price tag for such a military organization would be many, many times the entire budget of the present United Nations system, with current ad hoc expenditures for peacekeeping forces thrown in for good measure. This, too, is likely to remain a distant goal.

A third hypothetical scenario is one in which the world's security forces serve the kind of peacekeeping missions now performed by the United Nations. In these situations, either the Security Council or the General Assembly serves as a third party with sufficient influence to convince most nonnuclear states in conflict with each other to accept a standstill cease-fire and allow a United Nations peacekeeping force to police the voluntary truce until the conflict can be resolved at the negotiating table. In such a scenario, the United Nations peacekeeping force remains relatively small, is financed for short periods of about six months at a time, remains on duty at the pleasure of both parties to the conflict, and carries a minimum of weaponry. As we shall see, such peacekeeping missions are the current concept of collective security and an extremely practical response to the political and military requirements of conflicts between nonnuclear states at this time.[10]

Having documented the nuclear threat, the arms race, and the rampant political distrust that still prevail among the world's leaders, it is easy to feel despair and helplessness. However, closer examination of certain historical trends and their extrapolations into the future may leave us with some hope that systems of institutionalized trust and collective security may yet emerge in time to head off holocausts and catastrophes. Closer examination of relevant historical processes may also provide the world's leaders with guidelines for relevant immediate policies.

Round tables and world conferences are hardly likely to bring the golden age of peace in one grand transaction. However, with greater knowledge about the world's elites, their conflicts, and the conditions necessary to promote trust among them, such round tables and conferences, together with the daily security decisions of working politicians and statesmen, may hasten the evolution of the relevant historical processes through their critical stages and transitions into an irreversible period of world political integration. To this end, today's relatively primitive system of peacekeeping and fumbling efforts at arms control may well be making substantial contributions, and may be even more constructive when institutionally put together again, as prescribed in Chapter VII of the United Nations Charter.

# References

1. Karl W. Deutsch, *Politics and Government* (Boston: Houghton Mifflin, 1980), p. 175.
2. David B. Truman, *The Governmental Process* (New York: Knopf, 1951), Chap. 2.
3. For a survey of relevant theories, Ralph M. Goldman, *Contemporary Perspectives on Politics* (New Brunswick, N.J.: Transaction Books, 1976). For a paradigm that explains how negotiations contribute to social order, Anselm Strauss, *Negotiations* (San Francisco: Jossey-Bass, 1978). Also, Robert Jervis, "Cooperation Under the

Security Dilemma," *World Politics* (January 1978). For a typology of "political currencies" pertinent to transactions leading to political trust and arms control, Ralph M. Goldman, "A Transactional Theory of Political Integration and Arms Control," *American Political Science Review*, 62 (September 1969), 719-733. In brief, the political currencies include *incumbencies* in office, *shares* of political prerogative, and *commodities* such as government funds, goods, services, and armaments. Political integration (institutionalization) is a consequence of successful transactions among political elites using these currencies. Political trust follows from the successful transactions, in tandem with political integration. Arms control is, in this theory, the end product of a process that gives incumbents in governmental offices shares in the control and management of military commodities (armaments).

4. Paul Wehr, *Conflict Regulation* (Boulder, Colo.: Westview Press, 1979), which contains an invaluable annotated bibliography; Albert E. Eldridge, *Images of Conflict* (New York: St. Martin's Press, 1979); Robert Lyle Butterworth, *Moderation from Management: International Organizations and Peace* (Pittsburgh: University of Pittsburgh Center for International Studies, 1978); Dennis Pirages, *Managing Political Conflict* (London: Thomas Nelson and Sons, 1976); Morton Deutsch, *The Resolution of Conflict; Constructive and Destructive Processes* (New Haven: Yale University Press, 1973); Lewis A. Coser, *Continuities in the Study of Social Conflict* (New York: Free Press, 1967); "Conflict," *International Encyclopedia of the Social Sciences* (New York: Macmillan, 1968). A closely related literature on negotiation has recently become prolific. See, Anselm Strauss, *Negotiations* (San Francisco: Jossey-Bass, 1978); I. William Zartman, *The 50% Solution* (Garden City, N.Y.: Anchor Press/Doubleday, 1976); I. William Zartman, ed., *The Negotiation Process* (Beverly Hills: Sage, 1978).

5. Robert L. Butterworth, *Managing Interstate Conflict, 1945-74; Data with Synopses* (Pittsburgh: University of Pittsburgh Center for International Studies, 1976).

6. This review and analysis is begun in Ralph M. Goldman, "Military and Party Institutions in the Arms Control Process: English and Mexican Cases" (Unpublished paper delivered at the 95th Annual Meeting of the American Historical Association, December 28-30, 1980), which is based on a monograph in preparation entitled *The Arms Control Process*. The panel paper will appear in Ralph M. Goldman, ed., *Transnational Parties in World Affairs* (Santa Barbara, CA: Clio Press, forthcoming).

7. For a description of the trends and their implications, Ralph M. Goldman, "The Emerging Transnational Party System and the Future of American Parties," in Louis Maisel and Joseph Cooper eds., *Political Parties: Development and Decay* (Beverly Hills, CA.: Sage, 1978), Chap. 3. More detailed discussion of the emerging role of transnational parties will be found in Ralph M. Goldman, ed., *Transnational Parties in World Affairs*. Also in preparation by the

same author, *Transnational Parties and Movements* (Santa Barbara, CA: Clio Press, forthcoming), an extensive annotated bibliography of source materials in this field.

8. The U.S. Department of Defense has adopted the term "collective security" as a way of describing its alliance systems, such as NATO.

9. For analysis of the probable requirements of such a "world police force," Lincoln P. Bloomfield, *The Power to Keep Peace* (Boston: Little, Brown, 1971).

10. For excellent analyses and evaluations of contemporary United Nations peacekeeping, Larry L. Fabian, *Soldiers Without Enemies: Preparing the United Nations for Peacekeeping* (Washington, D.C.: Brookings Institution, 1971). Also, General Indar Rikhye et al., *The Thin Blue Line* (New Haven: Yale University Press, 1974); D.W. Wainhouse, *International Peacekeeping at the Crossroads* (Baltimore: Johns Hopkins University Press, 1973).

# CHAPTER 6

# The Security Services of the Trusted Peacekeepers

Although peacekeeping is a time-honored pursuit of statesmen and diplomats in international politics, the concept has acquired special meaning since the passage of the General Assembly's Uniting for Peace Resolution in 1950. Many view current peacekeeping practice as the most feasible response to the real world of power politics in which nuclear giants must be left to keep the peace between themselves, United Nations resources and budgets are likely to remain relatively minuscule, civil and internation wars must be expected as a consequence of the institutional rigidity of conflict and change processes in most parts of the world, and nonnuclear nations have yet to learn how to resolve their conflicts more efficiently within the framework of available supranational organizations. It also has become increasingly evident that arms control treaties in a world without conflict-resolving and military peacekeeping institutions are reduced to mere hardware contracts.

A brief survey and interpretation of selected instances of peacekeeping experience by the United Nations leads to the conclusion that this function has been expanding in scope and significance and that it may well be, incrementally speaking, one of the major trust-promoting activities in contemporary international politics. This observation does not deny that peacekeeping is still a weak enterprise, but so are the activities of all infants. As with infants, international peacekeeping requires nurturance if it is to mature to its maximum potential.

## Historical Background of Peacekeeping

During different periods of history, the major conflicts of the world were in one way or another resolved by some peacekeeping process or by a predominant power. What follows is a brief account of that experience. In classical times, one way of keeping the peace was to conquer the enemy or subdue "troublemakers" militarily. As the wealth and commercial traffic of the Mediterranean Sea increased, the warrior-leaders of ancient empires and city-states had various motives for embarking upon military adventures and conquests: personal ambition; aggrandizement of territory and riches; destruction of a hated adversary; and, not insignificantly, the protection of commerce and maintenance of the order and peace that enables commerce to thrive. In the latter regard, the Roman Empire was the principal peacekeeper of the Mediterranean world for several generations. A similar development could be observed along the main rivers of China, where nobles fought over the control of waterways, commerce, and territory from the twelfth century B.C. to the founding of the Sung dynasty in A.D. 960. Nonetheless, years of order and peace were the accomplishment of skillful peacekeepers, particularly under the Han dynasty (202 B.C. to A.D. 221) when China at times surpassed Rome in size, wealth, and power.

Despite countless local wars among ambitious nobles, the medieval Catholic Church, the Holy Roman Empire, and the feudal structure of society brought a sometimes unappreciated degree of order and political stability to an otherwise crude, primitive, and contentious Western world. At a later time, when the concepts of territoriality, nationhood, non-Catholic roads to salvation, and divine origins of royal power began to emerge, significantly accompanied by the breakup of feudal military coalitions that had supported papal supremacy, Europe became a war-torn place whose devastation was limited only by the volunteer character of its tiny armies and its primitive weaponry. However, these conflicts spread distrust among political leaders and spurred the development of new military technologies, even in that untechnological age. From the fifteenth to the seventeenth centuries, mankind created cannons, muskets, armed warships, guerrilla warfare, and other unfortunate products of human ingenuity. Militarily, periods of European peace came only when royal alliances sustained them, empire-building preoccupied the elites, and English control of the seas deterred wars. It was also during these centuries that scholars and jurists such as Hugo van Groot, or Grotius, and Richard Zouche (in 1625 and 1650, respectively) wrote their first treatises on international law and international relations in the hope that careful analysis and wise prescription would provide international leaders with the understanding and guidelines needed for resolving their conflicts in the interest of all.

With the end of the Napoleonic wars at the advent of the nineteenth century, the modern era of international relations and peacekeeping began. In 1815, the Congress of Vienna inaugurated the first systematic multilateral approach to the settlement of European disputes through international conferences. During the remainder of the nineteenth century, the Congress system conducted thirty such conferences. Since so much of the non-European world was possessed or controlled by the imperial powers of Europe, the Congress system, in effect, evolved a set of rules of imperial competition. When the Congress of Berlin established the first international secretariat in 1878, the new bureaucracy was another indication of the importance that the major powers attached to the peacekeeping work of the Congress system.

World War I was a consequence of the inadequacies of the Congress system. Intense distrust among European leaders, escalating alliance systems, and rigid, automatic military doctrines led to the collapse of the fragile peacekeeping system. However, European leaders did build on the experience, encouraged in part by the Wilsonian enthusiasm for constitutionalism and world order, by creating the League of Nations. Europe continued to be the center of world politics; the League legitimized and facilitated much of its conduct. The capture and dismemberment of the losers' empires was carried on through a League mandate system. New rules for peacekeeping were designed. Unfortunately, the twentieth century was well ahead of nineteenth-century concepts.

The League of Nations consisted of two bodies: the Assembly, made up of all forty-four members, and the Council, including the major powers. The League and its secretariat were dominated by the French and the British. Two of the largest nations in the world were not members during the 1920s: the United States, as a consequence of isolationism at home, and the Soviet Union, the fearsome Red Menace of the day. The League acted on the basis of the existing substantial body of international law and as though the requirements of a collective security system were available. The League system included the outlines of two other institutions of conflict resolution: a Permanent Court of International Justice and a Court of Arbitration.

By the end of its first decade, the inadequacies of the League of Nations were starkly evident. The Soviet Union joined but was xenophobic in its relations with other members and the organization as a whole. In 1931, the League found that it was unable to deal with the Japanese invasion of Manchuria. Nor could it halt the devastating but almost forgotten war between Bolivia and Paraguay in 1933. By 1935, the fascist ambitions of Mussolini led to savage attack upon Ethiopia. In his historic address to the League, Emperor Haile Selassie warned that the League's incapacity to halt aggression could only lead to its demise. Hitler's invasion of Austria in 1938 was the final blow. All of the techniques of collective security—censure, condemnation, economic sanctions, and so on—had proven ineffectual. The Axis powers were unconstrained predators.

The United Nations picked up the collective security legacy of the League of Nations and, theoretically, gave it teeth in the provisions of Chapter VII of its Charter. In effect, the U.N. was created as the policing system for a victorious coalition. The defeated Axis was disarmed and excluded. A trusteeship system replaced the mandate system for dismantling former empires. An International Court of Justice replaced the defunct Permanent Court of International Justice. An International Law Commission was created to promote the development of international law and its codification.

The General Assembly was to deal with matters of membership, budget, and, through its deliberations and recommendations, promote (not *legislate*) international cooperation for the maintenance of peace and security, the development of international law, and the advancement of the economic, social, cultural, educational, health, human rights, and political goals of all mankind. The Security Council, with its powerful five permanent members, was assigned primary responsibility for the maintenance of international peace and security and the settlement of international disputes. The secretariat, whose secretary-general is appointed by the General Assembly upon the recommendation of the Security Council, was to build the bureaucracy that would serve and implement the policies of all agencies of the United Nations system. Article 99 of the Charter also gave the secretary-general an unprecedented political prerogative: the right to bring to the attention of the Security Council any matter that, in his opinion, may threaten the maintenance of international peace and security.

Although so many components of a collective security system were theoretically in place, the United Nations was from the outset buffeted about by international conflicts and forces greater than itself. Nationalist leaders and movements in the territories of former empires impatiently demanded independence from their war-weary European possessors, and so the next quarter century witnessed the birth pangs of one hundred new states joining the original fifty members of the United Nations. The Cold War created a bipolar Soviet-American world that, at the end of three decades, was transformed into a multipolar world including the People's Republic of China, Japan, and the European Community. In another generation, others would undoubtedly join that company: Brazil, South Africa, India, and Vietnam. The community of nations today is very different from the one that established the United Nations system, and the year 2000 will undoubtedly see even more dramatic differences.

More than 400 internation conflicts have taken place since the founding of the U.N. In a century of such dangerous military technology and such rapid change in the social and political structure of the world, it is indeed a miracle that the world has not yet destroyed itself during one of these conflicts. Perhaps the real miracle is the restraint and caution inspired by shared fear. Perhaps the world's leaders have learned how vital it is to build, incrementally, the structure of institutionalized trust.

The first steps, however, were hardly auspicious. Between 1946 and 1950, collective security meant little more than United Nations troops and observation missions trying to discourage major power interventions into domestic civil wars and wars of independence from former empires. In 1950, the Korean "police action" inspired the General Assembly's Uniting for Peace Resolution, which put the General Assembly and the secretary-general into the business of peacekeeping whenever the Security Council failed at it. This was, as we have noted, the turning point for a new style of United Nations peacekeeping.

Arab-Israeli wars since 1948, the Suez Crisis in 1956, the Congo from 1960 to 1964, and Cyprus from 1960 to the present have been the largest, the most expensive, and the most militarily difficult of the peacekeeping missions. These and other missions have raised profoundly difficult questions of peacekeeping procedure, the structure of the military component, the method of financing, and a host of other issues. On the functional side, the new style of peacekeeping has come to mean investigation, observation, mediation between willing and "nonguilty" equal parties to a conflict, and truce maintenance. The experience to date has also seen the emergence of a middle-power peacekeeping constituency, ready and willing to provide standby forces for peacekeeping missions: Sweden, Canada, Denmark, Norway, Ireland, Finland, the Netherlands, New Zealand, Italy, India, and, more recently such communist countries as Yugoslavia and Poland. The principal suppliers of quartermaster, intelligence, and combat gear have been the United States and Great Britain, and their experience, too, has been invaluable.[1]

As an outcome of the Yom Kippur War of 1973, there was a resumption of peacekeeping responsibilities by the Security Council. The Security Council reestablished the United Nations Emergency Force (UNEF) to supervise the cease-fire. The five permanent members of the Council were excluded from participating in a pacekeeping force in the area, a negative response to the Soviet proposal that the superpowers provide such a force. A United Nations Disengagement Observer Force (UNDOF) was created to supervise the disengagement of forces and the creation of buffer zone between them. When, in 1978, provoked by the operations of the Palestine Liberation Organization from bases in Lebanon, Israel sent a major military expedition into that country, the United Nations added yet another peacekeeping force to the troubled area: the United Nations Interim Force in Lebanon (UNIFIL). UNIFIL became the most recent of the United Nations peacekeeping missions. Its troops joined the roster of more than 300,000 men who have served in such missions since the founding of the United Nations.

## Selected Cases Since 1945 and Selected Conclusions

The United Nations has been a direct agent of conflict-resolution in well over 100 cases since 1945. By broadening the definition of "conflict case," we may include occasions of U.N. "quiet diplomacy" and "good offices" that would easily double the number. Some cases have been more salient than others because of the significance of the parties, the degree of violence involved, difficulties of resolution, implications for politics of the United Nations, or the nature of the precedents, failures, and successes coming out of the peacekeeping mission. The survey that follows will give particular attention to the accretion of institutional arrangements resulting from the missions and the military-political implications of the experience.[2]

### Greece: U.N. Special Committee on the Balkans (UNSCOB)

A civil war in Greece began with the departure in 1945 of the German occupiers. Two underground resistance organizations—the National Liberation Front and the National People's Liberation Army, both dominated by the Greek Communist Party—established a provisional government to challenge the returning Royalist Party and the king. When Great Britain terminated its assistance to the king's government in 1947, the Truman Doctrine was promulgated and the United States undertook responsibility for assistance to Greece and Turkey.

With the collusion of the Soviet Union, arms and supplies were shipped to the Communist guerrillas through Yugoslavia, Albania, and Bulgaria. The Greek guerrillas also used these countries as sanctuaries and training areas. More than 150,000 lives were lost in the civil war and some 25,000 Greek children were evacuated (some said kidnapped) by the guerrillas from border communities and relocated in the surrounding countries.

The Greek civil war engaged the United Nations in its first peacekeeping mission. Although the Security Council promptly sent a mission to investigate the frontier incidents, a number of Soviet vetoes prevented meaningful action by that body. The United States urged the General Assembly to take up the matter. In September and October 1947, the General Assembly called on Greece's neighboring states to cease aiding the guerrillas and created the Special Committee on the Balkans (UNSCOB) to investigate and report on the situation.

On the basis of UNSCOB reports submitted from 1948 to 1951, the General Assembly issued a series of recommendations:

that Greece renew diplomatic relations with its neighbors; that the 25,000 Greek children be returned; that Albania and Bulgaria cease assistance to the guerrillas (Tito broke with the Soviet Union in 1949 and withdrew Yugoslav aid at that time); and that Greek army soldiers held captive in Balkan states be repatriated. In 1951, UNSCOB was replaced by a U.N. Peace Observation Commission, hostilities declined, and the civil war ended through attrition.

This first peacekeeping mission revealed important difficulties, enjoyed limited successes, and set some significant precedents. The most serious difficulty was the stalemate in the Security Council. A disagreement among the permanent members, more specifically, the United States and the Soviet Union, meant that the Council could not act as a conflict managing agency. The immobilization of the Security Council led to the important precedent of having the General Assembly become involved in a nonmilitary fashion. A further difficulty, to recur frequently, was the impracticality of thorough field investigations in a conflict of this character: long and open borders over which guerrillas and their supplies could pass readily; guerrilla warfare as a difficult kind of military operation to investigate; poor coordination of observation teams functioning under many different commands. Despite these difficulties, UNSCOB did succeed in casting the light of authoritative information and publicity upon a conflict that otherwise might have been obscured from world view. The General Assembly persisted in making recommendations that eventually constrained the parties. In sum, the Greek case put the General Assembly into peacekeeping and demonstrated that investigation and observation could be significant sources of pressure for ending a conflict.

### Palestine: U.N. Truce Supervision Organization (UNTSO)

As the birthplace of three of the world's great religions, Palestine has had a special religious, emotional, and territorial significance for Jews, Christians, and Moslems throughout the world. In 1897, the World Zionist Congress was established with the prime objective of making Palestine the "Jewish National Home." At that time, Palestine was part of the Turkish Empire. At the end of World War I, control of much of the Middle East fell to the British and the French. The British were responsible for Palestine. In 1917, British Foreign Secretary Balfour announced his government's willingness to help the Jewish people establish a national home in Palestine provided that "nothing shall be done which may prejudice the civil and religious rights of existing non-Jewish communities in Palestine."

As part of the Allied strategy for defeating the Central Powers in World War I, the British encouraged various Arab nationalist movements to seek independence from the Turks. After the war, the British, responsible for Palestine under a League of Nations mandate, were obligated to both Jews and Arabs for the development of their respective homelands in the area. The situation in the Middle East was aggravated in the 1930s by the exodus of Jews from Germany and other parts of Europe to escape Nazi persecution and concentration camps. Jewish immigration and land purchases in Palestine reached major proportions and were strenuously resisted by the leaders of the Arab nationalist movements. In 1937, the Peel Commission, a British royal commission, recommended partitioning Palestine between Jews and Arabs, a proposal that was rejected by the Arabs. In 1939, the British announced that Jewish immigration into Palestine would be limited to 75,000 over a period of five years, at which time it would be ended. Further, the sale of land to the Jews would be restricted. At the end of a ten-year period, Palestine would be given its independence under a special treaty relationship with Britain.

This policy did not respond realistically to the hundreds of thousands of Jews who were leaving Europe for Palestine. Jewish terrorist organizations emerged in Palestine to protest the British decision and to protect the immigrants. Equally frustrated, the Arabs engaged in their own terrorism with strikes against both Jews and British officials.

In May 1942, the American Zionist Association endorsed a plan to create a Jewish state of the whole of Palestine, open it up for unlimited immigration, and establish a Jewish army. By 1947, two years before they expected to establish an independent Palestine, the British, weakened by the economic, political, and social costs of World War II, turned to the United Nations for a solution. A United Nations Special Committee on Palestine came up with a plan to partition Palestine into two independent states—one Jewish and the other Arab—and to form a federation of these two as one independent nation. The Arabs opposed partition; the Jews favored it with some changes. Hostilities broke out in Palestine. The Security Council called for a truce. On May 14, 1948, the British mandate ended, and the Jews proclaimed the state of Israel. Within hours, the United States recognized the new nation. The following morning Arab troops from Egypt, Jordan, Syria, and Lebanon invaded Palestine to prevent the new state from coming into existence. At the United Nations, both the United States and the Soviet Union condemned the Arab action.

During the next eight months, fighting was sporadic, halted from time to time by temporary cease-fires and truces. The

General Assembly sent Dr. Ralph Bunche as its mediator, and by February 1949, he succeeded in negotiating an armistice agreement between Egypt and Israel, followed shortly by similar agreements with Jordan, Lebanon, and Syria. The agreements established Mixed Armistice Commissions, under which a United Nations Truce Supervision Organization (UNTSO) would supervise their implementation. These arrangements were underwritten by the Security Council. UNTSO has been on duty for thirty years.

UNTSO's main task has been to observe and report on compliance with the armistice agreements of 1949 and, subsequently, the cease-fire arrangements following the Suez crisis of 1956, the Six-Day War of 1967, and the Yom Kippur War of 1973. In performing these duties, UNTSO cooperated with subsequent United Nations Emergency Forces (UNEF) and the United Nations Disengagement Observer Force (UNDOF) established in 1974. At various times UNTSO has consisted of 30 to 567 officers from as many as 21 nations.

UNTSO brought the fledgling United Nations directly to the center of one of the most stubborn conflicts of modern times. Both the General Assembly and the Security Council had roles to play. The General Assembly sent mediators who succeeded in bringing the parties to the negotiating table. The Security Council gave its support to a small, nonmilitary observation mission that has been performing its task far longer than anyone could have predicted. The neutrality of United Nations agencies was painstakingly established by excluding the superpowers from the mission and bringing in a large number of participating middle powers. The UNTSO experience also demonstrated how successful the United Nations can be in a third-party role when the interests of the two superpowers coincide.

## Indonesia: U.N. Commission for Indonesia (UNCI)

Following World War I, both the indigenous population and the Dutch settlers of the Netherlands Indies sought a new relationship with the Netherlands. Some preferred greater self-government within the existing constitution, others a federal union with the Netherlands, and still others complete independence for a new United States of Indonesia. Strong economic ties existed between the colony and the mother country.

When the Japanese won control of the country in 1942, they encouraged the formation of an Indonesia Volunteer Army and cooperated with nationalist leaders in the preparation of a constitution. When the Japanese surrendered in August 1945, these nationalist leaders, led by Sukarno, proclaimed the independent Republic of Indonesia.

The transition was not an easy one. The Dutch suspected leaders who had been sponsored by the Japanese. The Indonesian leaders were divided among themselves about the degree of independence that the new country should seek and the amount of force that should be used in doing so. Further, it was difficult for the new government to organize itself administratively in many areas that were presumably to be included in the Republic: Java, Sumatra, Borneo, East Indonesia, the Malino States, West Irian (Western New Guinea), and other islands.

The British assumed responsibility for disarming the surrendering Japanese in 1945 and, almost immediately, found themselves trying to end fighting between Republican forces and the returning Dutch army. In January 1946, the Ukrainian SSR and the Soviet Union charged in the Security Council that British troops and Japanese armed forces were collaborating in military action against the local population and interfering with the national liberation movement in Indonesia. The Security Council refrained from taking action because direct negotiations between Indonesia and the Netherlands were about to begin in a matter of days. Late in 1946, the British withdrew their troops but assigned a mediator to assist in direct negotiations. Meanwhile, in the Netherlands, a national election brought leaders to office who were interested in early settlement of the dispute.

The negotiations proceeded through 1947. However, midyear, Dutch troops invaded Republic of Indonesia territories in what came to be known as the First Police Action. On August 1, 1947, the Security Council called upon the parties to cease hostilities and urged them to settle their dispute peacefully. As fighting continued, the Security Council established a three-member Good Offices Committee consisting of Australia, Belgium, and the United States. By January 1948, the Good Offices Committee achieved a truce agreement between the parties, only to have the Netherlands denounce the agreement eleven months later and embark upon a Second Police Action. The Security Council now recommended the formation of a federal, independent, United States of Indonesia and converted the Good Offices Committee into a United Nations Commission for Indonesia (UNCI) with instructions to assist the parties in implementing this resolution. In a unilateral action designed to elicit greater Dutch cooperation, the United States partially suspended Marshall Plan aid to that country. Under UNCI direction, negotiations proceeded toward a final settlement. Dutch forces were withdrawn, Indonesia agreed to respect Dutch economic rights, including fair compensation under any nationalization of property, and the Republic of the United States of Indonesia was recognized as an independent and sovereign state.

The transfer of sovereignty took place on December 27, 1949, and Indonesia became a member of the United Nations on September 28, 1950. UNCI maintained its contingent of military observers until early 1951, at which time it was disbanded.

The peacekeeping lessons of the Indonesian independence conflict were numerous. Resolution of the conflict was undoubtedly facilitated because it was not an issue loaded with East-West implications. In fact, the Communist members rather enjoyed watching Western powers trying to dismember the former empire of one of their number. The Security Council made a number of substantial third-party moves: attempting arbitration; providing a good-offices channel of communication that succeeded in bringing the parties to direct negotiations; and even going so far as to condemn one of the parties (the Dutch) and subjecting it to economic pressure. A facilitating factor was the military weakness of the Netherlands at the end of World War II and its inability to escalate the conflict beyond a certain point. One substantial difficulty for the United Nations, and one that would appear again as former colonies became new nations, was the question of U.N. jurisdictional competency in the case. The Indonesian independence problem was perceived as a domestic matter by the Dutch, hence its two "police actions" against the Indonesians and its reluctance to admit third parties to mediate the dispute.

### Kashmir: U.N. Military Observer Group in India and Pakistan (UNMOGIP)

Under British rule, the Hindu majority and the Moslem minority of colonial India succeeded in minimizing their religious conflicts within the framework of imperial government. However, as the time for British withdrawal approached, the Moslems insisted upon having a separate sovereign community. The British statute that established Indian independence in 1947 created three territorial entities: India, East Pakistan, and West Pakistan. The two parts of Moslem Pakistan were separated from each other by nearly 1,000 miles of Indian territory. There were also 565 princely states to which the British gave the choice of joining India, Pakistan, or remaining independent. Only three chose independence, one of which was Kashmir, a highly strategic area of approximately 85,000 square miles. Both India and Pakistan considered Kashmir a significant element in their national security, particularly against each other.

Some three million Moslems and about 800,000 Hindus comprised the population of Kashmir. The Maharajah, Hari Sing, was himself a Hindu. While Kashiri Moslems resented having a Hindu as their leader, they were also reluctant to be incorporated into Pakistan. Rather than make a choice between India and Pakistan, the Maharajah arranged a "standstill agreement" postponing a decision until internal strife had subsided.

Moslems in southwest Kashmir began a revolt against the Maharajah and set up a provisional government. As the Maharajah attempted to cope with this situation, the Pakistan government protested that Hindu attacks were being made on Moslem villages. Moslem tribesmen began crossing the border from Pakistan into Kashmir on the pretext of aiding their coreligionists. The Maharajah turned to India for military aid and offered to accede, which he did in October 1947. Pakistan promptly denounced the accession as a fraud. Indian troops were sent to Kashmir in time to halt Moslem tribesmen as they approached the capital. At this point, Pakistan sent its own troops into the fray.

On January 1, 1948, India asked the Security Council to take action against Pakistan. The Council called for a cease-fire and established a United Nations Commission for India and Pakistan (UNCIP) whose five members included Argentina, Belgium, Colombia, Czechoslovakia, and the United States. UNCIP recommended a truce agreement under which Pakistan would withdraw its troops at once, the Indian forces would withdraw in stages, and the local Kashmiri authorities would govern the evacuated territories until a solution was reached. UNCIP also recommended a plebiscite to determine the future of Kashmir. The cease-fire came into effect on January 1, 1949, and a U.N. Military Observer Group (UNMOGIP) was stationed along the cease-fire line.

UNMOGIP consisted of 30 to 65 observers recruited from about a dozen contributing countries. The mission's principal responsibility was to report on compliance with the cease-fire agreement and provide general surveillance of the cease-fire line. So few officers supervising a line extending thousands of miles was asking too much. Subsequent fighting in the area and recurring crises in Kashmir have underscored this difficulty. On the other hand, Kashmir peacekeeping did attempt to arrange a plebiscite and did lead to acceptance of mediation by the parties and a cease-fire. Unfortunately, between 1949 and 1953, the efforts of three U.N. mediators came to naught.

Discussion of the Kashmir conflict returned to the Security Council in January 1957. A resolution was offered calling for the demilitarization of Kashmir and the use of United Nations forces to provide appropriate conditions for a plebiscite. This was vetoed by the Soviet Union. The Kashmir question came up again in the Security Council in 1962 when hundreds of cease-fire violations were noted. Meanwhile, a religious campaign for the liberation of

Kashmir began to gather momentum in Pakistan. Suggestions from the United States and the United Kingdom regarding internationalizing the Kashmir Valley and the disposition of the waters of the Indus River system were rejected. By August 1965, Pakistan began infiltrating large numbers of regular armed forces into Kashmir.

The plebiscite was never held. The cease-fire had hardly been maintained. Mediation efforts failed. Yet, for fifteen years, third-party interventions, negotiations, and suggestions for resolution succeeded in postponing the holy war that simmered just beneath the surface. From a peacekeeping perspective, Kashmir demonstrated the importance of sustained discussion and insistent external pressures for negotiation.

### Korea: A Police Action

This is the classic case in which the United Nations endeavored to implement the provisions of Chapter VII of the Charter calling for collective military measures against an aggressor. The Korean War also cast the United States in the unhappy role of "policeman for the world." When it was over, the collective security action cost South Korea, the United States, and other United Nations forces some 438,000 battle casualties and approximately 500,000 other South Korean deaths from war-related events. On the North Korean and Chinese side, there were approximately 2 million battle and civilian casualties. This war ended the Security Council's effectiveness as the world's collective security agency, buried the concept of collective security for some time to come, and brought the General Assembly into peacekeeping through its Uniting for Peace resolution.

Before World War II, Korea had been a Japanese colony. During the war, the Allies agreed to divide Korea at the 38th parallel for the purpose of accepting the Japanese surrender. The North was to be the Soviet zone of occupation and the South under American military government. From 1945 to 1947, a US-USSR commission attempted to form a provisional government, but without success. In 1947, the United States asked the United Nations to take up the problem. The General Assembly established a nine-nation United Nations Temporary Commission on Korea (UNTCOK) to observe elections for a Korean national assembly and to arrange for the withdrawal of the occupying powers. The Soviet Union refused to go along with the plan and the Soviet commander refused to admit UNTCOK into North Korea. Instead, UNTCOK verified elections held in the American zone in May 1948 and observed the convening of the South Korean National Assembly, in which one-third of the seats were left vacant for future North Korean representatives. The Soviet Union vetoed repeatedly the Republic of Korea's (ROK) application for membership in the United Nations.

Meanwhile, the Democratic People's Republic of Korea (DPRK) was established in September 1948 in North Korea and a Supreme People's Council elected. In September 1948, the Soviet Union announced the withdrawal of its troops. North Korea applied for admission to the United Nations in 1949, but the application was not considered on grounds that the ROK was the only legal government in Korea. In May 1949, the United States began withdrawing its forces from South Korea. Within eight months, in June 1950, North Korea attempted to reunify that country militarily by invading South Korea. The United Nations Commission for Korea, UNCOK, which had replaced UNTCOK, immediately reported the invasion to the secretary-general.

In the Security Council, the United States offered a resolution demanding the immediate cessation of hostilities and the withdrawal of North Korean forces to the 38th parallel. This passed unanimously but only because of the Soviet boycott of the Council, which had been going on since March over the issue of the seating of the People's Republic of China. Two days later the Security Council urged all members of the United Nations to assist the South Koreans. President Truman had already ordered United States forces into action in support of the ROK.

On July 7, 1950, the Security Council established a unified military command under the direction of the United States General Douglas MacArthur. MacArthur proceeded with the apparent goal of conquering North Korea and thereby reunifying that country. In August, however, the Soviet representative returned to the Security Council and began to use the veto to end that body's participation in the conflict. At the instigation of the United States, a Uniting for Peace Resolution was adopted by the General Assembly on November 3, 1950. The resolution stated that if the Security Council failed to act in a serious conflict because of a permanent member's veto, the issue could then be tranferred to the General Assembly for consideration. A two-thirds majority of the General Assembly could then recommend—but not require—collective action. The resolution thus circumvented the veto and brought the General Assembly into the global security process directly. At this same time, the General Assembly also created the United Nations Commission for the Unification and the Rehabilitation of Korea (UNCURK) to supervise reconstruction once North Korea had been defeated.

In October, General MacArthur's forces crossed the 38th parallel and advanced almost to the Chinese border. Despite warnings from the People's Republic of China (PRC), MacArthur insisted upon continuing his advance. By the end of November, PRC forces launched major attacks against MacArthur's forces. The PRC eventually captured Seoul, the ROK capital. Not until March 1951 did the opposing armies stabilize their positions close to the 38th parallel. In June, the United States suggested that it might agree to a restoration of the pre-June 1950 territorial lines. The Soviet ambassador to the United Nations indicated that the terms might be acceptable to the other side. Cease-fire and armistice negotiations began on July 10, 1951. Not until Stalin's death in March 1953 did the negotiations accomplish very much. Thereafter, with India serving as a third party on the issue of prisoner repatriation, negotiations proceeded rapidly. In July, an armistice agreement was signed.

Such was the first and only attempt by the United Nations to implement the theory of collective security. It was a costly and tragic test from the point of view of human suffering and wasted resources. However, the Korean experience was not without its important institutional consequences for peacekeeping. Under the Uniting for Peace Resolution, the General Assembly and the secretary-general would henceforth be regularly and significantly involved in the United Nations' peacekeeping functions. The Security Council veto would frequently be circumvented. Although handicapped by the ad hoc character of most peacekeeping missions, their limited budgets, and the necessity of using temporary military advisors for their management, the secretary-general and the United Nations bureaucracy could expect to and did accumulate a substantial body of experience regarding the administration of peacekeeping missions. Korea, like the Berlin airlift in 1948, was another instance in which the United States made explicit its determination, even at great cost, to draw the line against breaches of trust and the peace. Korea, in many respects, tested the mettle and resolve of the postwar world's new leadership and produced a stalemate. The battlefield did indeed reflect the conditions in the Security Council. New approaches to keeping peace in this world now had to be found.

## Vietnam

For Americans at the time, Vietnam was an extension of the Korean conflict. Ho Chi Minh and the Vietminh (Vietnam Independence League) came into the consciousness of American leaders as one of many crisis centers developing in connection with the Cold War. Most were unfamiliar with the thousands of years of conflict and war among the heterogeneous populations of Indochina. Even the French conquest of the various kingdoms of Indochina during the latter part of the nineteenth century seemed like distant history.

During World War II, the Japanese exercised control over Indochina through the Vichy French governor-general. This control was tenuous because of guerrilla war being carried on against it by Ho Chi Minh, who had organized the Vietnamese Communist Party in 1930, and General Vo Guyen Giap, who drew together a liberation army in 1944. Anticipating their own defeat in 1945, the Japanese dismissed the Vichy French and set up governments under the kings of Cambodia and Laos and the Emperor of Annam, Bao Dai. With the surrender of Japan, Bao Dai abdicated, and the Vietminh proclaimed the Democratic Republic of Vietnam in September of that year. Ho Chi Minh became president and began to extend his control into the south.

Under the Potsdam agreements, the Nationalist Chinese were to accept the Japanese surrender in Indochina north of the 16th parallel, and the British to the south. Meanwhile, the French were to reestablish themselves in Cambodia and Laos. Ho Chi Minh negotiated with the French and won their recognition on condition that the Republic of Vietnam, together with Cambodia and Laos, would be part of an Indochinese federation and a member of a French Union. Negotiations broke down when French forces tried to take control of Vietnamese customs in November 1946. In December, the Vietminh army attacked French garrisons and an eight-year war began.

The Cold War gradually incorporated this Vietnamese nationalist movement into a working section of international Communism. American policy then became one of bolstering French efforts to regain control in Indochina. In May 1950, a United States mission of inquiry to Vietnam recommended $23 million in economic assistance and $15 million in military aid to the French. A few days after the outbreak of the Korean War in June, President Truman authorized a shipment of aircraft to Indochina and subsequently sent $119 million in further military aid. In 1952, the amount of military aid was increased to $300 million. The Communists in North Vietnam and the Communist-led Vietminh of Hanoi were now perceived in the United States as part and parcel of a unified Communist attack upon the free world, directed by a Moscow-Peking collaboration. One source of confusion in this perception of a Communist monolith was the breaking up of old empires under pressure of nationalist movements. Where did international Communism end and indigenous nationalism begin?

By 1953, the United States was financing approximately one-third of the French war effort in Indochina. When President Eisenhower and Secretary of State John Foster Dulles came to office, they anticipated a Chinese Communist intervention in the Indochina war in the same manner as in North Korea. They, too, increased American military assistance to France until, in 1954, it reached $1 billion.

The cycle of fear and distrust deepened with each development in the war. With Eisenhower and Dulles expecting a North Korean style invasion and the United States supporting France to the tune of one-half the latter's cost in the Indochina war, the Vietminh defeat of the French at Dien Bien Phu in March 1954 produced a profound crisis for the Eisenhower administration. Vice President Nixon and the Joint Chiefs of Staff recommended direct military intervention on the side of the French. President Eisenhower rejected the plan for intervention and instead encouraged the work of the Geneva Conference.

At that conference were France, China, the United States, Great Britain, the Soviet Union, the governments of North and South Vietnam, Cambodia, and Laos. The Geneva agreements created Laos, Cambodia, and Vietnam. In Vietnam, the French forces were to withdraw below the 17th parallel and the Vietminh were to move to its north. Each side would be responsible for the administration of its half of Vietnam until an election, to be held in July 1956, could reunite the country under a single government. The Geneva agreements were to be implemented under the supervision of an International Control Commission consisting of Canada, India, and Poland. The United States did not sign the Geneva Accords but, instead, pledged to refrain from disturbing the settlement and unilaterally promised to view any violation with grave concern.

Within weeks, however, the United States concluded the formation of the Southeast Asia Treaty Organization whose eight members pledged themselves to the collective defense of each other and the new states of Cambodia, Loas, and *South* Vietnam. Ho Chi Minh complained that SEATO was a violation of the spirit of the Geneva Accords but, expecting to win a majority in the 1956 election, nonetheless withdrew his forces to the north.

In October 1955, Ngo Dinh Diem, with the support of the United States, replaced the government of Emperor Bao Dai, declared the formation of the Republic of Vietnam (South Vietnam), and appointed himself president. Meanwhile, Ho Chi Minh had concluded mutual aid agreements with the Soviet Union and the People's Republic of China.

Even before he became president, Diem had taken the position that, since the new Republic of Vietnam had not signed the Geneva Accords, he was not committed to permitting elections in 1956, particularly since there was no opportunity to campaign in the North. The United States not only supported this position, but also began a program of aid to Diem. Thus, no Vietnamese elections were held in July 1956. The North Vietnamese prepared for guerrilla warfare in the South. The Eisenhower administration began to send large numbers of military advisers—almost 1,000 by 1960—to help Diem. Mutual distrust was now overwhelming and escalation of the conflict in Vietnam took on a life of its own.

When John Kennedy came to the presidency, he found the Vietnamese policy of the United States long on military action and short on political and diplomatic effort. Dissident elements in South Vietnam had formed a National Liberation Front to overthrow Diem. As the NLF was increasingly reinforced by North Vietnamese supplies and troops trained for guerrilla warfare, Diem's situation became desperate. Kennedy's military advisers, as might be expected, analyzed the situation in military terms and strongly recommended an increase in military advisers and supplies. By authorizing the dispatch of additional advisers, Kennedy breached the understandings of the Geneva Accords. He sent Vice President Lyndon Johnson on an Asian tour that conspicuously included South Vietnam. Recognizing that Diem was the sole representative of the American interest, Johnson joined the military in urgently recommending additional military aid. Kennedy also sent two trusted advisers—General Maxwell Taylor and Walter Rostow—to investigate the situation. Their advice was to send United States combat troops and use American airpower. Instead, Kennedy authorized an additional 15,000 military advisers and substantial amounts of military equipment. What Kennedy and his advisers failed to appreciate was the extent to which the Soviet Union and Communist China were willing to augment their aid to the North Vietnamese and, through them, to the Vietcong. This phase ended with the assassination of President Diem, and three weeks later, of President Kennedy.

The Johnson administration undertook a program of military escalation which was matched by Soviet-Chinese aid to North Vietnam and an expansion of Communist guerrilla warfare in the South. When Clark Clifford succeeded Robert McNamara as secretary of defense, Clifford undertook a reevaluation of American involvement in Vietnam and urged the President to reconsider the escalatory process. Efforts to bring in the United Nations were made, only to run into the facts that Vietnam was not a member of the United Nations and the United States refused to allow the Soviet veto to become another hurdle. Nearly 545,000 American troops were then in Vietnam. Massive but ineffectual bombing raids against the North were the order of the day. The loss in American lives, which reached 56,000 before the American withdrawal, was touching an increasing number of American homes. American popular opinion was deeply divided and chances for Johnson's renomination and reelection in 1968 disappeared.

It next became the task of President Nixon and his principal adviser, Henry Kissinger, to "Vietnamize" the war by turning combat operations over to the South Vietnamese and gradually withdrawing American troops. Nixon and Kissinger undertook negotiations with the North Vietnamese, the Soviet Union, and the Chinese, each at a different level. The Soviet Union was interested in promoting detente. The Chinese, who had just been seated at the United Nations in the place of the Nationalist Chinese as result of United States acceptance of a new arrangement, were also interested in disengagement. Thus, in time for the 1972 presidential election, Kissinger was able to announce that "peace was at hand."

In January 1973, a Vietnamese cease-fire was arranged under the terms of Paris Accords. The International Control Commission was revived to supervise the truce until an election could take place. However, cease-fire violations continued. Some 48,000 soldiers were killed during the first year of the "cease-fire." By the end of 1974, this figure reached 75,000. After Nixon resigned, President Gerald Ford found himself in the difficult position of withdrawing the last American troops, watching the North Vietnamese army mount a devastating offensive, and witnessing the South Vietnamese forces crumble and surrender. At the same time, the Communist Khmer Rouge swept to power in Cambodia. The Vietnam War cost more than 56,000 American lives, hundreds of thousands of Vietnamese dead, and more than $150 billion. What had started as a sideshow to the Korean war as far as the United States was concerned, ended as an American military and political defeat and an extension of the Vietnamese version of Communism across Southeast Asia.

From the perspective of international peacekeeping, the lessons were profound. First, any war that engaged the direct interest of one of the superpowers could not end in victory for either side. Vietnam underscored the experience in Korea. Second, the failure to involve the United Nations in the resolution of the conflict prevented public investigation of the true circumstances of the war and denied the conflict a substantial moderating force. The large role of deception in the conduct of all parties, particularly the

American leadership, deeply divided American and world opinion over the legitimacy of United States involvement. Third, nuclear bombs and sophisticated military technology were demonstrably meaningless against guerrilla warfare. American military inventiveness was seriously discredited by the experience. Fourth, the world had developed a two-tier international security system: one for the nuclear superpowers and the other for the nonnuclear members of the world community. At the superpower level, the balance-of-terror kept the peace. At the nonnuclear level, conflict resolution would have to turn increasingly to the new and expanding United Nations peacekeeping process. Finally, and most significantly, rapprochement and detente among the leaders of the world's most powerful nations—the United States, the Soviet Union, and the Peoples's Republic of China—was, by the end of the 1970s, the principal potential solvent of political distrust among the competing political elites of the world. With trust increasing, the international future seemed to depend largely on their capacity to develop systems of institutionalized trust. Their basic approach was to promote United Nations peacekeeping and speed up the pace of arms control negotiations.

## Suez: U.N. Emergency Force (UNEF-I)

In 1952, a coup led by Egyptian officers overthrew the regime of King Farouk and installed Gamal Abdel Nasser as president. Having distinguished himself in the Palestine war, Nasser vowed to lead the cause of Arab nationalism and return the million Palestinians who had been displaced by that war to their homeland. He soon prohibited Israeli ships from passing through the Suez Canal and began to harass Israeli ships going through the Straits of Tiran. By 1955, Israeli-Egyptian relations were at the point of explosion. France was also perturbed by Nasser on grounds that he was providing aid to Algerian revolutionaries. Meanwhile, under an agreement that came into effect in 1954, the British evacuated the Suez Canal Zone, only to have Nasser nationalize the Canal on July 26, 1956. Because the Suez Canal had been their lifeline to the Far East, the British led the protest of maritime nations, but to no avail.

Leaders of the three offended nations concluded a secret arrangement that called for an Israeli attack against Egypt to be followed by a Franco-British intervention for "peacekeeping" purposes. On October 29, 1950, Israel launched its attack in the Sinai. An Anglo-French ultimatum called for a cease-fire and a pullback of forces. When the United States introduced a similar resolution in the Security Council, however, the British and French representatives vetoed its passage. The Soviet Union, even as its tanks entered Budapest to crush a Hungarian rebellion, sided with Nasser and threatened England and France with atomic bombs, a threat to which the United States had to respond in kind. Then, with American and Soviet acquiescence, Yugoslavia submitted a resolution in the General Assembly calling for a peacekeepig mission under the Uniting for Peace Resolution. The Assembly created the United Nations Emergency Force on November 5, 1956, and instructed it to separate Egyptian and Israeli forces and supervise a truce. Meanwhile, chagrined by the discovery of their secret strategy for overthrowing Nasser and disappointed by President Eisenhower's failure to support their objectives in the Middle East, the British and French withdrew and, in effect, turned over that sphere of influence to the Americans.

UNEF-I eventually reached a maximum of 6,000 troops, the largest military force put together by the United Nations up to that time. It was to oversee compliance with the cease-fire and armistice, supervise the withdrawal of British, French, and Israeli forces, and patrol the border and Sharm el Sheik. Contingents were sent by Brazil, Canada, Colombia, Denmark, Finland, India, Indonesia, Norway, Sweden, and Yugoslavia. For the next ten years, UNEF performed commendably until Arab terrorist groups began harassment tactics. Finally, on May 16, 1967, President Nasser formally requested that UNEF be withdrawn. Secretary-General U Thant saw no alternative but to accede to the request of a host state. At the same time, Egyptian troops and large amounts of Soviet-made military equipment were moved into the Sinai, and Nasser closed the Gulf of Aqaba to Israel.

The Suez crisis added much to the stature of United Nations peacekeeping operations. Despite brandishing their nuclear arsenals, the two superpowers had cooperated in forcing two major powers, the United Kingdom and France, to end their unilateral military intervention and step aside in favor of a United Nations Emergency Force. The size of the peacekeeping mission was substantial and was carried off successfully for a decade. Secretary-General Dag Hammarskjold took the occasion of UNEF to offer a general proposal for the creation of standby units for future peacekeeping missions. In his proposed system, Hammarskjold made no mention of the Military Staff Committee of the Security Council but rather placed the secretariat at the center of preparedness and peacekeeping operations. In fact, the secretariat was thereafter at the center of all United Nations peacekeeping missions.

UNEF not only focused the debate about United Nations preparedness but also placed substantial strain on the financial arrangements supporting peacekeeping missions. The United Nations has two methods of financing its operations: an assessment upon each member proportionate to that member's capacity to pay, and a system of voluntary contributions that any member can make for whatever purpose it designates. Under Article 19 of the Charter, members who fall in arrears in payment of assessed dues may be denied their vote in the General Assembly. Financial support of UNEF, with its 6,000 troops, became a difficult issue. How much support should come from the general budget and how much from voluntary contributions? What was to be done if a country, specifically the Soviet Union, disapproved of the peacekeeping mission; could it be forced to help finance it?

Finally, the UNEF mission was the first to be terminated abruptly at the request of a host country, raising numerous questions about how this was done. The request came unilaterally from Egypt and was implemented immediately by Secretary-General U Thant. Should not such a request receive special emergency attention by the Security Council or General Assembly? Should not the United Nations pressure the reneging party to reconsider its request?

Possibly the most important lesson of UNEF-I was that the United Nations could be trusted to organize and sustain a significant military operation. Awkwardly and suspiciously, the superpower leaders cooperated to make this possible and, not coincidentally, to alter the balance of power in the Middle East.

## Lebanon: U.N. Observation Group in Lebanon (UNOGIL)

During the mid-1950s, President Chamoun of Lebanon, only a decade and a half after Lebanese independence, assumed a strong pro-Western posture, received military aid from the United States, and generally opposed the Arab nationalism represented by Egyptian President Nasser. Pro-Nasser opponents of Chamoun were substantially aided in their cause when Egypt and Syria merged to form the United Arab Republic on February 1, 1958. Anti-Chamoun forces united during the spring of that year, issued a call for a national strike, and embarked upon civil war. The rebels won control of the Lebanese-Syrian border. They received arms and munitions from the Syrians and propaganda support from the press of the United Arab Republic. On May 13, 1958, President Chamoun asked the United States for assistance. Units of the United States Sixth Fleet were ordered to the vicinity of Lebanon. The United States also expressed its willingness to send tanks and troops into Lebanon if requested.

Chamoun next appealed to the Arab League and to the Security Council of the United Nations. On June 6, the Council established the United Nations Observation Group in Lebanon (UNOGIL) to serve as an observer mission investigating the Lebanese charges of military infiltration from Syria.

As the civil war approached a stalemate, Nasser suggested that Chamoun should step down upon completion of his term of office, General Chehab, commander of the Lebanese army, should succeed him, and Lebanon should declare amnesty for all rebels. In July, however, a revolt against the king of Iraq, who had offered to assist Chamoun, complicated the picture. The Iraqi coup was interpreted by United States policymakers as a Communist move. Therefore, when Chamoun again asked for aid, the United States landed 14,000 troops and the British 2,000 in Lebanon. On July 15, the United States requested an emergency session of the United Nations Security Council, but this meeting was predictably deadlocked. Secretary-General Hammarskjold, exercising an unprecedented prerogative, asserted that he discerned an "implicit consensus" for expanding UNOGIL and that he would proceed to do so, subject to review by the Security Council.

The crisis subsided when, on July 31, General Chehab was elected to succeed Chamoun. Several days later, Chehab requested that American troops leave Lebanon. On August 8, the General Assembly passed a resolution instructing the secretary-general to have UNOGIL facilitate the United States withdrawal.

UNOGIL never exceeded 214 officer-observers supplied by 21 nations. Its presence in the area did serve as a constraining influence upon the parties, but, as in the Kashmir case, the number of observers was extremely small for so extended a border.

The Lebanese crisis was particularly interesting in that at least five "conflict managers" became involved. The Security Council took notice of the conflict but remained inert for all practical purposes. The General Assembly was actively concerned, creating UNOGIL, but held back while other peacekeeping moves were taking place. The secretary-general assumed an unusual administrative prerogative by undertaking to expand UNOGIL upon his own initiative. The United States and the United Kingdom sent troops, upon the request of the Lebanese president, to maintain order. However, the final solution originated with the fifth conflict manager, Nasser and the Arab League. The concept of regional peacekeeping was importantly implemented in this case and would be again in the future. Regional peacekeeping assumes that the members of a regional organization such as the Arab League prefer to handle their own conflicts without "outside intervention." This motivation was particularly strong in the

Lebanese case because of Nasser's claim to leadership of the cause of Arab nationalism.

## The Congo: U.N. Operation in the Congo (UNOC)

For a decade following World War II, Belgian policy in the Congo was primarily concerned with economic and social programs. Political change was expected to come at some unspecified future time. The Congo was peaceful until 1955 when various nationalist movements demanded independence. Riots broke out in January 1959, and the Belgians, hoping to avoid the kind of costly struggle the French had experienced in Algeria, set June 30, 1960, as the date of independence.

The Congo consisted of six provinces, each inhabited by numerous tribes. Various nationalist political parties were essentially coalitions of tribes. Joseph Kasavubu's party was based in the Leopoldville province and preferred a loose federation of the provinces. Patrice Lumumba's party sought a centralized governmental system and was extremely critical of tribalism. The dominant party in Katanga province was led by Moise Tshombe, whose principal aim was to prevent the exploitation of the province's vast mineral wealth by the rest of the Congo. Belgian mining companies were also extremely interested in protecting their large investment in Katanga's extractive industry.

At independence, Kasavubu became president and Lumumba prime minister. However, the army continued to be led by Belgian officers, and this arrangement provoked a mutiny within a week of independence. Disorder spread, Belgian residents began to leave the country, and the Belgians sent in paratroops to reinforce their bases in Leopoldville and Katanga provinces. The second week after independence, Tshombe declared Katanga's secession from the new nation.

On July 12, 1960, Kasavubu and Lumumba requested aid from the United Nations. The Security Council passed a resolution asking Belgium to withdraw its troops and authorizing the secretary-general to provide military assistance until such time as the Congolese government could restore internal order with its own security forces. Secretary-General Hammarskjold established the Organization des Nations Unis au Congo (ONUC), whose troops eventually numbered 20,000 drawn from twenty-five nations. ONUC was almost entirely supplied by the United States and the United Kingdom.

ONUC found a difficult situation. The Belgians were refusing to withdraw. Tshombe said that U.N. troops would not be permitted in Katanga. The Soviet Union had begun to send arms and equipment to the Lumumba faction. Kasavubu dismissed Lumumba. Lumumba charged Kasavubu with high treason. By September 14, Joseph Mobutu, commander of the Congolese army, announced that the army had taken over the government.

At the United Nations, the Soviet Union vigorously opposed the entire Congolese operation, hoping thereby to place itself on the side of African nationalist movements, of which Lumumba's party was a leading exemplar. It was also a Soviet intention to disrupt the Belgian, British, and French effort to protect their economic interests in Katanga. Tshombe had considerable resources with which to resist Soviet and Lumumba maneuvers: substantial revenues from mining taxes; Belgian and other foreign mercenaries in large numbers to lead his troops; considerable support in Europe and the United States; and support from international business interests.

On August 24, 1961, the Kasavubu-Mobutu government of the Congo ordered the expulsion of non-Congolese from Katanga's security forces and, for this, asked for the assistance of ONUC. Within a few days, ONUC began to arrest and evacuate the mercenaries. On September 17, Secretary-General Hammarskjold was killed in a plane crash en route to negotiate with Tshombe. Soon after, a cease-fire was concluded between ONUC and the Katanga government. However, attacks on ONUC forces continued, and the Security Council, with Britain and France abstaining, authorized Acting Secretary-General U Thant "to take vigorous action, including the use of requisite measures of force, if necessary," to arrest and deport the mercenaries. After heavy fighting, the United States ambassador and the United Nations Special Representative, Dr. Ralph Bunche, succeeded in bringing Congolese Prime Minister Adoula and Katanga's Tshombe together on an eight-point unity agreement. Fighting broke out once again, however. ONUC, with American backing and Soviet withdrawal, finally brought the Katanga secession to an end in January 1963. ONUC forces remained on duty, at the request of the Congolese central government, until June 30, 1964.

ONUC was the largest peacekeeping force to that date and the most expensive, costing the United Nations $402 million. The mission precipitated the first serious financial crisis at the United Nations. On January 1, 1964, the Soviet Union became legally delinquent because of its refusal to pay assessed peacekeeping dues. Ten other nations were also in arrears, and France soon became an eleventh. Under Article 19, the penalty for nonpayment of dues was loss of vote in the General Assembly. The American position was that Article 19 should be imposed at the opening of the next General Assembly session. The Soviet Union threatened to withdraw from the United Nations. Most members of the General Assembly sought to avoid a confrontation.

The United States wanted peacekeeping costs to be widely shared. The Soviet Union was pressing for the return of all peacekeeping functions to the exclusive authority of the Security Council where its veto could carry decisive weight. As a way out of the stalemate, the General Assembly created in February 1965 the Special Committee on Peacekeeping Operations, better known as the Committee of 33. The 33 members were widely representative politically and geographically. Their charge was to examine the entire question of peacekeeping operations. In time, the Committee of 33 became the forum in which the superpowers addressed themselves directly to a large range of peacekeeping issues. Because of veto and mutual distrust, the Military Staff Committee of the Security Council failed to provide such a forum two decades earlier. The Committee of 33 provided an acceptable place in which to set down systematically the issues in dispute. In the drawn-out process of institutionalizing a function such as peacekeeping, the Committee of 33 must be viewed as an undramatic but important facilitator of international political trust.

### Cyprus: U.N. Force in Cyrus (UNFICYP)

The island of Cyprus in the Mediterranean Sea has had strategic significance for Turkey, Greece, and Great Britain over many centuries. In 1878, Turkey ceded the island to Britain for administrative purposes. The British annexed Cyprus in 1914 and established it as a Crown Colony in 1925. The population of the island is approximately four-fifths Greek and one-fifth Turkish, with intense ethnic hatreds dominating the relationship between the two.

The Greek majority have tended to favor union with Greece, *enosis*. This movement has been encouraged by the Greek government, the Greek Orthodox Church hierarchy, and, at times, the international community. In 1950, Archbishop Mikhail Makarios became the spokesman for Greek Cypriots. Turkish Cypriots, considering themselves a persecuted minority, have opposed *enosis* and rely upon the government of Turkey for the protection of their interests. Turkey has been particularly concerned about the strategic importance of Cyprus for its national defense. The British also have opposed *enosis* on grounds that it would aggravate the already serious ethnic divisions. Further, Cyprus was British headquarters for their Middle East military forces and an important part of the British line of communication to the Middle and Far East.

As time passed, these five parties to the Cyprus conflict were joined by the leadership of NATO, of which both Greece and Turkey were members, the United States, whose responsibilities in the Middle East were increasing, and the Soviet Union, whose interest lay in support of anti-imperial nationalist movements generally but, in this case, concern over the possibility that its Greek and Turkish neighbors might go to war.

In 1954, the Greek government asked the U.N. General Assembly to consider the Cyprus problem. In 1955, Greek Cypriots began attacking British buildings and residences. The British, unsuccessfully, tried to confer with Greece and Turkey. As the conflict continued, the Greeks sought self-determination, the Turks preferred partition, and the British eventually expressed a willingness to abandon their sovereignty over the island on condition that they could maintain a military base there.

In 1957, the secretary-general of NATO made an unsuccessful offer to mediate. The Greeks remained adamant about achieving *enosis*. But, in 1958, Archbishop Makarios indicated that he would settle for independence. A London Agreement was negotiated in 1959 that included a constitution and three treaties. The Treaty of Alliance involved Cyprus, Greece, and Turkey and provided for 950 Greek troops and 650 Turkish troops to be stationed on the island to train the Cypriot army. The Treaty of Guarantee permitted Britain, Greece or Turkey to act singly or collectively to maintain the independent status of the island, that is, prevent either *enosis* or partition. The Treaty of Establishment created a sovereign Cypriot republic, with the exception of two military bases to be kept under British rule. The constitution established a Cypriot president who was to be a Greek and a Cypriot vice president who was to be Turkish, each with veto power. The agreement came into effect on August 16, 1960.

Soon after, severe disagreements emerged. By December 1963, there was an outbreak of violence between the two Cypriot communities. With the acquiescence of Archbishop Makarios, the British formed a joint British-Turkish-Greek peacekeeping force and subsequently proposed a NATO peacekeeping force. Makarios preferred to involve the United Nations. When the temporary truce was broken, Turkey threatened to intervene. The British agreed to take the Cyprus matter to the Security Council on February 15, 1964. On March 4, the Council established a United Nations Force in Cyprus (UNFICYP), whose mission was to help prevent communal fighting. UNFICYP at various times ranged from 4,500 to 7,000 troops. Its mandate was extended every three to six months.

Meanwhile, both Greece and Turkey began sending arms and soldiers to the island. There was serious fighting during August

1964. A military coup in Greece in April 1967 brought in a regime strongly in favor of *enosis*. Greek Cypriot forces attacked and Turkey countered with a large-scale military intervention. Eventually, UNFICYP was able to separate the conflicting forces.

In time, Greek Cypriot extremists, impatient with Makarios' conciliatory efforts and abandonment of *enosis*, tried to assassinate him. In June 1974, Makarios began to remove army officers who were supporters of *enosis*. When he tried to remove as many as 600 Greek officers from the Cypriot National Guard, a military coup sent him into exile. On July 19, 1974, Makarios addressed the Security Council in an appeal for assistance. The British arranged talks between Turkish and Greek representatives, but on July 30, Turkey landed more than 6,000 soldiers on Cyprus and started bombing operations against the Greek Cypriots.

The failure of the military regime in Greece to accomplish *enosis* led to its resignation and the restoration of civilian government. Turkish forces meanwhile extended their occupation to the entire northern section of Cyprus, citing the 1960 Treaty of Guarantee. In August 1974, the Security Council expanded UNFICYP's responsibility in an effort to put an end to the fighting. The Turkish Cypriot zone had, in effect, partitioned the island. On February 24, 1975, a Turkish Cypriot Constituent Assembly was convened to establish the Turkish Cypriot Federated State.

Early in 1977, Makarios, reinstated as president, and Turkish Cypriot leader Denktash agreed on principles for a settlement. Cyprus was to become a sovereign, bizonal, bicommunal federal republic, with appropriate territorial adjustments to be negotiated. Under United Nations auspices and with United States encouragement, negotiations continue to this day.

U.N. peacekeeping in Cyprus, as in the Lebanese crisis, was the occasion for involvement of regional organizational representatives, in this case, NATO. The presence of UNFICYP contributed substantially over the years to the maintenance of internal order on the island. The mission rarely used force, except in self-defense, and developed a substantial intellignece network designed to discover and head off imminent violence. In more recent years, both Greece and Turkey have become increasingly solicitous of their relationships with NATO and the European Community and have been more predisposed toward settlement. The United States, as a supplier of weapons to both Greece and Turkey, has applied pressure to both sides by refraining or threatening to refrain from delivering arms. The most active center for proposals and negotiations to resolve the conflict has been the secretariat of the United Nations. Despite centuries of hatred and violence on the island, the forces of moderation and improved political trust continue to grow and the prospects for settlement improve.

## India-Pakistan: U.N. India-Pakistan Observation Mission (UNIPOM)

With the status of Kashmir still unresolved, relations between India and Pakistan worsened during 1964 and 1965. This was in part a consequence of a boundary agreement reached by China and Pakistan in which the latter claimed to represent Kashmir and in part a consequence of a renewed boundary dispute over the Rann of Kutch. Kutch was one of the princely states that had acceded to India at the time of independence. The Rann was an area of about 3,500 square miles claimed by Pakistan. In 1956, Pakistani and Indian forces clashed in the area. During 1959-1960, the two countries conducted a series of talks about this border problem. In 1965, Pakistani forces again began to patrol the area and charged India with violations of its air space. In April 1965, the Pakistani commenced a large-scale military attack.

The United Kingdom immediately offered to serve as a third party in the dispute and suggested a cease-fire. The British succeeded in bringing the parties together in the Kutch Agreement on June 30, which called for a cease-fire, troop withdrawals, and further negotiations before an ad hoc Indo-Pakistani Western Boundary Case Tribunal.

Although the conflict over Kashmir was resumed at about this same time, the Tribunal began hearings on the Kutch issue. By February 1968, it awarded 90 percent of the Rann to India and about 10 percent to Pakistan.

Meanwhile, during August 1965, Pakistani "freedom fighters" began infiltrating into Kashmir across the cease-fire line established in 1949. When Indian forces resisted, Pakistan sent its regular forces into the battle which soon became a full-scale war. Secretary-General U Thant traveled to the scene to try to initiate talks. The United States and the United Kingdom suspended their respective military aid programs to the parties.

Secretary-General U Thant officially learned of the cease-fire line violations from UNMOGIP (United Nations Military Observer Group in India and Pakistan) reports. The permanent members of the Security Council agreed that the cease-fire had to be reestablished and the Kashmir problem resolved. UNMOGIP forces were enlarged, and a new United Nations India-Pakistan Observer Mission (UNIPOM) was established to supervise troop withdrawals. However, U Thant's efforts were unsuccessful.

The initiative for third-party mediation passed to the Soviet Union, which had offered its good offices. This was followed by a conference at Tashkent, arranged by Soviet Premier Kosygin, during January 1966. The resulting Tashkent Declaration provided for troop withdrawals and repatriation of prisoners of war. UNIPOM, consisting of about 100 observers, assisted in the troop withdrawals and reestablishment of the cease-fire line. Observation of the cease-fire line was resumed by UNMOGIP when UNIPOM was terminated.

The 1965 India-Pakistan disputes once again demonstrated the usefulness of observation teams as the "eyes" of the United Nations. In this instance, the Security Council was able to intervene on the basis of the UNMOGIP report in the absence of any other complaint or information. It was, of course, impossible for the small mission to patrol the entire border. Nor could it identify an aggressor, which was unnecessary under the principal assumption of contemporary peacekeeping, that is, there are no aggressors, only equal parties to a dispute. This conflict also demonstrated the usefulness of having the United Nations in the background as others attempt mediation. In a sense, the Indians and Pakistani were thereby encouraged to "settle out of court." This led to the Western Boundary Tribunal and acceptance of the good-offices intervention of a nearby superpower, the Soviet Union. Given the territorial ambiguities, the strategic importance, and the religious emotions surrounding the India-Pakistan disputes, it was no small cooperative achievement to have the Security Council so effectively bring the parties together.

## Middle East: U.N. Emergency Force (UNEF-II)

By early 1967, Palestine guerrilla units, under the command of El Fatah and the Palestine Liberation Organization, began to escalate border attacks against Israel and step up their call for Arab unity in a war of liberation. Syria provided the principal base from which El Fatah made its forays and was itself the most radical Arab voice in the campaign against Israel. King Faisel of Saudi Arabia and King Hussein of Jordan assumed a more conservative and cautious approach. In April 1967, a major skirmish between Israel and Syria occurred. President Nasser immediately proclaimed a state of emergency for the Egyptian armed forces and consummated a defense agreement with the Syrians. As demonstrations against Israel mounted throughout the Arab world, Nasser requested that the United Nations Emergency Force, which had been stationed on the Egyptian side of the border with Israel, be withdrawn.

Secretary-General U Thant acknowledged Egypt's right, as the host country, to demand the withdrawal but referred the problem to the UNEF Advisory Committee. India and Yugoslavia, whose contingents were the largest in UNEF, expressed their desire to withdraw their contingents, which left little choice but to end the mission. The matter was bitterly debated at the United Nations as Israel and Egypt mobilized troops along their borders.

On May 22, 1967, Nasser closed the Straits of Tiran at the entrance of the Gulf of Aqaba, which in effect was a blockade of the strategic Israeli port of Elath. Israel had previously withdrawn her forces from the Straits of Tiran on condition that the Western powers would guarantee freedom of passage for Israeli shipping. Israeli appeals to Paris, London, and Washington, however, brought little response. On May 26, Nasser, in a public address, defined the issue as greater than one of territorial water; the problem was the very existence of Israel.

On June 1, General Moshe Dayan, the hero of the 1956 Sinai campaign, was appointed Israeli minister of defense. On June 2, the leader of the Palestine Liberation Organization called for a holy war to liberate Palestine. On June 5, Israel embarked upon a preemptive attack on Egyptian airfields. Within the week, Israeli forces occupied the Sinai Peninsula, the Gaza Strip, the West Bank of the Jordan River, the City of Jerusalem, and the Golan Heights. The Arabs suffered the destruction or loss of 430 planes and, 800 tanks, 15,000 troop fatalities, and the capture of 5,500 prisoners. Israel suffered about 700 dead and 40 aircraft lost. The Six Day War was a stunning defeat for the Arab states and a costly investment for the Soviet Union, whose large aid in military equipment had been either destroyed or captured by the Israelis. The outcome of the war altered the balance of power in the Middle East.

The Six Day War also demonstrated the weakness of a United Nations role if it responded to a crisis hesitantly. The Israelis ignored United Nations calls for a cease-fire until they had accomplished their military objectives. On June 9 and 10, Egypt and Syria agreed to a cease-fire to which the Israelis were now ready to subscribe. With UNEF gone, supervision of the ensuing cease-fire was placed in the hands of the United Nations Truce Supervision organization (UNTSO). The United Nations did little more than adopt principles for reconciling the Middle East conflict. The single resolution, 242, passed on November 22, 1967, called for secure and recognized boundaries for Israel in exchange for her withdrawal from occupied territories.

Meanwhile, cease-fire violations were frequent. Israel began to plan for the establishment of Jewish settlements in the occupied territories. The Soviet Union replaced the lost military hardware. Egyptian and Syrian military forces engaged in strenuous training programs. The Palestine Liberation Organization stepped up its harassments. Arab demands for the return of the occupied territories became increasingly shrill.

When Nasser died in 1970, he was succeeded by General Anwar Sadat as Egypt's president. Sadat worked assiduously to repair and coordinate Egyptian and Arab military capacity. On Yom Kippur, the Jewish Day of Atonement, that is, October 6, 1973, Egypt and Syria began a surprise attack across the Suez Canal and against the Golan Heights. Israelis literally rushed from their synagogues to the battlefield to fend off the attack. The Israelis, anticipating some early Arab military action, believed that it could be more or less readily contained. This time, the Isaelis did not want to put themselves in an unfavorable political light by preempting. What was surprising—in fact, shocking—was the competency of the Arab troops and the deadly accuracy of the Soviet-supplied ground-to-air and other missiles. The Israelis lost a near-fatal number of tanks, planes, and lives.

As casualties grew, the Soviet Union began to pour in weapons and supplies for their Arab clients. The United States airlifted similar materials to Israel. The Soviet Union then began to supply tanks and planes, and this was matched by the United States. By the second week, Israeli forces had advanced to within twenty miles of the Syrian capital and had encircled some 100,000 Egyptian troops on the East Bank in the Sinai.

On October 21, Soviet and American leaders put together a cease-fire resolution which they jointly sponsored in the Security Council. Two such calls for a cease-fire failed to end the fighting, and the Soviet Union proposed that a joint Soviet-American peacekeeping force be dispatched to the area. This proposal promptly sank in the sea of distrust that surrounded superpower relations. When the United States rejected the plan, the Soviet Union announced that it would unilaterally move its own troops in as a peacekeeping mission. President Nixon responded by placing American armed forces worldwide on military alert. The pace of escalation was fearsome.

The nonaligned nations in the Security Council offered a resolution authorizing the secretary-general to dispatch a new United Nations Emergency Force to the area. Permanent members were excluded from providing troops for the peacekeeping force but were allowed to send a few observers. The first of the 7,000-contingent UNEF-II began to arrive on October 27.

The Israelis were deeply chastened by their "victory" and President Sadat made the most of the "restored honor" of his nation. Secretary of State Henry Kissinger, who had been the key figure in the timing and conditions of the cease-fire, undertook intensive negotiations with all parties in an effort to use the new balance of power as the basis for peace negotiations. He shuttled back and forth between Jerusalem and Cairo in one of the most dramatic diplomatic missions of modern times.

In addition to UNTSO (the United Nations Truce Supervision Organization) and UNEF-II, the United Nations also put into the field a Disengagement Observer Force (UNDOF). This mission's assignment, begun in May 1974, was to observe Israeli and Syrian compliance with the disengagement agreement pertaining to the Golan Heights. UNDOF was the force that policed the demilitarized zone in that area. In addition, the United States provided 200 American civilian technicians to man the sophisticated early warning technology that was placed in the Sinai between Israeli and Egyptian forces. Distrustful of United Nations peacekeeping missions, the Israelis were comforted by this American trip-wire arrangement.

A peace process had indeed begun. By 1977, Menachem Begin, a former Zionist terrorist and hard-liner, had become prime minister of Israel. Jimmy Carter had just become president of the United States. Then, in November, President Sadat made a sudden and spectacular visit to Jerusalem and addressed the Israeli Knesset. The deed itself recognized Israeli sovereignty and initiated the long and difficult face-to-face negotiations that followed. In 1978, President Carter brought Sadat and Begin together at Camp David for an unprecedented round of summit negotiations. In 1979, a peace treaty between Egypt and Israel was signed over the objections of most Arab states and mounting threats from the Palestine Liberation Organization.

In retrospect, the Security Council peacekeeping resolutions of October 1973 were extremely important from a number of perspectives. With superpower agreement, the resolutions once again returned the peacekeeping function to the Security Council. The command of UNEF-II was vested in the secretary-general rather than the Military Staff Committee. Whereas the Soviet Union and its allies had previously been excluded from peacekeeping operations, Poland was now incorporated into the mission as a representative of the Communist bloc. Possibly of greatest significance was the Council's decision that UNEF-II, unlike other peacekeeping operations, would be supported financially as a regular expense of the United Nations to be borne by the membership in accordance with Article 17, paragraph 2. These provisions represented a significant demonstration of political trust and cooperation and a major step forward in the evolution of United Nations peacekeeping.

## Lebanon: U.N. Interim Force in Lebanon (UNIFIL)

If Israel has been battered by external attack, Lebanon has almost equally been torn by internal strife during most of its existence. The Lebanese political structure was created in 1943 when it received its independence from France. A small country with about two million population, in contrast to most of its Arab neighbors, Lebanon has a heterogeneous people consisting primarily of Maronite Christians, Shi'ite Moslems, and Sunni Moslems. Reflecting the population balance of the 1940s, the Chamber of Deputies distributed representation on a six-to-five basis between Christians and Moslems, respectively. The custom also developed that the presidency should go to a Maronite Christian, the premiership to a Sunni Moslem, and the speakership of the Chamber of Deputies to a Shi'ite Moslem. The Lebanese armed forces were carefully balanced by ethnic and religious considerations.

After the expulsion of Palestinian guerrilla units from Jordan in September 1970, southern Lebanon became the primary military base for the Palestine Liberation Organization. PLO units were large and heavily armed. In time, the Palestinian troops exceeded the total strength of the Lebanese army and remained free of Lebanese governmental control. The situation was further aggravated by the immigration of some 400,000 Palestinian refugees, adding yet another dimension to the religious and ethnic tensions within the country.

By the mid-1970s the situation in Lebanon was almost entirely out of control. Palestinian troops were actively using southern Lebanon for artillery attacks and frequent raids into Israeli territory. This brought Israeli reprisals. In the rest of the country, what had been a Maronite Christian majority was now a minority as a consequence of a dramatic growth in the Moslem population. On April 13, 1976, a Christian Phalangist attack on a bus carrying Palestinian civilians killed twenty-two of them. This ignited a civil war in which Christian forces fought Moslem elements. The Palestinian commandoes, although aligned with the Moslems, attempted to moderate the conflict. By 1977, Christians were attacking Palestinian refugee camps, and war atrocities were common.

Syria became involved in order to prevent the partition of Lebanon, a development that would possibly put a non-Arab buffer state on Israel's northern borders and create a potential ally for the Israelis. Syria was also interested in curbing the influence of the Palestine Liberation Organization in a region of vital interest to itself. Meanwhile, Israel was beginning to provide military assistance to the Christian Phalangists.

In 1977, the Arab League assigned Syria responsibility for imposing a cease-fire in Lebanon. This brought Syrian troops dangerously close to the Israeli border along southern Lebanon. Israel stepped up aid to the Maronite Christian forces as their client buffer troops in the area. As this aid escalated, the Syrians permitted the Palestinians to launch counteroffensives. By early 1978, Israel had become a de facto participant in the Lebanese civil war.

Elsewhere, President Sadat of Egypt was embarking upon his peace moves with Israel. In an attempt to block these developments, the PLO committed a series of terrorist acts. On March 12, 1978, one of these attacks was made on a bus in Tel Aviv, killing over twenty persons. On March 19, the Israelis made a large-scale attack upon Palestinian bases, landing forces in southern Lebanon and preparing to remain there as long as necessary.

Condemnation of the Israeli action came quickly at the United Nations. An American resolution, passed on March 21, asserted that Lebanese sovereignty must be respected and the Israeli military action cease. A United Nations Interim Force in Lebanon (UNIFIL) was created to maintain peace in the area. Thus, the Arabs were able to achieve an early Israeli withdrawal through political means at the U.N., the Lebanese were able to retain their sovereignty, and the Israelis, although apparently set back by the United Nations action, succeeded in having a United Nations peacekeeping force provide yet another buffer at its most exposed border in the north.

On March 23, the first units of a 4,000-man UNIFIL force arrived in Lebanon. From the outset, UNIFIL troops were greeted as targets to be shot at by virtually all parties to the conflict. After all, no one ever promised that United Nations peacekeeping would take place in a rose garden. They were the smallest, least armed, and most politically constrained military unit in the area. Yet, in time, UNIFIL was able to defuse much of the fighting.

## Issues and Prospects for Peacekeeping

Numerous institutional trends can be discerned from the United Nations peacekeeping experience thus far, as sampled in the preceding case studies. The following recapitulation of the new institutionally relevant developments in each case reveals the accretion of organizational behaviors, political precedents, and formalization of expectations that has taken place since the founding of the United Nations.

Greece:

(a) Charter's assignment of peacekeeping function to the Security Council is assumed for the first time by General Assembly.

**(b)** Neutrality of United Nations observers is established.

**(c)** UNSCOB investigations and reports demonstrate effectiveness of publicity as a counter to covert operations (of Russia, in this case).

Palestine:

**(a)** United Nations recommends conditions for creating a sovereign nation (Israel).

**(b)** General Assembly is an effective third-party mediator in armistice negotiations.

**(c)** Implementation of armistice is assigned to United Nations. Exclusion of superpowers from UNTSO is seen as assuring neutrality.

Indonesia:

**(a)** Dutch consider Indonesian independence a domestic problem. Issue of United Nations jurisdiction in the conflict is raised and resolved in favor of United Nations.

**(b)** United Nations again recommends creation of a sovereign nation (United States of Indonesia).

**(c)** United Nations assumes a good-offices role.

**(d)** Evidence that the absence of superpower disagreement facilitates conflict resolution.

Kashmir:

**(a)** United Nations-supervised plebiscite recommended.

**(b)** Importance of sustained external pressure for continuation of negotiations is demonstrated.

Korea:

**(a)** Risks and costs of classic collective security "police" operation are demonstrated.

**(b)** Uniting for Peace Resolution redefines function of peacekeeping and enlarges role of General Assembly.

**(c)** Evidence that intense superpower involvement on opposing sides assures stalemate of the conflict.

Vietnam:

**(a)** Demonstrated the risks and costs of excluding the United Nations from a third party role.

Suez:

**(a)** A major military role assigned to the Secretary-General.

**(b)** Financing of United Nations peacekeeping missions emerges as a serious difficulty.

**(c)** Unilateral termination of a peacekeeping mission emerges as another serious difficulty.

Lebanon:

**(a)** Regional peacekeeping mission established (by Arab League).

Congo:

**(a)** Largest armed peacekeeping mission to date.
**(b)** Led to serious financial crisis and establishment of Committee of 33 at United Nations.

Cyprus:

**(a)** Outstanding intelligence work by United Nations peacekeeping mission contributes to reduction of communal strife.

Indian-Pakistan:

**(a)** Evidence that superpower cooperation may facilitate conflict resolution.

Middle East:

**(a)** Soviet Union proposes a joint superpower peacekeeping force, which is rejected.
**(b)** Security Council assumes principal role in setting peacekeeping mission with superpowers excluded but a member of the Soviet bloc (Poland) represented on the mission.

Lebanon:

**(a)** United Nations peacekeeping mission employed as counter to guerrilla (PLO) operations.

Several generalizations about the United Nations peacekeeping experience should be made. First, regardless of its military weakness, the United Nations has provided a vital third-party role in an impressive number of conflict cases. Whether the Security Council, the General Assembly, or the secretary-general, at least one organ of the world body has been available as a channel of communication, a focus of publicity, and a source of mediatory pressure for most major international conflicts since its founding. It has even served this function during confrontations between the superpowers.

Second, the United Nations experience has demonstrated the critical importance of timely intervention between parties locked in military combat. The United Nations has provided the prime influence for bringing a cessation of military violence and a transfer of the conflict to the negotiation table.

Third, United Nations peacekeeping has become a widely shared international activity. When the world's major powers cooperate, peacekeeping functions are usually carried off promptly and smoothly. When the major powers are at opposite ends of the argument, the middle and nonaligned powers are nonetheless able to impelement significant initiatives.

Perhaps most important, as power within the United Nations has dispersed from an American-dominated organization to a bipolar and then a multipolar balance, the occasions for confrontation, fear, and distrust have lessened in frequency and intensity. As the representatives of national elites have become preoccupied with arguments and decisions regarding when and how to employ peacekeeping missions, they also have developed a certain clarity about the nature of this function and a substantial degree of camaraderie about surmounting the difficulties associated with it. Three decades of United Nations peacekeeping may seem militarily unimpressive to those who equate order with might. However, if we could design an objective measure of political trust, we would undoubtedly find substantial correlation between the United Nations peacekeeping experience and the expansion of trust among the world's leaders. The three decades of peacekeeping have been three decades of confidence-building and institutional development.

The basic peacekeeping contract is, as we have seen, Chapter VII of the United Nations Charter. While the words continue to read as a collective security mandate, the practicalities of international politics and history have converted them into a set of peacekeeping guidelines. Words and guidelines, however, have raised issues of implementation. A brief survey of some of these issues will make explicit many of the political objectives and dilemmas that are inherent in the function as prescribed in Chapter VII.

*Who authorizes?* Chapter VII declares that the Security Council shall "determine" when a threat to the peace warrants action by the United Nations. The 1950 Uniting for Peace Resolution allows the General Assembly to assume that responsibility when the Security Council does not. Under Article 99, the secretary-general may not only bring to the attention of either or both bodies any threat to the peace but may, upon his own initiative, investigate, observe, report, and offer his good offices as initial peacekeeping measures in any crisis. The charter also welcomes regional and local peacekeeping interventions. This has been variously interpreted as including actions by regional organizations, such as NATO or the Arab League, as well as the good offices of major powers in whose sphere of influence the conflict may occur, as in the case of the Soviet Union's assistance to India and Pakistan at Tashkent in 1966.

This many potential sources of peacekeeping intervention in international conflicts is in marked contrast to the situation prior to the Congress of Vienna in 1815. Today, it is difficult to conceive of a serious conflict that could escape notice, fail to receive prompt attention, or avoid being subjected to the conciliatory pressures of the international community. In a profoundly important way, so many peacekeepers and peacemakers are reassuring to competing national leaders who must occasionally engage in brinkmanship. The high probability of such intervention was part of the Israeli military calculation when it embarked upon a preemptive strike in 1967. Similarly, it must have been a factor in the Egyptian planning in 1973. Each side could be positive that no war between them would be allowed to last longer than a matter of days.

There is some dispute over which of these many institutional agencies has the prime prerogative and responsibility for peacekeeping. In this debate, the United States has been a loose constructionist in its interpretation of Chapter VII. The American premise is that *any* agency and *anybody* who can bring a military engagement to an end should have the right to do so by peaceful means. It was the United States that sponsored the Uniting for Peace Resolution that has become the basis for the enlargement of the General Assembly's involvement in peacekeeping operations. The United States has also supported several plans for broadening and regularizing the military management responsibilities of the secretary-general. On the other hand, the Soviet Union has been a strict constructionist regarding Chapter VII. According to the Soviet view, the Charter places responsibility for collective security with the Security Council, and that is where it should be exercised. In this connection, the Soviet Union has from time to time recommended full activation of the Military Staff Committee and the assignment of serious functions to it. Implicit in the Soviet position, of course, is the special veto prerogative that it may exercise as a permanent member of the Council. As the exercise of the veto declines and the conditions of detente improve, we may anticipate that the superpowers and other major powers may cooperate more intensively in helping carry out the United Nations peacekeeping and collective security functions. Signs of this have already appeared in UNEF-II, as noted earlier. We shall return to this tendency in the next chapter.

Those favoring a large peacekeeping role for the General Assembly rest their case upon several propositions. Their first argument usually is that there can be no veto power on the question of a breach of or threat to the peace. A military crisis is a military crisis, and those who refuse to face up to it must be considered a party to it. Modern wars may lead too directly and too readily to the ultimate catastrophe. There is no room for naysayers. Second, the General Assembly is populated by middle and smaller powers, and these are the nations most likely to profit from a resolution of serious conflicts as well as most likely to participate in peacekeeping missions. Third, the members of the General Assembly tend to have an easier and more varied relationship with the secretary-general, who has acquired most of the management responsibilities for peacekeeping missions. Fourth, there could be those serious confrontations between the major powers that could be headed off only with the authority of the full membership of the international community, and the General Assembly is where that community is best mobilized for such a grave task.

It should not be forgotten that a major source of authority for a peacekeeping mission comes from the parties in conflict themselves. Two features of contemporary peacekeeping are that the consent of the parties is essential and that the peacekeeping mission remain in the field only so long as that consent continues. Yet the experience with UNEF-I in 1967 raised serious doubt about the propriety of unilateral actions by a host government. A demand for withdrawal of a peacekeeping mission should, it is contended, be immediately referred to the organ that authorized the mission in the first place, that is, the Security Council or the General Assembly.

*When may an authorization be made?* This question addresses the issues of procedure and immediacy of response. The usual course has been for a party to complain to the Security Council. If the Security Council fails to respond, the matter may be taken to the General Assembly under the Uniting for Peace Resolution. If a regional organization or major power is interested in interceding in the conflict, this must be taken into account. If a crisis is imminent and time is of the essence, the secretary-general may put it on the agenda in the absence of any other complainant. The facts of the case, usually difficult to ascertain in the heat of an international confrontation, must be put together authoritatively and objectively as a basis for the judgment to send or not to send a peacekeeping force. These and other procedural requirements take time, staff, and effort, all of which may be in very short supply at the moment of crisis.

The problem of timing is perhaps the most significant. Since surprise attacks are so much a feature of military advantage, it is rare for a party to announce an intended military action: one such rare case was the invasion of Vietnam in 1979 by the People's Republic of China "to teach the former a lesson." Speed of response and timing of an intervention may make all the difference in the outbreak and course of a military conflict. Elaborate and prolonged institutional procedures of decision making are hardly effective responses. The need for an immediate response capability raises a number of extremely difficult issues. Should United Nations peacekeeping missions consist of standing military forces instead of the standby forces now employed? Should an executive such as the secretary-general be allowed, as is the American president, for example, to order peacekeeping forces into action at a moment's notice? The issues have generated several proposals and much debate.

In 1948, the first secretary-general, Trygve Lie, proposed the formation of a United Nations Guard. He conceived of the Guard as a standing unit of the secretariat, available for such operational duties as protecting United Nations property and personnel, patrolling cease-fire zones, or supervising elections. He proposed an initial force of only 800 international volunteers, 300 of whom would be permanently located at U.N. headquarters. He anticipated that the guard might eventually number between 1,000 to 5,000 men. He denied that the guard would be a substitute for the enforcement army that the Military Staff Committee was presumably responsible for creating. The Lie plan found absolutely no support. The major powers had already reached a consensus against development of standing international forces for the United Nations.

In 1958, Secretary-General Hammarskjold prepared a Summary Study of the UNEF-I experience. It was a through going statement of all of the requirements and issues associated with the development of a peacekeeping force that "could be activated on short notice in future emergencies."[3] The Summary Study and its recommendations were never approved. The Soviet Union distrusted any such plan; other nations were concerned about the financial burdens; the United States wanted to remain free to send in the Marines unilaterally, and so on. Instead, Hammarskjold began to expand the secretariat's Field Operations Service section, created by Lie in 1949. This was the staff that would increasingly absorb the civilian administrative support of peacekeeping missions. Hammarskjold also gave renewed attention to the preparation of standby agreements with a substantial number of nations. If enough nations were willing to keep peacekeeping units in full preparedness for immediate assignment in a crisis, such standby units could possibly circumvent the problem of immediacy of response.

*Who may participate?* It was the obvious assumption of the authors of the United Nations Charter that the members of the Security Council, particularly the permanent members, would provide the forces necessary to punish an aggressor or maintain the peace. According to Chapter VII, other nations would be invited to help. The Cold War and the Korean War effectively set aside that assumption. Instead, peacekeeping missions authorized by the Security Council or the General Assembly came to be manned by troops volunteered by a slowly expanding company of nations. At first, the Nordic powers—Sweden, Norway, Denmark, and Finland—were the principal providers. Equipment, supplies, and finances came chiefly from the United States and the United Kingdom. Canada, the Netherlands, Austria, Iran, New Zealand, Italy, and others began to develop special peacekeeping units during the 1960s. These nations made standby agreements with the secretary-general and have been called to duty over the years.

In more recent years, there has been concern that participation in peacekeeping missions be widely distributed among the five regions of the world. This was explicitly sought in the composition of UNEF-II, which included a member of the Communist bloc. Calling up peacekeeping units from all parts of the world has the distinct symbolic purpose of giving such forces an aura of universality and worldwide support. Recruitment from such dispersed sources also tends to spread the opportunities for gaining peacekeeping experience and insights. Further, participation tends to reinforce middle and small power commitment to the United Nations generally.

The question of participation by the permanent members of the Security Council continues to be a touchy one. Initially, distrust between the superpowers ran so deep that each side was certain the other would become a spoiler in any peacekeeping mission if given the opportunity to introduce its own troops. With occupied Eastern Europe and Berlin in mind, the West was particularly sensitive to Soviet reluctance to remove its military forces once they have set foot in a community. However, during the debate over Resolution 340 of October 1973, in which UNEF-II was established, several of the permanent members indicated a desire to participate in future peacekeeping missions. As the prospects for such participation increase over the years, United Nations peacekeeping missions may assume some of the characteristics of military alliances in which commanders and troops must learn how to work together, employ standardized equipment, and coordinate their implementation of specific missions. Such a development, particularly as it tends to involve substantial military cooperation between the superpowers, is likely to be a major step toward the centralization of world military institutions whose analogue we have observed in the centralization of military institutions within nations.

Meanwhile, middle-sized nations are likely to continue to provide most of the peacekeeping forces. The motivations are several and reasonable. Middle-sized nations are likely to prefer having international disputes resolved by mediation rather than by military might. Contributed troops have an opportunity to receive special training and skills in the use of specialized equipment. The costs of national contingents are reimbursed by the United Nations, resulting in a financial savings for the contributor. Participation in peacekeeping missions lends prestige and influence in both the particular crisis and in world affairs generally. Finally, such participation nurtures the image of nonalignment and a strong commitment to peace.

*What is to be contributed?* This question refers to numbers of troops, kinds and amounts of pertinent equipment, supplies and other logistical support, and financial resources. Manpower contributions have varied widely, ranging from individual officers with special skills to one or more battalions. The special nature of peacekeeping missions increasingly calls for special training. Soldiers ordinarily trained to kill must be taught how to return fire only in self-defense. Mediating and pacifying skills are particularly appropriate in many on-site situations. The gathering of evidence in investigatory or observational missions must be learned. Skills in intelligence work, particularly with respect to modern sophisticated early warning systems, is necessary. Most difficult of all is the need to function as a kind of sitting duck for unhappy extremists eager to remove peacekeepers who stand between them and their chosen enemy.

The provision of equipment and supplies for peacekeeping missions has become a high-cost item. The United States has absorbed the greatest share of this burden not only because of its desire to have missions succeed but also as part of its role as the world's principal arms supplier. The United Kingdom has been the second principal supplier. But equipment and supplies require elaborate logistical arrangments. In this area, the secretariat has developed a substantial staff and body of experience with respect to acquisition, storage, delivery, and replacement of the material needed by its peacekeeping missions.

*Who pays?* This is the unpleasant question raised most stubbornly at the conclusion of the U.N. operation in the Congo. Should the financial resources for peacekeeping be drawn from the regularly assessed funds of the United Nations, or should reliance be placed upon either a special scale of assessment or voluntary contributions? Those who resist the development of a truly international peacekeeping force with substantial autonomy will resist including peacekeeping among the regular costs of the United Nations. Mandatory financial support for missions would inhibit those who may object from using their purse strings as a means for discouraging such enterprises. Also, the universal experience with military expenditures is that they tend to become the largest item in a governmental budget, and that degree of financial support is not yet forthcoming in the United Nations. There is already serious objection to the United Nations budget of a half billion a year, even though this amount seems a pittance given the scope of the United Nations' functions.

The consensus seems to be leaning in the direction of employing *all* options: regular assessment, special assessment, and voluntary contributions. The important goal is to get the peacekeeping job done. There are those who look forward to the time when the United Nations, like any public agency, will have regular and independent sources of income, for example, royalties from ocean mining operations. However, that seems far in the future.

Once beyond the questions of financial contributions, there are other fiscal issues to be resolved. Pay scales for military personnel from different nations vary, and the question of standardizing these scales for peacekeeping missions has already been debated. Special training costs for standby units are a matter of concern. A wider sharing of the costs of equipment and supplies is likely to become a troublesome issue as the United States reduces its contribution.

*Who shall have operational control of missions?* The charter presumably assigns this duty to the Military Staff Committee, but history has given it to the secretary-general. This has been a mixed blessing. The secretary-general has been unable to gather a permanent staff of military advisers; most of the arrangements have been ad hoc. Administrative support services have been absorbed in the Field Operations Service within the secretariat. These are headquarters issues. In the field, peacekeeping missions face a more difficult real world. Many field commanders have been permitted substantial autonomy and have exercised it with consummate skill and excellent results. Their story, when fully told and appreciated, may emerge as the principal glory of United Nations peacekeeping.

This brief survey of United Nations peacekeeping describes not only some of the major examples of that experience and some of the broad issues raised in connection with its future development, it also reveals the large extent to which a great many nations and agencies have become involved in this process. Past, present, and future arrangements for peacekeeping are the continuing concern of the Security Council, the General Assembly, and the secretary-general, not to mention the Committee of 33, regional organizations, and a large number of NonGovernmental Organizations (NGOs) promotive of stronger future peacekeeping institutions. Perhaps the most immediate, yet least visible, consequence of all this activity and development is the growth in trust among world leaders that flows from such efforts. In a sense, the nations that peacekeep together are collectively more secure together. The pathway of peacekeeping, as currently practiced, may well be a direct route to collective security.

*What goals for peacekeeping?* Perhaps the most fundamental question relates to the functions to be served by the peacekeeping activities of the United Nations or, for that matter, regional and other peacekeepers. Several functions come to mind, the most important of which is the promotion of a system of institutionalized trust in world affairs.

One elementary function of peacekeeping of even the mildest sort is its inherent collective disapproval of and resistance to war and other military approaches to internation conflict. This disapproval is usually manifest in (a) Security Council or General Assembly decisions to view the particular conflict as a threat to the general peace, (b) similar decisions to investigate such conflicts and offer third-party good offices toward their resolution, (c) United Nations willingness to organize and pay for costly peacekeeping missions, and (d) sustained United Nations attention to the conflict until it does reach some degree of resolution. In the short term, such collective disapproval may seem a weak and ineffectual way of confronting serious conflicts. In the long term, however, consistent, firm, and formal world disapproval of military methods of conflict is likely to contribute significant negative reinforcement in constraining warlike behavior by competing international elites. There are those optimists who believe that such constraints are already beginning to take effect.

A second function of peacekeeping has been to hasten the termination of military hostilities. Cease-fires and truces are essential steps in moving adversaries from the battlefield to the conference table, and the implementation of cease-fires and truces requires monitoring by a peacekeeper. Clearly, conflict resolution is easier to accomplish when words and negotiations replace weapons and violence.

A third function is to strengthen, incrementally, the collective security capabilities of the United Nations As we have seen, it is already the case that successful U.N. peacekeeping missions have increased the confidence of nations in this United Nations role and have prompted many countries to assume some degree of participation in such missions. Because the United Nations so predictably and promptly expresses a peacekeeping interest in every internation conflict, it now appears that some national leaders are willing to risk military engagement on the assumption that U.N. peacekeeping intervention will keep the engagement brief.

A fourth, and perhaps most important, function of peacekeeping is the promotion of institutionalized trust in world affairs. As we have seen in an earlier chapter, institutionalized trust requires (a) predictable behavior that (b) produces positive consequences for the transactors in an exchange. Well-established and assertive third-party peacekeeping interventions by the United Nations or regional organizations such as the European Community tend to encourage predictable behavior by the adversaries in a number of ways. When a neutral third party mounts public pressure on both adversaries to negotiate rather than battle, it tends to be difficult for the adversaries to refuse; most adversaries are reluctant to be identified as the one who prefers bloodshed. Most adversaries are likely to want a cease-fire in order to preserve their military resources for another day. Finally, an adversary can respond favorably to the peacemaking good offices of a neutral third party without loss of "face" or indication of weakness before the enemy. Thus, as the United Nations and other supranational organizations persist in providing regular and reliable peacekeeping efforts and as the political habits of responding positively to such peacekeeping interventions become established, the predictability of internation conflict scenarios—from military engagement to negotiating table—will increase and strengthen the structure of international institutionalized trust.

Institutionalized trust also requires that political transactions produce positive consequences for the embattled adversary parties. Successful peacekeeping can promote the probability of such positive outcomes by making it easier and cheaper for the adversaries to negotiate the substantive issues that led to their war making. The attention of the world is likely to remain fixed on the grievances and issues until they are to some extent resolved. The formal and informal influence of outside parties is likely to encourage moderation and reasonableness in demands. The very process of negotiation improves the prospect that each side will come away from the conflict with "half a loaf," that is, something rather than nothing or everything. The more successive profitable transactions of this type, the more enduring is likely to be the trust that competing elites extend to each other and the greater their confidence in the peacekeeping institutions that facilitated the resolution of their disagreements.

# References

1. For evaluative analyses, Larry L. Fabian, *Soldiers Without Enemies: Preparing the United Nations for Peacekeeping* (Washington, D.C.:

Brookings Institution, 1971), and Indar Jit Rikhye et al., *The Thin Blue Line* (New Haven: Yale University Press, 1974).

2. Data for each case are drawn from several sources: M. D. Donelan and M. J. Grieve, *International Disputes: Case Histories 1945-1970* (New York: St. Martin's Press, 1973); Robert L. Butterworth, *Managing Interstate Conflict, 1945-74: Data with Synopses* (Pittsburgh: University of Pittsburgh Center for International Studies, 1976); John G. Stoessinger, *Why Nations Go To War* (2nd ed. New York: St. Martin's Press, 1978); *UNITAR News,* 5, no. 1 (1973), United Nations case materials collected by this author in connection with a National Science Foundation grant (1968) for an inquiry into "Integrative Consequences of Organizational Conflict Strategies."

3. U.N. General Assembly, *Official Records*, 12th sess., Sup. 1A (1957). The full Hammarskjold document is *United Nations Emergency Force: Summary Study of the Experience Derived from the Establishment and Operation of the Force,* U.N. Doc. A/3943, October 9, 1958.

# CHAPTER 7

# Arms Control: Backing into a Collective Security Alliance?

War and preparation for war are costly, risky, and primitive techniques of protection from or influence over distrusted adversaries. When antagonistic elites understand this, they often become predisposed to negotiate cheaper, less risky, and more civilized systems of political conflict resolution and mutual safety. The problem then becomes one of negotiating skill within particular contexts of events and distributions of power.

Historically, each negotiating context presents a different set of practical problems for such predisposed elites. In one context, for example, militarily victorious elites may dictate to the vanquished what new institutional arrangements are going to prevail. Usually this calls for the loser to be incorporated into the victor's system, as were the Central Powers under the League of Nations system. In another context, relatively equal or stalemated adversaries may create new institutional arrangements that usually preserve the political status quo yet afford improved opportunities for nonviolent techniques of competition and conflict management, for example, the prospects inherent in the Egyptian-Israeli peace treaty.

Another example of this latter context may be the detente policy of the two stalemated superpowers, according to which, as we have seen in the previous chapter, contemporary United Nations peacekeeping may provide one opportunity for negotiating more efficient and stable institutions of nonviolent conflict resolution while, as we shall discuss in this chapter, arms control negotiations may present an opportunity for rearranging the world's military institutions so that they are less organized for destruction of the enemy and more organized for maintenance of order. The distinction between enemy-destruction and order-maintenance is not only perceptual ("them-versus-us" being reduced simply to "us") but also motivational (conflict-resolution becoming more important than victory) and organizational (management responsibilities shared by all interested parties and even by potential adversaries). If this is a valid expectation, then what is most important about contemporary arms control negotiations is the confidence-building, trust-promoting political process that they evolve rather than the specific content of any particular arms control agreement. Through successful negotiations over the years, the superpowers and their allies may be backing rather than pushing the world into a viable, efficient, and stable collective security system.

Meanwhile, the world's dominant elites function in a political-military environment that compels them to distrust each other and to prepare militarily against threatening competitors. If, however, the world's institutional arrangements for nonviolent conflict—for example, representative assemblies, party systems, judicial systems, and so on—were available, substantial, efficient, and stable, the violent techniques of elite conflict, that is, wars and revolutions, would become obsolescent because of their sheer lack of cost effectiveness. Why make war or revolution when less costly means of contest, with greater chances of victory, are available? In such a world, arms control agreements would be unnecessary and disarmament would become an issue of maintaining order rather than enemy-destroying security services. As nonviolent methods grow in scope and influence, political trust and motivation for political cooperation are also likely to thrive. But the transition from armed distrust to institutionalized trust and from pervasive conflict to sturdy cooperation is, unfortunately, a long, tedious, incremental, backsliding human process. Successfully negotiated phases of this transition may be reflected and recorded in constitutions and treaties; such documents cannot command the transition to take place.

We now turn to a review and evaluation of this arms control and disarmament process. What is the extent of its achievements as a negotiating process promotive of the conditions of institutionalized trust, as a source of constraints upon the arms race, and as the producer of a world collective security system. Before embarking upon such a review, it is useful to examine current usage of such terms as "arms control," "arms limitation," and "disarmament." The 1976 annual report of the U.S. Arms Control and Disarmament Agency is a good place to start.

> **Arms control includes all those actions, unilateral as well as multilateral, by which we *regulate* the levels and kinds of armaments in order to reduce the likelihood of armed conflicts, their severity and violence if they should occur, and the economic burden of military programs. Disarmament, a somewhat older term, describes a particular kind of arms control—efforts specifically to *reduce* military forces and perhaps ultimately to eliminate them.[1]**

While "arms control" is the more popularly used generic term for this field of public policy, most of today's agreements and negotiations may be more strictly referred to as "arms limitation." As suggested in the quoted definition above, the parties to an arms limitation agreement place mutually acceptable constraints upon particular types of military forces and weapons systems. Examples are the treaties achieved at the Washington Disarmament Conference of 1921-1922 where the United States, the United Kingdom, Japan, France, and Italy set a 5:5:3:1.75:1.75 ratio for the number of capital ships each would float. Similarly, the Soviet-American Strategic Arms Limitation Talks (SALT I and SALT II) placed limits on the number and types of strategic systems—bombers, intercontinental ballistic missiles, and submarine-launched ballistic missiles—for delivering nuclear bombs to their targets. Arms limitation agreements, as the ACDA report indicates, presumably help reduce the likelihood of armed conflicts, their severity, and the associated economic burdens. Such agreements also strive to stabilize an established military balance of power, slow an arms race without loss of military advantage or security, reduce international tension, and introduce predictability into the military balance.

One characteristic of arms limitation agreements that may be easily overlooked is that they seem to place limits on weapons systems that may become obsolete within the foreseeable future. For example, the capital ship, one of the world's mightiest weapons in 1921, would soon be displaced in that exalted position by the airplane. Today, there is already the expectation that the almighty nuclear bomb may be superseded by even more devastating weaponry before the end of the century. If this is a valid characterization of arms limitation agreements, then we can assert with even greater confidence that the content of such agreements may be less important than the confidence-building political process, if any, that they engender. In this respect, arms limitation and arms control negotiations and agreements may help generate political trust among competing elites by, among other things, (a) enabling them to control their respective military budgets, particularly in countering the pressures of their own domestic Hawks, (b) providing forums for regularized discussion of military issues, (c) moderating the surprise of technological breakthroughs or drastic policy changes on one side or the other, and (d) perhaps most important, affording representatives of adversary leaderships an opportunity to come to know each other personally and to develop a degree of camaraderie in their search for compromises and peace.

"Disarmament" is not only an "older term" but also a more emotional and ideological term. Extreme proponents of disarmament also tend to be extreme antimilitarists, pacifists, and advocates of brotherly love as the solvent of human conflict. As antimilitarists, these disarmers see military leaders as bloodthirsty managers of human carnage, ever delighted by new weapons and by opportunities for battle (a view that most generals and admirals, content with their peacetime sinecures and perquisites, would hardly share). As pacifists, these disarmers rarely offer a program for deterring unwarranted attacks and maintaining order and physical safety. In fact, some disarmers seriously propose one or another form of unilateral disarmament in the belief that other nations, including serious adversaries, may be trusted to follow the noble example; such proposals assume, erroneously, that trust is something that is given rather than a set of attitudes that parties earn transactionally. As advocates of brotherly love, these disarmers tend to forget the inevitability and often constructive consequences of serious but not necessarily deadly human conflict. Disarmament is further burdened by its incorporation into one or another ideological rhetoric, for example, war and preparation for war as "a sign of capitalism's decay" or as the "tool of a Communist dictatorship."

Despite these emotional and ideological burdens, disarmament is regularly placed on the agenda of world politics: in Chapter VII of the United Nations Charter; in proposals for a world disarmament conference (interestingly, never for a world *security* conference); in the convening of General Assembly special sessions on disarmament; in the titles of programs and agencies, such as the U.S. Arms Control and Disarmament Agency; and in the rhetoric of world leaders as they try to identify themselves with their people's universal yearning for an end to war and violence. Once on the public policy agenda, disarmament usually refers to the liquidation of all national military forces except those needed to maintain domestic order. This goal is presumably to be achieved by phased, simultaneous, and balanced reductions in the military forces and weapons stockpiles of all nations.

Such a policy and process is, of course, contrary to all human experience and an unfortunate example of placing the cart before the horse. Political elites disarm only when they (a) have been conquered, (b) have become a coalition member or satellite of some larger military power, or (c) have agreed to subordinate themselves and their military forces to a centralized military institution controlled by a system of collective decision making in which they have a share, for example, civilian parliamentary control over military policies and budgets. Otherwise, no leadership will disarm itself until the requirements of physical safety and military security are established and assured. The necessary antecedent condition of world disarmament is a system of world security that includes arrangements for institutionalized trust.

The latter proposition raises the special usage given the term "arms control" in sections of this book. In this usage, arms control refers to the situation in which competing elites share, through some efficient system of representation, control over the structure, resources, and uses of a centralized military institution within a political community. In this situation, civilian elites are separate from and senior to the military. Thus, for example, the United States Congress and the British Parliament can have no members who are on active military duty. Through statute and purse string, these bodies determine the structure, resources, and uses of their national military forces, perhaps overly influenced by their respective military-industrial complexes. Under these circumstances of shared civilian control of military institutions, the military becomes the instrument of the elites' mutual protection during serious internecine contests for political power. Such contests may instead be terminated in legislative actions or electoral competitions between political parties rather than on the battlefield. This definition of "arms control," however, is particular to this volume. The elements of this definition are familiar in integrated and stable national political systems such as the United States or the United Kingdom. They have yet to emerge as elements in a supranational political system. Nonetheless, what is particularly useful about this definition of arms control is that (a) it places in relationship to each other such factors as military institutions, institutional alternatives for nonviolent elite competition, civilian-military relations, community political integration, and arms control and (b) it clarifies the developmental sequence, namely, that assured collective security is the necessary antecedent condition of disarmament.

With these terminological considerations in mind, we may now examine when, where, by whom, and by what negotiating procedures the issues of international arms control, arms limitation, and disarmament have been dealt with since the end of World War II.

## The Significance of Changing Forums

Negotiating forums on questions of arms control and disarmament consist of many elements that may reflect a power struggle, reveal trends in the evolution of a political institution, or measure the level of political trust among the parties. Therefore, it is empirically useful to examine these elements: the occasion for a negotiation; the parties to the negotiation; the topic of concern; the procedures of decision and settlement; the duration of the negotiation (and particularly whether this is due to complexity of issues or dilatory tactics), and the outcomes in terms of tradeoffs, formal treaties or agreements, the creation of institutional or bureaucratic structures, and contextually, the improvement of political relations and trust.

The first such arms control and disarmament forum was conducted before the end of World War II at the San Francisco Conference, which wrote the Charter of the United Nations. The charter was signed June 25, 1945, and came into effect on October

24, 1945. Between these dates, events took place that altered many of the basic assumptions of the charter and radically changed the nature of world politics. On July 16, the United States secretly exploded the first nuclear bomb on the desert of New Mexico. In August, squadrons of the United States Air Force dropped atom bombs on Hiroshima and Nagasaki. The charter's arrangements for dealing with issues of arms control and disarmament were thus outmoded even before they came into effect.

Under the charter's original design, the Security Council, and particularly the five permanent members, was to have primary responsibility for maintaining international peace and providing for collective security. This was to be accomplished with "the least diversion for armaments of the world's human and economic resources (Article 1)." To assist the Security Council in performing these responsibilities, Article 47 established the Military Staff Committee (MSC) consisting of the chiefs of staff of the five permanent members of the council: the United States, the Soviet Union, the United Kingdom, France, and China.

The Military Staff Committee was charged with advising and assisting the Council "on all questions relating to the Security Council's military requirements for maintenance of international peace and security, the employment and command of forces placed at its disposal, the regulation of armaments, and possible disarmament." If the discharge of its responsibilities required, MSC could invite other states to serve with the Committee. Following the traditional function of chiefs of staff, MSC was to be responsible for "the strategic direction of any armed forces placed at the disposal of the Security Council." According to Chapter VII of the Charter, member states are expected to hold military units immediately available for collective international enforcement actions when authorized by the Security Council.

At the close of World War II, collective security, in practical terms, meant collective enforcement actions by the five permanent members against any international "outlaw" engaging in acts of aggression or other breaches of the peace. But the invention of the atom bomb made traditional notions of military action obsolete, and the Cold War made the expectation of collective military action defunct. These consequences were quickly manifest in the demise of the MSC as a forum for arms control negotiations and collective security preparedness. To address the totally unprecedented issues raised by nuclear weapons, in January 1946 the General Assembly created the United Nations Atomic Energy Commission—composed of representatives of all states on the Security Council and Canada. UNAEC was to be the nuclear forum. It lasted, however, only until January 1952, when the

General Assembly replaced it with the Disarmament Commission.

American proposals before the UNAEC, generally known as the Baruch Plan (after Bernard Baruch, a famous financier and adviser to United States presidents), offered to turn over to the United Nations full information about nuclear technology and full control over sources of raw materials (uranium, thorium, and so on) and means of production, provided that the veto power of permanent members be abrogated in enforcement decisions pertaining to the development and control of atomic energy and further provided that an International Atomic Development Authority be created with powers to control and inspect all atomic activities throughout the world.

The Soviet Union, taking the position that the United Nations was merely an organ of American power, persistently rejected the Baruch proposal, particularly with respect to the veto and inspection of all atomic activities. The former was viewed as diminishing Soviet influence in the United Nations and the latter as an invasion of Soviet sovereignty. In September 1949, the Soviet Union tested its first atomic weapon and thereby ended the American monopoly. American, Soviet, Canadian, and other nuclear arms proposals remained stalemated in both AEC deliberations and the General Assembly until January 1950 when the Soviet Union withdrew from the discussions in order to apply pressure to have Nationalist China replaced at the United Nations by a representative of the People's Republic of China. As indicated earlier, this forum for possible nuclear arms control was abandoned in 1952.

Meanwhile, MSC was faring poorly, too. At its first meeting on February 4, 1946, MSC embarked upon a study of the organizational implications of Article 43. Under this article member states were to make armed forces available to the Security Council "on its call and in accordance with a special agreement or agreements" with regard to numbers and types of forces, their degree of readiness and general location, and so forth. While the permanent members agreed that they were likely to be the principal suppliers of national contingents for peacekeeping, they were in almost complete disagreement about the structure and composition of such forces. MSC's report of April 30, 1947, to the Security Council reflected the impasse. While the report's forty-one articles contained many broad areas of consensus, each of the five powers made extensive comments on points of disagreement. By August 1948, MSC abandoned its efforts and held its last substantive meeting. MSC has since met perfunctorily every fortnight for a few minutes "as a symbol of disappointed hopes which are not dead, but have been put aside for a better day."[2]

Unable to determine what its collective security forces should be, MSC was even less able to deal with arms control and disarmament questions. On December 14, 1946, the General Assembly addressed itself to the latter concerns in a unanimously adopted resolution that noted the relationship between world security and disarmament, called for reduction and regulation of armaments and armed forces under an international system of control and inspection, and recommended the withdrawal of armed forces from former enemy territories, the latter referring to the massive Allied occupation forces in Europe and elsewhere. Two months later, the Security Council established the Commission for Conventional Armaments (CCA) to examine these issues.

CCA consisted of representatives of all members of the Security Council. The reports of the Commission between 1948 and 1950 ran up against counterproposals from the Soviet Union and the Ukrainian SSR. The commission recommended, among other things, that full publication of level of armed forces and conventional armament be reported by all members. The Soviets argued that such a requirement was "militaristic" in its assumption that security should precede disarmament. The General Assembly adopted the commission's proposals. However, in April 1950, the Soviet Union challenged the membership of the representative of Nationalist China and boycotted the work of the commission. Thus, another forum was hurt by the Cold War, and, very shortly, destroyed by the Korean War.

Hoping to keep alive the security, peacekeeping, and arms control discussions begun in the Atomic Energy Commission and the Commission on Conventional Armaments, the General Assembly, in 1952, created a Disarmament Commission to consist of representatives from all Security Council states plus Canada. The new commission was directed to examine (a) questions of disclosure and verification of force levels of all states, (b) limitation and reduction of the size of these forces, (c) nuclear as well as conventional armament limitations, and, what turned out to be most significant, (d) procedures by which states could more readily negotiate arms limitation treaties. By 1954, the Disarmament Commission had received a substantial number of arms limitation and disarmament proposals from its principal members and decided to create a Subcommittee on Disarmament to facilitate negotiations. The subcommittee included Canada, France, the Soviet Union, the United Kingdom, and the United States. This membership included the powers with nuclear programs and avoided the distracting issue of the two Chinas.

The proposals in the Subcommittee on Disarmament during the 1950s were many and the debates often acrimonious. The competing views were well prepared and vigorously presented. By

1956, it was evident to the members of the subcommittee that their efforts were not likely to bring forth any comprehensive program of arms limitation or disarmament. Instead, it appeared more reasonable to work toward limited rather than comprehensive disarmament objectives. The subsequent proposals and deliberations of the subcommittee have been credited with paving the way for the establishment of the International Atomic Energy Agency in 1957, the Antarctic Treaty of 1959, the Limited Test Ban Treaty of 1963, the Outer Space Treaty of 1967, and the Non-Proliferation Treaty of 1968. All of these treaties related to problems of nuclear weaponry and nuclear energy, and the Subcommittee on Disarmament, made up of five nuclear powers, was indeed the most competent forum for exploring these problems.

In 1956, the Western members of the subcommittee began to suggest that forums and agencies outside the United Nations be created to negotiate and implement arms limitation agreements. The veto, the composition of the Security Council, and the politics of the General Assembly were obstacles to the serious negotiating tasks at hand. Further, with the United States and the Soviet Union now embarked on a nuclear arms race, the power structure of the world had become bipolar, thoroughly dominated by the two superpowers and their respective alliance systems. When the Disarmament Commission of twelve members was expanded in 1959, at the Soviet Union's behest, to include *all* members of the United Nations, it was recognized that the commission could no longer be, if ever it was, an effective forum. The commission met from time to time during the 1960s and early 1970s to receive reports and hear proposals for a World Disarmament Conference, but it remained otherwise inactive. At the General Assembly's Special Session on Disarmament in 1978, the *Final Document* called for reactivation of the full Disarmament Commission, and this occurred in 1979.

With the Disarmament Commission going out of business in 1959, a new forum came into being: the Ten-Nation Disarmament Committee (TNDC). The Committee reflected the new global balance of power: Canada, France, Italy, the United Kingdom, and the United States for the West; Bulgaria, Czechoslovakia, Poland, Romania, and the Soviet Union for the Communist bloc. TNDC immediately fell into charges and countercharges, the West claiming that the Eastern powers were unwilling to undertake the necessary planning for a real reduction of armaments under effective international controls, the East declaring that the West was avoiding the General Assembly's declared objective of general and complete disarmament. As the 1960s began, the arms competition was further complicated by the American commitment to the development of MIRVs (*m*ultiple *i*ndependently-targetable *r*eentry *v*ehicles), which made it possible for each side to have many more warheads than the other side had missiles. (The destabilization resulting from MIRV became a major dilemma during the SALT II negotiations in later years.) A further source of tension was the shooting down of an American U-2 reconnaissance plane by the Soviet Union just prior to a scheduled Eisenhower-Khrushchev summit meeting. The dispute led to the demise of TNDC and creation of a successor Eighteen-Nation Disarmament Committee (ENDC) in 1962, which was enlarged in 1969 to twenty-six members and renamed the Conference of the Committee on Disarmament (CCD).

ENDC and CCD were both arrangements for moving arms control and disarmament questions out of the formal structure and constraints of the United Nations organization. Although formally detached from the United Nations, both forums have been staffed by the secretariat and financed by the General Assembly, to which they have submitted annual reports. Both ENDC and CCD, through expansions of membership, have sought to represent not only the superpower alliances but also the growing number and influence of nonaligned nations. In 1969, the CCD balance was seven members from the West, seven from the Soviet bloc, and twelve nonaligned. In 1975, five other nonaligned states were added to make a total membership of thirty-one. The United States and the Soviet Union have served as cochairmen of both ENDC and CCD.

When Secretary-General U Thant recommended the transformation of ENDC into CCD in 1969, he also proposed that the General Assembly declare 1970-1980 a Disarmament Decade, which it did. Unburdened by glittering publicity and dramatic confrontations and all too often discounted as an ineffectual academic seminar and debating club, ENDC had nonetheless served as an indispensable site for communication and negotiation about difficult questions of arms control and disarmament. ENDC's composition was also politically realistic, for the nonaligned nations had come to realize the vital importance and risks that the superpower and other arms races held for their own security and development. The nonaligned states have not only served as a third force in global military and political affairs but have also become a relentless pressure group for the design and achievement of multilateral arms limitation agreements. This nonaligned role emerged in ENDC and was expanded in CCD during the Disarmament Decade.

As the seedbed of arms control and disarmament initiatives, proposals, and agreements, the record of ENDC and CCD, often unnoticed, has been impressive. ENDC picked up and carried forward the work of the Disarmament Commission. ENDC also did the drafting and other preparatory work of major treaties and agreements, many of which were concluded in other forums. ENDC became a clearinghouse and codification committee for nearly every significant security, arms control, and disarmament proposal put forth before and during its tenure. Even draft proposals that were shelved were highly important as a record of official governmental thinking about many issues and as a source of ideas that subsequently bore fruit.

The major documents initially before the Eighteen-Nation Disarmament Committee in 1962 were the "Draft Treaty on General and Complete Disarmament under Strict International Control," submitted by the Soviet Union on March 15, and the "Outline of Basic Provisions of a Treaty on General and Complete Disarmament in a Peaceful World," submitted by the United States on April 18. Early versions of these proposals were offered by the Soviet Union in April and June 1957 and by the four Western powers on the Subcommittee on Disarmament in August of that year. More detailed plans were submitted to the Ten-Nation Disarmament Committee by both sides in March 1960. The 1962 documents became the basis for discussions over the next three years. By 1964, the GCD proposals revealed the best official Soviet and American thinking about how the superpowers might lead the world into an era of disarmament and international peacekeeping at the end of a three-stage process. Although all but forgotten, the two competing approaches reflect principles of action that are of more than passing interest, particularly in their recognition that any reduction in armaments must be accompanied by a related increase in United Nations peacekeeping forces. Furthermore, features of the two proposals may be discerned in several of the arms control treaties actually consummated during the late 1960s and thereafter.[3]

The topics and concepts introduced, analyzed, and refined in ENDC and CCD have been wide-ranging. Discussions of nuclear weapons test bans prepared the ground for the Limited Test Ban Treaty (1963), the Threshold Test Ban Treaty (1974), the Peaceful Nuclear Explosions Treaty (1976), and current negotiations toward a comprehensive test ban. The concept of nuclear-weapons-free zones spawned the Outer Space, the Latin American Nuclear-Free Zone, and the Seabed treaties (1967, 1967, and 1971, respectively), and has kept alive proposals for other regional nuclear-free zones of peace. Attention to the economic and social consequences of the arms race and disarmament has succeeded in linking the plight and prospects of developing nations to the wastefulness of excessive military expenditures and unwanted wars. Proposals for the reduction and elimination of nuclear weapons stockpiles have led to the

Non-Proliferation Treaty (1968), the Strategic Arms Limitation Talks (SALT) between the two superpowers, and the broadening of the responsibilities of the International Atomic Energy Agency. Another major concern has been the achievement of a comprehensive ban on chemical and biological weapons, which eventually produced a Biological Weapons Convention to which the United States, reluctant for years to do so, has subscribed. In sum, ENDC and CCD have been notable and effective arms control and disarmament planning negotiating forums, so much so that the 1978 Special Session of the General Assembly (SSOD) took steps to more fully incorporate CCD into the operations of the United Nations.

The *Final Document* of SSOD noted that "for maximum effectiveness, two kinds of bodies are required in the field of disarmament—deliberative and negotiating," the former to include all members and the latter a much smaller number (paragraph 113). Declaring that the General Assembly "has been and should remain the main deliberative organ" in the disarmament field, SSOD's *Final Document* restricted the future work of the Assembly's First Committee to security and disarmament questions, and reactivated the Disarmament Commission composed of all members to conduct deliberations regarding a comprehensive program for disarmament. As a consequence, France and China were brought into the negotiating process and transformed CCD into a Committee on Disarmament open to all nuclear-weapon states plus thirty-two to thirty-five other states to comprise the negotiating body for this field.

By declaring itself *the* main deliberative organ in the disarmament field, the General Assembly assumed a major role in a function initially assigned to the Security Council. This action is comparable to the Assembly's assumption of a key role in peacekeeping through its Uniting for Peace Resolution in 1950. As students of two-house legislatures will confirm, this type of arrogation of function is a predictable feature of normal political competition within bicameral legislatures. As evidence of this tendency, the General Assembly concluded the first Special Session on Disarmament by scheduling a second Special Session for 1982. From the point of view of progress in the field of arms control and disarmament, the growing involvement of the General Assembly may be a salutory effort to overcome the failure of the Security Council in providing an effective forum in this field.

Not all security, arms control, and disarmament forums are global (General Assembly) or bilateral (SALT) in composition. Regional forums and negotiations have also been undertaken, with perhaps less striking achievements thus far. The European region is the principal case in point. In 1973 the Conference on Security and Cooperation in Europe (CSCE), made up of thirty-three nations of Europe plus the United States and Canada (as members of the NATO alliance), began meetings that led to the signing of a Final Act in 1975. Aimed at reducing barriers between Western and Eastern Europe, the Final Act set forth three sets (or "baskets") of principles for governmental action by the thirty-five states. The principles dealt with "confidence-building measures" bearing upon the improvement of human rights, protection of the environment, movement of people, scientific and technological exchanges, settlement of disputes, and military security. The latter, of particular interest here, included agreements to give prior notification of major military maneuvers, exchange observers to these maneuvers, and encourage negotiations for effective arms control. CSCE established a Commission on Security and Cooperation in Europe to receive and consolidate semiannual reports on the implementation of the Final Act. Thus, the subjects—human rights, security, environmental protection, and so on—are now matters of public information, institutionalized attention, and inevitably, propaganda and debate. The process of implementation is expected to be continuous and has already generated innumerable meetings, exchanges, and other activities hitherto difficult to initiate.

In 1973 another regional forum got under way: the Conference on Mutual and Balanced Force Reduction (MBFR). MBFR is composed of seven voting members representing NATO (the United States, the United Kingdom, Canada, Belgium, West Germany, Luxembourg, and the Netherlands), four from the Warsaw Pact (Russia, East Germany, Poland, and Czechoslovakia), and eight nonvoting participants (five from NATO and three others from the Warsaw Pact). The objective of MBFR has been to reduce the size and weaponry of the armed forces in Central Europe and to make their distribution less confrontational. This forum has been less productive. According to its 1978 Annual Report, the U.S. Arms Control and Disarmament Agency indicates that Warsaw Pact forces in East Germany, Poland, and Czechoslovakia total 58 divisions made up of over 960,000 ground force personnel equipped with 16,000 tanks and 3,000 tactical aircraft. Facing these are NATO forces—in West Germany, Belgium, the Netherlands, and Luxembourg—totaling 27 divisions made up 790,000 ground force personnel, 7,000 tanks, and 1,000 tactical aircraft. The two sides disagree about the manpower data that should be used as the basis for reducing forces (there is a 150,000-man discrepancy regarding the size of the Warsaw Pact forces), the method for computing manpower and other ceilings (the use of absolute or proportional limits), and the technological equations for reducing armaments (American neutron bombs versus Soviet tanks, for example).

Progress in MBFR negotiations has been almost imperceptible. What is perhaps most impressive is the fact that they are being conducted at all. It has been in Europe that major wars of the past several centuries have begun. It is in Europe that the two most powerful alliance systems in the contemporary world—NATO and the Warsaw Pact—confront each other, bolstered by the most technologically sophisticated weaponry known in human history. It is over the security of Europe that the two superpowers are most likely to become embroiled in World War III.[4] In addition to its European concerns, perhaps the most significant feature of MBFR is the fact that it is the first serious attempt to deal with the control of conventional arms.

From the point of view of popular interest, the Strategic Arms Limitation Talks (SALT) have undoubtedly been the most dramatic of the arms control forums. In the SALT discussions, the two nuclear giants have been face to face on a problem that vividly threatens the survival of human civilization and perhaps even life on this planet. SALT has been the big forum. The drama has been heightened by the high level of senior leaders and governmental agencies involved in the negotiations. The United States SALT delegations, whose negotiating positions have been coordinated through the National Security Council, have included representatives of the secretary of state, the secretary of defense, the chairman of the Joint Chiefs of Staff, the director of the Arms Control and Disarmament Agency, and the director of the Central Intelligence Agency. On the Soviet side, there have been two overlapping decision-making structures: the Communist party and the Soviet government. The Politburo of the party, backed up by the staff of the Central Committee, has been the principal center for SALT decisions. In the governmental bureaucracy, SALT policy research preparations have been the concerns of the Supreme Military Council, of which Brezhnev has been chairman, the Ministry of Defense, the Ministry of Foreign Affairs, and the Academy of Sciences' Institute of World Economy and International Relations, and Institute on the U.S.A. With such agencies and officials on each side, there is little doubt that the two governments place supreme importance upon the SALT process, commensurate with their responsibility to themselves and to the rest of humanity.

In 1962, the Soviet Union deployed a limited *anti*ballistic *m*issile (ABM) system around Leningrad. In 1964, the Russians displayed an ABM missile during a parade in Moscow, thereby anticipating the deployment of an ABM system, called the Galosh, around Moscow. The purpose of ABMs was to intercept and destroy incoming nuclear missiles. The technology for ABM systems was available in the early 1960s, but it soon became clear to most planners that no antiballistic system could be created that would provide a completely effective shield against attack. Nevertheless, Congress insisted upon appropriating funds for an ABM system.

After many attempts by Presidents Kennedy and Johnson to draw the Soviets into a negotiation about ABM, Johnson, in responding to congressional pressure in 1967, agreed to begin deployment of an ABM system unless the Soviet Union promptly and seriously entered into an arms limitation discussion. Premier Kosygin agreed to do so in 1967, but the Russians were unwilling to commence until after the pending Non-Proliferation Treaty (NPT) had been completed. Bilateral SALT negotiations between the two nuclear powers were therefore announced on July 1, 1968, the date that the NPT agreement was available for signature by subscribing parties. The first SALT sessions were held in Vienna from April 16 to August 15, 1970, and in Helsinki from November 2 to December 18, 1970. Their purpose was the "limitation and reduction of both offensive and defensive strategic nuclear-weapon delivery systems and systems of defense against ballistic missiles."

SALT negotiations have been in progress since 1969 and are currently considered an ongoing process. Results thus far have been the SALT I treaties and agreements, SALT II, and the expectation that SALT III will commence as soon as SALT II has been ratified. The first SALT talks produced two agreements in 1972: the Anti-Ballistic Missile (ABM) Treaty, still in effect, which limited each side to two ABM sites, subsequently reduced to one; and a five-year Interim Agreement on strategic offensive nuclear weapons, which froze the number of ICBM and submarine launchers on both sides at the levels deployed or under construction in 1972. Strategic heavy bombers were not restricted. The Interim Agreement allowed the Soviet Union more launchers than the United States—2,350 to 1,710—but also prohibited further deployment of Soviet launchers, which they were doing at the rate of several hundred per year. The object of the subsequent SALT II negotiations was to convert the Interim Agreement into a permanent arms arrangement.[5]

In August 1972, the United States Senate approved the ABM Treaty. During the second half of September, both houses of Congress approved the Interim Offensive Arms Agreement. This paved the way for the SALT II negotiations. SALT II began on November 21, 1972, in Geneva. The agenda included the extension of numerical restrictions on strategic weapons and their delivery systems, the development of qualitative restrictions on the rapidly advancing missile technology, and the inclusion of bombers, antisubmarine warfare (ASW) systems, and other new systems in the accounting of a strategic balance between the superpowers.

The issues before the SALT II negotiating forum were intrinsically difficult. The negotiating situation was further complicated, however, by the fact that the United States had replaced almost all the personnel of its SALT I delegation, and the Soviet Union had significantly changed the composition of its SALT decision structure by admitting the Soviet defense minister to full membership in the Politburo. In addition, Watergate was, by 1974, distracting the Nixon-Kissinger leadership.

During 1973, a Nixon-Brezhnev statement expressed the hope that a new SALT agreement would be reached by 1974. When it appeared that this would be impossible, two side agreements were concluded instead: a protocol to the ABM Treaty limiting each side to one ABM system instead of the two in the original treaty, and a new Threshold Test Ban Treaty restricting underground nuclear tests to explosions with a yield no greater than 150 kilotons. Both agreements were signed on July 3, 1974.

Domestic political, bureaucratic, and technological developments continued to harass the SALT II negotiations. Another major difficulty was the definition of "parity" between the two strategic weapon and delivery arsenals. As a consequence, the regular delegation negotiations were intermittently supplemented by summit meetings between President Nixon and General Secretary Brezhnev, and, later, President Ford and Brezhnev. In November 1974, the latter two met in Vladivostok and agreed in principle to equal aggregate ceilings for strategic nuclear delivery vehicles, including bombers. However, when the negotiators resumed their discussions in Geneva in 1975, new disagreements appeared regarding the classification and treatment of certain new delivery technology, namely, the American cruise missile and the Soviet Backfire bomber.

Shortly after the inauguration of President Carter in 1977, the new administration proposed lower ceilings than those agreed upon at Vladivostok, thereby reopening several issues and prolonging the negotiation process. When the Interim Agreement expired in 1977, both parties continued to conduct themselves as though it were still in effect. Not until June 1979 was a SALT II agreement signed by President Carter and now President Brezhnev as heads of state, subject to ratification by Congress and the Supreme Soviet.

The SALT II agreement consists of three parts: (1) a treaty setting quantitative limits on numbers of delivery systems and qualitative constraints on new types of weapons, to last until the end of 1985; (2) a short-term protocol effective until December 1981, dealing with mobile ICBM launching systems and cruise missiles; and (3) a joint statement of principles and guidelines for subsequent SALT III negotiations. The timing of the SALT II treaty-signing was less than fortuitous. It took place amid growing strains in Soviet-American detente and at the beginning of the quadrennial American presidential election contest. Before 1979 concluded, the American hostage crisis in Iran and the invasion of Afghanistan by Russia propelled Soviet-American relations into a major clash, with SALT II ratification a major victim. Nevertheless, there seemed little doubt among foreign policy officials on both sides that the SALT negotiating process would eventually be resumed. There were those, particularly at the United Nations, who looked forward not only to SALT III but also to an eventual SALT IV that would bring into the negotiating process the other principal nuclear powers. With no other equally potent forum dealing with the issues of nuclear weaponry, the superpowers and the world could ill afford to close down the SALT process. In what way it would evolve, from a bilateral to a multilateral negotiation, remains for the future to reveal. One possibility may be a revival of the United Nations Military Staff Committee as the appropriate and permanent supranational forum for future strategic arms limitation talks.

There is one type of arms control forum that has been given relatively little attention as such but which may carry the seeds of enduring success in this field, namely, the various ongoing, sometimes tiny, bureaucracies created in connection with post-World War II arms control agreements. These bureaucracies consist of the permanent staff of several supranational agencies such as: the International Atomic Energy Agency (IAEA) created in 1956; the Agency for the Prohibition of Nuclear Weapons in Latin America (OPANAL) established under the Treaty of Tlatelolco, Mexico, in 1967; the Standing Consultative Commission (SCC) established by the United States and the Soviet Union in 1972 to monitor the SALT I agreements; and the United Nations Centre for Disarmament organized in 1977.

There are other bureaucratic forums: e.g. the Conferences on Security and Cooperation in Europe (CSCE) to administer periodic reviews of the Helsinki agreements of 1974. Also, in March 1977, the United States and the Soviet Union established eight task forces or "working groups," each to deal with one of the following problem areas: a comprehensive test ban; control of radiological weapons; arms limitation in the Indian Ocean zone; control of conventional arms transfers; civil defense; antisatellite capabilities; and arrangements for prior notification of missile test flights.

Many bureaucracies, including the supranational ones just cited, have qualities that may make them excellent long run forums for arms control negotiations. A substantial and well-organized bureaucracy often represents diverse concepts, theories, and interests relevant to the public policy issue with which it is concerned. Personnel usually have long tenure with the advantages and disadvantages of daily and continuing interaction with each other. This results not only in familiarity with each other's modes of thought and actions but also tends to inhibit dramatic surprises in behavior of the parties. In time, the staff of such bureaucracies develop a shared interest in their common goals and take on the perspectives and style of third parties mediating competing interests. Bureaucracies also become a repository of essential information and experience relevant to the agreements and policies they administer. They serve as a clearinghouse for proposals and plans that otherwise would be lost or ignored. Bureaucracies also tend to break up larger policy issues into smaller, more manageable ones, a process that often is critical for conflict resolution.

To return to the International Atomic Energy Agency as one of the major supranational bureaucratic forums related to arms control, it will be recalled that the IAEA had its origin in President Eisenhower's 1953 Atoms-for-Peace proposal. With the endorsement of the General Assembly in 1954, the American proposal creating IAEA became a statute that was signed by seventy governments. IAEA came into operation in 1957. Its General Conference is the annual meeting of all signatory members, now numbering over a hundred. The conference elects half of the members of a thirty-four–member board of governors, approves the selection of the director general, and fixes the IAEA budget. IAEA has become a staff of several hundred with responsibilities for nuclear research and development, health and safety standards, civil liability, technical assistance, and, since the adoption of the Nuclear Non-Proliferation Treaty in 1968, the administration of a safeguard program to ensure that peaceful atomic energy activities are not diverted to military uses. As a consequence of India's surprise nuclear explosion in 1974, IAEA has accelerated its efforts to tighten nuclear safeguard controls. It is in this function that IAEA's staff has expanded most rapidly to perform activities increasingly significant for nuclear arms control. Further rapid growth of the agency's arms control responsibilities over the next decades may be expected.

Regional agencies such as OPANAL and CSCE conferences may also be expected to evolve in keeping with their broadening experience and assignments. OPANAL consists of a General Conference made up of all contracting nations, a five-member council selected by the General Conference, and a secretariat whose staff is concerned with administering meetings, verifying compliance, negotiating IAEA safeguard agreements, conducting special inspections upon request and acquiescence by contracting parties, maintaining relations with other international organizations, and carrying out other arms control and mediating duties.

The Final Act of the Conference on Security and Cooperation in Europe adopted in 1975 by the thirty-five participating nations sought to establish a "CSCE process" that would maintain a continuing oversight of the implementation of its provisions on military security in Europe, cooperation in the fields of economics, science, and technology, and cooperation in the fields of human rights and related humanitarian matters. The vehicle for this process was to be follow-up conferences, the first of which was held in Belgrade from October 4, 1977, to March 9, 1978. A second review conference began in Madrid on November 11, 1980.

The business of the Belgrade conference consisted of reports of compliance and noncompliance with the provisions of the Helsinki Final Act, demands and proposals for improved implementation, and debates over the political activities of various nongovernmental monitoring groups seeking to promote CSCE implementation. While the conference proceedings themselves were secret and unrecorded, a substantial volume of public documents was compiled in preparation for and following upon the meeting. This was particularly true of the reports of the United States Commission on Security and Cooperation in Europe, a commission established by Congress in June 1976, composed of six representatives, six senators, and three executive branch appointees. CSCE will undoubtedly continue well into the future as a forum for exposure, dispute, and pressure as East and West document each other's failings.

The Standing Consultative Commission established by a memorandum of understanding between the United States and the Soviet Union in 1972 was charged with implementing the provisions of various strategic arms agreements, including the ABM Treaty, the 1972 Interim Agreement, and the 1971 Agreement on Measures to Reduce the Risk of Outbreak of Nuclear War. The SCC meets in private, deals with questions of compliance, endeavors to remove uncertainties and misunderstandings about the agreements, and entertains proposals for improving implementation of the agreements. Each side has a "component," or delegation, supported by a small staff that engages in almost continuous review, discussion, and negotiation. It may be assumed that this particular forum also serves as a convenient place for sharing intelligence about each other's nuclear and strategic technology and policies. The SCC is perhaps the most likely agency for preventing either side from carrying off any technological surprises in the strategic weapons field. Relatively unnoticed, the SCC may be one of the more successful means for promoting institutionalized trust between the two major nuclear powers.

Yet another growing bureaucracy is the United Nations Centre for Disarmament. The centre, previously the Disarmament Affairs Division of the Secretariat, was upgraded in 1977 and assigned an assistant secretary-general as director. The centre's responsibilities were expanded by the 1978 Special Session On Disarmament (SSOD). These new responsibilities include an augmented program of study, research, information, and contact with nongovernmental organizations (NGOs). Prior to SSOD, the centre's staff numbered about thirty-five to forty, and its biennial budget was $2,145,700. SSOD also created a board of eminent persons to advise the secretary-general on various studies and policies in the field of arms control and disarmament, this board to be administered by the staff of the centre. There is little doubt that the Centre for Disarmament has only begun its career as a forum in the arms control negotiating process.

The large number of arms control and disarmament forums noted in this brief survey reinforces the impression that problems of international security, the arms race, arms control, and disarmament are high on the agenda of the world's elites and receive a substantial investment of leadership time and thought. With struggle for international power and influence always in the background, much more than talk and propaganda have come out of these forums. The large accumulation of treaties and agreements in the historically brief period of thirty to thirty-five years has been impressive.

So has the quality of their involvement in the arms control process. Unilateral gestures such as the Baruch Plan and several testing moratoriums have been supplemented by bilateral and multilateral negotiations. Middle and small powers have insisted upon enlarging their participation and have been relatively effective in bringing pressure for action on the superpowers. The General Assembly, by conducting special sessions on disarmament and augmenting its organizational capacity for dealing with disarmament matters, has been a major factor in universalizing attention to and planning for security and arms control questions.

The importance of universalizing arms control forums cannot be overstated. All nations have a vital interest. The respective members of the NATO and Warsaw Pact alliance systems have an interest in keeping their leaders—the United States and the Soviet Union—from nuclear excesses and misjudgments, for they as well as the superpowers are the likeliest targets of any potential nuclear holocaust. The nonaligned nations of the world have a tremendous interest in reducing their own and superpower military expenditures better to afford developmental budgets. Universal negotiating forums also hold promise of replacing the bipolar balance of power with a more dispersed and less confrontational system of international power. Universal forums are more likely to maintain arms control negotiations as a public process subject to popular pressures. Above all, the large array of negotiating forums reviewed here reveals how numerous are the marketplaces for security, arms control, and disarmament transactions where almost none existed before.

## The Functions of the Negotiating Process

There is a rapidly growing body of behavioral science theory and inquiry regarding negotiation and transaction in politics and other fields of human interaction. William Zartman declares simply: "Ours is an age of negotiation." Anselm Strauss observes: "A social order—even the most repressive—without some forms of negotiation would be inconceivable. Even dictators find it impossible and inexpedient simply and always to order, command, demand, threaten, manipulate, or use force; about some issues and activities they must persuade and negotiate." According to Peter Blau, social exchange relations evolve slowly, usually starting with minor transactions in which little trust is required, but neither is there much risk. By discharging obligations for goods and behaviors received, individuals demonstrate their trustworthiness, leading to gradual expansion of exchanges *accompanied by growth of mutual trust*. This latter theoretical view, noted in an earlier chapter, is, of course, of profound importance for the security and arms control matters that concern us here.[6]

Negotiations are an essential communications process that precedes any transaction. It specifies the goods, behaviors, or other currencies available for exchange between the transactors. It compels each transactor to clarify his or her value priorities sufficiently to be able to decide according to his or her *own subjective criteria* whether the thing to be received is worth more than that which is to be given in exchange. This can be money for goods or services (the typical economic transaction), deference for advice (as suggested by Homans and Blau in connection with behavioral exchanges), a vote for a political favor (common in legislative logrolling), or cruise missiles for Backfire bombers (as in SALT II negotiations). Negotiations also help reveal those values that transactors may share more or less equally. Knowing these shared values often facilitates exchanges and cooperation. Thus, for example, the shared values that seem to motivate powerful adversaries to negotiate arms control agreements include (a) common fear of mutual destruction, (b) upredictable and uncontrollable consequences of military engagement, (c) satisfaction with the status quo, and (d) the economies of preventable competition.

Social and political transactions differ from economic ones in that the currencies exchanged are somewhat less clearly specified. The units of currency exchanged in social and political transactions are not as precisely measurable as in most economic exchanges. Nonetheless, the other attributes of transaction are present in all types of exchange. One of these is time, which can be an important aspect of transaction. The simplest transactions are those in which two parties transfer goods between themselves simultaneously. However, when the transfers take place at different times, anticipation and trust become significant elements in the situation. Mortgage loans are the example referred to earlier. A bank will extend a mortgage loan to be repaid with interest in specified amounts over some future period of years. The borrower receives immediate cash for the immediate purchase of a house; the lender gains the expectation of being repaid with interest over a future period or, in case of default, unqualified ownership of the house. Similarly, but somewhat more ambiguously, a friend will invite another to dinner in the expectation that such an invitation will be reciprocated at some future time. As each time-extended transaction concludes successfully, each of the parties develops a greator feeling of trust toward the other. As stated in transaction theory, each exchange has been profitable for each of the parties. The resulting satisfactions have improved the degree of trust each holds in the other. According to the definition of "trust" set forth earlier, each party is able to feel confident (a) about the predictability of the behavior of the other and (b) that the other's predicted behavior has favorable consequences for themselves.

These theoretical observations about negotiating and transacting permit us to better appreciate the special significance of arms control negotiations and treaties as activities and events promotive of international institutionalized trust. A brief examination of negotiations per se and of treaties and agreements may further illuminate this view.

Arms control negotiations serve a number of confidence-building functions. Negotiations help clarify adversary values. In the case of the CSCE Helsinki agreements and follow-up conferences, it has been evident that the Soviet Union is most interested in the security arrangements, particularly those that confirm its dominance of Eastern Europe, whereas the United States prefers to focus on issues of human rights. Negotiations may be revealing of adversary military and other strategies. For example, as a vast land mass with one-fourth of the world's population, the People's Republic of China is more interested in modern conventional weaponry rather than nuclear bombs, feeling safe enough perhaps by helping maintain the nuclear stalemate between the Soviet Union and the United States.

During negotiations, opposing expectations may become explicit, whether accepted by the other party or not. Thus, during the SALT II negotiations, the United States made clear its expectation that the Soviet Union would refrain from stepping up the rate of production of its Backfire bombers, and eventually the Soviets acknowledged and conceded this. Continuing negotiations may be a vital preventive of surprise maneuvers and unexpected crises. This is certainly one of the functions of the SALT negotiating process, the CSCE process, the MBFR negotiations, the "hot lines," and similar ongoing discussions and arrangements.

Two other trust-promoting functions of negotiations may be less evident but are nonetheless equally, if not more, significant. As we noticed earlier, the various negotiating forums have, over the years, served to give structure to the world's "marketplaces" for the "sale" of security services. Thus, there has evolved a set of nuclear marketplaces in which the superpowers have arranged a duopolistic dominance over strategic weapons systems; near-nuclear powers have continued to try to break into this market, and the smaller nonnuclear nations have begun to challenge the very existence of nuclear weaponry as a source of global security. There have been conventional weapons marketplaces. There are security marketplaces that are global in scope and others that are regional. As we have seen, these marketplaces, or forums, are increasingly visible and organized. Over future decades, these are the places within which and the processes whereby international security is most likely to be negotiated.

A second, less evident, function of negotiation is its role in the pursuit of "exact knowledge," as described earlier, of each other's military capabilities. Hitherto, this pursuit has been almost entirely the function of military intelligence. More recently, the negotiating process has presented its own occasions for learning about the military capabilities of others. Just as Harry Truman told Joseph Stalin of the detonation of the first atom bomb during their conversations at Yalta, we must assume that such developments as the neutron bomb, cruise missiles, antisatellite satellites, Backfire bombers, and similar technological advances have been shared between negotiating parties at some time before the news reached the popular press. As for arms control negotiations proper, these would be literally impossible if each side did not have precise and verified data about the other's military hardware and deployments.

Turning to treaties and international agreements, we find similar confidence-building implications. Treaties and agreements, after all, are literally the creations of the contracting parties. Each party not only assumes that the other is less than trustworthy but also is vitally concerned with agreeing only to those arrangements that are unilaterally verifiable and enforceable. There is no developed world judicial process as yet that can determine, on the basis of presented evidence, whether one or another party has breached the contract. Nor is there a world enforcement agency at hand to punish the guilty party. Nevertheless, treaties and international agreements do comprise much of the body of international law such as it is. As do laws of any kind, treaties and international agreements serve as public instruments for clarifying and stabilizing expectations about each other's behavior. Such clarification and stabilization are essential for the development of social and political order at all levels of human self-governance.

Treaties and agreements enable the contracting parties to publicly specify areas of common interest as well as shared goals. Even though such declarations are often dismissed as "mere verbiage," they are an indispensable antecedent for cooperation and organized activity. The "verbiage" becomes more compelling if it spells out specific guidelines for behavior. Such behavioral requirements and expectations may subsequently be the basis for signaling danger if one of the parties is preparing to breach the contract. For example, in the case of the Helsinki security arrangements, the conduct of NATO or Warsaw Pact military maneuvers without due notice to the other party may in time be interpreted as a clue that something unsavory is going on. Israel's preemptive strike against its Arab neighbors in 1967, as another example, was justified by the former as a defensive action in response to threatening maneuvers by Egypt, Syria, and others.

Treaties and agreements may also provide opportunities for preparation and response to potential breaches or betrayals by one of the contracting parties. This is usually provided in abrogation, inspection and verification clauses. A nation that seeks to abrogate rather than renegotiate a treaty is undoubtedly preparing to make trouble. If inspection or verification arrangements are obstructed, a similar conclusion may be drawn. The inclusion of such provisions in treaties and agreements provides a device whereby each party may have some warning of danger and some opportunity for preparation and response.

Finally, treaties and agreements may provide organizational mechanisms, such as the aforementioned bureaucratic forums, for continuing, perhaps permanent, negotiation about issues too difficult to resolve immediately or in the near future. Such are the arrangements that lead to the social order alluded to by Anselm Strauss. In this sense, theoreticians speculate that conflict is an important prerequisite of political integration so long as conflict is accompanied by negotiations and some successful political transactions. If this is a valid proposition, then arms control and disarmament negotiations, treaties, and agreements have been an essential avenue toward world political integration and security. According to such a theory, successful arms control and disarmament negotiations and agreements are vital steps in the development of institutionalized trust and shared control over the security services of the world. Given the present intensity of political distrust between the superpowers and among other adversaries throughout the world, it, of course, seems impossible that such adversaries may yet become "allies" as a consequence of the arms control process.

## Treaties and Agreements as Building Blocks of Institutional Development

The quantity and quality of public discussion, official negotiations, and international agreements and treaties dealing with arms control, disarmament, global security, and international peacekeeping since the end of World War II have been unprecedented in human history. What has all this activity accomplished in building political institutions that can provide security services sufficient for all to feel safe in this world? What have the treaties and agreements provided as building blocks in the construction of systems of institutionalized trust among the world's competing elites?

Political institutions grow as a consequence of enduring agreements about political relationships to be formally organized, uniform patterns of political conduct to be expected of members or participants, and the ratio between conflict and consensus that is to be maintained in stable equilibrium. When the recurrent actions and events of a group or a community attain a high degree of formality, uniformity, and stability, these actions and events are said to be institutionalized. Thus, for example, as the lawmaking actions of a community acquire formality, uniformity, and stability, that community's legislative institution takes shape and tends to endure. Bureaucratic, judicial, party, commercial, family, religious, and other human institutions emerge in the same way, by uniform, hence predictable, behavioral responses to recurrent and similar social or political situations.

Political institutions promote trustworthy conduct and attitudes of trust when they (a) help make the conduct of members and participants predictable and (b) facilitate transactions among members and participants from which they derive positive consequences, that is, satisfactions and a "sense of profit." In the economic realm, for example, we have seen how institutionalized trust has evolved in the fields of mortage loans, automobile financing, credit cards, and similar standarized commercial transactions. How, then, have the arms control treaties and agreements that have accumulated since the end of World War II contributed to the development of international institutions promoting interelite trust? What has been the content of the consensus among the parties to these treaties and agreements, particularly with respect to security? What aspects of relationship and conduct have been formalized, made uniform, and stabilized, hence made sufficiently predictable to be institutions? Are the outcomes of these arms control treaties and agreements substantial building blocks for the construction of systems of international trust and security?

Examination of the arms control treaties and agreements of the past thirty or so years reveals a two-tier structure, as alluded to earlier: nuclear and nonnuclear. At the nuclear tier, with its awesome risks of mass annihilation, errors in strategic judgment, theft, and proliferation, motivation to cooperate has been high and treaties numerous. At the nonnuclear or conventional tier, little has been accomplished, for reasons to be examined later.

## Preventive Treaties

One series of treaties, often referred to as nonarmament treaties, have been preventive in character. Their object has been to prevent arms competition where none has yet taken place but seems imminent. Although never agreed upon, the Baruch Plan (June 1946) was the earliest attempt at prevention. The nonarmament series includes the Antarctic Treaty (signed December 1, 1959), the Outer Space Treaty (January 27, 1967), the Latin American Nuclear-Free Zone Treaty (February 14, 1967), and the Seabed Arms Control Treaty (February 11, 1971). Of current interest along these same lines are discussions regarding the establishment of nuclear-free zones in the Indian Ocean region, the Middle East, and Africa.

The Baruch Plan, presented by the United States to the United

Nations Atomic Energy Commission, offered to cease the manufacture of atomic bombs, destroy those then in existence, and establish an international agency to which all information pertaining to the production of energy could be given. All this was to be implemented as soon as a reliable system of inspection and control could be established to apprehend and punish violators. In other words, the United States, fully aware of the unprecedented nature of the weapon it had created, was willing to forgo its nuclear monopoly and move toward international collective controls. The United States monopoly was likely to be short term. Self-interested actions, as would be an inclination to confess in the Prisoners' Dilemma model, would unquestionalby lead to a costly nuclear arms race. The logical escape from the dilemma seemed to be via some system of international cooperation and control, together with procedures of inspection that would help build a system of institutionalized trust.

The Soviet Union rejected the Baruch Plan as a potential invasion of Soviety sovereignty, a plot against Soviet economic development, and a threat to Soviet security. What the Soviet representatives did not say was that Stalin was intent upon producing a Russian atomic bomb, an effort well along even as the Baruch Plan was debated in New York. In retrospect, one may speculate what the military state of the world might now be if the Baruch Plan had been adopted and an institution for shared control of atomic energy created in 1946. One may also speculate if and how current competing international elites may find their way back to the system envisaged by the Baruch Plan as a reasonable approach to collective control over nuclear arms and nuclear energy.

By the early 1950s some fifteen nations had explored the Antarctic continent, and several had registered claims of sovereignty over some of its areas. Most of the activity in Antarctica was scientific in character, reinforced by the collaborations taking place during the International Geophysical Year of 1957-1958. In May 1958, the United States proposed a conference aimed at keeping Antarctica international and demilitarized. The treaty written by the ensuing conference prohibits military bases, fortifications, tests, maneuvers, and similar activities on that continent. It also prohibits nuclear explosions or the deposit of nuclear wastes. However, all parties may use Antarctica for peaceful purposes, have free access to all parts of the continent at any time, and freely inspect any installations on it. Disputes may be referred to the International Court of Justice.

Drawn up with a minimum of fanfare, the Antarctic Treaty is loaded with precedents of a confidence-building type: military and scientific cooperation instead of competition; defined demilitarized territory; free access and open inspection of the facilities of all nations; an institution for dealing with disputes. As the first postwar arms control agreement, the Antarctic Treaty offered a hopeful sign despite the view of some that it dealt with a continent that was remote, barren, and militarily uninteresting. Quite the contrary. Relevant technologies are reducing the distance to Antarctica, discovering its rich resources, and increasing its military potential. The treaty was a positive diplomatic achievement and a model and stimulus for subsequent negotiating efforts.

In October 1957, the Soviet Union launched Sputnik, the first earth-orbiting satellite. The United States' Explorer 1 satellite followed in January 1958. Shortly after becoming president, John F. Kennedy called for a space program that would land American astronauts on the moon, a goal accomplished by the Apollo program in 1969. The decade of the 1960s witnessed a crescendo of manned satellites orbiting the earth and raising qualms about the prospect that nuclear-armed satellites might also be sent aloft or stationed on the moon. In September 1960, President Eisenhower, in an address before the General Assembly of the United Nations, recommended that the demilitarized-zone approach of the Antarctic Treaty be applied to outer space and celestial bodies. Prolonged negotiations eventually led to the Outer Space Treaty of 1967.

The treaty signatories agreed not to place in orbit around the earth, install on the moon or any other celestial body, or otherwise station in outer space nuclear or any other weapons of mass destruction. The agreement limited the use of the moon and other celestial bodies to peaceful purposes only, calling for international cooperation in space exploration and, in a precedent-setting provision in Article VII, holds launching states "internationally liable for damage" to states or persons caused by objects launched into space. The treaty has not only prevented an arms race in space but has led to numerous Soviet-American scientific collaborations in space experiments.

Also signed in 1967 was the Treaty of Tlatelolco (Mexico) prohibiting nuclear weapons in Latin America. The Cuban missile crisis of 1962 had pointedly reminded the leaders of Latin America of the risks of involvement in the nuclear arms race and led many of them to propose an agreement to make Latin America a nuclear-free zone along the lines of the nonarmament treaties. The treaty requires the contracting parties to refrain from receiving, producing, testing, or otherwise using nuclear weapons in their respective territories. Nuclear materials and facilities are to be devoted only to peaceful purposes. The contracting parties also agree to follow IAEA safeguard procedures and to cooperate with the verification procedures of OPANAL, the treaty's newly established Agency for the Prohibition of Nuclear Weapons in Latin America. Protocol I to the treaty requires signatory states outside the nuclear-free zone to abide by the treaty's provisions. Protocol II requires signatory nuclear-weapons states to respect the denuclearized status of the zone and to avoid contributing to violations of the pact.

Although enhancing the security of the United States and discouraging the proliferation of nuclear weapons, this treaty presented problems for the United States that led to a later statement of understanding. This statement became part of the U.S. Senate's instrument of ratification in 1971. With Cuba not a party, the United States affirmed that nonparties within the zone would not be protected by the treaty provisions. With Brazil actively interested in nuclear energy, America insisted that the explosion of any nuclear device should be prohibited. As a voluntary constraint upon itself, the United States agreed to detonate its own nuclear devices only under appropriate international arrangements according to the recently signed (1968) Nuclear Non-Proliferation Treaty. In general, however, the Latin American Nuclear-Free Zone Treaty gave substantial encouragement to proponents of other regional nuclear-free zones: the Indian Ocean region, the Middle East, and Africa in particular.

Oceanographic developments during the 1960s opened the possibility that the ocean floor could be used to launch nuclear and other weapons of mass destruction. Verification of such weapons emplacements was technically difficult. The concept of the seas as the common heritage of mankind was also gaining popularity at this time. Disputes over the extent (12 miles, 200 miles, and so on) of a nation's territorial waters were becoming increasingly intense. There was, nonetheless, international consensus that the question of peaceful uses of the oceans and seas was urgent, and the General Assembly appointed a committee to study the issue. The problem was also referred to the Eighteen-Nation Disarmament Committee. Early in 1969, the Soviet Union and the United States both presented draft treaties that, by the end of the year, had become a joint draft treaty. The definition of territorial waters and the procedures for verification were the principal subjects of discussion for the next two years. By February 11, 1971, however, the Seabed Arms Control Treaty was written and open for signature.

The treaty prohibits contracting parties from emplacing nuclear and other weapons of mass destruction on the seabed and the ocean floor beyond a twelve-mile coastal zone. Both unilateral and international verification procedures are permitted. A five-year review conference was called for and subsequently held in June 1977.

In contrast to the above preventive treaties, the spreading militarization of the Indian Ocean region, the Middle East, and Africa reflects ongoing elite contests for national and regional power. Further, it is fairly evident, but never acknowledged, that at least one nation in each of these regions already has a nuclear weapon capability: India in the Indian Ocean area, Israel in the Middle East, and South Africa in Africa. Closing an opened nuclear Pandora's box is a very different exercise from keeping it closed in the first place.

Perhaps even more important than the preventive features of these nonarmament treaties are their promotion of cooperation in several aspects of international security. Exploration and scientific research have been the principal beneficiaries in the Antarctic and Outer Space treaties. The Seabed Treaty has undoubtedly facilitated the ongoing conferences to develop a law-of-the-seas treaty under which the world's oceans and seas may be the shared resource and responsibility of all nations. Somewhat more difficult to implement has been the Latin American Nuclear-Free Zone Treaty. As experience with the administration of the Latin American Treaty accumulates, it is likely to serve as a prototype for other regional arms control arrangements.

In sum, the nonarmament treaties have specified important areas of collective security interest and set in place significant expectations and arrangements in the structure of institutionalized trust. The fact that these treaties are multilateral and relatively undramatic—in contrast, for example, to the SALT treaties—is itself a great assurance that they will endure and provide the basis for more comprehensive arrangements.

### Duopoly-Maintaining Treaties

In industry or commerce, a duopoly exists when the market is dominated by two sellers often acting implicitly in collusion to set prices, allocate production, and control distribution. This exercise of economic power is not only profitable but also allows a controllable competition that reduces the probability of devastating surprises, overwhelming marketing victories, or serious challenges by lesser sellers. These same conditions characterize the nuclear duopoly of the United States and the Soviet Union. The nuclear duopolists are, of course, interested in military might rather than profit, global political prestige rather than price setting. They are surely competitive but seeking to be so in a managed fashion, as in the SALT treaties. They are deeply concerned about the production and distribution of nuclear weapons, and this is manifest in the test ban and nonproliferation treaties.

In the absence of a Baruch Plan system of international controls and in the presence of an inexorably advancing nuclear technology, is the Soviet-American nuclear duopoly a form of institutionalized trust that facilitates superpower communication about a particularly dangerous weapons system and achieves arms limitations that would otherwise be impossible? As prolonged and difficult as the SALT talks have been, it is argued, they would be even more so if a larger number of nations were involved. The Soviet-American talks have at least completed SALT I and SALT II agreements. While the British have now joined the superpowers in the negotiations for a Comprehensive Test Ban Treaty, this opens the duopolistic process only slightly. The participation of the French and the Chinese, the two other established nuclear-weapon powers, in negotiations to maintain control over the nuclear tier of the arms race, has been problematical; each has preferred to go its own way in building a nuclear stockpile. As though keeping the lid on nuclear weaponry among the five nuclear-weapon states were not difficult enough, there are some thirty other nations ready and eager to detonate atom bombs and join the prestigious and exclusive nuclear club.

Nuclear weapons have been present on earth since 1945. Given the Cold War and the intensity of international distrust since World War II, the pace at which the duopoly superpowers and others have written treaties banning nuclear tests and limiting nuclear stockpiles has been unprecedented and impressive. The list of dates that follows not only describes that pace but also reveals the interaction between technological developments and proliferation on the one hand and treaty signing on the other.

In the deliberate and cautious realm of diplomatic negotiation, the duopolists have been relatively speedy and prolific in the production of nuclear arms control treaties. The negotiations have had not only to deal with complex technical issues but also to reconcile competing bureaucratic interests that underlay each party's posture. Over the years, superpower negotiators have acquired insight into each other's needs and thinking, experience with negotiating strategies and tactics, and personal friendships built on a shared desire to prevent unwanted catastrophe. At the nuclear tier of the arms race, negotiations and treaties have accomplished much in laying the foundations for systems of institutionalized trust.

When the United States and the Soviet Union exploded their first hydrogen bombs in 1952 and 1953, respectively, the terrifying size of the explosions and the uncontrollable radioactive fallout

**Table 7.  The Pace of Detonations and Treaties**

| | Detonations | | Treaties |
|---|---|---|---|
| | Fission Bombs | Fusion Bombs | |
| 1945 | U.S. | | |
| 1949 | U.S.S.R. | | |
| 1952 | U.K. | U.S. | |
| 1953 | | U.S.S.R. | |
| 1957-1958 | (ICBMs; satellites) | | |
| 1960 | France | | |
| 1963 | | | Limited Test Ban |
| 1964 | P.R.C. | | |
| 1967 | | | P.R.C. |
| 1968 | | | Non-Proliferation |
| 1972 | | | SALT I |
| 1973 | India | | |
| 1974 | | | Threshold Test Ban Peaceful Nuclear Explosions Vladivostok Agreement |
| 1979 | South Africa? Israel? | | SALT II |

caused worldwide concern about the dangers of testing. Scientists, military planners, politicians, and the public embarked upon an angry debate about the effects of radiation: hereditary defects caused by mutation of reproductive cells; leukemia and bone cancer caused by strontium 90; and the life-shortening consequences of radiation to the body as a whole.[7] But even as the test-ban debate grew in intensity, the technology for monitoring compliance with test bans was being invented and produced by the superpowers. High-resolution photoreconnaissance equipment was developed by the mid-1950s and carried by high-flying U-2 aircraft. The first U-2 flights over the Soviet Union began in 1956. Sputnik arrived in 1957. By 1960, the United States began orbiting its reconnaissance satellites for detecting nuclear tests and photographing nuclear installations. Remarkably, within the span of a single decade, the superpowers had created programs of dangerous nuclear weapons tests, the technical means for monitoring such tests, and a treaty to ban the most dangerous tests in the atmosphere, in outer space, and underwater.

The Limited Test Ban Treaty (LTB) was signed on August 5, 1963, the outcome of a negotiating process begun in July 1958. Scientific representatives of eight nations met in Geneva in 1958 to discuss how to monitor a ban on nuclear explosions, that is, how to distinguish a nuclear test from an earthquake and how to know a test a long distance from its site. Meanwhile, the United States, the United Kingdom, and the Soviet Union, each unilaterally, began a temporary nuclear test moratorium that lasted until October 1961 when the Soviet detonated a 57-megaton H-bomb, the largest to that date. LTB negotiations were continued in 1962 and 1963; the final three-power treaty was concluded within ten days.

The parties to LTB agreed not to carry out any nuclear weapon test explosion, or any other nuclear explosion, in the atmosphere, underwater, in outer space, or in any other environment if the explosion would cause radioactive debris beyond the borders of the state conducting the explosion. Thus, in the absence of adequate verification controls, Peaceful Nuclear Explosions (PNEs) as well as weapons tests were prohibited. Underground tests continued to be permitted. Over 100 nations have since signed the treaty; France and the People's Republic of China have not.

During LTB negotiations numerous treaty proposals and clarifications of technical issues did much to advance trust-promoting institutional arrangements. For example, in June 1957 the Soviet Union proposed, for the first time, the creation of an international test-ban supervisory commission and a system of inspection installations on the territories of the three nuclear powers in the Pacific Ocean. The Soviets sought an immediate suspension of tests. The United States insisted upon an adequate system of controls.

The requirements of a control system became the focus of contention: (a) the Soviet Union wishing to retain the veto, the United States opposing any limits on the inspection process; (b) the Soviet Union wishing to limit on-site inspections, the United States opposing quotas, geographical limits, or limits on types of events to be inspected; (c) the Soviet Union desiring national ownership of control installations, the United States arguing for internationally owned and operated control posts; and (d) the Soviet Union proposing a tripartite ("troika") administrative council for the international control commission, the United States favoring a single administrator. These differences, appearing at a time of Cold War and severe international distrust, were relatively minor and legitimate when measured against the usual demands of national self-interest and security. In fact, the substance of these differences represented a "great leap forward" from the extreme and stubborn disagreement evoked by the Baruch Plan a decade earlier.

When France in 1960 and the People's Republic of China in 1964 detonated their first nuclear devices, it was at least generally acknowledged that nuclear materials were widely available and that nuclear technology was less difficult to master than previously assumed. Further, by 1966, five nations were operating or constructing nuclear reactors for the generation of electric power. Since reactors also produce plutonium, a fissionable material usable in the manufacture of nuclear weapons, it was imperative that antiproliferation measures be developed promptly. It was estimated that by 1985 some 300 reactors throughout the world would be operating and producing sufficient plutonium to construct between 20 and 25 nuclear bombs *daily*.

As early as August 1957, nonproliferation proposals were submitted to the United Nations Disarmament Commission. In 1961, the General Assembly urged the preparation of a nonproliferation agreement. On January 21, 1964, President Johnson offered a nonproliferation plan to the Eighteen-Nation Disarmament Committee. The Soviet Union responded with expressions of doubt about American motivations, noting that the United States was even then discussing a *m*ultilateral *n*uclear *f*orce (MLF) with its NATO allies. The MLF project was perceived by the Soviets as a form of proliferation that would eventually give West Germany access to nuclear weapons.

By 1966, the United States gave up plans for MLF, at the same time assuring its NATO allies that a nonproliferation treaty would cover only nuclear weapons and not delivery systems. The United States also assured NATO that the emerging treaty would not prohibit development of U.S.-controlled nuclear weapons on the territory of nonnuclear NATO members nor would it bar a newly federated European community from succeeding to the nuclear status of one of its members. The latter assurance anticipated the time when a united European state would evolve from that continent's steady progress toward political and military integration.

On July 1, 1968, a Nuclear Non-Proliferation Treaty (NPT) was ready for signature. The treaty provided that each nuclear-weapon state party to the agreement would refrain from transferring and each nonnuclear-weapon state party to the agreement would decline to receive any nuclear weapons or other nuclear explosive device. The parties agreed to accept international, that is, IAEA, safeguard procedures for preventing the diversion of peaceful nuclear activities to the development of nuclear weapons. The peaceful uses of nuclear energy, including nuclear explosion technology, were to be made available to nonnuclear parties under appropriate international control arrangements. The parties to NPT expressed the determination to work toward comprehensive nuclear arms control and disarmament agreements. The treaty called for an NPT review conference, and one was subsequently held in May 1975. A further review conference is scheduled for the year 1995. About 110 nations have signed the treaty; Brazil, France, India, Pakistan, the People's Republic of China, South Africa, and several other near-nuclear states have not.

Several significant concerns emerged during the NPT negotiations that are worth noting. Some were dealt with in whole or in part by the treaty. Regional nonnuclear states, such as those in the European Atomic Energy Community (EURATOM), were eager to maintain their regional safeguard system, and this was made possible by allowing them to have collectively direct negotiations with IAEA. Developing countries were apprehensive about the availability of nuclear energy for their rapidly growing energy needs, and the treaty gave assurances in this regard. Nonnuclear states feared military disadvantages if they renounced nuclear weapons, and this brought forth agreement from the nuclear powers that steps toward a cessation of the nuclear arms race would be speeded up. In addition, the United States, the Soviet Union, and the United Kingdom each made formal declarations before the U.N. Security Council that it would seek immediate Security Council action to provide assistance to any nonnuclear-weapon state party to NPT that was the object of nuclear aggression or threats.

During the 1960s the Soviet Union, as the junior duopolist at the time, made major strides toward achieving nuclear stockpile parity with the United States. As noted in Table 4 (Chap. 2, pg. 34), from 1965 to the signing of the SALT I agreements in 1972, Soviet ICBM delivery vehicles grew from 270 to 1,618, surpassing the 1,054 vehicles in the American arsenal. The same rate of growth occurred in submarine-launched ballistic missiles (SLBM): from 120 in 1965 to 740 in 1972, the latter figure representing 84 SLBMs more than the American. The Soviet missiles also carried a much heavier payload, or throw-weight, than the American. The United States, on the other hand, remained ahead in strategic bombers: 457 to 140 in 1972, and in the target accuracy of its missiles.

What was thoroughly clear during the SALT I negotiations from 1969 to 1972 was that the duopolists' production of nuclear weapons and delivery systems had reached a point of diminishing returns. About 400 nuclear bombs are sufficient to almost completely destroy either the United States or the Soviet Union. With *thousands* of nuclear warheads in their respective stockpiles, the two superpowers had enough to destroy each other several times over. As overkill capacity grew, the utility of each additional warhead and delivery vehicle diminished. The American development of MIRVs (*m*ultiple *i*ndependently-targetable *r*eentry *v*ehicles) after 1967 only underscored the trend toward diminishing returns in national security. MIRVs enabled an individual missile to carry a number of nuclear warheads, each of which could be directed toward a separate target. A MIRVed "bus" could carry, at that time, from three to ten warheads. The Soviet Union tested its first MIRV in 1973, a year after the SALT I agreements were concluded.

The first series of Strategic Arms Limitation Talks (SALT I) opened up all of the issues pertinent to arms limitation efforts in general. How is parity between dissimilar weapons to be measured, for example, superior Soviet throw-weight versus superior American target accuracy? How should agreements deal with technological advances that are achieved even as limitation agreements are being negotiated, for example, the Soviet decision to place an antiballistic missile (ABM) defense system around Moscow versus the American decision to build MIRVs? In the absence of a neutral and powerful international monitoring agency, how would verification of compliance be assured? How could each party's different defense needs be taken into account, for example, the Soviet fear of encirclement by NATO at its west, China at its east, and general uncertainty at its south in the Middle East and the Asian subcontinent versus the United States' commitments to overseas allies in Europe and Asia? How would defensive measures such as antiballistic missile systems and civil defense preparations be balanced against offensive strategic systems such as ICBMs, SLBMs, and strategic bombers?

On May 26, 1972, the first round of SALT negotiations concluded with two documents: an Anti-Ballistic Missile (ABM) Treaty and a five-year Interim Agreement on strategic offensive nuclear weapons. The underlying assumptions of the ABM Treaty were that (a) no antiballistic missile system could effectively defend either country against the downpour of nuclear missiles each could deliver and (b) the retaliatory second-strike capability of each was sufficient to destroy the entire population of the other in the event of all-out attack. These were chastening admissions of indefensibility and the capacity to hold each other's populations hostage to a second strike.

The provisions of the ABM Treaty allowed each side to have two ABM deployment areas of a restricted size and location. One area could protect the nation's capital, the other an ICBM launch area. The two sites were to be at least 1,300 kilometers apart. (A protocol to the treaty was signed in 1974 reducing the allowed sites to one: the Moscow system for the Soviets and the Grand Forks, North Dakota, missile defense system for the United States.) Each side could have 100 interceptor missiles and 100 launchers per site. Both agreed to restrict qualitative improvement of ABM technology and to consult with each other if technological breakthroughs occurred. (Some American experts have complained in recent years that the Soviets have secretly been stretching the latter provision on qualitative improvement.) Finally, the treaty provided for a U.S.-U.S.S.R. Standing Consultative Commission to promote the treaty's objectives and implementation.

The Interim Agreement placed a temporary limit on the numbers and types of strategic missile delivery systems, in effect freezing them at their level in 1972. This meant a limit of 1,054 ICBMs for the United States and 1,618 for the Soviet Union, 710 SLBMs for the United States and 950 for the Soviets. Each side could improve or replace older missiles but neither could significantly enlarge the dimensions of the silo launchers. Mobile ICBM systems and strategic bombers were not included in the limitations. Both parties agreed to pursue further negotiations without delay, that is, embark on SALT II discussions. (When the Interim Agreement expired in 1977, SALT II had not been concluded. Both parties conducted themselves as though the agreement remained in effect.)

Two further trust-promoting agreements were achieved in the Threshold Test Ban Treaty (TTBT) of 1974 and the Peaceful Nuclear Explosions (PNE) Treaty of 1976. Together, these agreements represented further steps toward a sharing of "exact knowledge" about each other's nuclear weaponry and toward the conclusion of a comprehensive test ban. The parties to the Limited Test Ban Treaty of 1963 had pledged to work toward a comprehensive and final ban on nuclear weapons test explosions, and TTBT was one outcome of that pledge. The treaty prohibits underground nuclear tests having a yield exceeding 150 kilotons (150,000 tons of TNT). Further, for the first time, each party agreed to make available to the other important scientific information regarding test sites and nuclear weapons test programs, for example, location and geological characteristics of the test sites in order to facilitate verification, numbers of tests, and so on. There was to be prompt consultation if explosions accidentally exceeded the 150-kiloton threshold.

In negotiating TTBT, both parties recognized the difficulty in distinguishing between a nuclear weapons test explosion and a peaceful nuclear explosion or series of explosions such as might be employed in digging a river channel or a reservoir. The Treaty on Underground Nuclear Explosions for Peaceful Purposes, that is, the PNE Treaty of 1976, was the response to these concerns.

The treaty put an aggregate ceiling of 1,500 kilotons on "group" PNEs, that is, two or more explosions within five seconds. For the first time a provision for on-site inspection by the other party during a test was included, along with mandatory exchanges of technical information. The number of inspecting observers, the geographical extent of their access, and similar details were spelled out. A joint consultative commission would be established to discuss compliance measures and additional on-site inspection arrangements. Not yet ratified by the U.S. Senate, the TTBT and PNE treaties may eventually be superseded by a Comprehensive Test Ban Treaty. Meanwhile, the willingness to move toward a comprehensive ban, exchange technical information, and tolerate on-site inspection are to be counted as additional building blocks in the structure of institutionalized trust.

SALT II commenced shortly after the SALT I agreements were signed. But SALT II promptly bogged down in old issues and new technologies: the definition of nuclear parity; the inclusion of MIRVs and strategic bombers in the ceilings; the counting of Soviet Backfire bombers and American cruise missiles as strategic delivery vehicles; the inclusion or exclusion of NATO nuclear forces. At a 1974 summit meeting between President Ford and General Secretary Brezhnev in Vladivostok, the principle of equal aggregate ceilings for strategic nuclear delivery vehicles was agreed upon. Each side would be allowed 2,400 vehicles, of which 1,320 could be MIRVed systems. The 2,400-vehicle ceiling included ICBMs, SLBMs, and strategic bombers, but the classification of cruise missiles and Backfire bombers remained unresolved.

The SALT II agreement signed in 1979 consists of three parts: a treaty that expires in 1985; a protocol that expires on December 31, 1981; and a joint statement of guidelines for future negotiations in SALT III. The treaty restricts the United States and the Soviet Union to an equal overall limit of 2,400 strategic nuclear delivery vehicles, a ceiling that is to be reduced to 2,250 by December 31, 1981. Within the 2,250 ceiling, each side may have a maximum of 1,320 MIRVed ICBMs, SLBMs, strategic bombers equipped with long-range (over 350 miles) cruise missiles, and air-to-surface ballistic missiles (ASBMs) with ranges over 350 miles. Within the total of 1,320 MIRVed vehicles, neither side may have a combined total of more than 1,200 ICBMs, SLBMs, and ASBMs. Within the total of 1,200, neither side is permitted more than 820 MIRVed ICBMs. The various sublimits are intended to keep MIRVing under control, particularly MIRVed ICBMs. ICBMs may be

MIRVed with no more than ten warheads; SLBMs with no more than fourteen. The treaty endeavors to place limits on missile throw-weight. Each side is permitted to test and deploy only one new type of ICBM for the duration of the treaty, thus allowing the United States to proceed with an M-X missile. Long-range cruise missiles are limited to twenty to twenty-eight per aircraft. Each side is forbidden to interfere with the other's national technical means of verifying compliance. Numerous other provisions complete the treaty.

The protocol places temporary (to 1981) limits on certain systems. Deployment of mobile ICBM launchers is banned, but testing is allowed. Flight-testing and deployment of long-range ASBMs is banned. Deployment of long-range ground-launched or sea-launched cruise missiles is limited to those with less than a 350-mile range.

The joint statement speaks of SALT as a continuing process, and both sides agree to work for further numerical limitations and qualitative constraints. In a separate memorandum, the Soviet Union agrees to limit its production of Backfire bombers to its present rate of about 30 per year.

SALT II, as we have seen, was signed at a time when Hawks in both the United States and the Soviet Union seemed to be on the ascendant. The Soviet buildup in nuclear and conventional arms continued unabated. The United States and its NATO allies undertook to modernize European tactical nuclear forces. The Soviet Union continued to use surrogate military forces, such as the Cubans, to shore up pro-Soviet political parties and movements in Africa and the Middle East. Soviet unwillingness to support the condemnation of Iran for holding American diplomats hostage at the United States embassy in Tehran and the Soviet invasion of Afghanistan all but ended talk of detente and initiated what has been referred to as Cold War II. Congress planned steep increases in the defense budget. The years 1979 and 1980 hardly lent themselves to the advancement of trust-promoting agreements such as SALT II. At no point, however, did the executive leadership of either superpower speak or act as though SALT II would be cast aside. Negotiations had been too painstaking, the SALT process too essential, resumption of a nuclear arms race likely to be too costly, and the undermining of the duopoly too destabilizing to allow the treaty to be set aside permanently.

In an exclusive article written for *Newsweek* (May 28, 1979), Dr. Georgi Arbatov, director of the Soviet Union's Institute of U.S. and Canadian Studies and a member of the Supreme Soviet, expressed the Soviet view as follows:

**Obviously, the agreement does not and cannot resolve all the problems or remove all the reasons for concern. We are worried about the development of some U.S. weapons systems not covered by the agreement. We, like the Americans, would like to ensure the complete invulnerability of our ICBMs and have even more than 100 percent confidence in verification.**

● ● ●

**I would like to reiterate that we conducted negotiations in good faith with representatives of three U.S. administrations and in the course of those negotiations we agreed to such compromises that we considered possible and admissible. The Americans, in all probability, would not agree to make concessions if they were demanded by our Supreme Soviet during its discussion of the agreement. There is no reason to believe that we would behave differently under pressure from the U.S. Senate.**

Dr. Arbatov's confidence in the verification arrangements is shared by Congressman Les Aspin of the House Armed Services Committee. Writing in *Scientific American*, Aspin described all of the conceivable methods by which the Soviet Union could cheat and dismissed them all as having little or no potential for going undetected. The one exception is a possible upgraded Backfire bomber, and this delivery system is the subject of a separate SALT memorandum and high on the agenda for negotiation in SALT III.[8]

Furthermore, there were other compelling nuclear problems in the wings. Laser technology was progressing rapidly, and there were those who believed laser weaponry would make atom bombs and strategic delivery systems obsolete within a decade or two. This expectation seemed implicit in the comprehensive test ban negotiations, a kind of recognition that the most and the worst had already been accomplished in nuclear weapons technology and that a new era in the science of weaponry was in the offing. On the other hand, CTB discussions also held promise of devising ways of returning to the kind of international cooperation and institutionalized trust envisaged in the Baruch Plan. One of the CTB treaties is expected to consist of an agreement among the United States, the Soviet Union, and the United Kingdom to coordinate their respective systems for verifying the occurrence of nuclear tests in the atmosphere, over water, and on the ground. Another CTB treaty is expected to establish a worldwide system of seismic stations designed to detect underground nuclear tests. If these treaties organize a permanent agency to carry out their provisions, it will be a major step toward effective supranational control of developments at the first tier of the arms race. Such arrangements could well convert the duopoly into a multilateral and internationally controlled monopoly of the world's principal instruments of violence. Such a monopoly is the hallmark of a self-governing political community. There was also the problem of designing effective nuclear energy safeguards and discouraging the nuclear hide-and-seek being played by the near-nuclear states eager to test a big explosion. Finally, there was the growing prospect of nuclear theft and terrorism, a brand of international lawlessness that could eventually compel the community of nations to hire themselves a global sheriff.

## Emergency Communication Treaties

This general category of arms control treaties since World War II aims to avoid the most serious pitfall of prisoners' dilemmas, namely, failure or incapacity to communicate with an adversary. Difficulty in judging the trustworthiness of the other party is increased manifold by lack of communication. The search for common goals and nonviolent strategies is impossible without communication. Emergencies, accidents, errors, and misperceptions cannot be handled adequately without communication. In a nuclear age, when the survival of civilization may depend upon the ability to communicate with an adversary within minutes, emergency communication treaties and agreements have an obvious special importance.

The first of these was the "Hot Line" Agreement of 1963 between the United States and the Soviet Union. The Soviet Union expressed its concern about surprise attack in 1954, and a 1958 Conference of Experts on Surprise Attack focused professional attention on the problem. American and Soviet general and complete disarmament (GCD) proposals in early 1962 mentioned the need for prompt and reliable military communications. This need was dramatized by the Cuban missile crisis of October 1962 during which prompt, direct communication between heads of state was lacking. By June 1963, the two superpowers completed the first "hot line" agreement establishing a direct telegraphic communication link between Washington and Moscow to be used only in crisis situations involving the security of either nation. The original "hot line" had teletype equipment at both terminals, one full-time duplex wire telegraph circuit using a northern route through Copenhagen, Stockholm, and Helsinki, and one full-time duplex radio telegraph circuit via Tangiers.

Advances in satellite communications technology made it reasonable before long to improve the "hot line," and this was done in 1971 with a "Hot Line" Modernization Agreement. A system of multiple terminals was installed at each end in Washington and Moscow, and two new circuits were established using the United States Intelsat satellite system and the Soviet Molniya II satellite. The line has been used several times, particularly during the Middle East crises of 1967, 1973 and 1979.

During the SALT I talks negotiators on both sides were impressed by the risks of technical malfunction, human error, misinterpreted incidents, or unauthorized actions that could lead to nuclear disaster. As a consequence, two separate working groups were established, one to arrange for the "hot line" link just described and the other to explore measures to reduce the risk of outbreak of nuclear war. The latter concluded an "Accidents Measures" Agreement in 1971. In this agreement both sides pledged to take measures to improve organizational and technical safeguards against accidental or unauthorized use of nuclear weapons. Arrangements were made for immediate notification should a risk of nuclear war arise from ambiguous incidents, unidentified objects reported by early warning systems, or unexplained detonations of nuclear weapons. Planned missile launches beyond one's own territory and in the direction of the other party would require advance notification.

A second consultative agreement was signed shortly after SALT II talks began and as the era of Soviet-American detente got under way. This was the 1973 Agreement on the Prevention of Nuclear War. The superpowers agreed to make the removal of the danger of nuclear war a primary objective of their policies and to practice restraint in their relations toward each other and all countries. They also agreed to consult with each other in situations that involved a danger of nuclear confrontation. These consultations are also to be communicated to the United Nations and to other countries such as the NATO or Warsaw Pact allies.

Innocuous though it may seem, the inclusion of the responsibility to notify third parties, particularly the United Nations, may prove to be a profoundly significant acknowledgement of the vital role of third parties in international conflict resolution and may be another step in the long-term process of removing the prisoners' dilemma predicament in which the nuclear powers often find themselves.

Communication and third parties are essential elements of any system for promoting institutionalized trust, and these elements have been put in place by the several emergency communication agreements just examined. In many ways, these particular agreements help bring the nuclear tier of the arms race back to earth by acknowledging the human frailties of the leaders and agencies of nuclear-weapon states. Like other humans, these leaders and agencies are subject to misinformation, misperception, error, and accident. The difference lies in the potential consequences for the human race. Every institutional arrangement and procedure that helps make the behavior of such powerful adversaries more predictable and less likely to produce negative consequences for each other and the rest of mankind is a contribution to the growing international structure of institutionalized trust.

### Conventional Arms Treaties

At the second tier of the world's arms race are the conventional arms transfers and buildups. Most of the activity in this second tier is still in the discussion stage: the Conference on Mutual and Balanced Force Reduction (MBFR) in Central Europe, begun in 1973; the conventional arms transfers (CAT) working group established by the United States and the Soviet Union in 1977; and the references to conventional arms in the *Final Document* of the General Assembly's Special Session on Disarmament in 1978.

One weapons system became the subject of intense negotiations immediately after World War I, namely, biological and chemical weapons. The use of chemical weapons during World War I had excited great outrage in world opinion, and the United States led efforts to ban them. By 1925, a Geneva Protocol was concluded which prohibited the use of bacteriological weapons, but, ironically, the U.S. Senate refused to ratify it. The Geneva Protocol, it was argued, was poorly drafted, contained ambiguous provisions, included no procedure of verification, and failed to include chemical weapons. The subject was raised again by the Conference of the Committee on Disarmament and the U.N. General Assembly in 1966. Discussions bogged down until the questions of biological and chemical weapons were separated, at the suggestion of the British. Soon after, the United States and the Soviet Union presented a joint draft of a Biological Weapons Treaty to CCD and the General Assembly. This treaty banned the development, production, or stockpiling of biological agents except for peaceful purposes such as immunization. This ban included toxins—that is, chemicals such as botulin—that are produced by biological processes. It was clear to all parties that biological weapons were not controllable systems, had a technology too readily available to all nations, and carried experimental risks not worth bearing. The U.S. Senate ratified this treaty along with the 1925 Geneva Protocol in 1974.

As described in an earlier chapter, the motivations for buying and supplying conventional arms are still very strong. Old empires continue to be dismantled. The new nations emerging from this process continue to experience internal political instability and security threats from hostile neighbors. Developing nations purchase arms not only in reaction to purchases by neighbors but also as ways of promoting their regional and global political prestige. Sellers continue to do so not only for profit, domestic employment, and balance-of-trade considerations, but, also as a technique for building or maintaining alliances. As a consequence, the conventional arms race has become a meeting ground for the twin problems of conventional arms control and United Nations peacekeeping. Civil wars and regional wars are fed by conventional arms transfers on the one hand; the resulting conflicts activate the U.N. peacekeeping process on the other. This interaction is likely to go on until all nations acquire stable domestic institutions and clarify sovereign relations between themselves and their neighbors, developments that are likely to require a long time.

The Conference on Mutual and Balanced Force Reductions in Central Europe (MBFR) is both a nuclear and a conventional arms limitation negotiation. The goal is to arrive at some optimal distribution of military forces and weapons so as to assure the safety of all parties. The perceived Soviet threat to Europe lies in the presence of large numbers of Soviet troops in East European countries, the proximity of the Soviet Union to Central Europe, and the great numbers of modern offensive weaponry, such as tanks, stationed along the Soviet border. The perceived European threat to the Soviet Union lies in the stockpile of nuclear bombs in Great Britain and France, the presence of American troops armed with tactical nuclear weapons, and the revival of Germany as a military power. The normalization of American and European relations with the People's Republic of China is another source of Soviet anxiety. MBFR has been a relatively ineffectual forum for resolving these concerns.

The continued integration of the nations of Western Europe into a united European Community (EC) further complicates MBFR. The nine member nations of the European Community have now had their first direct transnational election of representatives to the European Parliament, and in the next decade or so this body is likely to arrogate to itself many of the powers of a continental legislature. The Commission of the European Community has already functioned for some time as a supranational bureaucracy. Although NATO is likely to remain the principal defense organization of Europe and the North American continent, it seems inevitable that long-standing proposals for an exclusively European Defense Community under the control of the European Community will be revived. EC members have been considering ways in which to better coordinate their respective national foreign policies. Such coordination will necessarily deal with fundamental European security problems, hence further appear to confront and resist the Soviet "threat." In short, the trend toward a more integrated and independent European defense establishment runs in the opposite direction from the purpose of MBFR, which is to reduce and limit military forces in Europe. The inability of MBFR to reach a conventional arms limitation agreement may be explained in part by this apposition of trends.

We have already noted that by 1978 fully two-thirds of the world's conventional weapons transfers involved the United States (32 percent) and the Soviet Union (34 percent) as suppliers. In May 1977, President Carter announced a policy intended to restrain United States arms exports, particularly to nations in the more volatile regions of the world. Whereas previously United States military aid to another government was automatically considered a positive contribution to American security, the new policy would view arms transfers as an "exceptional" foreign policy-instrument, that is, the burden of proof that the proposed transfer will contribute to United States national security rests with those who favor such a proposal. Guidelines were also established for limiting the level of sophisticated weaponry that could be exported. The policy further stated that the United States would refrain from being the first supplier to introduce advanced weapons into a region.

The new arms transfer policy thus acknowledged that, one of the principal suppliers, the United States had a special responsibility for initiating the search for limitations on the trade in conventional weaponry. Therefore, in 1977, the United States called on supplier and recipient nations to join together in such an effort. Discussions with numerous supplier nations commenced, the most important of which promised to be in the Soviet-American CAT working group established in 1977. In these first discussions the two nations agreed that their status as principal suppliers warranted continuing bilateral consultations as well as restraint. Three rounds of CAT talks were held by the working group in 1978, during which it was agreed that a system of concrete restraints was necessary and should be designed in future talks. Given the multiplicity of suppliers and buyers of conventional arms, the CAT talks are likely to be difficult and prolonged, particularly with respect to arrangements that include others than the United States and the Soviet Union. Yet, such talks and the treaties or agreements that may result are precisely the way to build institutional structures and procedures promotive of international trust.

The first formal document explicitly supporting the concept of limitations on conventional arms transfers was the *Final Document* of the U.N. General Assembly's 1978 Special Session on Disarmament. The 149 members of the United Nations at that time agreed in paragraphs 22–24, 54, and 81–85 that the question of conventional arms transfers required prompt consultation and agreement among suppliers and recipients regarding methods for limiting all types of international trade in such weapons. Significantly, SSOD urged that such talks be "based on the principle of undiminished security of the parties" and "also taking into account the inalienable right to self-determination and independence of peoples under colonial or foreign domination." These were references to the very conditions that seem most to propel the conventional arms race, namely, the desire for regional security on the part of new and developing nations recently risen from the ashes of old empires and the difficulties in achieving domestic order within many of these new and developing nations. These have been perhaps the most serious hurdles to limitation of the conventional arms trade.

In conclusion, MBFR, the Soviet-American CAT working group, and the *Final Document* of SSOD suggest that the conventional arms race has during the 1970s at last come into the focus of attention of the world's major suppliers and buyers of such weaponry. It has also become evident that if some international agency had the capacity to help maintain internal order and justice within new and developing nations—that is, the most active conventional arms buyers—and to assure these nations safety from nearby predators, many of the most compelling motivations for the international conventional arms trade would be reduced or removed. If, for example, United Nations or regional peacekeeping forces were sufficient to keep unfriendly neighbors from invading each other or to discourage foreign powers from promoting domestic civil wars, national regimes would have far less need to arm themselves to the point of economic ruin and gross militarization of their maturing societies. At this level of international politics, the need for a global sheriff may once again be recognized.

## Domesticating Security: The Ranchers Hire a Sheriff

When all the bits and pieces of international arms control activity since the end of World War II are tied together, do they add up to a structure sufficient to house the attitudes, conduct, and guarantees of international institutionalized trust among the world's competing elites? The answer is an optimistic "yes." Highly dangerous and lethal weaponry, profound ideological differences, bitter political diatribe, and cumbersome bureaucracies notwithstanding, the superpowers, the grand alliances of NATO and the Warsaw Pact, and hosts of middle-sized and small states have involved themselves in elaborate and sustained negotiations, bilateral and multilateral agreements and treaties, universal declarations of arms control and peacekeeping policy postures, and new supranational bureaucratic operations that have welded together whole networks of cooperation and institutionalized trust. By these means, expectations about the conduct of international actors have been clarified, constrained, and made more predictable. The consequences of "good" conduct have become more decisively positive for most parties: restrained cost of military preparations; less risk of accidental war; growing awareness of cheaper nonmilitary modes of conflict and conflict resolution, and greater opportunity for identifying and pursuing common goals worldwide.

Several conclusions may be drawn from this survey and analysis. *First*, the arms race is not likely to be ended without the development of systems of institutionalized trust among the world's competing elites. *Second*, among the most critical systems of institutionalized trust are those pertaining to arms control agreements and supranational—United Nations or regional—peacekeeping missions.

*Third*, the negotiation and implementation aspects of arms control agreements, because of their potential for promoting and institutionalizing relationships of trust, are equally important to, if not more important than, the military weaponry and force-level features of these agreements. The quantitative treaty provisions about military hardware give an illusion of objectivity about military "balance." Yet, the negotiation and implementation procedures acknowledge that "balance" is inevitably a subjective judgment. By institutionalizing negotiation and implementation processes, the parties to arms control agreements are better able to update, match, and discuss their different subjectivities, senses of security or insecurity, and solutions, thereby discovering on an ongoing basis common security goals and testing each other's trustworthiness.

*Fourth*, world security services are likely to evolve on a two-tier basis. At the nuclear tier, whether the nuclear duopoly continues or becomes an internationalized monopoly, the greatest risks of nuclear disaster are likely to come from horizontal proliferation, nuclear theft, and terrorist possession. International nuclear policing agencies will probably develop rapidly, perhaps jarred into place by some unfortunate—and possibly preventable—nuclear disaster. At the nonnuclear tier, world security services are likely to evolve from the present peacekeeping function. To the extent that United Nations and regional peacekeeping missions eventually provide security forces capable of displacing the unilateral, armed, self-defense forces of individual nations, to that degree will the arms race(s) at the nonnuclear tier diminish and collective security be achieved. The process of building collective security organizations, that is, supranationalizing national armed forces, is likely to be a long and challenging one.

In matters of world security services, the notion of a supranational sheriff may be something more than an interesting figure of speech. The history and functions of sheriffs provide a relevant, human, institutional experience for the needs of a contemporary world in which international crime, terrorism, and aggression abound and grow increasingly dangerous. The office of sheriff had its origins in pre-Conquest England and persists to this day as a county law enforcement office in the United Kingdom and the United States. During the first century after the Conquest, the English sheriff convened and led the military forces of the shire (county), executed all writs, and judged criminal and civil cases. Over time the sheriff's judicial functions were taken over by the king's itinerant justices, and his remaining duties involved investigation of allegations of crime, preliminary examination of the accused, trial of lesser crimes, and detention of the accused in major crimes. In modern England the sheriff also brings together panels of jurors, provides for the safe custody of prisoners, and conducts the returns in parliamentary elections.

In the United States the sheriff is usually an elected public officer of his county. He has major police, court, and penitentiary duties related to the enforcement of the criminal law. In literature and in film, American sheriffs, particularly those in the West, have been glamorized and glorified as civic protectors against gangs of rustlers, gamblers, murderers, and other evildoers. In order to preserve public order, the sheriff has had the power to call out the *posse comitatus*, that is, to deputize persons to serve temporarily as an armed force in the county. Such sheriff's posses could be compared to U.N. peacekeeping missions gathered by the secretary-general in ad hoc circumstances. U.N. peacekeeping missions do not quite ride to capture an outlaw; the criminality of nations does not have an established place in international law and practice. However, the time may not be too distant when such missions may include the capture of nuclear thieves or gangs of terrorists.

It is also worth noting that the election of county sheriffs as well as the financial and military support of international peacekeeping missions both succeed when endorsed and funded by elites with a common security interest, for example, by wealthy ranchers in the American West and by powerful states in contemporary international peacekeeping. In a practical sense, the sheriff or the peacekeeping mission has been a "hired gun" charged with maintaining order within a particular system of law and justice.

If the development of world and regional peacekeeping and security services follows along the same historical lines as that of sheriffs, the way may well be paved for the gradual integration of national armed forces into a network of supranational security organizations. In this way, the military organizations of competing national elites, under the guidance of some representative civilian institution such as the Security Council or the General Assembly or both, may be able to merge step-by-step into a collectively controlled world security force. The institutional elements are already established; what lies ahead are phases of arms control and peacekeeping arrangements yet to unfold.

It should be noticed, however, that these developments would involve the special usage of the concept "arms control" alluded to earlier in this chapter. In this sense, arms control places the management of military forces under the shared control of all elites, including actual or potential adversaries. Civilian representative assemblies appear, historically, to be best suited as institutions for such shared control over military institutions. And, as we have noted, political party systems have, historically, been the most effective alternative to competing armies as systems of elite competition. Through parties, the citizenry control elites. Through representative assemblies, elites control each other and the military. These alternatives thereby place control of arms—on a shared basis—into the hands of those most likely to use them against each other.

With arms control, international peacekeeping, and collective security thus viewed as pieces of the same cloth, for what developments and trends should the concerned observer watch in the coming years? A number of critical factors have been mentioned in the course of this survey and may be recapitulated by asking the following questions:

**1.** At the nuclear tier, will the bilateral SALT talks and agreements become a multilateral negotiation among the five known nuclear-weapon states? If so, will the responsibilities for implementation be transferred to the United Nations, specifically, the U.N. Military Staff Committee?

**2.** Will the forthcoming Comprehensive Test Ban Treaty establish an effective permanent nuclear monitoring system and bureaucracy that, together with the IAEA, may serve as the world's nuclear detective force responsible not only for discouraging weapons testing but also for maintaining nuclear energy safeguards, preventing nuclear theft, and pursuing nuclear terrorists?

**3.** Will the principles of prevention found in the nonarmament treaties, now mainly geographic in nature, be adapted to "collectivize" qualitative breakthroughs in weaponry such as PBW (*particle-beam weaponry*)?

**4.** Will the U.N. Military Staff Committee or the United Nations Centre for Disarmament be assigned the task of inventorying the stockpiles and transfers of military weaponry and armed forces throughout the world? Will such a supranational military intelligence center reduce the need for expensive national intelligence agencies? Will such a center also be assigned responsibility for an international arms transfer licensing system?

**5.** Will the Security Council resume, as it has to a large degree in the case of UNEF II, the peacekeeping responsibilities assigned to it in the charter? If so, will the years of work of the Special Committee on Peacekeeping Operations (the Committee of 33) help resolve some of the difficult issues regarding organization, command structure, standby forces, deployment, finances, size, supply, and so forth? Will the veto be modified to accommodate the need for prompt United Nations response to crises? Will a combination of United Nations and regional peacekeeping forces acquire a relationship similar to that between state militia and county sheriffs in the United States? Will the proposals of Secretaries-General Trygve Lie and Dag Hammarskjold for a United Nations guard be revived, particularly in connection with the protection of diplomats, embassies, and U.N. missions?

**6.** Will the United Nations and the various regional organizations become increasingly responsible for moderating civil wars, for example, the United Nations in the Congo and Cyprus and the Arab League in Lebanon, on grounds that such internal instabilities are a threat to international peace?

**7.** Will alternative nonmilitary modes of international elite competition, most notably transnational political parties, develop as less costly and less risky institutions of political conflict? Will transnational parties, functioning through a representative institution such as the General Assembly, provide the mechanism of shared civilian control over any emergent world collective security force?

The institutionalizing trends alluded to in each of these questions will, in the light of this survey, probably be among the most critical in any advance toward arrangements for promoting and maintaining an environment of trust in a world seeking to end the arms race and conduct its disagreements without war. Some of these trends have been going on for some time, others have just begun, and still others have yet to appear. Optimists and Doves will pay attention to the undramatic and the gradually aggregating institutional developments. Pessimists and Hawks will focus on the dramatic confrontations and dangers that are an inescapable part of the human conflict process. Both perspectives will be laden with subjectivity, distinct attitudes of trust and distrust, and widely differing senses-of-security. The architects of a world without arms races and wars will necessarily continue to cope with both, undoubtedly for a long time, as they build that world a block at a time.

# References

1. U.S. Arms Control and Disarmament Agency, *Arms Control Report* (July 1976), p. 3.
2. Trygve Lie, *In the Cause for Peace* (New York: Macmillan, 1954), p. 98.
3. The full texts continue to provide important insights into Soviet and American policies and proposals. Texts may be found in Department of Political and Security Council Affairs, United Nations, *The United Nations and Disarmament, 1945–1970* (United Nations, 1970), Appendixes II and III.
4. For a scenario contemplated by a group of NATO officers, see, John Hackett et al., *The Third World War, August 1985* (New York: Macmillan, 1978). From a military point of view, the account is strikingly realistic. It describes, in retrospect, the one-month war in which the Soviet Union makes a lighting strike into Central Europe at a time when the Allies are ill prepared. There is a limited nuclear exchange which triggers the internal collapse of the Soviet Empire. In this "report," presumably written after the war, the authors observe: "The purpose of the war had after all been largely political—to exploit the conventional weakness of the West in order to humiliate the U.S. and to re-establish absolutism in Eastern Europe as the only safeguard against dissidence and fragmentation."
5. Details of the SALT I negotiations are available in several publications. For example, see John H. Barton and Lawrence D. Weiler, *International Arms Control: Issues and Agreements* (Stanford, CA: Stanford University Press, 1976), Chap. 9, and Mason Willrich and John B. Rhinelander eds., *SALT, The Moscow Agreement and Beyond* (New York: Free Press, 1974).
6. I. William Zartman, *The 50% Solution* (Garden City, N.Y.: Anchor Books, 1976), p. 2; Anselm Strauss, *Negotiations: Varieties, Contexts, Processes, and Social Order* (San Francisco: Jossey-Bass, 1978), p. ix; Peter M. Blau, *The Dynamics of Bureaucracy* (Chicago: University of Chicago Press, 1955); Ralph M. Goldman, "A Transactional Theory of Political Integration and Arms Control," *American Political Science Review,* 62 (September 1969), 719–733; and *Contemporary Perspectives on Politics* (New

Brunswick, N.J.: Transaction Books, 1976), Chap. 4. See also, George Homans, *Social Behavior: Its Elementary Forms* (New York: Harcourt, Brace and World, 1961); Alfred Kuhn, *The Study of* *Society* (Homewood, IL: Dorsey Press, 1963); I. William Zartman, ed., *The Negotiation Process; Theories and Applications* (Beverly Hills: Sage Publications, 1978); Thomas A. Reilly and Michael W. Sigall, *Political Bargaining* (San Francisco: W. H. Freeman, 1976).

7. Details may be found in Herbert F. York, ed., *Arms Control* (San Francisco: W. H. Freeman, 1973), Section 3.

8. Les Aspin, "The Verification of the SALT II Agreement," *Scientific American*, 240, no. 2 (February 1979), 38–45.

# Appendix A

## Further Information:
## An Annotated Bibliography

In an introductory fashion, this book has endeavored to reconnect several fields of public policy—arms control, disarmament, peacekeeping, and collective security—that have become disconnected in the thinking and writings of experts and policy makers. The serious student of these profoundly significant subjects, upon examination of the literature identified in this bibliography, will become informed not only about these connections but also aware of (a) the anxiety that has produced a voluminous literature, (b) the variety of authors —scholars, journalists, propagandists, religious leaders, military experts, and others—who have given their best attention to these subjects, and (c) the lack of well-confirmed predictive knowledge that could help produce "cures" for the political pathologies of global insecurity and war. Without deprecating all that has been thought and written, there is still great need for sound analysis, new knowledge, and applied skills directed toward mankind's search for a safe world in which serious conflicts can be constructively harnessed to the dynamics of social change.

This bibliography chiefly notes books in the various fields that deal with topics covered in the text of this book: modern war and the arms race; arms control and disarmament; international peacekeeping; and international collective security. The annotated entries, particularly for the basic reference works, will lead the reader to the vast stores of journal articles, reports, press reports, and other literature on these subjects. I apologize for any relevant and significant works that may have been overlooked.

## GOVERNMENT REPORTS AND PERIODICAL JOURNALS AND NEWSLETTERS

### Government Reports

United Nations, New York 10017 (Attention: Office of Public Information). For general orientation to the U.N. and its organizational development, *Everyman's United Nations; Handbook of Activities and Evolution Since 1945*. Other periodically published reports from the U.N. include: *Demographic Yearbook* (1948–); *Disarmament Yearbook* (1977–);

*United Nations Documents Index* (1950-); *Yearbook of International Statistics* (1950-); *Yearbook of the United Nations* (1970-); and *United Nations Monthly Chronicle* (1964-).

United Nations Institute for Training and Research, 801 United Nations Plaza, New York 10017 (Publications Unit).: *UNITAR News.*

United States Arms Control and Disarmament Agency, Washington, D.C. 20451: *Arms Control; Annual Report to Congress; Arms Control and Disarmament Agreements; Texts Documents on Disarmament* (with references to other relevant governmental reports).

United States Department of Defense, Washington D.C. 20402: *Report of the Secretary of Defense to Congress.* Superintendent of Documents, annual.

United States Department of State, Washington, D.C. 20520: *Bulletin* (Attention: Bureau of Public Affairs), weekly.

## Periodical Journals and Newsletters

*Armed Forces and Society.* An interdisciplinary journal of the Inter-University Seminar on Armed Forces and Society, University Chicago, Chicago 60637.

*Arms Control Today.* Newsletter (monthly) of The Arms Control Association, 11 Dupont Circle N.W., Washington, D.C. 20036. Each issue contains an invaluable current bibliography and authoritative short articles on current arms control issues.

*Bulletin of Atomic Scientists.* 1020 E. 58th Street, Chicago 60637.

*Bulletin of Peace Proposals.* Reports on scientific efforts, social problems, and current conflicts, International Peace Research Institute, Box 142, Boston 02113. Quarterly.

*Conflict Resolution.* Quarterly scholarly journal. Sage Publications, 275 South Beverly Drive, Beverly Hills, CA 90212.

*Defense Monitor.* Monthly publication of the Center for Defense Information, 122 Maryland Avenue N.E., Washington, D.C. 20002.

*Disarmament Times.* Covers major arms control and disarmament events. Published at irregular intervals by World Conference on Religion and Peace, 777 United Nations Plaza, New York 10017.

*Foreign Affairs.* Council on Foreign Relations, 58 East 68th Street, New York 10021. Quarterly. Contains annotated bibliography of current books and governmental documents.

*Foreign Policy.* Foreign Policy Association, 345 East 46th Street, New York 10017. Quarterly. Commentaries by leading authorities.

*International Security.* Scholarly articles. Center for Science and International Affairs, Harvard University, 79 Boylston Street, Cambridge, MA 02138.

*Orbis.* Foreign Policy Research Institute, University of Pennsylvania, Philadelphia 19174. Quarterly.

*War/Peace Report.* Center for War/Peace Studies, 218 East 18th Street, New York 10003. Monthly.

## MODERN WAR AND THE ARMS RACE

### Bibliographies and Data Sources

Arkin, William. *Research Guide to Current Military and Strategic Affairs.*
Washington, D.C.: Institute for Policy Studies, 1981.
A comprehensive guide to public information sources dealing with U.S.
military affairs, Soviet and other foreign military policies, and global
strategic issues. Specific topics include: U.S. military defense policy and
posture; the U.S. defense budget; arms sales and military aid; weapons
systems; NATO arms control and disarmament policies; and intelligence
operations.

Burt, Richard, and Geoffrey Kemp. *Congressional Hearings on American
Defense Policy: An Annotated Bibliography.* Lawrence: University
Press of Kansas, 1973.

*Civil Defense, 1960-1967: A Bibliographic Survey:* Washington, D.C.:
Government Printing Office, 1967.

Greenberg, Martin H., and Augustus R. Norton. *International Terrorism; An Annotated Bibliography.* Boulder: Westview Press, 1980.

Greenwood, John, et al. *American Defense Policy Since 1945: A
Preliminary Bibliography.* Lawrence: University Press of Kansas, 1973.

Hanreider, Wolfram F., and Larry V. Beal. *Words and Arms: A Dictionary of Security and Defense Terms.* Boulder: Westview Press, 1979.
A source book on the jargon of national security and defense policies.
Part 1 defines some 800 terms relating to weapons systems, military
organization, and strategic theories. Part 2 contains brief essays about
major policy concepts such as "counterforce strategies." Part 3 provides
statistics, tables, and charts summarizing U.S. and Soviet defense
capabilities, with projections for the mid-1980s.

International Institute for Strategic Studies. *The Military Balance,
1979-1980.* New York: Facts on File, 1979.
An annual statistical reference and assessment of the distribution of
military power in the world. Provides data about the size and composition of the armed forces in each state of the world as well as analyses of
the NATO–Warsaw Pact conventional and nuclear balance as of 1979.

Keegan, John. *World Armies.* New York: Facts on File, 1979.
A world-wide survey of the army as an institution within the context of
each country's social fabric. This is the first edition of what is planned to
be a regular reference publication.

Lang, Kurt. *Military Institutions and the Sociology of War: A Review
of the Literature with Annotated Bibliography.* Beverly Hills, CA: Sage,
1972.

Leitenberg, Milton. *USSR Military Expenditures and Defense Industry;
An Introduction and Guide to Sources.* Los Angeles: Center for the

Study of Armament & Disarmament (California State University), 1980. A description and analysis of the available data and data sources on the Soviet Union's economy and national budget, particularly as the latter relates to military expenditure, research, and development. The bibliographic portion of this booklet includes a great many difficult-to-find sources.

Robinson, Julian Perry, and Richard Dean Burns. *Chemical /Biological Warfare: A Selected Bibliography*. Rev. ed. Los Angeles: Center for the Study of Armament & Disarmament (California State University), 1979. A bibliography of general reference works and studies dealing with chemical and biological warfare, the technological and medical aspects of these weapons systems, the CBW policies of various major powers, the use of CB weapons in the past and under contemporary circumstances, and efforts to achieve arms control agreements on CBW.

Sellers, Robert C. *Armed Forces of the World; A Reference Handbook*. New York: Praeger, 1976. Data on the military establishments of all countries in the world including totals for defense budgets and manpower, number and types of aircraft, vessels, and other principal items of equipment, defense agreements, and sources of military assistance. Also provides data on international security forces and local conscription laws.

Stockholm International Peace Research Institute (SIPRI). *World Armaments and Disarmament; SIPRI Yearbook*. Stockholm: SIPRI, annual. An authoritative annual series of data on world military expenditures, arms production, and arms trade. Describes new weapons technology, recent arms control agreements or negotiations, and related activities of exporters and importers of arms.

Westing, Arthur H. *Herbicides as Weapons; A Bibliography*. Los Angeles: Center for the Study of Armament and Disarmament (California State University), 1973

Herbicides (plant poisons) are a special type of chemical warfare agent developed by the U.S. Army in the early 1940s and used extensively in Vietnam as a means of denying forest cover to the enemy. The bibliography includes approximately 300 items.

## Books and Collections of Papers

Aron, Raymond; trans. by Ernest Powell. *The Great Debate; Theories of Nuclear Strategy*. Garden City, N.Y.: Doubleday, 1965. Lectures presented in 1962–1963 at the University of Paris review the evolution of American strategic thought, the problems confronting the Atlantic Alliance, and the various points of view regarding France's independent deterrent.

Art, Robert, J., and Kenneth N. Waltz (eds.). *The Use of Force: International Politics and Foreign Policy*. 2nd ed. Washington, D.C.: University Press of America, 1980.

A collection of recent essays by scholars, which with technology, strategy, and the use of force (in twentieth century international politics) from theoretical and historical perspectives.

Bader, William. *The United States and the Spread of Nuclear Weapons.* New York: Pegasus, 1967.
A review of U.S. nuclear policy by a staff consultant to the Senate Foreign Relations Committee. Bader anticipates the acquistion of nuclear weapons by India, Japan, West Germany, Israel, and others. He is critical of the U.S. approach to proliferation although acknowledging that the Nuclear Non-Proliferation Treaty could provide a framework for U.S.–Soviet cooperation on this problem.

Barron, John. *KGB; The Secret Work of Soviet Secret Agents.* New York: Bantam, 1974.
A volume on the intricate complexities of the Soviet Security service. Much of it consists of stories of particular KGB actions abroad. There are two primary sources of data about the KGB; (1) former Soviet citizens who had been KGB officers or agents; (2) security services that knew the most about the KGB as a result of daily contact with it.

Beres, Louis René. *Terrorism and Global Security: The Nuclear Threat.* Boulder: Westview Press, 1979.
Nuclear terrorism involves the use of nuclear explosives or radioactivity by insurgent groups. The author identifies factors that tend to foster nuclear terrorism, the forms such terrorism may take, and the probable consequences of each form. He also identifies a coherent strategy of counter-nuclear terrorism.

Blechman, Barry M., and Stephen S. Kaplan. *Force Without War: U.S. Armed Forces as a Political Instrument.* Washington, D.C.: Brookings Institution, 1978.
A survey and analysis of the use and efficacy of military force short of war as an instrument of diplomacy in the period since World War II. The survey covers 215 shows-of-force and their impact in helping attain U.S. foreign policy objectives. It also examines the influence of such factors as Soviet and Chinese actions and U.S. domestic political considerations during particular conflict situations.

Boston Study Group. *The Price of Defense.* New York: Times Books, 1979.
The Boston Study Group is a private and informal group concerned with the risks, the costs, the adequacy, and the excesses of U.S. military policy today. This book provides a concise yet comprehensive analysis of U.S. military needs. It describes the forces and spending needed to defend the United States, to support the defense of Western Europe, Japan, and Israel, and to deter war.

Brodie, Bernard, and Fawn M. Brodie. *From Crossbow to H-Bomb.* Bloomington: Indiana University Press, 1973.
The history of the application of science to war is considered in this volume. The authors discuss the many and varied applications of science

to the development and/or improvement of weapons and weapons systems, from 480 B.C. up to the present.

Chayes, Abram, and Jerome B. Wiesner (eds.). *ABM: An Evaluation of the Decision to Display an Anti-Ballistic Missile System.* New York: Harper & Row, 1969.
This report represents an independent, nongovernmental evaluation of the ABM issue in which a number of distinguished experts from the scientific and academic worlds, and others with extensive governmental experience in these matters, were asked to prepare papers on specialized aspects of the ABM problem, political as well as technical. The result is a comprehensive work that presents the *abcs* of the ABM in detail.

Congressional Quarterly. *U.S. Defense Policy; Weapons, Strategy and Commitments.* Washington, D.C.: Congressional Quarterly, Inc., 1978.
Collection of articles from Congressional Quarterly describing and analyzing Congressional actions on matters of American security policy.

Douglass, Joseph D., Jr. and Amoretta M. Hoeber. *Soviet Strategy for Nuclear War.* Stanford: Hoover Institution, 1979.
An examination of Soviet military literature to discover Soviet thinking and rationale for the growth of the U.S.S.R.'s military capability and approaches to the possibility of nuclear war. The literature analyzed was written for purposes of internal policy debates within the Soviet Union.

Douglass, Joseph D., Jr. *Soviet Military Strategy in Europe.* New York: Pergamon Press, 1980.
An analysis of Soviet military doctrine and strategy for war in Europe. Soviet development of conventional and nuclear arms, the structure of military command, control, and intelligence, and principles for the conduct of war.

Dupuy, Trevor N., et al. *The Almanac of World Military Power.* 4th ed. San Rafael, CA: Presidio Press, 1980.
This volume divides the world into ten regions and describes for each its military geography, strategic significance, regional alliances, and recent international conflicts. The countries within each region, listed alphabetically, are described for their militarily relevant resources (area, population, armed forces, gross national product, etc.), defense structure, politico-military policy, strategic problems, military assistance, alliances, military facts and statistics, and paramilitary data.

Endicott, John E., and Roy W. Stafford, Jr. (eds.). *American Defense Policy.* 4th ed. Baltimore: Johns Hopkins University Press, 1977.
A collection of papers on the evolution of U.S. defense strategy, arms control policies, defense policymaking processes, and the role of changing institutional contexts. Compiled by two officers who are faculty of the U.S. Air Force Academy.

Enthoven, Alain, and K. Wayne Smith. *How Much Is Enough? Shaping the Defense Program, 1961-1969.* New York: Harper & Row, 1971.
The authors, as participants in the process, describe the strategy, force, and financial planning policies and procedures developed in the 1950s

and 1960s as these were applied to defense issues in the 1960s. The analysis examines the role of the Secretary of Defense in this process and the function of analysis as such in defense decision-making. Most of the period covered was during Robert S. McNamara's incumbency as Secretary of Defense and Charles J. Hitch as Defense Comptroller.

Farrar, Lancelot L., Jr. *War: A Historical, Political, and Social Study.* Santa Barbara, CA: ABC-Clio Press, 1978.
A collection of scholarly papers providing an interdisciplinary approach to the study of war. Topics range from theories about war, the evolution of war from ancient Greece to the industrial era and the nuclear age, to the legal, moral, and emotional aspects of war.

Greenberg, Martin H., and Augustus R. Norton. *Studies in Nuclear Terrorism.* Boston: G. K. Hall, 1979.
A collection of articles on the consequences of nuclear proliferation, with particular attention to the problem of nuclear terrorism.

Greenwood, Ted. *Making the MIRV; A Study of Defense Decision-Making.* Cambridge, MA: Ballinger, 1976.
The author identifies the many actors and complex considerations in the decision process leading up to the development of the MIRV. He concludes the analysis with a set of propositions regarding the control of technological development.

Griffiths, Franklyn, and John C. Polanyi (eds.). *The Dangers of Nuclear War.* Toronto: University of Toronto Press, 1979.
A collection of papers and comments by an expert group meeting for a Pugwash Symposium in Toronto in 1978. The topics are wide-ranging: nuclear crises and the escalation of local wars, problems of command and control over nuclear weaponry, the spread of nuclear weapons, the likelihood of nuclear terrorism, probable future weapons developments, and the risk of nuclear war between superpowers.

Harkavy, Robert E., and Edward A. Kolodziej (eds.). "American Security Policy and Policy-Making," *Policy Studies Journal* (Special issue; Autumn 1979).
A symposium with papers on the historical and contemporary settings for the use and control of force, policy issues in current American security policy, process issues in this field, and approaches to the use and control of force.

Harkavy, Robert E. *The Arms Trade and International Systems.* Cambridge, MA: Ballinger, 1978.
The author traces the arms trade in its historical context based on data from the M.I.T. Center for International Studies, the Stockholm International Peace Research Institute, and the Modern Military Division of the U.S. National Archives. He assesses the impact of weapons technology on the distribution of power among major nations, international business practice, and ideological conflicts.

Haselkorn, Avigdor. *The Evolution of Soviet Security Strategy: 1965-1975.* New York: Crane, Russak & Co., 1978.

On the basis of his analysis of historical developments, the author argues that the Soviet Union has been since 1965 putting in place the components of a Soviet collective security system. He also offers a critique of the modes of strategic analysis used by many Western analysts.

Hilsman, Roger. *The Politics of Policy Making in Defense and Foreign Affairs.* New York: Harper & Row, 1971.
This book focuses on the process of policymaking in the field of foreign and defense policy. It tries to place foreign policy and its making in the broader context of the workings of American politics and government.

Holst, John, and William Schneider, Jr. (eds.). *Why ABM? Policy Issues in the Missile Defense Controversy.* New York: Pergamon, 1969.
A collection of papers defending the development of the ABM. Discusses the ABM in relation to the arms race generally, European defense, and strategic arms control.

Joshua, Wynfred. *Nuclear Weapons and the Atlantic Alliance.* New York: National Strategy Information Center, 1973.
A survey of nuclear strategy as an element in NATO defense. Strategic issues are seen as causing doubts and tensions among the Western allies.

Kahan, Jerome H. *Security in the Nuclear Age: Developing U.S. Strategic Arms Policy.* Washington, D.C.: Brookings Institution, 1975.
The author analyzes the complex elements of U.S. policy, which he traces from the Eisenhower Administration to the end of the Nixon presidency, in relation to changing Soviet nuclear policy. He investigates doctrinal and budgetary issues that will influence the fundamental features of America's future strategic posture, the U.S.–Soviet nuclear relationship, and the outcome of SALT. He offers guidelines for establishing a national policy of "stable deterrence."

Kahn, Herman. *On Thermonuclear War.* Princeton, N.J.: Princeton University Press, 1961.
An influential analysis of the prospects for a nuclear war, the probable consequences, and the need to think about the "unthinkable."

Kapur, Ashok. *International Nuclear Proliferation; Multilateral Diplomacy and Regional Aspects.* New York: Praeger, 1979.
A comprehensive study of nuclear proliferation. Part I concerns itself with multilateral diplomacy, nonproliferation, and the problems of nuclear safeguards and disarmament. Part II deals with select nuclear powers of the future, i.e., South Africa, South Asia, Northeast Asia, and South America.

Kupperman, Robert, and Darrell Trent. *Terrorism; Threat, Reality, Response.* Stanford: Hoover Institution, 1979.
An analysis of the problem of domestic and international terrorism and the role government must play in maintaining security against terrorists. The authors consider the potential of technological response. The volume includes eight essays by theorists and scholars in the field.

Lee, William T. *Understanding the Soviet Military Threat; How CIA*

*Estimates Went Astray.* New Brunswick, N.J.: Transaction Books, 1977.

A critique of what the author describes as the systematic optimism about Soviet intentions and capabilities that has characterized the American intelligence community for twenty years. The author sees the Soviet Union's program of indefinite political expansion, based on the rapid growth of Soviet military forces, as a design to achieve visible superiority in every category and to determine the direction of world political development.

Lefever, Ernest W. *Nuclear Arms in the Third World; U.S. Policy Dilemma.* Washington, D.C.: Brookings Institution, 1979.

Despite heavy cost and substantial political risk, several Third World countries will probably produce nuclear arms during the next two decades. The author examines the prospects in India, Pakistan, Iran, Israel, Egypt, South Korea, and Taiwan. He urges stronger U.S. security commitments to these nations in order to reduce regional threats and fears of abandonment by nuclear allies.

Liska, George. *Nations in Alliance.* Baltimore: Johns Hopkins Press, 1962.

The author offers a theory of international relations that focuses on the factors relevant to the formation and dissolution of alliances.

Lucas, William A., and Raymond H. Dawson. *The Organizational Politics of Defense.* Pittsburgh: University Center for International Studies (University of Pittsburgh),; 1974.

Describes the organizational dynamics of the Department of Defense from the 1940s to the tenure of Secretary Robert S. McNamara. Applying the analytical approach of theories of complex organizations, a series of key case studies in Pentagon politics—the B-36-supercarrier debate, the Thor-Jupiter and Nike-Bomarc conflicts, etc.—are used to illustrate the dynamics. The book focuses on such issues as the origins and tactics of duplication in strategic nuclear forces, the political consequences of organizational risk and uncertainty, the use of systems analysis, and the role of inter-service conflict.

Martin, Laurence, *Arms and Strategy.* New York: David McKay, 1973.

Describes major nuclear powers and their relationships, the various types of non-nuclear limited wars and how these might occur, the places where armed conflict seems most threatening, and the arms trade with the Third World. Data is drawn from SIPRI and Institute of Strategic Studies (London) sources.

McGowan, Pat, and Charles W. Kegley, Jr. (eds.). *Threats, Weapons, and Foreign Policy.* Beverly Hills, CA: Sage, 1980.

An examination of the relationships between defense and foreign policy using such behavioral science methodologies as simulations and formal modeling. Topics include: the overt behavior of states in conflict; Soviet perceptions of crises; threat, public opinion, and American military spending; legislative control of British and American weapons acquisitions; and similar subjects. Contains a bibliography of recent comparative foreign policy studies.

Melman, Seymour. *The Permanent War Economy; American Capitalism in Decline*. New York: Simon and Schuster, 1974.

The author argues that the war economy, with its billions for defense, is eroding the private sector of the economy by (a) its sheer drain on capital and (b) the "cost maximization" philosophy of Defense officials and subcontractors. The latter refers to the policy that creating jobs, rather than production, is the principal objective of defense business. As a consequence, the system created to protect our national security is actually undermining it. Melman believes that the defense budget should be cut by two-thirds.

Midlarsky, Manus I. *On War; Political Violence in the International System*. New York: Free Press, 1975.

An investigation of the circumstances under which the onset of political violence—internationally, regionally, and domestically—is most likely, and those circumstances which most affect the intensity and duration of the conflict. Conclusions are based on statistical analyses of the war experience of over 100 countries in the modern period of 1815-1945.

Millis, Walter. *Arms and Men; A Study in American Military History*. New York: Putnam, 1956.

A commentary on the history of American military policy. As such, it is an experimental attempt to discover if it is possible, by retraversing the history of American military institutions in the light of newer attitudes, to shed any illumination upon the extraordinarily difficult and seemingly insoluble military problems which confront the nation today.

Myrdal, Alva. *The Game of Disarmament; How the United States and Russia Run the Arms Race*. New York: Pantheon, 1976.

The policy questions of disarmament from an international point of view. The author attempts to encompass the multifarious problems relating, on the one hand, to the arms race, and, on the other, to disarmament measures. In principle, the first part deals with the complex problem from some broad angles: as part of the general malaise of our era, particularly the unreason of competing for military might. It also retells the disarmament history of political failures machinated by the superpowers. The second part deals with the main issues that disarmament negotiations and debates have centered around since World War II.

Nef, John U. *War and Human Progress*. Cambridge, MA: Harvard University Press, 1950.

A survey and analysis of the effects of past wars on human welfare. The book is divided into three parts with each part covering a specific period of history. Part I concerns itself with warfare and the genesis of industrialism circa 1494-1640. Part II discusses the developing concept of limited war and covers the period of 100 years following 1640. Part III considers industrialism and the theory of total war covering the period from 1740 to 1950.

Neuman, Stephanie G., and Robert E. Harkavy (eds.). *Arms Transfers in*

*the Modern World*. New York: Praeger, 1979.
The escalating trade in international arms allows political as well as economic and social manipulation by supplier and receiver alike. This volume includes theoretical and policy analyses of the arms trade. Particular attention is given to the rapid extension of arms to less developed nations, the growing global diffusion of advanced weaponry, and the acceleration of nations' indigenous capacities in weapons development and production.

Noel-Baker, Philip. *The Arms Race*. Dobbs Ferry, New York: Oceana, 1958.
A classic history and analysis of the conditions for disarmament.

Office of Technology Assessment, Congress of the United States. *The Effects of Nuclear War*. Washington, D.C. 20510: June 1979.
This is the OTA report to the Senate Committee on Foreign Relations regarding the effects of nuclear war on the populations and economies of the United States and the Soviet Union. The report covers the direct effects from blast and radiation and the indirect effects causing economic, social, and political disruption. "The effects of nuclear war that cannot be calculated in advance are at least as important as those analysts attempt to quantify." The main chapters include a summary of the report, a "tutorial" on the effects of nuclear weapons over Detroit or Leningrad, the role of civil defense, three case studies of a possible attack, and other long-term effects.

Pierre, Andrew J. (ed.). *Arms Transfers and American Foreign Policy*. New York: New York University Press, 1979.
A collection of articles that discuss the history, magnitude, and impact of arms sales and grants.

Quanbeck, Alton H., and Barry M. Blechman. *Strategic Forces: Issues for the Mid-Seventies*. Washington, D.C.: Brookings Institution, 1973.
The authors assume the balance of terror as a given and proceed to describe the characteristics of land-based missiles, bombers, and missile submarines. They evaluate the likely costs and strategic consequences of alternative force postures.

Ra'anan, Uri, Robert L. Pfaltzgraff, Jr., and Geoffrey Kemp (eds.). *Arms Transfers to the Third World; The Military Buildup in Less Industrial Countries*. Boulder: Westview Press, 1978.
Although the U.S. is the largest supplier, the authors raise questions about the policies of other suppliers as well. Specialists discuss the military, political, and economic aspects of arms transfers and the weapons diffusion process.

Richardson, Lewis F. *Statistics of Deadly Quarrels*. Pittsburgh: Boxwood Press, 1960.
An early and influential quantitative inquiry into attributes and casualties associated with civil and international wars.

Roberts, Chalmers. *The Nuclear Years*. New York: Praeger, 1970.
This book grew from an effort to summarize the history of the nuclear years—both the arms race and the efforts to control or curb it. The book

is meant to be a short history for those who wish to re-explore the past quarter century.

Rosi, Eugene J. (ed.) *American Defense and Detente*. New York: Dodd, Mead & Co., 1973.
A collection of thirty-five authoritative articles on military security policy previously published elsewhere. The subjects covered include: national values and the pursuit of the national interest; factors in the contemporary world security environment; domestic dimensions of the security problem; and the relationships between world and domestic factors.

Sanders, Ralph. *The Politics of Defense Analysis*. New York: Dunellen, 1973.
A comparative analysis of the systems analysis approaches of the Eisenhower, Kennedy, Johnson, and Nixon administrations. The author's asessment describes the difficulty of separating political preferences from the "objectivity" of systems analysis. Sanders also comments on the tensions among policy makers, analysts, Congress, and the uniformed military.

Schelling, Thomas C. *Arms and Influence*. New Haven: Yale University Press, 1966.
An analysis of the relationship between war and diplomacy. In a world of nuclear weapons, military power is not so much exercised as threatened. The new diplomacy of violence is essentially bargaining power and the exploitation of this power to preserve peace or threaten war. The author identifies ways in which military capabilities are used as bargaining power, illustrating how the U.S. moves during the Berlin and Cuban crises as well as the bombing of North Vietnam were signals to the enemy intended to influence their making certain decisions rather than merely preparations for military engagement.

Schelling, Thomas C. *The Strategy of Conflict*. Cambridge: Harvard University Press, 1960.
A series of interrelated essays concerning themselves with a field that has been described as "theory of bargaining" or "theory of conflict." The essays themselves are a mixture of pure and applied research.

Schilling, Warner R., W. T. R. Fox, C. M. Kelleher, and D. J. Puchala. *American Arms and a Changing Europe: Dilemmas of Deterrence and Disarmament*. New York: Columbia University Press, 1973.
This report is from a major research project by the Institute of War and Peace Studies at Columbia University and presents eight model security arrangements made possible by military, economic, and political forecasts about the next decade. It examines choices the U.S. will face as it tries to maintain both the European balance of power and the Soviet-American balance of terror.

Singer, J. David, and Melvin Small. *The Wages of War, 1816-1965: A Statistical Handbook*. New York: Wiley, 1972.
Over seven years in preparation, this collection of data emerging from

the Correlates of War Project offers the first full operational set of data on modern international war. The study covers 93 interstate, imperial, and colonial wars, their severity, magnitude, dates, and participants, the rank position of each war on several scales, battle-death ratios between initiators and defenders, the number of wars between pairs of nations, and other quantitative data designed to facilitate the scientific study of war.

Singer, J. David (ed.). *The Correlates of War*. 2 vols. New York: Free Press, 1979.
In the first volume fifteen articles, written by Singer alone or in collaboration with others, describe the difficulties of identifying the events and conditions which have correlated with the occurrence of war, offering solutions to some of these problems. Volume II, mainly a collection of papers by political scientists, discusses the incidence of war, the validity of balance-of-power models for explaining international conflict, and the range of variables relevant to the causes of war.

Singer, J. David. *Explaining War: Selected Papers from the Correlates of War Project*. Beverly Hills CA: Sage, 1979.
Singer and his associates in the Correlates of War Project have maintained a research tradition—begun in the works of Quincy Wright, Lewis F. Richardson, and Karl Deutsch—that seeks to explain the causes that underlie a nation's decision to go to war. These papers deal with the problems and strategies of war and peace research, the incidence of war, the role of alliance systems, the function of military capability, and the impact of other variables in the causal sequence.

Sivard, Ruth Leger. *World Military and Social Expenditures*. New York: Institute for World Order, annual.
Records and summarizes the military and human services expenditures of the nations of the world in an annual (since 1974) compendium of statistics, graphs, and charts. An authoritative source for comparative data on the spending of 140 nations on military forces, health care, education, international peacekeeping, foreign aid, and similar outlays.

Stockholm International Peace Research Institute. *The Arms Trade with the Third World*. Rev. ed. Stockholm: SIPRI, 1975.
This study examines the most recent statistical data on arms supply policies of each of the five leading supplying nations—the U.S., the Soviet Union, Great Britain, France, and China—and the importing policies of the Third World countries in the Far East, the Indian subcontinent, the Middle East, Africa, and Latin America. It also examines the indigenous arms production in Third World countries and assesses proposals for regulating the trade in arms.

Stockholm International Peace Research Institute. *Weapons of Mass Destruction and the Environment*. New York: Crane, Russak & Co., 1978.
A description of several weapons of mass destruction (nuclear, chemical, biological, and geophysical) and their spatial and temporal effects on the environment. The authors conclude that the environmental issue is hard-

ly a secondary one but rather a central consideration in the arms race.

Tammen, Ronald L. *MIRV and the Arms Race: An Interpretation of Defense Strategy.* New York: Praeger, 1973.
First behind-the-scenes study of how MIRV's (Multiple Independent Reentry Vehicles) were conceived and how their development was justified. The author raises some interesting as well as perturbing questions with regard to the process by which MIRV and the various government and military policies influencing the continuation of the MIRV program evolved over the years. A former military specialist for the CIA and currently Legislative Assistant for Military Affairs to Senator Proxmire, the author in his controversial conclusion finds that MIRV was developed largely in response to internal domestic pressures rather than to enemy threats.

United Nations. *Economic and Social Consequences of the Arms Race and of Military Expenditures.* New York: UNIPUB, 1978.
Focuses on the arms build-up, with special attention to the role of emerging powers that have developed regional military pre-eminence. Topics include: dynamics of the arms race; diversion of resources to military ends; the arms race and economic and social development; military budgets.

United Nations. *Napalm and Other Incendiary Weapons and All Aspects of Their Possible Use.* New York: UNIPUB, 1973.
Assesses the broad implications of incendiary warfare for the future and covers medical and nonmedical effects as well as social and economic consequences.

Van Cleave, William R., and W. Scott Thompson. *Strategic Options for the Early 80s: What Can Be Done?* New Brunswick, N.J.: Transaction Books, 1979.
An examination of the options for "closing the window of opportunity" now opening to the Soviet Union as a consequence of growing vulnerability of U.S. strategic forces. Recommendations for building upon present technology initially, with the intention of avoiding a desperate launch-on-warning strategy.

Willrich, Mason, and Theodore B. Taylor. *Nuclear Theft: Risks and Safeguards.* Cambridge, MA: Ballinger, 1974.
A report to the Energy Policy project of The Ford Foundation that analyzes the possibility of nuclear violence using fissionable material that might be stolen from the U.S. nuclear power industry. Develops suggestions for safeguards against such an event.

Wright, Quincy. *A Study of War.* 2 vols. Chicago: University of Chicago Press, 1942.
A classic and comprehensive study of war from the perspectives of several disciplines. Attempts to clarify the problem of war by exhibiting the relativity of war (a) to history, (b) to point of view, and (c) to social and political controls.

York, Herbert F. *Race to Oblivion; A Participant's View of the Arms*

*Race.* New York: Simon and Schuster, 1970.
York has been involved in nuclear weapons development from the outset, first as a professor and most recently as head of President Carter's delegation negotiating a Comprehensive Test Ban Treaty. He describes in anecdotal fashion the personalities and interpersonal relationships of those concerned with developing MIRV, nuclear airplanes, and other technological advances in weaponry. Warns that the arms race may have momentum of its own and believes that the U.S. has a particular responsibility for cooling the race down.

York, Herbert F. *The Advisors.* San Francisco: W. H. Freeman, 1976.
A look at the early years of the arms race with special consideration given to the development of the H-bomb. The conflicts that arose between the advisory personnel, i.e., Dr. Oppenheimer and Teller, and the resultant decision by then President Truman to proceed with development of the bomb. The book also examines in some detail the intellectual content of the Superbomb debate itself.

Young, Elizabeth. *A Farewell to Arms Control?* London: Penguin, 1972.
A survey of the nuclear-weapons policies of the U.S., Soviet Union, Great Britain, France, and China, arriving at the conclusion that the arms race is going forward without pause.

## ARMS CONTROL AND DISARMAMENT

### Bibliographies and Data Sources

Ball, Nicole, and Milton Leitenberg. *Disarmament, Development and Their Interrelationship.* Los Angeles: Center for the Study of Armament & Disarmament (California State University), 1980.
A critical essay and selected bibliography on the links between disarmament and the social and economic development of developing nations in particular.

Burns, Richard Dean, and Susan Hoffman Hutson. *The SALT Era; A Selected Bibliography.* Rev. ed. Los Angeles: Center for the Study of Armament & Disarmament (California State University), 1979.
A bibliography that covers the background to SALT, SALT I, SALT II, and related issues of superpower, Chinese, and European views of the SALT process, SALT economics, nonproliferation, test bans, the military and strategic balance, civil defense, and the consequences of nuclear warfare.

Burns, Richard Dean. *Arms Control and Disarmament; A Bibliography.* Santa Barbara, CA: ABC-Clio, 1977.
Probably the most comprehensive bibliography on theory, movements, issues, history, treaties, proposals, and war/peace environment of arms control and disarmament available. Nearly 9,000 books and articles cited. Includes references to records of treaties and negotiations from 1100 B.C. to the present. Drawn from law, economics, philosophy, psychology, political science, and history.

Clemens, Walter C., Jr. *Soviet Disarmament Policy, 1917-1963: An Annotated Bibliography.* Stanford, CA: Hoover Institution Press, 1968.
A comprehensive list of basic documents, books, and serials dealing with the ideological, economic, legal, strategic, and historical aspects of disarmament in Soviet policy.

League of Nations. *Annotated Bibliography on Disarmament and Military Questions.* Geneva: League of Nations Publications, 1931.

Larson, Arthur D. (ed.). *National Security Affairs: A Guide to Information Sources.* Detroit: Gale Research Co., 1973.
A compilation of information about principal sources on peace and nonviolence, arms control, international conflict, U.S. foreign relations and defense policies, and theories and research about conflict resolution.

Lloyd, Lorna, and Nicholas Sims. *British Writing on Disarmament, 1914-1978.* New York: Nicholas, 1979.
A comprehensive bibliography of books, articles, papers, essays, and pamphlets of British origin on the subject of disarmament, arranged by historical periods. Subjects include arms trade, atomic energy and nuclear weapons, chemical and biological warfare, seabed arms control, unilateral disarmament, etc. Also covered are the scientific, economic, military, legal, and foreign policy aspects of disarmament.

Roswell, Judith. *Arms Control, Disarmament, and Economic Planning; A List of Sources.* Los Angeles: Center for the Study of Armament and Disarmament (California State University), 1973.
The focus of this bibliography is on the economic and developmental consequences of disarmament, that is, the cost of defense, the impact of defense spending on employment and distribution of income, and similar economic questions.

U.S. Arms Control and Disarmament Agency. *A Quarterly Bibliography with Abstracts and Annotations.* Washington, D.C.: U.S. Arms Control and Disarmament Agency, Winter, 1964-1965.

United States Development of the Army. *Disarmament: A Bibliographic Record, 1916-1960.* Washington, D.C.: Department of Defense, 1960.
A survey of publications dealing with the historical background of disarmament, its problems and proposed solutions, disarmament efforts in the U.N., and disarmament policies of the U.S., the Soviet Union, and other Western powers. Provides descriptive annotations and abstracts. Updated in 1961 and 1965 under title *U.S. Security, Arms Control and Disarmament.*

## Books and Collections of Papers

American Assembly. *Arms Control: Issues for the Public.* Englewood Cliffs, N.J.: Prentice-Hall, 1961.
Papers presented at a 1961 American Assembly conference. The papers endeavor to clarify the role of the citizen in the control of armaments, the search for disarmament, foreign policy relevant to arms control, and

the perspectives of the Soviet Union, Europe, and the U.S. on these matters.

Barton, John H., and Lawrence D. Weiler. *International Arms Control; Issues and Agreements.* Stanford: Stanford University Press, 1976.
Written for the general reader, this book deals with the history, philosophy, cultural context, technology, economic and political ramifications, achievements and future prospects of international arms control.

Barnet, Richard J., and Richard A. Falk (eds.). *Security in Disarmament.* Princeton, N.J.: Princeton University Press, 1965.
The essays have to do with the technical and political feasibility of choosing arms control and disarmament as a national security strategy. Examines inspection problems, international police issues, unilateral interventions *vs.* supranational authority.

Becker, Abraham S. *Military Expenditure Limitation for Arms Control: Problems and Prospects.* Cambridge, MA: Ballinger, 1979.
A short history and analysis, with documents and recent proposals, of efforts to limit military expenditures as a process for achieving arms control.

Bull, Hedley. *The Control of the Arms Race: Disarmament and Arms Control in the Missile Age.* 2nd ed. New York: Praeger, 1965.
An inquiry into the modern arms race and the measures by which it might be controlled. There are two ideas which have a central place in this study: disarmament and arms control. These are examined both in general and in the context of the strategies, weapons, and political tensions of the present time. Author believes that arms control is achievable, but disarmament is not.

Burns, Richard Dean, and Donald Urquidi. *Disarmament in Historical Perspective.* Washington, D.C.: U.S. Arms Control and Disarmament Agency, June 1968.
An analysis of selected arms control and disarmament agreements made between World Wars from 1919 to 1941.

Cahn, Anne, et al. *Controlling Future Arms Trade.* New York: McGraw-Hill, 1977.
This is a publication of the 1980s Project of the Council on Foreign Relations. The various authors describe the economic motives for Western arms sales and the dangers of uncontrolled arms transfers. Several proposals suggest linking economic aid to security aid as a device for reducing the latter, unilateral U.S. restraint in providing arms aid, and other approaches.

Clarke, Duncan L. *Politics of Arms Control; The Role and Effectiveness of the U.S. Arms Control and Disarmament Agency.* New York: Free Press, 1980.
A comprehensive history of ACDA and its successes and frustrations. Much of the research is based on 250 interviews. The book describes the personalities involved, the impact of the internal workings of the federal

bureaucracy on the major arms control issues of the previous twenty years, and, with particular emphasis, the period of Paul Warnke's directorship of the agency.

Clemens, Walter C. Jr. *The Arms Race and Sino-Soviet Relations*. New York: Columbia University Press, 1967.
The author anticipates an arms race between China and the Soviet Union during the 1970s. The military potential of each power and their attitudes towards arms control will de determined by the balance of power and economic factors.

Clemens, Walter C., Jr. *The Superpowers and Arms Control; From Cold War to Interdependence*. Lexington, MA: D.C. Heath and Co., 1973.
A review of the history of the Cold War and the arms race between the superpowers, viewing arms control agreements as an instrument for containing the arms race. Performs a logical analysis of the domestic and external conditions in which the adversaries believe it in their interest to enter into tacit or explicit agreements with each other regarding armaments. Stresses importance of preventive arms control.

Clough, Ralph N., A. Doak Barnett, Morton H. Halperin, and Jerome H. Kahan. *The United States, China, and Arms Control*. Washington, D.C.: Brookings Institution, 1975.
A discussion of the strategic nuclear force that China has been constructing since 1964, the implications for China's foreign policy, and the responses available to U.S. policymakers. The authors examine the relationship between the size and composition of the U.S. nuclear arsenal, the U.S.–Soviet strategic balance, and U.S. relations with its allies on the one hand and the new Chinese nuclear "presence" on the other. Among the recommendations: mutual no-first-use pledges between the U.S. and China and a nuclear-free zone on the Korean peninsula.

Dougherty, James (ed.). *The Prospects for Arms Control*. New York: MacFadden Books, 1965.
An anthology by authors with a tendency to prefer national military strength rather than arms control. Selections are written by Herman Kahn, Sidney Hook, Robert Levine, Thomas Schelling, and others.

Dougherty, James E. *How to Think About Arms Control and Disarmament*. New York: Crane, Russak & Co., 1973.
A recapitulation of the concepts and issues pertinent to the arms control problem, digesting the past experience up through SALT I.

Dupuy, Trevor N., and Gay M. Hammerman. *A Documentary History of Arms Control and Disarmament*. Ann Arbor, MI: R.R. Bowker, 1973.
From a disarmament conference in the Yangtze Valley in 546 B.C. to the SALT I agreements of 1973, this volume contains 158 treaties, resolutions, agreements, declarations, conventions, plans, conferences, and proposals in their original text. An essay at the beginning of each of the five sections of the book places the materials in historical perspective. The sections cover ancient and medieval arms control efforts, the rise of the nation-state and the accompanying technological revolution,

1919–1939 as the post-World War I period, and the nuclear age from 1945 on.

Epstein, William. *The Last Chance: Nuclear Proliferation and Arms Control*. New York: Free Press, 1976.
The author surveys and analyzes the various problems relating to the non-proliferation of nuclear weapons and the future of the so-called "non-proliferation regime." The study analyzes the effectiveness and adequacy of the non-proliferation regime and, in particular, of the Non-Proliferation Treaty as well as the extent to which the nuclear powers have carried out their obligations and responsibilities under the Partial Test Ban Treaty and the Non-Proliferation Treaty, and what more they must do.

Grodzins, Morton, and Eugene Rabinowithch (eds.). *The Atomic Age; 45 Scientists and Scholars Speak*. New York: Basic Books, 1963.
A collection of articles drawn from the *Bulletin of the Atomic Scientists*, 1945–1962. The documents and articles collected in this volume represent the views of scientists dealing directly with political issues. Divided into three parts, Part I deals with unsuccessful efforts, immediately after World War II, to achieve international control over nuclear weapons. Parts II and III address themselves, respectively, to the international and national consequences of the failure of control.

Jensen, Lloyd. *Return from the Nuclear Brink; National Interest and the Nuclear Non-Proliferation Treaty*. Lexington, MA: D.C. Heath, 1973.
Examines the viability of the Nuclear Non-Proliferation Treaty, the reluctance of important powers to sign the treaty, and the views of the near-nuclear states. The author finds that reservations about the security implications of the treaty tend to be more important than economic concerns.

Kaplan, Morton A. (ed.). *SALT: Problems and Prospects*. Morristown, N.J.: General Learning Press, 1973.
A collection of papers written from different perspectives on the SALT I process. The papers comment on precedents for SALT in arms control history, the postures of the superpowers, the language, strategy, and technology pertinent to the SALT negotiations, the impact on Europe and near-nuclear powers, and the consequences for the entire international system.

Keesing's. *Disarmament; Negotiations and Treaties, 1946-1971*. Research Report 7. New York: Charles Scribner's Sons, 1972.
Survey of United Nations efforts and reports since 1946. Description of Geneva Conference on Testing, Ten-Power Disarmament Committee, Eighteen-Power Disarmament Committee, Nuclear Test Ban Treaty, regional and nuclear-free zone treaties and proposals, and SALT.

Kincade, William H., and Jeffrey D. Porro (eds.). *Negotiating Security*. Washington, D.C.: Carnegie Endowment for International Peace, 1979.
A collection of 47 articles from *Arms Control Today*, the newsletter of the Arms Control Association, on nuclear weapons and strategy, nuclear

proliferation and testing, non-nuclear arms control, and regional arms control. Contains glossary and excellent bibliography.

Kintner, William R., and Robert L. Pfaltzgraff (eds.). *SALT: Implications for Arms Control in the 1970s.* Pittsburgh: University of Pittsburgh Press, 1973.
Assesses the self-interested reasons why the U.S. and the U.S.S.R. agreed to SALT. The impact of the treaty on U.S., U.S.S.R., Chinese relations, military strategy, proliferation, the Middle East, Japan, and international security.

Kolkowicz, Roman, et al. *The Soviet Union and Arms Control: A Superpower Dilemma.* Baltimore: Johns Hopkins University Press, 1970.
Analysis of the influences upon the Soviet approach to arms control, particularly with respect to SALT. These include the achievement of strategic parity with the United States, the drain on economic resources created by Soviet military expenditures, the growing Soviet concern about developments in China, and the internal politics of the Soviet Union, particularly with regard to the opposition to strategic arms talks from Communist Party ideologues and the Soviet version of the "military-industrial complex."

Labrie, Roger (ed.). *SALT Handbook: Key Documents and Issues, 1972-1979.* Washington, D.C.: American Enterprise Institute, 1979.
This volume traces the history of the Strategic Arms Limitation Talks and the evolution of major issues in strategic nuclear arms policy since the signing of the first SALT agreements in May 1972. The volume includes actual texts of the treaties and agreements, statements and testimony before Congress by important participants, background essays, annotated bibliographies, and a glossary of technical terms.

Lawrence, Robert M. *Arms Control and Disarmament; Practice and Promise.* Minneapolis: Burgess, 1973.
A brief introduction to the field, with particular attention paid to the military-strategic evolution of the Cold War.

Long, Franklin A., and George W. Rathjens (eds.). *Arms, Defense Policy, and Arms Control.* New York: W.W. Norton, 1976.
Twelve essays by experts in the arms control field dealing with fifteen years of change in the field. The interconnections between arms control and international political relations, crisis stabilization, and weapons development are examined. At least two essays are on the domestic aspects of the problem.

McVitty, Marion H. *A Comparison and Evaluation of Current Disarmament Proposals.* New York: World Law Fund, 1964.
Comparison is between the Draft Treaty on General and Complete Disarmament Under Strict International Control, as presented by the U.S.S.R. in September 1962 and February 1964, and the Outline of Basic Provisions of a Treaty on General and Complete Disarmament Under Strict International Control, presented by the U.S. in April and August 1962 and August 1963. "The current United States and Soviet

proposals have in common a recognition of the mutual distrust from which the disarmament process must begin," according to the author.

Marks, Anne W. (ed.). *NPT: Paradoxes and Problems*. Washington, D.C.: Arms Control Association, 1975.
In anticipation of the first review conference of signatories of the Treaty on Non-Proliferation of Nuclear Weapons to be held in May 1975, a group of arms control experts held an unofficial meeting to identify issues likely to come before that review conference and to suggest other issues relevant to nuclear arms control. This volume contains six working papers of this meeting, the report of the meeting, and other information related to the status of NPT.

Marwah, Onkar, and Ann Schulz (eds.). *Nuclear Proliferation and the Near-Nuclear Countries*. Cambridge, MA: Ballinger, 1975.
The Non-Proliferation Treaty of 1968 has done little to discourage serious nuclear aspirants. The original expectations that nuclear capacities would not be sought by Third World countries failed to recognize the independent foreign policy conceptions and requirements of these countries. Further, continuing competition among the present nuclear powers has fueled the current diffusion of weapons and technology. The list of countries likely to possess nuclear weapons within the next few years numbers almost a dozen (at the time of publication of this book). The papers in this collection examine the process of proliferation and its consequences for the international political system.

Newhouse, John. *Cold Dawn: The Story of SALT*. New York: Holt, Rinehart and Winston, 1973.
An account of the negotiating process at Helsinki and Vienna and an analysis of the negotiating issues.

Panofsky, Wolfgang K. H. *Arms Control and SALT II*. Seattle: University of Washington Press, 1979.
The Director of the Stanford Linear Accelerator Center urges the continuation of arms control efforts, citing SALT II as an important step in the process. A discussion of the central issues in the treaty ratification debate.

Platt, Alan. *The U.S. Senate and Strategic Arms Policy, 1969–1977*. Boulder, CO.: Westview Press, 1978.
The author analyzes Congress' changing participation in one important security policy area: strategic arms. The experience evolves from SALT I, SALT II, and the issue of selective counterforce targeting. A comparison is made between the first year of the Carter Administration and the Nixon-Ford-Kissinger era.

Platt, Alan, and Lawrence D. Weiler. *Congress and Arms Control*. Boulder: Westview Press, 1978.
An examination of the changing role of Congress with respect to various arms control issues—SALT, nonproliferation, arms sales, weapons procurement. Also discusses the problem of secrecy in arms negotiations, the involvement of the Senate Foreign Relations Committee in the arms

control policy process, European perspectives on Congressional involvement in defense issues, and prospective tendencies in future legislative interests and in arms control issues.

Prendergast, William B. *Mutual and Balanced Force Reduction: Issues and Prospects*. Washington, D.C.: American Enterprise Institute, 1978.
A description of the prolonged negotiations between the NATO alliance and the Warsaw Pact on the problem of force reductions in Central Europe, clarifying the issues that divide the two sides. The author also describes the complex process of negotiating and decision making.

Ranger, Robin. *Arms and Politics, 1958-1978; Arms Control in a Changing Political Context*. Toronto: Macmillan of Canada, 1979.
An analysis of all significant attempts to reach agreement on arms control since the end of World War II, relating leadership personalities and goals to the context of the Cold War to show how they produced such outcomes as the 1958 Surprise Attack Conference, the 1963 Partial Test Ban, the 1968 Non-Proliferation Treaty, and the SALT talks. The author argues that the Soviets have regularly forced Western negotiators to settle for political rather than technical limitations on armaments, thus reinforcing the Soviet hard-line policies.

Robles, Alfonso. *The Denuclearization of Latin America*. Washington, D.C.: Carnegie Endowment, 1967.
A leading proponent of a Latin American nuclear-free zone describes how this was achieved in the negotiations for the Treaty of Tlatelolco.

Russett, Bruce M., and Bruce G. Blain. *Progress in Arms Control?* San Francisco: W.H. Freeman, 1979.
A collection of articles from *Scientific American* dealing with arms control and nuclear strategy. Articles trace the development of U.S. and Soviet nuclear policies, the debate over the development of the hydrogen bomb, the nuclear testing negotiations, the first SALT agreements, the changing technology, and problems of nuclear proliferation.

Shaker, Mohamed Ibrahim. *The Nuclear Non-Proliferation Treaty: Origin and Implementation, 1959-1979*. Dobbs Ferry, N.Y.: Oceana, 1980.
A full account of the negotiating history of the Nuclear Non-Proliferation Treaty of 1968, its interpretation and implementation over a period of twenty years. The account begins with the early negotiations culminating in the Irish Resolution of 1961 and the General Assembly Resolution 2028 (XX) of 1965. The volume includes all relevant documents.

Singer, J. David. *Deterrence, Arms Control, and Disarmament; Towards a Synthesis of National Security Policy*. Columbus: Ohio State University Press, 1962.
The author proposes a three-stage approach to the problem of armaments which would carry the world through the dangerous but imperative transition from deterrence to disarmament, with arms control providing the bond and bridge between the two.

Stone, Jeremy. *Strategic Persuasion; Arms Limitation Through Dialogue*.

New York: Columbia University Press, 1967.

The author focuses on the problem of credibility in arms control negotiations and argues that the direct exchange of information through both official and unofficial channels can help achieve agreement.

Talbott, Strobe. *Endgame: The Inside Story of SALT II*. New York: Harper & Row, 1979.

The author, *Time* diplomatic correspondent, gives a report of the SALT II negotiations, focusing on the individuals principally involved in working out the agreement: Brezhnev and Dobrynin on the Soviet side; Carter, Vance, Brzezinski, Brown, Warnke, and Turner on the American. The volume describes the problem of reconciling national responsibilities with the hope of achieving international security and peace.

United Nations. *The United Nations Disarmament Yearbook, 1976*. New York: UNIPUB, 1977.

First issue of an annual publication documenting current national and international developments in the field of disarmament. Covers such topics as: nuclear-weapon-free zones; cessation of nuclear weapon tests; Treaty on the Non-Proliferation of Nuclear Weapons; spread of nuclear technology; Strategic Arms Limitation Talks; measures relating to non-nuclear weapons; regional arms control; reduction of military budgets; limitation of trade in conventional arms.

United Nations. *Comprehensive Study of the Question of Nuclear-Weapon-Free Zones in All Its Aspects*. New York: UNIPUB, 1976.

Provides historical background of military denuclearization, responsibilities of states within the zone and of other states, verification and control issues, principles for defining the zone, relationship of zone to international law, and peaceful uses of nuclear energy.

United Nations Department of Political and Security Affairs. *The United Nations and Disarmament, 1945-1970*. New York: United Nations, 1970.

Official and comprehensive review of all arms control and disarmament activities going on at or in connection with the United Nations during this period.

United Nations Department of Political and Security Affairs. *The United Nations and Disarmament, 1970-1975*. New York: United Nations, 1976.

Brings the previous volume to date for 1970-1975.

UNESCO. *Social and Economic Consequences of the Arms Race and Disarmament*. New York: UNIPUB, 1978.

Reviews research trends, including those in socialist countries; impact of arms transfers on militarization and development. Bibliography covers the military establishment and society, arms race, disarmament and the economy, arms trade and military assistance, military research and development and its impact on scientific institutions.

U.S. Arms Control and Disarmament Agency. *Arms Control.*

Washington, D.C.: U.S. Arms Control and Disarmament Agency, annual. This is the Agency's annual report to the President, who in turn submits it to the Congress. It describes the principal negotiations, treaties, arms transfer data, research activities, and other functions performed by the Agency during the preceding year. It includes information about the status of several multilateral arms control agreements. The 1976 report was prepared with the ordinary citizen in mind, i.e., providing an overview of major arms control and disarmament concepts, recent history of developments in the field, and major current issues.

U.S. Arms Control and Disarmament Agency. *Arms Control and Disarmament Agreements; Texts and Histories of Negotiations*. Washington, D.C.: U.S. Arms Control and Disarmament Agency, annual.
Issued in annual editions, this compendium of treaty texts and their negotiating background includes the Geneva Protocol of 1925 and all treaties to which the U.S. has been party since World War II.

U.S. Arms Control and Disarmament Agency. *Economic Impact of Disarmament*. Washington, D.C.: Superintendent of Documents, 1962.
An assessment of the problems that the United States would confront if a disarmament agreement were adopted, particularly problems arising from the impact on jobs and defense contractors.

Wainhouse, David, et al. Arms Control Agreements. Baltimore: Johns Hopkins Press, 1968.
Particular attention is paid to inspection and verification problems. Recommends a single international verification organization.

Willrich, Mason, and John B. Rhinelander. *SALT; The Moscow Agreements and Beyond*. New York: Free Press, 1974.
A collection of ten scholarly papers and related treaties and other public documents that examine the background of the Moscow agreements and analyze them in the light of the weapons systems to which they pertain. The agreements are also assessed from Soviet, European, and Asian perspectives. The roles of the U.S. Executive Branch and Congress are included.

Wolfe, Thomas W. *The SALT Experience*. Cambridge, MA: Ballinger, 1979.
An in-depth study of the political and strategic impact of SALT upon U.S.–Soviet relations and upon the processes of national-security decision-making in the two countries. The author describes the institutional setting of the SALT process, the principal issues, the evolution of superpower strategic postures, the events at Vladivostok, and the continued efforts to reach an accord.

Wolfers, Arnold, Robert E. Osgood, et al. *The United States in a Disarmed World*. Baltimore: Johns Hopkins Press, 1966.
Several scholars evaluate the United States outline proposals for general and complete disarmament offered during the early 1960s.

Wu, Yuan-li. *Communist China and Arms Control; A Contingency Study*. Stanford: Hoover Institution, 1968.

This study attempts to forecast China's foreign and domestic attitudes and policy goals pertinent to arms control.

York, Herbert F. *Arms Control: Readings*. San Francisco: W.H. Freeman, 1973.
Articles from *Scientific American* explaining nuclear weapons technology and strategic issues for the lay reader. The articles focus on the history of nuclear weaponry, current efforts to limit nuclear weapons, potential peaceful uses of nuclear technology, and general problems of arms control.

## INTERNATIONAL PEACEKEEPING

### Bibliographies and Data Sources

Cook, Blanche Wiesen (ed.). *Bibliography on Peace Research in History*. Santa Barbara, CA: ABC-Clio Press, 1969.
A wide-ranging bibliographical collection covering such topics as religious pacifism, pacifism, anti-militarism, non-violence, arbitration, world law, histories of peace organizations, leaders in peace movements, propaganda related to peace and war, contemporary peacekeeping operations, and studies in disarmament. Provides a guide to manuscript sources, bibliographical aids, and organizations helpful to peace researchers.

Durkee, Kinde. *Peace Research: Definitions and Objectives; A Bibliography*. Los Angles: Center for the Study of Armament and Disarmament (California State University), 1976.
The bibliography cites sources that provide various definitions and topics considered pertinent to "peace research." Articles and books identifying peace research centers, projects, and analytical approaches are also included.

Legault, Albert. *Peace-Keeping Operations: A Bibliography*. Paris: International Information Center on Peace-keeping Operations, 1967.

### Books and Collections of Papers

Bloomfield, Lincoln P. *The Power to Keep Peace*. Berkeley: World Without War Council Publications, 1971.
Problems associated with the development of a military peacekeeping capability at the United Nations. Evaluation of proposals to develop a world force, their relationship to disarmament and peacekeeping functions, and the Soviet view of such proposals. Includes brief observations by Hans J. Morgenthau, Stanley Hoffmann, Thomas C. Schelling, and Henry V. Dicks.

Bowett, D. W. *United Nations Forces: A Legal Study of United Nations Practice*. New York: Praeger, 1964.
This is a history of the creation of international forces during the last two decades and a handbook for those responsible for their future organization and administration. In its entirety, this was the first at-

tempt to examine comprehensively the problems of United Nations Forces and to state the case for the formation of a permanent U.N. Force.

Cox, Arthur M. *Prospects for Peacekeeping*. Washington, D.C.: Brookings Institution, 1967.
Recommendations to improve the practical management, preparation, and financing of U.N. peacekeeping operations.

Fabian, Larry L. *Soldiers Without Enemies; Preparing the United Nations for Peacekeeping*. Washington, D.C.: Brookings Institution, 1971.
Describes the transition from the concept of collective security to that of peacekeeping, the antecedents in the League of Nations and earlier, the initial U.N. efforts at collective enforcement, the emergence of a middle-power peacekeeping constituency, and the problems of U.N. consensus, organization, decision making, and action in international peacekeeping.

Forsythe, David P. *United Nations Peacemaking: The Conciliation Commission for Palestine*. Baltimore: Johns Hopkins University Press, 1972.
A diplomatic history of the Conciliation Commission for Palestine from 1949 to 1968, with special attention to the commission's structure, mandate, and other features. An analysis endeavors to draw general recommendations for other peacekeeping efforts.

Higgins, Rosalyn. *United Nations Peacekeeping; 1946-1967: Documents and Commentary*. 4 Volumes. New York: Oxford University Press, 1969-1980.
Four volumes of documents and commentary on United Nations Peacekeeping operations, covering all U.N. forces and Military Observer Groups. Describes the background of each mission, how the U.N. became involved, and the significance of different events. Vol. III is devoted entirely to the Congo operation.

James, Alan. *Politics of Peacekeeping*. New York: Praeger, 1968.
A rich source of historical detail about such peacekeeping operations as Kashmir and Cyprus. The author classifies the cases into three types: patching-up, prophylaxis, and proselytism.

Randle, Robert F. *Origins of Peace*. New York: Free Press, 1973.
An analysis of the factors in the peacemaking process that has in the past brought wars to a conclusion. The study draws upon samples of 500 wars between 1500 and 1971, describing the stages, procedures, and modes of peacekeeping, the content of peace settlements, and the effects of a number of important variables that could be identified in the environment of war and peace talks.

Rikhye, Indar Jit, Michael Harbottle, and Bjorn Egge. *The Thin Blue Line; International Peacekeeping and Its Future*. New Haven: Yale University Press, 1974.
The authors have had senior positions in United Nations peacekeeping operations. They analyze past experience, drawing mainly from the case study of the Middle East, the Congo, and the Cyprus missions. They examine major power involvement in the future, techniques for an-

ticipating conflicts and then controlling them, prospects and means for strengthening U.N. machinery, and the implications of the return of UNEF to the Middle East.

Russell, Ruth B. *United Nations Experience with Military Forces: Political and Legal Aspects*. Washington, D.C.: Brookings Institution, 1964.
A Staff Paper that provides a historical survey of United Nations experience with the use of mixed contingents of national military forces in the name of, through the machinery of, and to a limited extent under the control of the U.N.

Stoessinger, John G. *The United Nations; Financing Peace-Keeping Operations*. Washington, D.C.: Brookings Institution, 1964.
This book describes the ways the United Nations is financed and how its budgets are administered, treating in particular the special bond issued for paying its debts in 1962 and the assessments of the member nations for peace-keeping operations in 1963. In general, the analysis covers the U.N. crisis of the early 1960s when the U.N. was carrying the financial burden of two expensive peace-keeping operations in the Middle East and in the Congo.

Wainhouse, David W., et al. *International Peace Observation; A History and Forecast*. Baltimore: Johns Hopkins Press, 1966.
A comprehensive historical study of the successes and failures in 70 peace-observation and peacekeeping attempts during the previous 45 years by the League of Nations, the Organization of American States, and the United Nations.

Wainhouse, David, et al. *International Peacekeeping at the Crossroads*. Baltimore: Johns Hopkins University Press, 1973.
Several contributors discuss the political, financial, manpower, and logistical aspects of international, national, and local levels of support for United Nations peacekeeping initiatives over the past 25 years. The papers analyze the nature and scope of national support for several United Nations peacekeeping operations and also assess the role of regional organizations in peacekeeping. The book includes a summary of costing problems, logistical management, and planning issues.

## COLLECTIVE SECURITY AND INSTITUTIONAL DEVELOPMENT

### Bibliographies and Data Sources

LaBarr, Dorothy F., and J. David Singer. *The Study of International Politics; A Guide to the Sources*. Santa Barbara: Clio Books, 1976.
A comprehensive bibliography in the general area of international politics that includes many references to literature and other sources dealing with arms control, disarmament, peacekeeping, conflict resolution, collective security, and global integration. Also includes citations for other master bibliographies.

Prosad, Devi. *Non-Violence and Peacemaking: A Bibliography*. London:

Commonweal Trust for War Resisters International, 1963.

Williams, Stillman P. *Toward a Genuine World Security System: An Annotated Bibliography for Layman and Scholar*. Washington, D.C.: United World Federalists, 1964.

## Books and Collections of Papers

Benoit, Emile (ed.). *Disarmament and World Economic Interdependence*. New York: Columbia University Press, 1966.
Analyses presented at the International Conference on Economic Aspects of World Disarmament and Interdependence held in Oslo in 1965. Examines strategies that would use economic resources released by arms reductions for expanding East-West trade, for initiating East-West joint scientific ventures, and for projects aimed at improving the world environment and restraining international violence.

Butterworth, Robert Lyle. *Managing Interstate Conflict, 1945-74: Data with Synopses*. Pittsburgh: Center for International Studies (University of Pittsburgh), 1976.
Some 310 conflicts are narrated briefly and analyzed as problems in conflict management. A codebook is included as a quantification of certain aspects of each case.

Butterworth, Robert Lyle. *Moderation from Management: International Organizations for Peace*. Pittsburgh: Center for International Studies (University of Pittsburgh), 1978.
An empirical assessment of the international collective security organizations—the United Nations, Organization of American States, Arab League, Council of Europe, Organization of African Unity—created since 1945 and their effectiveness as conflict managers.

Claude, Inis L., Jr. *Swords Into Plowshares*. 3d ed. New York: Random House, 1964.
An analysis of various theories and approaches to the achievement of peace within the state system.

David Davies Study Group on the Peaceful Settlement of International Disputes. *Report of the Study Group*. London: David Davies Memorial Institute of International Studies, 1966.
The Institute's distinguished Study Group was created in 1963 and reported in 1966. Various parts of the report deal with international negotiation, mediation and good offices, conciliation, arbitration, the International Court of Justice, the experience of the United Nations in peaceful settlement, and the settlement of disputes in special fields. The analysis examines the legal and political character of international disputes, the international machinery for their settlement, and an evaluation of the adequacy of that machinery.

Donelan, M. D., and M. J. Grieve. *International Disputes; Case Histories, 1945-1970*. New York: St. Martin's Press, 1973.
This is the third of a series of studies prepared under the sponsorship of

the David Davies Memorial Institute of International Studies, London. Fifty case study accounts dealing with major post-World War II internation conflicts in which U.N. peacekeeping often had a major role.

Falk, Richard A., and Saul H. Mendlovitz (eds.). *The Strategy of World Order: Toward a Theory of War Prevention*. Vol. 1. New York: World Law Fund, 1966.
An extensive collection of reprinted articles on the causes of war and peace, the nature of international society, the legal issues related to the bombing of Hiroshima, the state of the international legal order, the institutions of international law, the United Nations, the procedures of pacific settlement and peace-keeping, and the problem of arms control and disarmament.

Ferencz, Benjamin B. *Defining International Aggression: The Search for World Peace*. 2 vols. Dobbs Ferry, N.Y.: Oceana, 1976.
A documentary history and analysis of efforts during the past fifty years to achieve a definition of those acts by states that constitute international aggression. The author, a former U.S. Prosecutor at the Nuremberg war crimes trials, discusses the condemnation of aggressive war at Nuremberg and Tokyo and traces the debates that led to the consensus definition of aggression adopted by the U.N. General Assembly in 1974. In a word-by-word analysis he examines the understandings and misunderstandings that relate to the ambiguous provisions of the definition.

Finkelstein, Marina S., and Lawrence S. (eds.). *Collective Security*. San Francisco: Chandler, 1966.
A compilation of definitions and views on collective security.

Haas, Ernst B. *Beyond the Nation-State: Functionalism and International Organization*. Stanford: Stanford University Press, 1965.
A theoretical analysis of the factors and varying forms of international integration.

Larus, Joel (ed.). *From Collective Security to Preventive Diplomacy*. New York: John Wiley, 1965.
Documentary and interpretative material on the League of Nations and the United Nations, their diplomacy and their problems. The latter part of the book describes the emergence of preventive diplomacy and its application in the Suez and Congo crises.

Leebaert, Derek (ed.). *European Security: Prospects for the 1980's*. Lexington, MA: D.C. Heath, 1979.
European security has been made more complex by such new issues as energy supply, technological sharing, and ideological drift. Previously, this security rested primarily on military strength, economic vigor, and national stability. The mixture of the new issues and the old bases will present serious challenges in the 1980s.

Levi, Werner. *The Coming End of War*. Beverly Hills, CA: Sage, 1981.
Levi offers evidence that the likelihood of nuclear war between the superpowers is declining. Ever-increasing interaction between the major

developed nations, particularly economic interactions, makes nuclear war less and less palatable. Levi anticipates that future conflicts between the superpowers will be conducted through proxy of smaller nations, or on economic rather than military battlegrounds.

Luard, Evan. *The International Regulation of Civil Wars*. New York: New York University Press, 1972.
Several essays examine recent civil wars in Spain, Greece, Lebanon, Laos, the Congo, Yemen, and Cyprus, evaluate their impact on international relations, and consider the problem of regulating civil wars through law or institutions.

Northedge, F. S., and M. D. Donelan. *International Disputes; The Political Aspect*. New York: St. Martin's Press, 1972.
Analyses based upon the fifty case studies of post-World War II internation conflicts compiled under the auspices of the David Davies Memorial Institute. (See M. D. Donelan and M. J. Grieve, *International Disputes; Case Histories, 1945-1970*.) The analyses suggest why some conflicts were settled by force and others negotiated non-violently.

Parten, Daniel G. *Individual Responsibility Under a Disarmament Agreement in American Law*. Durham, N.C.: Duke Rule of Law Research Center, 1965.
Argues for a U.S. constitutional amendment that would establish individual responsibility for reporting national violations of international disarmament agreements. Unilateral U.S. action would presumably be a model and a challenge to other world powers.

Raman, K. Venkata. *Dispute Settlement Through the United Nations*. Dobbs Ferry, N.Y.: Oceana, 1977.
Published under the auspices of the United Nations Institute for Training and Research, this volume contains eight papers on various aspects of peaceful settlement of international disputes, including third-party roles, analysis for mediation, the function of law, procedural issues in U.N. mediation, and the use of "good offices." Contains a selected bibliography on peaceful settlement: about 125 books and 75 articles.

Stone, Julius. *Conflict Through Consensus; United Nations Approaches to Aggression*. Baltimore: Johns Hopkins University Press, 1977.
The Consensus Definition of Aggression adopted by the United Nations General Assembly in 1974 is analyzed and evaluated by an international legal scholar. The author identifies the ambiguities, silences, and self-contradictions that weaken the definition.

Study Group on the Peaceful Settlement of International Disputes. *Report*. London: David Davies Memorial Institute of International Studies, 1966.
The United Nations, the International Court of Justice, the Permanent Court of Arbitration, and similar institutions of negotiation and settlement are described, analyzed, and evaluated.

Zacher, Mark W. *International Conflicts and Collective Security, 1946-1977; The United Nations, Organization of American States, Organiza-*

*tion of African Unity, and Arab League.* New York: Praeger, 1979. The author offers a theory of collective security, with particular attention to the definitions of such terms as "war," "crisis," and "alignment." Patterns of security and peacemaking involvement by the U.N. and three regional organizations are compared.

# Appendix B

**Final Document of the Tenth Special Session of the General Assembly of the United Nations**

(Adopted by consensus on June 30, 1978, in the form of a resolution.)

*The General Assembly,*

*Alarmed* by the threat to the very survival of mankind posed by the existence of nuclear weapons and the continuing arms race, and recalling the devastation inflicted by all wars,

*Convinced* that disarmament and arms limitation, particularly in the nuclear field, are essential for the prevention of the danger of nuclear war and the strengthening of international peace and security and for the economic and social advancement of all peoples, thus facilitating the achievement of the new international economic order:

*Having resolved* to lay the foundation of an international disarmament strategy which, through co-ordinated and persevering efforts in which the United Nations should play a more effective role, aims at general and complete disarmament under effective international control,

*Adopts* the following Final Document of this special session of the General Assembly devoted to disarmament:

## I. INTRODUCTION

**1.** Attainment of the objective of security, which is an inseparable element of peace, has always been one of the most profound aspirations of humanity. States have for a long time sought to maintain their security through the possession of arms. Admittedly, their survival has, in certain cases, effectively depended on whether they could count on appropriate means of defence. Yet the accumulation of weapons, particularly nuclear weapons, today constitutes much more a threat than a protection for the future of mankind. The time has therefore come to put an end to this situation, to abandon the use of force in international relations and to seek security in disarmament, that is to say, through a gradual but effective process beginning with a reduction in the present level of armaments. The ending of the arms race and the achievement of real disarmament are tasks of primary importance and urgency. To meet this historic challenge is in the political and economic interests of all the nations and peoples of the world as well as in the interests of ensuring their genuine security and peaceful future.

**2.** Unless its avenues are closed, the continued arms race means a growing threat to international peace and security and even to the very survival of mankind. The nuclear and conventional arms build-up threatens to stall the efforts aimed at reaching the goals of development, to become an obstacle on the road to achieving the new international economic order and to hinder the solution of other vital problems facing mankind.

**3.** Dynamic development of detente, encompassing all spheres of international relations in all regions of the world, with the participation of all countries, would create conditions conducive to the efforts of States to end the arms race, which has engulfed the world, thus reducing the danger of war. Progress on detente and progress on disarmament mutually complement and strengthen each other.

**4.** The Disarmament Decade solemnly declared in 1969 by the United Nations is coming to an end. Unfortunately, the objectives established on that occasion by the General Assembly appear to be as far away today as they were then, or even further because the arms race is not diminishing but increasing and outstrips by far the efforts to curb it. While it is true some limited agreements have been reached, "effective measures relating to the cessation of the nuclear arms race at an early date and to nuclear disarmament" continue to elude man's grasp. Yet the implementation of such measures is urgently required. There has not been either any real progress that might lead to the conclusion of a treaty on general and complete disarmament under effective international control. Furthermore, it has not been possible to free any amount, however modest, of the enormous resources, both material and human, that are wasted on the unproductive and spiralling arms race, and which should be made available for the purpose of economic and social development, especially since such a race "places great burden on both the developing and the developed countries."

**5.** The Members of the United Nations are fully aware of the conviction of their peoples, that the question of general and complete disarmament is of utmost importance and that peace, security and economic and social development are indivisible and have therefore recognized that the corresponding obligations and responsibilities are universal.

**6.** Thus a powerful current of opinion has gradually formed, leading to the convening of what will go down in the annals of the United Nations as the first special session of the General Assembly devoted entirely to disarmament.

**7.** The outcome of this special session, whose deliberations have to a large extent been facilitated by the five sessions of the Preparatory Committee which preceded it, is the present Final Document. This introduction serves as a preface to the document which comprises also the following three sections: a Declaration, a Programme of Action and recommendations concerning the international machinery for disarmament negotiations.

**8.** While the final objective of the efforts of all States should continue to be general and complete disarmament under effective international control, the immediate goal is that of the elimination of the danger of a nuclear war and the implementation of measures to halt and reverse the arms race and clear the path towards lasting peace. Negotiations on the entire range of those issues should be based on the strict observance of the purposes and principles enshrined in the Charter of the United Nations, with full recognition of the role of the United Nations in the field of disarmament and reflecting the vital interest of all the peoples of the world in this sphere. The aim of the Declaration is to review and assess the existing situation, outline the objectives and the priority tasks and set forth fundamental principles for disarmament negotiations.

**9.** For disarmament, the aims and purposes of which the Declaration proclaims, to become a reality it was essential to agree on a series of specific disarmament measures, selected by common accord as those on which there is a consensus to the effect that their subsequent realization in the short term appears to be feasible. There is also a need to prepare through agreed procedures a comprehensive disarmament programme. That programme, passing through all the necessary stages, should lead to general and complete disarmament under effective international control. Procedures for watching over the fulfilment of the obligations thus assumed had also to be agreed upon. That is the purpose of the Programme of Action.

**10.** Although the decisive factor for achieving real measures of disarmament is the "political will" of States, and especially of those possessing nuclear weapons, a significant role can also be played by the effective functioning of an appropriate international machinery designed to deal with the problems of disarmament in its various aspects. Consequently, it would be necessary that the two kinds of organs required to that end, the deliberative and the negotiating organs, have the appropriate organization and procedures that would be most conducive to obtaining constructive results. The fourth and last section of the Final Document has been prepared with that end in view.

## II. DECLARATION

11. Mankind today is confronted with an unprecedented threat of self-extinction arising from the massive and competitive accumulation of the most destructive weapons ever produced. Existing arsenals of nuclear weapons alone are more than sufficient to destroy all life on earth. Failure of efforts to halt and reverse the arms race, in particular the nuclear arms race, increases the danger of the proliferation of nuclear weapons. Yet the arms race continues. Military budgets are constantly growing, with enormous consumption of human and material resources. The increase in weapons, especially nuclear weapons, far from helping to strengthen international security, on the contrary weakens it. The vast stockpiles and tremendous build-up of arms and armed forces and the competition for qualitative refinement

of weapons of all kinds to which scientific resources and technological advances are diverted, pose incalculable threats to peace. This situation both reflects and aggravates international tensions, sharpens conflicts in various regions of the world, hinders the process of detente, exacerbates the differences between opposing military alliances, jeopardizes the security of all States, heightens the sense of insecurity among all States, including the non-nuclear-weapons States, and increases the threat of nuclear war.

12. The arms race, particularly in its nuclear aspect, runs counter to efforts to achieve further relaxation of international tension, to establish international relations based on peaceful coexistence and trust between all States, and to develop broad international cooperation and understanding. The arms race impedes the realization of the purposes, and is incompatible with the principles, of the Charter of the United Nations, especially respect for sovereignty, refraining from the threat or use of force against the territorial integrity or political independence of any State, peaceful settlement of disputes and non-intervention and non-interference in the internal affairs of States. It also adversely affects the rights of peoples freely to determine their systems of social and economic development, and hinders the struggle for self-determination and the elimination of colonial rule, racial or foreign domination or occupation. Indeed, the massive accumulation of armaments and the acquisition of armaments technology by racist regimes, as well as their possible acquisition of nuclear weapons, present a challenging and increasingly dangerous obstacle to a world community faced with the urgent need to disarm. It is, therefore, essential for purposes of disarmament to prevent any further acquisition of arms or arms technology by such regimes, especially through strict adherence by all States to relevant decisions of the Security Council.

13. Enduring international peace and security cannot be built on the accumulation of weaponry by military alliances nor be sustained by a precarious balance of deterrence or doctrines of strategic superiority. Genuine and lasting peace can only be created through the effective implementation of the security system provided for in the Charter of the United Nations and the speedy and substantial reduction of arms and armed forces, by international agreement and mutual example leading ultimately to general and complete disarmament under effective international control. At the same time, the causes of the arms race and threats to peace must be reduced and to this end effective action should be taken to eliminate tensions and settle disputes by peaceful means.

14. Since the process of disarmament affects the vital security interests of all States, they must all be actively concerned with and contribute to the measures of disarmament and arms limitations, which have an essential part to play in maintaining and strengthening international security. Therefore the role and responsibility of the United Nations in the sphere of disarmament, in accordance with its Charter, must be strengthened.

**15.** It is essential that not only Governments but also the peoples of the world recognize and understand the dangers in the present situation. In order that an international conscience may develop and that world public opinion may exercise a positive influence, the United Nations should increase the dissemination of information on the armaments race and disarmament with the full co-operation of Member States.

**16.** In a world of finite resources there is a close relationship between expenditure on armaments and economic and social development. Military expenditures are reaching ever higher levels, the highest percentage of which can be attributed to the nuclear weapon States and most of their allies, with prospects of further expansion and the danger of further increases in the expenditures of other countries. The hundreds of billions of dollars spent annually on the manufacture or improvement of weapons are in sombre and dramatic contrast to the want and poverty in which two-thirds of the world's population live. This colossal waste of resources is even more serious in that it diverts to military purposes not only material but also technical and human resources which are urgently needed for development in all countries, particularly in the developing countries. Thus, the economic and social consequences of the arms race are so detrimental that its continuation is obviously incompatible with the implementation of the new international economic order based on justice, equity and co-operation. Consequently, resources released as a result of the implementation of disarmament measures should be used in a manner which will help to promote the well-being of all peoples and to improve the economic conditions of the developing countries.

**17.** Disarmament has thus become an imperative and most urgent task facing the international community. No real progress has been made so far in the crucial field of the reduction of armaments. However, certain positive changes in international relations in some areas of the world provide some encouragement.

Agreements have been reached that have been important in limiting certain weapons or eliminating them altogether, as in the case of the Convention on the Prohibition of the Development, Production and Stockpiling of Bacteriological (Biological) and Toxin Weapons and on Their Destruction, and excluding particular areas from the arms race. The fact remains that these agreements relate only to measures  of limited restraint while the arms race continues. These partial measures have done little to bring the world closer to the goal of general and complete disarmament. For more than a decade there have been no negotiations leading to a treaty on general and complete disarmament. The pressing need now is to translate into practical terms the provisions of this Final Document and to proceed along the road of binding and effective international agreements in the field of disarmament.

**18.** Removing the threat of a world war—a nuclear war—is the most acute and urgent task of the present day. Mankind is confronted with a choice: we must halt the arms race and proceed to disarmament or face annihilation.

**19.** The ultimate objective of the efforts of States in the disarmament process is general and complete disarmament under effective international control.

The principal goals of disarmament are to ensure the survival of mankind and to eliminate the danger of war, in particular nuclear war, to ensure that war is no longer an instrument for settling international disputes and that the use and the threat of force are eliminated from international life, as provided for in the Charter of the United Nations.

Progress towards this objective requires the conclusion and implementation of agreements on the cessation of the arms race and on genuine measures of disarmament taking into account the need of States to protect their security.

**20.** Among such measures, effective measures of nuclear disarmament and the prevention of nuclear war have the highest priority. To this end, it is imperative to remove the threat of nuclear weapons, to halt and reverse the nuclear arms race until the total elimination of nuclear weapons and their delivery systems has been achieved, and to prevent the proliferation of nuclear weapons.

At the same time, other measures designed to prevent the outbreak of nuclear war and to lessen the danger of the threat or use of nuclear weapons should be taken.

**21.** Along with these, agreements or other effective measures should be adopted to prohibit or prevent the development, production or use of other weapons of mass destruction. In this context, an agreement on elimination of all chemical weapons should be concluded as a matter of high priority.

**22.** Together with negotiations on nuclear disarmament measures, negotiations should be carried out on the balanced reduction of armed forces and of conventional armaments, based on the principle of undiminished security of the parties with a view to promoting or enhancing stability at a lower military level, taking into account the need of all States to protect their security. These negotiations should be conducted with particular emphasis on armed forces and conventional weapons of nuclear-weapon States and other militarily significant countries. There should also be negotiations on the limitation of international transfer of conventional weapons, based, in particular, on the same principle, and taking into account the inalienable right to self-determination and independence of peoples under colonial or foreign domination and the obligations of States to respect that right, in accordance with the Charter of the United Nations and the Declaration on Principles of International Law concerning Friendly Relations and Cooperation Among States, as well as the need of recipient States to protect their security.

**23.** Further international action should be taken to prohibit or restrict for humanitarian reasons the use of specific conventional weapons, including those which may be excessively injurious, cause unnecessary suffering or have indiscriminate effects.

**24.** Collateral measures in both the nuclear and conventional fields, together with other measures specifically designed to build confidence, should be undertaken in order to contribute to the creation of favourable conditions for the adoption of additional disarmament measures and to further relaxation of international tension.

**25.** Negotiations and measures in the field of disarmament shall be guided by the fundamental principles set forth below.

**26.** All States Members of the United Nations reaffirm their full commitment to the purposes of the Charter of the United Nations and their obligation strictly to observe its principles as well as other relevant and generally accepted principles of international law relating to the maintenance of international peace and security.

They stress the special importance of refraining from the threat or use of force against the sovereignty, territorial integrity or political independence of any State, or against peoples under colonial or foreign domination seeking to exercise their right to self-determination and to achieve independence; non-intervention and non-interference in the internal affairs of other States; the inviolability of international frontiers; and the peaceful settlement of disputes, having regard to the inherent right of States to individual and collective self-defence in accordance with the Charter.

**27.** In accordance with the Charter, the United Nations has a central role and primary responsibility in the sphere of disarmament. In order effectively to discharge this role and facilitate and encourage all measures in this field, the United Nations should be kept appropriately informed of all steps in this field, whether unilateral, bilateral, regional or multilateral, without prejudice to the progress of negotiations.

**28.** All the peoples of the world have a vital interest in the success of disarmament negotiations. Consequently, all States have the duty to contribute to efforts in the field of disarmament. All States have the right to participate in disarmament negotiations. They have the right to participate on an equal footing in those multilateral disarmament negotiations which have a direct bearing on their national security. While disarmament is the responsibility of all States, the nuclear-weapons States have the primary responsibility for nuclear disarmament, and, together with other militarily significant States for halting and reversing the arms race. It is therefore important to secure their active participation.

**29.** The adoption of disarmament measures should take place in such an equitably and balanced manner as to ensure the right of each State to security and that no individual State or group of States may obtain advantages over others at any stage. At each stage the objective should be undiminished security at the lowest possible level of armaments and military forces.

**30.** An acceptable balance of mutual responsibilities and obligations for nuclear and non-nuclear-weapons States should be strictly observed.

**31.** Disarmament and arms limitation agreements should provide for adequate measures of verification satisfactory to all parties concerned in order to create the necessary confidence and ensure that they are being observed by all parties. The form and modalities of the verification to be provided for in any specific agreement depend upon and should be determined by the purposes, scope and nature of the agreement. Agreements should provide for the participation of parties directly or through the United Nations system in the verification process. Where appropriate, a combination of several methods of verification as well as other compliance procedures should be employed.

**32.** All States, and in particular nuclear weapon States, should consider various proposals designed to secure the avoidance of the use of nuclear weapons, and the prevention of nuclear war. In this context, while noting the declarations made by nuclear-weapon States, effective arrangements, as appropriate, to assure non-nuclear-weapon States against the use or the threat of use of nuclear weapons could strengthen the security of those States and international peace and security.

**33.** The establishment of nuclear-weapon-free zones on the basis of agreements or arrangments freely arrived at among the States of the zone concerned, and the full compliance with those agreements or arrangements, thus ensuring that the zones are genuinely free from nuclear weapons, and respect for such zones by nuclear-weapon States, constitute an important disarmament measure.

**34.** Disarmament, relaxation of international tension, respect for the right to self-determination and national independence, the peaceful settlement of disputes in accordance with the Charter of the United Nations and the strengthening of international peace and security are directly related to each other. Progress in any of these spheres has a beneficial effect on all of them; in turn, failure in one sphere has negative effects on others.

**35.** There is also a close relationship between disarmament and development. Progress in the former would help greatly to the realization of the latter. Therefore resources released as a result of the implementation of disarmament measures should be devoted to economic and social development of all nations and contribute to the bridging of the economic gap between developed and developing countries.

**36.** Non-proliferation of nuclear weapons is a matter of universal concern. Measures of disarmament must be consistent with the unalienable right of all States, without discrimination, to develop, acquire and use nuclear technology, equipment and materials for the peaceful use of nuclear energy and to determine their peaceful nuclear programmes in accordance with their national priorities, needs and interests, bearing in mind the need to prevent the proliferation of nuclear weapons. International co-operation in the peaceful uses of nuclear energy should be conducted under agreed and appropriate international safeguards applied on a non-discriminatory basis.

**37.** Significant progress in disarmament, including nuclear disarmament, would be facilitated by parallel measures to strengthen the security of States and to improve in general the international situation.

**38.** Negotiations on partial measures of disarmament should be conducted concurrently with negotiations on more comprehensive measures and should be followed by negotiations leading to a treaty on general and complete disarmament under effective international control.

**39.** Qualitative and quantitative disarmament measures are both important for halting the arms race. Efforts to that end must include negotiations on the limitation and cessation of the qualitative improvement of armaments, especially weapons of mass destruction and the development of new means of warfare so that ultimately scientific and technological achievements may be used solely for peaceful purposes.

**40.** Universality of disarmament agreements helps create confidence among States. When multilateral agreements in the field of disarmament are negotiated, every effort should be made to ensure that they are universally acceptable. The full compliance of all parties with the provisions contained in such agreements would also contribute to the attainment of that goal.

**41.** In order to create favourable conditions for success in the disarmament process, all States should strictly abide by the provisions of the Charter of the United Nations, refrain from actions which might adversely affect efforts in the field of disarmament, and display a constructive approach to negotiations and the political will to reach agreements. There are certain negotiations on disarmament under way at different levels, the early and successful completion of which could contribute to limiting the arms race. Unilateral measures of arms limitation or reduction could also contribute to the attainment of that goal.

**42.** Since prompt measures should be taken in order to halt and reverse the arms race, Member States hereby declare that they will respect the above-stated objectives and principles and make every effort faithfully to carry out the Programme of Action set forth in section III below.

## III. PROGRAMME OF ACTION

**43.** Progress towards the goal of general and complete disarmament can be achieved through the implementation of a programme of action on disarmament, in accordance with the goals and principles established in the Declaration on disarmament. The present Programme of Action contains priorities and measures in the field of disarmament that States should undertake as a matter of urgency with a view to halting and reversing the arms race and to giving the necessary impetus to efforts designed to achieve genuine disarmament leading to general and complete disarmament under effective international control.

**44.** The present Programme of Action enumerates the specific measures of disarmament which should be implemented over the next few years, as well as other measures and studies to prepare the way for future negotiations and for progress toward general and complete disarmament.

**45.** Priorities in disarmament negotiations shall be: nuclear weapons; other weapons of mass destruction; including chemical weapons; conventional weapons, including any which may be deemed to be excessively injurious or to have indiscriminate effects; and reduction of armed forces.

**46.** Nothing should preclude States from conducting negotiations on all priority items concurrently.

**47.** Nuclear weapons pose the greatest danger to mankind and to the survival of civilization. It is essential to halt and reverse the nuclear arms race in all its aspects in order to avert the danger of war involving nuclear weapons. The ultimate goal in this context is the complete elimination of nuclear weapons.

**48.** In the task of achieving the goals of nuclear disarmament, all the nuclear-weapon States, in particular those among them which possess the most important nuclear arsenals, bear a special responsibility.

**49.** The process of nuclear disarmament should be carried out in such a way, and requires measures to ensure, that the security of all States is guaranteed at progressively lower levels of nuclear armaments, taking into account the relative qualitative and quantitative importance of the existing arsenals of the nuclear-weapon States and other States concerned.

**50.** The achievement of nuclear disarmament will require urgent negotiation of agreements at appropriate stages and with adequate measures of verification satisfactory to the states concerned for:

* cessation of the qualitative improvement and development of nuclear-weapon systems;

* cessation of the production of all types of nuclear weapons and their means of delivery, and the production of fissionable material for weapons purposes;

* a comprehensive phased programme with agreed time-frames, whenever feasible, for progressive and balanced reduction of stockpiles of nuclear weapons and their means of delivery, leading to their ultimate and complete elimination at the earliest possible time.

Consideration can be given in the course of the negotiations to mutual and agreed limitation or prohibition, without prejudice to the security of any State, of any types of nuclear armaments.

**51.** The cessation of nuclear-weapon testing by all States within the framework of an effective nuclear disarmament process would be in the interest of mankind. It would make a significant contribution to the above aim of ending the qualitative improvement of nuclear weapons and the development of new types of such weapons and of preventing the proliferation of nuclear weapons. In this context the negotiations now in progress on a "treaty prohibiting nuclear-weapon tests, and a protocol covering nuclear explosions for peaceful purposes, which would be an integral part of the treaty," should be concluded urgently and the result submitted for full consideration by the multilateral negotiating body with a view to the submission of a draft treaty to the General Assembly at the earliest possible date.

All efforts should be made by the negotiating parties to achieve an agreement which, following General Assembly endorsement, could attract the widest possible adherence.

In this context, various views were expressed by non-nuclear-weapon States that, pending the conclusion of this treaty, the world community would be encouraged if all the nuclear-weapon States refrained from testing nuclear weapons. In this connection, some nuclear-weapon States expressed different views.

**52.** The Union of Soviet Socialist Republics and the United States of America should conclude at the earliest possible date the agreement they have been pursuing for several years in the second series of the strategic arms limitation talks (SALT II). They are invited to transmit in good time the text of the agreement to the General Assembly. It should be followed promptly by further strategic arms limitation negotiations between the two parties, leading to agreed significant reductions of, and qualitative limitations on, strategic arms. It should constitute an important step in the direction of nuclear disarmament and ultimately of establishment of a world free of such weapons.

**53.** The process of nuclear disarmament described in the paragraph on this subject should be expedited by the urgent and vigorous pursuit to a successful conclusion of ongoing negotiation and the urgent initiation of further negotiations among the nuclear-weapon States.

**54.** Significant progress in nuclear disarmament would be facilitated both by parallel political or international legal measures to strengthen the security of States and by progress in the limitation and reduction of armed forces and conventional armaments of the nuclear-weapons States and other States in the regions concerned.

**55.** Real progress in the field of nuclear disarmament could create an atmosphere conducive to progress in conventional disarmament on a world-wide basis.

**56.** The most effective guarantee against the danger of nuclear war and the use of nuclear weapons is nuclear disarmament and the complete elimination of nuclear weapons.

**57.** Pending the achievement of this goal, for which negotiations should be vigorously pursued, and bearing in mind the devastating results which nuclear war would have on belligerents and non-belligerents alike, the nuclear-weapon States have special responsibilities to undertake measures aimed at preventing the outbreak of nuclear war, and of the use of force in international relations, subject to the provisions of the Charter of the United Nations, including the use of nuclear weapons.

**58.** In this context, all States and in particular nuclear-weapon States should consider as soon as possible various proposals designed to secure the avoidance of the use of nuclear weapons, the prevention of nuclear war and related objectives, where possible through international agreement and thereby ensure that the survival of mankind is not endangered. All States should actively participate in efforts to bring about conditions in international relations among States in which a code of peaceful conduct of nations in international affairs could be agreed upon and which would preclude the use or threat of use of nuclear weapons.

**59.** In the same context, the nuclear weapon States are called upon to take steps to assure the non-nuclear-weapon States against the use or threat of use of nuclear weapons. The General Assembly notes the declarations made by the nuclear-weapon States and urges them to pursue efforts to conclude as appropriate effective arrangements to assure non-nuclear-weapon States against the use or threat of use of nuclear weapons.

**60.** The establishment of nuclear-weapon-free zones on the basis of arrangements freely arrived at among the States of the region concerned, constitutes an important disarmament measure.

**61.** The process of establishing such zones in different parts of the world should be encouraged with the ultimate objective of achieving a world entirely free of nuclear weapons. In the process of establishing such zones, the characteristics of each region should be taken into account. The States participating in such zones should undertake to comply fully with all the objectives, purposes and principles of the agreements or arrangements establishing the zones, thus ensuring that they are genuinely free from nuclear weapons.

**62.** With respect to such zones, the nuclear-weapon States in turn are called upon to give undertakings, the modalities of which are to be negotiated with the competent authority of each zone, in particular:
**(a)** to respect strictly the status of the nuclear-weapon free zone;
**(b)** to refrain from the use of threat of use of nuclear weapons against the States of the zone.

**63.** In the light of existing conditions, and without prejudice to other measures which may be considered in other regions, the following measures are especially desirable:

**(a)** Adoption by the States concerned of all relevant measures to ensure the full application of the Treaty for the Prohibition of Nuclear Weapons in Latin America (Treaty of Tlatelolco), taking into account the views expressed at the special session on the adherence to it.

**(b)** Signature and ratification of the Additional Protocols of the Treaty for the Prohibition of Nuclear Weapons in Latin America (Treaty of Tlatelolco) by the States entitled to become parties to those instruments which have not yet done so;

**(c)** In Africa, where the Organization of African Unity has affirmed a decision for the denuclearization of the region, the Security Council shall take appropriate effective steps whenever necessary to prevent the frustration of this objective;

**(d)** The serious consideration of the practical and urgent steps, as described in the paragraphs above, required for the implementation of the proposal to establish a nuclear-weapon-free zone in the Middle East in accordance with the relevant General Assembly resolutions where all parties directly concerned have expressed their support for the concept and where the danger of nuclear-weapon proliferation exists. The establishment of a nuclear-weapon-free zone in the Middle East would greatly enhance international peace and security. Pending the establishment of such a zone in the region, States of the region should solemnly declare that they will refrain on a reciprocal basis from producing, acquiring, or in any other way, possessing nuclear weapons and nuclear explosive devices, and from permitting the stationing of nuclear weapons on their territory by any third party and agree to place all thier nuclear activities under International Atomic Energy Agency safeguards. Consideration should be given to a Security Council role in advancing the establishment of a Middle East nuclear-weapon-free zone;

**(e)** All States in the region of South Asia have expressed their determination of keeping their countries free of nuclear weapons. No action should be taken by them which might deviate from that objective. In this context, the question of establishing a nuclear-weapon-free zone in South Asia has been dealt with in several resolutions of the General Assembly which is keeping the subject under consideration.

**64.** The establishment of zones of peace in various regions of the world, under appropriate conditions, to be clearly defined and determined freely by the States concerned in the zone, taking into account the characteristics of the zone and the principles of the Charter of the United Nations, and in conformity with international law, can contribute to strengthening the security of States within such zones and to international peace and security as a whole.

In this regard, the General Assembly notes the proposals for the establishment of zones of peace, *inter alia*, in:

**(a)** South-East Asia where states in the region have expressed interest in the establishment of such a zone, in conformity with their views;
**(b)** Indian Ocean, taking into account the deliberations of the General Assembly and its relevant resolutions and the need to ensure the maintenance of peace and security in the region.

**65.** It is imperative as an integral part of the effort to halt and reverse the arms race, to prevent the proliferation of nuclear weapons. The goal of nuclear non-proliferation is on the one hand to prevent the emergence of any additional nuclear-weapon States beside the existing five nuclear-weapon States, and on the other progressively to reduce and eventually eliminate nuclear weapons altogether. This involves obligations and responsibilities on the part of both nuclear-weapon States and non-nuclear-weapon States, the former undertaking to stop the nuclear-arms race and to achieve disarmament by urgent application of measures outlined in the relevant paragraphs of this Document, and all States undertaking to prevent the spread of nuclear weapons.

**66.** Effective measures can and should be taken at the national level and through international agreements to minimize the danger of the proliferation of nuclear weapons without jeopardizing energy supplies or the development of nuclear energy for peaceful purposes. Therefore, the nuclear-weapon States and the non-nuclear-weapon States should jointly take further steps to develop an international consensus of ways and means, on a universal and non-discriminatory basis, to prevent the proliferation of nuclear weapons.

**67.** Full implementation of all the provisions of existing instruments on non-proliferation, such as the Treaty on the Non-Proliferation of Nuclear Weapons and/or the Treaty for the Prohibition of Nuclear Weapons in Latin America (Treaty of Tlatelolco) by States parties to those instruments will be an important contribution to this end. Adherence to such instruments has increased in recent years and the hope has been expressed by the parties that this trend might continue.

**68.** Non-proliferation measures should not jeopardize the full exercise of the inalienable rights of all States to apply and develop their programmes for the peaceful uses of nuclear energy for economic and social development in conformity with their priorities, interests and needs. All States should also have access to, and be free to acquire technology, equipment and materials for peaceful uses of nuclear energy, taking into account the particular needs of the developing countries. International co-operation in this field should be under agreed and appropriate international safeguards applied through the International Atomic Energy Agency on a non-discriminatory basis in order to prevent effectively proliferation of nuclear weapons.

**69.** Each country's choices and decisions in the field of the peaceful uses of nuclear energy should be respected without jeopardizing their respective fuel cycle policies or international co-operation, agreements, and contracts for the peaceful use of nuclear energy provided that agreed safeguard measures mentioned above are applied.

**70.** In accordance with the principles and provisions of Resolution 32/50, international co-operation for the promotion of the transfer and utilization of nuclear technology for economic and social development, especially in the developing countries, should be strengthened.

**71.** Efforts should be made to conclude the work of the International Nuclear Fuel Cycle Evaluation strictly in accordance with the objectives set out in the final communique of its Organizing Conference.

**72.** All States should adhere to the Protocol for the Prohibition of the Use in War of Asphyxiating, Poisonous or Other Gases, and of Bacteriological Methods of Warfare.

**73.** All States which have not yet done so should consider adhering to the Convention on the Prohibition of the Development, Production and Stockpiling of Bacteriological (Biological) and Toxin Weapons and on Their Destruction.

**74.** States should also consider the possibility of adhering to multilateral agreements concluded so far in the disarmament field which are mentioned below in this section.

**75.** The complete and effective prohibition of the development, production and stockpiling of all chemical weapons and their destruction represent one of the most urgent measures of disarmament. Consequently, conclusion of a convention to this end, on which negotiations have been going on for several years, is one of the most urgent tasks of multilateral negotiations. After its conclusion, all States should contribute to ensuring the broadest possible application of the convention through its early signature and ratification.

**76.** A convention should be concluded prohibiting the development, production, stockpiling and use of radiological weapons.

**77.** In order to help prevent a qualitative arms race and so that scientific and technological achievements may ultimately be used solely for peaceful purposes, effective measures should be taken to avoid the danger and prevent the emergence of new types of weapons of mass destruction based on new scientific principles and achievements. Efforts should be appropriately pursued aiming at the prohibition of such new types and new systems of weapons of mass destruction. Specific agreements could be concluded on particular types of new weapons of mass destruction which may be identified. This question should be kept under continuing review.

**78.** The Committee on Disarmament should keep under review the need for a further prohibition of military or any other hostile use of environmental modification techniques in order to eliminate the dangers to mankind from such use.

**79.** In order to promote the peaceful use of and to avoid an arms race on the sea-bed and the ocean floor and the subsoil thereof, the Committee on Disarmament is requested—in consultation with the States parties to the Treaty on the Prohibition of the Emplacement of Nuclear Weapons and Other Weapons of Mass Destruction on the Sea-Bed and the Ocean Floor and the Subsoil Thereof, and taking into account the proposals made during the 1977 Review Conference and any relevant technological developments—to proceed promptly with the consideration of further measures in the field of disarmament for the prevention of an arms race in that environment.

**80.** In order to prevent an arms race in outer space, further measures should be taken and appropriate international negotiations be held in accordance with the spirit of the Treaty on Principles Governing the Activities of States in the Exploration and Use of Outer Space including the Moon and other Celestial Bodies.

**81.** Together with negotiations on nuclear disarmament measures, the limitation and gradual reduction of armed forces and conventional weapons should be resolutely pursued within the framework of progress towards general and complete disarmament. States with the largest military arsenals have a special responsibility in pursuing the process of conventional armaments reductions.

**82.** In particular the achievement of a more stable situation in Europe at a lower level of military potential on the basis of approximate equality and parity, as well as on the basis of undiminished security of all States with full respect for security interests and independence of States outside military alliances, by agreement on appropriate mutual reductions and limitations would contribute to the strengthening of security in Europe and constitute a significant step towards enhancing international peace and security. Current efforts to this end should be continued most energetically.

**83.** Agreements or other measures should be resolutely pursued on a bilateral, regional and multilateral basis with the aim of strengthening peace and security at a lower level of forces, by the limitation and reduction of armed forces and of conventional weapons, taking into account the need of States to protect their security, bearing in mind the inherent right of self-defense embodied in the Charter of the United Nations and without prejudice to the principle of equal rights and self-determination of peoples in accordance with the Charter, and the need to ensure balance at each stage and undiminished security of all States. Such measures might include those in the following two paragraphs.

**84.** Bilateral, regional and multilateral consultations and conferences where appropriate conditions exist with the participation of all the countries concerned for the consideration of different aspects of conventional disarmament, such as the initiative envisaged in the Declaration of Ayacucho subscribed in 1974 by eight Latin American countries.

**85.** Consultations should be carried out among major arms suppliers and recipient countries on the limitation of all types of international transfers of conventional weapons, based, in particular, on the principle of undiminished security of the parties with a view to promoting or enhancing stability at a lower military level, taking into account the need of all States to protect their security as well as the inalienable right to self-determination and independence of peoples under colonial or foreign domination and the obligations of States to respect that right, in accordance with the Charter of the United Nations and the Declaration on Principles of International Law concerning Friendly Relations and Co-operation Among States.

**86.** The 1979 United Nations Conference on Prohibitions or Restrictions of Use of Certain Conventional Weapons which may be Deemed to be Excessively Injurious or to have Indiscriminate Effects should seek agreement, in the light of humanitarian and military considerations, on the prohibition or restriction of use of certain conventional weapons including those which may cause unnecessary suffering or which may have indiscriminate effects. The conference should consider specific categories of such weapons, including those which were the subject-matter of previously conducted discussions.

**87.** All States are called upon to contribute towards carrying out this task.

**88.** The result of the Conference should be considered by all States and especially producer States, in regard to the question of the transfer of such weapons to other States.

**89.** Gradual reduction of military budgets on a mutually agreed basis, for example, in absolute figures or in terms of percentage points, particularly by nuclear-weapon States and other militarily significant States would be a measure that would contribute to the curbing of the arms race, and would increase the possibilities of reallocation of resources now being used for military purposes to economic and social development, particularly for the benefit of the developing countries. The basis for implementing this measure will have to be agreed by all participating States and will require ways and means of its implementation acceptable to all of them, taking account of the problems involved in assessing the relative significance of reductions as among different States and with due regard to the proposals of States on all the aspects of reduction of military budgets.

**90.** The General Assembly should continue to consider what concrete steps should be taken to facilitate the reduction of military budgets bearing in mind the relevant proposals and documents of the United Nations on this question.

**91.** In order to facilitate the conclusion and effective implementation of disarmament agreements and to create confidence, States should accept appropriate provisions for verification in such agreements.

**92.** In the context of international disarmament negotiations, the problem of verification should be further examined and adequate methods and procedures in this field be considered. Every effort should be made to develop appropriate methods and procedures which are non-discriminatory and which do not unduly interfere with the internal affairs of other States or jeopardize their economic and social development.

**93.** In order to facilitate the process of disarmament, it is necessary to take measures and pursue policies to strengthen international peace and security and to build confidence among States. Commitment to confidence-building measures could significantly contribute to preparing for further progress in disarmament. For this purpose, measures such as the following and other measures yet to be agreed upon, should be undertaken:

(1) The prevention of attacks which take place by accident, miscalculation or communications failure by taking steps to improve communications between Governments, particularly in areas of tension, by the establishment of "hot lines" and other methods of reducing the risk of conflict.

(2) States should assess the possible implications of their military research and development for existing agreements as well as for further efforts in the field of disarmament.

(3) The Secretary-General shall periodically submit reports to the General Assembly on the economic and social consequences of the arms race and its extremely harmful effects on world peace and security.

**94.** In view of the relationship between expenditure on armaments and economic and social development and the necessity to release real resources now being used for military purposes to economic and social development in the world, particularly for the benefit of the developing countries, the Secretary-General should, with the assistance of a group of qualified governmental experts appointed by him, initiate an expert study on the relationship between disarmament and development. The Secretary-General should submit an interim report on the subject to the General Assembly at its thirty-fourth session and submit the final results to the Assembly at its thirty-sixth session for subsequent action.

**95.** The expert study should have the terms of reference contained in the report of the Ad Hoc Group on the Relationship between Disarmament and Development appointed by the Secretary-General in accordance with General Assembly resolution 32/88 A of 12 December 1977. It should investigate the three main areas listed in the report, bearing in mind the United Nations studies previously carried out. The study should be made in the context of how disarmament can contribute to the establishment of the new international economic order. The study should be forward-looking and policy-oriented and place special emphasis on both the desirability of a reallocation, following disarmament measures, of resources now being used for military purposes to economic and social development, particularly for the benefit of the developing countries and the substantive feasibility of such a reallocation. A principal aim should be to produce results that could effectively guide the formulation of practical measures to reallocate those resources at the local, national, regional and international levels.

**96.** Taking further steps in the field of disarmament and other measures aimed at promoting international peace and security would be facilitated by carrying out studies by the Secretary-General in this field with appropriate assistance from governmental or consultant experts.

**97.** The Secretary-General shall, with the assistance of consultant experts, appointed by him, continue the study of the interrelationship between disarmament and international security and submit it to the thirty-fourth session of the General Assembly, as requested in resolution A/RES/32/87C.

**98.** The thirty-third and subsequent sessions of the General Assembly should determine the specific guidelines for carrying out studies, taking into account the proposals already submitted including those made by individual countries at the special session, as well as other proposals which can be introduced later in this field. In doing so, the General Assembly would take into consideration a report on these matters prepared by the Secretary-General.

**99.** In order to mobilize world pubic opinion on behalf of disarmament the specific measures set forth below, designed to increase the dissemination of information about the armaments race and the efforts to halt and reverse it, should be adopted.

**100.** Governmental and non-governmental information organs and those of the United Nations and its specialized agencies should give priority to the preparation and distribution of printed and audio-visual material relating to the danger represented by the armaments race as well as to the disarmament efforts and negotiations on specific disarmament measures.

**101.** In particular, publicity should be given to the final documents of the special session.

**102.** The General Assembly proclaims a week starting 24 October, the day of the foundation of the United Nations, as a week devoted to fostering the objectives of disarmament.

**103.** To encourage study and research on disarmament, the United Nations Centre for Disarmament should intensify its activities in the presentation of information concerning the armaments race and disarmament. Also, the United Nations Educational, Scientific and Cultural Organization (UNESCO), is urged to intensify its activities aimed at facilitating research and publications on disarmament, related to its fields of competence, especially in developing countries, and should disseminate the results of such research.

**104.** Throughout this process of disseminating information about the developments in the disarmament field of all countries, three should be increased participation by non-governmental organizations concerned with the matter, through closer liasion between them and the United Nations.

**105.** Member States should be encouraged to ensure a better flow of information with regard to the various aspects of disarmament to avoid dissemination of false and tendentious information concerning armaments and to concentrate on the danger of escalation of the armaments race and on the need for general and complete disarmament under effective international control.

**106.** With a view to contributing to a greater understanding and awareness of the problems created by the armaments race and of the need for disarmament, Governments and governmental and non-governmental international organizations are urged to take steps to develop programmes of education for disarmament and peace studies at all levels.

**107.** The General Assembly welcomes the initiative of the United Nations Educational, Scientific and Cultural Organization in planning to hold a world congress on disarmament education and, in this connexion, urges that organization to step up its programme aimed at the development of disarmament education as a distinct field of study through the preparation *inter alia*, of teachers' guides, textbooks, readers and audio-visual materials. Member States should take all possible measures to encourage the incorporation of such materials in the curricula of their educational institutes.

**108.** In order to promote expertise in disarmament in more Member States, particularly in the developing countries, the General Assembly decides to establish a programme of fellowships on disarmament. The Secretary-General, taking into account the proposal submitted to the special session, should prepare guidelines for the programme. He should also submit the financial requirements of 20 fellowships at the thirty-third regular session of the General Assembly, for inclusion in the regular budget of the United Nations bearing in mind the savings that can be made within the existing bugetary appropriations.

**109.** Implementation of these priorities should lead to general and complete disarmament under effective international control, which remains the ultimate goal of all efforts exerted in the field of disarmament. Negotiations on general and complete disarmament shall be conducted concurrently with negotiations on partial measures of disarmament. With this purpose in mind, the Committee on Disarmament will undertake the elaboration of a comprehensive programme of disarmament encompassing all measures thought to be advisable in order to ensure that the goal of general and complete disarmament under effective international control becomes a reality in a world in which international peace and security prevail and in which the new international economic order is strengthened and consolidated. The comprehensive programme should contain appropriate procedures for ensuring that the General Assembly is kept fully informed of the progress of the negotiations including an appraisal of the situation when appropriate and, in particular, a continuing review of the implementation of the programme.

**110.** Progress in disarmament should be accompanied by measures to strengthen institutions for maintaining peace and the settlement of international disputes by peaceful means. During and after the implementation of the programme of general and complete disarmament, there should be taken, in accordance with the principles of the United Nations Charter, the necessary measures to maintain international peace and security, including the obligation of States to place at the disposal of the United Nations agreed manpower necessary for an international peace force to be equipped with agreed types of armaments. Arrangements for the use of this force should ensure that the United Nations can effectively deter or suppress any threat or use of arms in violation of the purposes and principles of the United Nations.

**111.** General and complete disarmament under strict and effective international control shall permit States to have at their disposal only those non-nuclear forces, armaments, facilities and establishments as are agreed to be necessary to maintain internal order and protect the personal security of citizens and in order that States shall support and provide agreed manpower for a United Nations peace force.

**112.** In addition to the several questions dealt with in this Programme of Action, there are a few others of fundamental importance, on which, because of the complexity of the issues involved and the short time at the disposal of the special session, it has proved impossible to reach satisfactory agreed conclusions. For those reasons they are treated only in very general terms and, in a few instances, even not treated at all in the Programme.

It should be stressed, however, that a number of concrete approaches to deal with such questions emerged from the exchange of views carried out in the General Assembly which will undoubtedly facilitate the continuation of the study and negotiation of the problems involved in the competent disarmament organs.

## IV. MACHINERY

**113.** While disarmament, particularly in the nuclear field, has become a necessity for the survival of mankind and for the elimination of the danger of nuclear war, little progress has been made since the end of the Second World War. In addition to the need to exercise political will, the international machinery should be utilized more effectively and also improved to enable implementation of the Programme of Action and help the United Nations to fulfil its role in the field of disarmament.

In spite of the best efforts of the international community, adequate results have not been produced with the existing machinery. There is, therefore, an urgent need that existing disarmament machinery be revitalized and forums appropriately constituted for disarmament deliberations and negotiations with a better representative character.

For maximum effectiveness, two kinds of bodies are required in the field of disarmament—deliberative and negotiating. All Member States should be represented on the former, whereas the latter, for the sake of convenience, should have a relatively small membership.

**114.** The United Nations, in accordance with the Charter, has a central role and primary responsibility in the sphere of disarmament. Accordingly, it should play a more active role in this field, and in order to discharge its functions effectively, the United Nations should facilitate and encourage all disarmament measures—unilateral, bilateral, regional or multilateral—and be kept duly informed through the General Assembly, or any other appropriate United Nations channel reaching all members of the Organization, of all disarmament efforts outside its aegis without prejudice to the progress of negotiations.

**115.** The General Assembly has been and should remain the main deliberative organ of the United Nations in the field of disarmament and should make every effort to facilitate the implementation of disarmament measures.

An item entitled "Review of the implementation of the recommendations and decisions adopted by the General Assembly at its tenth special session" shall be included in the provisional agenda of the thirty-third and subsequent sessions of the General Assembly.

**116.** Draft multilateral disarmament conventions should be subjected to the normal procedures applicable in the law of treaties. Those submitted to the General Assembly for its commendation should be subject to full review by the Assembly.

**117.** The First Committee of the General Assembly should deal in the future only with questions of disarmament and related international security questions.

**118.** The General Assembly establishes, as successor to the Commission originally established by resolution 502 (VI), a Disarmament Commission composed of all Members of the United Nations.

*The General Assembly decides that:*

**(a)** The Disarmament Commission shall be a deliberative body, a subsidiary organ of the General Assembly, the function of which shall be to consider and make recommendations on various problems in the field of disarmament and to follow up the relevant decisions and recommendations of the special session devoted to disarmament. The Disarmament Commission should, *inter alia*, consider the elements of a comprehensive programme for disarmament to be submitted as recommendations to the General Assembly and, through it, to the negotiating body, the Committee on Disarmament;

**(b)** The Disarmament Commission shall function under rules of procedure relating to the committees of the General Assembly with such modifications as the Commission may deem necessary and shall make every effort to ensure that, in so far as possible, decisions on substantive issues be adopted by consensus;

**(c)** The Disarmament Commission shall report annually to the General Assembly. It will submit for the consideration by the thirty-third session of the General Assembly a report on organizational matters. In 1979, the Disarmament Commission will meet for a period not exceeding four weeks, the dates to be decided at the thirty-third session of the General Assembly;

**(d)** The Secretary-General shall furnish such experts, staff and services as are necessary for the effective accomplishment of the Commission's functions.

**119.** A second special session of the General Assembly devoted to disarmament should be held on a date to be decided by the General Assembly at its thirty-third session.

**120.** The General Assembly is conscious of the work that has been done by the international negotiating body that has been meeting since March 14, 1962 as well as the considerable and urgent work that remains to be accomplished in the field of disarmament.

The General Assembly is deeply aware of the continuing requirement for a single multilateral disarmament negotiating forum of limited size taking decisions on the basis of consensus. It attaches great importance to the participation of all the nuclear-weapon States in an appropriately constituted negotiating body: the Committee on Disarmament.

The General Assembly welcomes the agreement reached following appropriate consultations among the member States during the Special Session of the General Assembly Devoted to Disarmament that the Committee on Disarmament will be open to the nuclear-weapon States, and 32 to 35 other States to be chosen in consultation with the President of the thirty-second session of the General Assembly; that the membership of the Committee on Disarmament will be reviewed at regular intervals; that the Committee on Disarmament will be convened in Geneva not later than January 1979 by the country whose name appears first in the alphabetical list of membership; and that the Committee on Disarmament will:

**(a)** Conduct its work by consensus;

**(b)** Adopt its own rules of procedures;

**(c)** Request the Secretary-General of the United Nations, following consultations with the Committee on Disarmament, to appoint the Secretary of the Committee, who shall also act as his personal representative, to assist the Committee and its Chairman in organizing the business and timetables of the Committee;

**(d)** Rotate the chairmanship of the Committee among all its members on a monthly basis;

**(e)** Adopt its own agenda taking into account the recommendations made to it by the General Assembly and the proposals presented by the members of the Committee:

**(f)** Submit a report to the General Assembly annually, or more frequently as appropriate, and provide its formal and other relevant documents to the Member States of the United Nations on a regular basis;

**(g)** Make arrangements for interested States, not members of the Committee, to submit to the Committee written proposals or working documents on measures of disarmament that are the subject of negotiation in the Committee and to participate in the discussion of the subject matter of such proposals or working documents;

**(h)** Invite States not members of the Committee, upon their request, to express views in the Committee when the particular concerns of those States are under discussion;

**(i)** Open its plenary meetings to the public unless otherwise decided.

**121.** Bilateral and regional disarmament negotiations may also play an important role and could facilitate negotiations of multilateral agreements in the field of disarmament.

**122.** At the earliest appropriate time, a world disarmament conference should be convened with universal participation and with adequate preparation.

**123.** In order to enable the United Nations to continue to fulfil its role in the field of disarmament and to carry out the additional tasks assigned to it by this special session, the United Nations Centre for Disarmament should be adequately strengthened and its research and information functions accordingly extended.

The Centre should also take account fully of the possibilities offered by United Nations specialized agencies and other institutions and programmes within the United Nations system with regard to studies and information on disarmament. The Centre should also increase contacts with non-governmental organizations and research institutions in view of the valuable role they play in the field of disarmament. This role could be encouraged also in other ways that may be considered as appropriate.

**124.** The Secretary-General is requested to set up an advisory board of eminent persons, selected on the basis of their personal expertise and taking into account the principle of equitable geographical representation, to advise him on various aspects of studies to be made under the auspices of the United Nations in the field of disarmament and arms limitation, including a programme of such studies.

**125.** The General Assembly notes with satisfaction that the active participation of the Member States in the consideration of the agenda items of the special session and the proposals and suggestions submitted to them and reflected to a considerable extent in the Final Document have made a valuable contribution to the work of the special session and to its positive conclusion.

Since a number of those proposals and suggestions, which have become an integral part of the work of the special session, deserve to be studied further and more thoroughly, taking into consideration the many relevant comments and observations made both in the general debate of the plenary and the deliberations the Ad Hoc Committee, the Secretary-General is requested to transmit, together with this Final Document, to the appropriate deliberative and negotiating organs dealing with the questions of disarmament all the official records of the special session of the General Assembly devoted to disarmament, in accordance with the recommendations which the Assembly may adopt at its thirty-third session. Some of the proposals put forth for consideration of the special session of the Assembly are listed below:

**(a)** Text of the decision of the Central Committee of the Romanian Communist Party concerning Romania's position on disarmament and, in particular, on nuclear disarmament, adopted on 9 May 1978 (A/S-10/14);

**(b)** Views of the Swiss Government on problems to be discussed at the tenth special session of the General Assembly (A/S-10/AC.1/2);

**(c)** Proposals of the Union of Soviet Socialist Republics on practical measures for ending the arms race (A/S-10/AC.1/4);

**(d)** Memorandum from France concerning the establishment of an International Satellite Monitoring Agency (A/S-10/AC.1/7);

**(e)** Memorandum from France concerning the establishment of an International Institute for Disarmament Research (A/S-10/AC.1/8);

**(f)** Proposal by Sri Lanka for the establishment of a World Disarmament Authority (A/S-10/AC.1/9 and Add. 1);

**(g)** Working paper submitted by the Federal Republic of Germany entitlted "Contribution to the seismological verification of a comprehensive test ban" (A/S-10/AC.1/12);

**(h)** Working paper submitted by the Federal Republic of Germany entitled "Invitation to atttend an international chemical-weapon verification workshop in the Federal Republic of Germany" (A/S-10/AC.1/13);

**(i)** Working paper on disarmament submitted by China (A/S-10/AC.1/17);

**(j)** Working paper submitted by the Federal Republic of Germany concerning zones of confidence-building measures as a first step towards the preparation of a world-wide convention on confidence-building measures (A/S-10/AC.1/20);

**(k)** Proposal by Ireland for a study of the possibility of establishing a system of incentives to promote arms control and disarmament (A/S-10/AC.1/21);

**(l)** Working paper submitted by Romania concerning synthesis of the proposals in the field of disarmament (A/S-10/AC.1./23);

**(m)** Proposal by the United States of America on the establishment of a United Nations Peace-keeping Reserve and on confidence-building measures and stabilizing measures in various regions, including notification of manoeuvres, invitation of observers to manoeuvres, and the United Nations machinery to study and promote such measures (A/S-10/AC.1/24);

**(n)** Proposal by Uruguay on the possibility of establishing a polemological agency (A/S-10/AC.1/25);

**(o)** Proposal by Belgium, Canada, Denmark, Germany, Federal Republic of Ireland, Italy, Japan, Luxembourg, the Netherlands, New Zealand, Norway, Sweden, the United Kingdom of Great Britain and Northern Ireland and the United States of America on the strengthening of the security role of the United Nations in the peaceful settlement of disputes and peacekeeping (A/S-10/AC.1/26 and Corr. 1 and 2);

**(p)** Memorandum from France concerning the establishment of an International Disarmament Fund for Development (A/S-10/AC.128);

**(q)** Proposal by Norway entitled "Evaluation of the impact of new weapons on arms control and disarmament efforts" (A/S-10/AC.1/31);

**(r)** Note verbale transmitting the text, signed in Washington on 22 June 1978, by the Ministers for Foreign Affairs of Argentina, Bolivia, Chile, Colombia, Ecuador, Panama, Peru and Venezuela, reaffirming the principles of the Declaration of Ayacucho with respect to the limitation of conventional weapons (A/S-10/AC.1/34);

**(s)** Memorandum from Liberia entitled "Declaration of a new philosophy on disarmament" (A/S-10/AC.1/35);

**(t)** Statements made by the representatives of China on 22 June 1978, on the draft Final Document of the tenth special session (A/S-10/AC.1/36);

**(u)** Proposal by the President of Cyprus for the total demilitarization and disarmament of the Republic of Cyprus and the implementation of the resolutions of the United Nations (A/S-10/AC.1/39);

**(v)** Proposal by Costa Rica on economic and social incentives to halt the arms race (A/S-10/AC.1/40);

**(w)** Amendments submitted by Dhina to the draft Final Document of the tenth special session (A/S-10/AC.1/L.2 to L.4, A/S-10/AC.1/L.7 and L.8);

**(x)** Proposals by Canada for the implementation of a strategy of suffocation of the nuclear arms race (A/S-10/AC.1/L.6);

**(y)** Draft resolution submitted by Cyprus, Ethiopa and India on the urgent need for cessation of further testing of nuclear weapons (A/S-10/AC.1/L.10);

**(z)** Draft resolution submitted by Ethiopa and India on the non-use of nuclear weapons and prevention of nuclear war (A/S-10/AC.1/L.11);

**(aa)** Proposal by the non-aligned countries on the establishment of a zone of peace in the Mediterranean (A/S-10/AC.1/37, para. 72);

**(bb)** Proposal by the Government of Senegal for a tax on military budgets (A/S-10/AC.1/37, para. 101);

**(cc)** Proposal by Austria for the transmission to Member States of working paper A/Ac.187/109 and the ascertainment of their view on the subject of verification (A/S-10/AC.1/37, para. 113);

**(dd)** Proposal by the non-aligned contries for the dismantling of foreign military bases from foreign territories and withdrawal of foreign troops from foreign territories (A/S-10/AC.1/37, para. 126);

(ee) Proposal by Mexico for the opening, on a provisional basis, of an *Ad Hoc* account in the United Nations Development Programme to use for development the funds which may be released as a result of disarmament measures (A/S-10/AC.1/37, para. 141);

(ff) Proposal by Italy on the role of the Security Council in the field of disarmament in accordance with Article 26 of the United Nations Charter (A/S-10/AC.1/37, para. 179);

(gg) Proposal by the Netherlands for a study on the establishment of an international disarmament organization (A/S-10/AC.1/37, para. 186).

**126.** In adopting this Final Document, the States Members of the United Nations solemnly reaffirm their determination to work for general and complete disarmament and to make further collective efforts aimed at strengthening peace and international security; eliminating the threat of war, particularly nuclear war; implementing practical measures aimed at halting and reversing the arms race; strengthening the procedures for the peaceful settlement of disputes; and reducing military expenditures and utilizing the resources thus released in a manner which will help to promote the well-being of all peoples and to improve the economic conditions of the developing countries.

**127.** The General Assembly expresses its satisfaction that the proposals submitted to its special session devoted to disarmament and deliberations thereon have made it possible to reaffirm and define in this Final Document fundamental principles, goals, priorities and procedures for the implementation of the above purposes, either in the Declaration or the Programme of Action or in both. The Assembly also welcomes the important decisions agreed upon regarding the deliberative and negotiating machinery and is confident that these organs will discharge their functions in an effective manner.

**128.** Finally, it should be borne in mind that the number of States that participated in the general debate, as well as the high level of representation and the depth and scope of that debate, are unprecedented in the history of disarmament efforts. Several Heads of State or Government addressed the General Assembly. In addition, other Heads of State or Government sent messages and expressed their good wishes for the success of the special session of the Assembly. Several high officials of specialized agencies and other institutions and programmes within the United Nations system and spokesmen of 25 non-governmental organizations and six research institutes also made valuable contributions to the proceedings of the session. It must be emphasized, moreover, that the special session marks not the end but rather the beginning of a new phase of the efforts of the United Nations in the field of disarmament.

**129.** The General Assembly is convinced that the discussions of the disarmament problems at the special session and its Final Document will attract the attention of all peoples, further mobilize world public opinion and provide a powerful impetus for the cause of disarmament.

# Name Index

# Subject Index

# ABOUT THE AUTHOR

Ralph M. Goldman is Professor of Political Science at San Francisco State University. He received a B.A. degree from New York University, and M.A. and Ph.D. degrees from the University of Chicago.

A former consultant to the Democratic National Committee, Professor Goldman's special interests include American political parties, national politics, international conflict, and theories of political behavior. He has served as a research associate for the Brookings Institution, and as Director of the Institute for Research on International Behavior at the San Francisco State University. He has taught at the University of California at Berkeley and at San Diego, the University of Chicago, Stanford University, and Michigan State University.

Professor Goldman is the author of *Search for Consensus: The Story of the Democratic Party,* and *Contemporary Perspectives on Politics,* and he is co-author of *The Politics of National Party Conventions* and *Presidential Nominating Politics in 1952* (5 vols.). The publications to which he has contributed include *American Political Science Review, U.S. News and World Report, Journal of Higher Education, National Civic Review.*